THE BOOK
of
IRC

Alexander Charalabidis

No Starch Press
San Francisco

THE BOOK OF IRC. Copyright ©2000 By Alexander Charalabidis

Printed in the United States of America

1 2 3 4 5 6 7 8 9 10—02 01 00

Trademarks

Trademarked names are used throughout this book. Rather than use a trademark symbol with every occurrence of a trademarked name, we are using the names only in an editorial fashion and to the benefit of the trademark owner, with no intention of infringement of the trademark.

Publisher: William Pollock
Project Editor: Karol Jurado
Technical Reviewer: M.D. Yesowitch
Cover and Interior Design: Derek Yee Design
Copyeditor: Gail Nelson
Composition: Derek Yee Design
Proofreader: John Carroll
Indexer: Nancy Humphreys

Distributed to the book trade in the United States and Canada by Publishers Group West, 1700 Fourth Street, Berkeley, California 94710, phone: 800-788-3123, fax: 510-528-3444.

For information on translations or book distributors outside the United States, please contact No Starch Press directly:

No Starch Press
555 De Haro Street, Suite 250, San Francisco, CA 94107-2365
phone: 415-863-9900; fax: 415-863-9950; info@nostarch.com; www.nostarch.com

The information in this book is distributed on an "As Is" basis, without warranty. While every precaution has been taken in the preparation of this work, neither the author nor No Starch Press shall have any liability to any person or entity with respect to any loss or damage caused or alleged to be caused directly or indirectly by the information contained in it.

Library of Congress Cataloging-in-Publication Data
Charalabidis, Alexander.
        The book of IRC / Alexander Charalabidis.
              p.   cm.
        Includes index.
        ISBN 1-886411-29-8
        1. Internet Relay Chat. I. Title.
    TK5105.886.C48   1999
    005.7'1376–dc21   99-10403

BRIEF CONTENTS

Chapter 0

Instructions for Internet Dummies

1

Chapter 1

IRC? What's That?

11

Chapter 2

Your IRC Survival Kit

19

Chapter 3

Windows IRC Clients

33

Chapter 4

Unix Clients

41

Chapter 5

IRCing on the Macintosh

55

Chapter 6

Connecting to a Server

73

Chapter 7

Channels

99

Chapter 8

Communication

125

Chapter 9

Finding People on IRC

147

Chapter 10

Creating and Managing a Channel

157

Chapter 11

Enhancing a Client with Scripts

187

Chapter 12

IRC Operators

201

Chapter 13

CTCP

207

Chapter 14
DCC
217

Chapter 15
Server and Network Commands
227

Chapter 16
Odds and Ends
239

Chapter 17
Abuse and Security Issues
253

Chapter 18
Installing, Running, and
Operating an IRC Server
265

Chapter 19
IRC Robots
289

Chapter 20
The Soapbox and More
295

Appendix A
Network and Server Lists
307

Appendix B
Terminology
313

Appendix C
Countries on IRC and Domain
Decoder
321

Appendix D
Useful Addresses
327

Appendix E
Server Numerics
331

Appendix F
Sample Server Configurations
339

CONTENTS IN DETAIL

0

INSTRUCTIONS FOR INTERNET DUMMIES

0.1	Help! Where's the On Button?	2
0.2	Equipment	2
0.3	Computing and the Internet for Beginners	5
0.4	Internet Service Providers	6
0.4.1	*Connecting to the Internet via a PPP Dial-Up*	7
0.4.2	*Connecting to the Internet via Dial-In*	7
0.5	Starting Out on the Internet and Using Basic Services	8
0.5.1	*Using the World Wide Web*	8
0.5.2	*Using FTP*	9
0.5.3	*Using Telnet*	9

1

IRC? WHAT'S THAT?

1.1	So . . . What's It All About?	12
1.2	Origin and History of IRC	13
1.3	Technical Concept	15
1.4	What IRC Has to Offer	16
1.5	IRC for Company Use	17

2

YOUR IRC SURVIVAL KIT

2.1	Saints and Sinners	19
2.2	Safety First	20
2.2.1	*Trojan Horses*	20
2.2.2	*Nukes*	22
2.2.3	*Insert Card to Continue*	22
2.3	The Virtual Tourist's Guide to IRC Networks	23
2.3.1	*Formation of IRC Networks*	23
2.3.2	*Bright Lights, Big City*	25
2.3.3	*Small-Town World*	25
2.3.4	*Foreign Exchange*	26

2.3.5	*All Things Special*	*26*
2.4	Somebody Asked Me to Meet Him . . . Where?	27
2.5	IRC Clients and Servers	27
2.5.1	*Differences among Clients*	*28*
2.5.2	*Differences among Servers*	*29*
2.5.3	*Client Commands versus Server Commands*	*29*
2.6	Software Licensing	30
2.7	Basic Commands	31

3

WINDOWS IRC CLIENTS

3.1	mIRC	33
3.1.1	*Setup and Use*	*34*
3.2	Pirch	36
3.2.1	*Setup and Use*	*37*
3.3	Visual IRC	37
3.3.1	*Setup and Use*	*38*
3.4	Other Windows Clients	39

4

UNIX CLIENTS

4.1	Getting a Client	42
4.2	ircII	43
4.3	sirc	44
4.4	BitchX	44
4.5	Installation of ircII and Related Clients	45
4.5.1	*tar, gzip, and Feather*	*45*
4.5.2	*Configuring ircII*	*48*
4.5.3	*Compile*	*50*
4.5.4	*Binaries*	*50*
4.5.5	*Setting the Environment*	*51*
4.5.6	*The .ircrc File*	*53*

5

IRCING ON THE MACINTOSH

5.1	Mac Users Do IRC with Style	55
5.1.1	General Downloading Instructions	56
5.1.2	Choosing the Right Client	57
5.2	Ircle	58
5.2.1	Setup and Use	60
5.3	ShadowIRC	61
5.3.1	Setup and Use	63
5.4	Snak	64
5.4.1	Setup and Use	66
5.5	MacIRC	66
5.5.1	Setup and Use	67
5.6	ChatNet	68
5.6.1	Setup and Use	70
5.7	Summary	71

6

CONNECTING TO A SERVER

6.1	Selecting a Network and Server, and Connecting	74
6.1.1	Internet Addressing	75
6.1.2	ircII	76
6.1.3	Graphical Clients and mIRC	76
6.2	Things That Can Go Wrong	78
6.2.1	K-lined, or You Are Not Welcome . . .	78
6.2.2	Ping Timeout	79
6.2.3	No More Connections/Server Full	80
6.2.4	Connection Refused	80
6.2.5	Unable to Resolve Server Name	81
6.2.6	Illegal Nickname	82
6.2.7	Nickname or Channel Temporarily Unavailable	82
6.2.8	Ending Up on a Different Server	82
6.2.9	No Authorization	83
6.2.10	Ident Required/Install Identd/Bad Username	83
6.3	Welcome to the Internet Relay	85
6.3.1	The Message of the Day	86
6.3.2	Your Identity on IRC	87
6.3.3	Nickname Registration and Ownership	88
6.3.4	The Realname Field	88
6.4	User Modes (Umodes)	89
6.4.1	Umode i	89

6.4.2	Umode w	90
6.4.3	Umode s	90
6.4.4	Umode o	90
6.4.5	Umode d	90
6.4.6	Umode r	90
6.4.7	Other Umodes	91
6.5	Changing Servers: The SERVER Command	91
6.6	Disconnecting from a Server	92
6.6.1	Nickname Collisions	93
6.6.2	Operator Kill	94
6.6.3	Server Downtime	94
6.6.4	Ping Timeout	95
6.6.5	Connection Reset by Peer	95
6.6.6	Excess Flood	95
6.6.7	Kill Line Active	96
6.6.8	Other Types of Connection	96

7

CHANNELS

7.1	Obtaining a List of Available Channels	101
7.1.1	Disconnecting When Using LIST	103
7.1.2	Strange Channel Names	104
7.1.3	Argh! The List Keeps Scrolling Off and I Miss Most of It	104
7.1.4	I Give Up—Nothing Is Working	105
7.2	Selecting a Channel from the List and Finding the Right Channel	105
7.3	Joining a Channel	106
7.3.1	No Such Channel	108
7.3.2	How Did I End Up on Channel #?	108
7.3.3	Banned from Channel	108
7.3.4	Bad Channel Key	109
7.3.5	Channel Is Full	110
7.3.6	Kick or Ban after Joining	110
7.3.7	I Joined a Channel on the List and It's Empty!	110
7.3.8	Nickname or Channel is Currently Unavailable	111
7.3.9	Invite-Only	111
7.4	Who Is on the Channel?	112
7.5	Channel Operators	113
7.5.1	Channel Bots	114
7.6	Moderated Channels and +Voice	116
7.7	Channel Events	116
7.7.1	Mode Changes	117
7.7.2	Joins, Parts, and Quits	117
7.7.3	Nick Changes	118

7.7.4	*Kicks*	*118*
7.8	Leaving a Channel	118
7.9	Joining Multiple Channels	119
7.9.1	*Switching between Multiple Channels*	*119*
7.10	Channel 0	120
7.10.1	*The Channel #2,000 Trick*	*120*
7.11	Netsplits and Lag	121
7.11.1	*Netsplits*	*121*
7.11.2	*Server-Server Lag*	*123*
7.11.3	*Client-Server Lag*	*124*

8

COMMUNICATION

8.1	Types of Messages You May Receive	126
8.1.1	*Public Messages on a Channel*	*126*
8.1.2	*Private Messages*	*126*
8.1.3	*Notices*	*127*
8.1.4	*CTCP Requests*	*127*
8.1.5	*DCC Requests*	*128*
8.1.6	*Wallops*	*128*
8.1.7	*Operator Notices*	*129*
8.1.8	*Local Machine Messages and Talk Requests*	*130*
8.1.9	*Actions*	*131*
8.1.10	*Server Notices*	*131*
8.1.11	*I Joined a Channel and Nothing's Happening!*	*131*
8.2	Etiquette	132
8.3	Ignoring Messages	133
8.3.1	*Ignoring with ircII*	*133*
8.3.2	*Ignoring with mIRC*	*134*
8.3.3	*The SILENCE Command*	*135*
8.4	Sending to a Channel	135
8.4.1	*Sending to a Channel While Not on It*	*136*
8.4.2	*Communicating with Multiple Channels*	*136*
8.5	Sending Private Messages	137
8.5.1	*Using QUERY*	*137*
8.6	Strange Characters in Messages	138
8.7	Colored Text and Highlights	138
8.7.1	*Using Highlights with ircII*	*139*
8.7.2	*Using Highlights and Color with mIRC*	*140*

8.8	Smile!	141
8.9	Actions	141
8.10	Common Abbreviations	142
8.11	Autogreets	143
8.12	Keeping Track of Events by Logging	143
8.12.1	*Logging with ircII*	*143*
8.12.2	*Logging with mIRC*	*144*
8.13	Communication Problems	144
8.13.1	*Can't Send to Channel*	*144*
8.13.2	*Text Is Scrolling on a Single Line*	*144*
8.13.3	*I Can't See My Nickname Before My Messages*	*145*

9

FINDING PEOPLE ON IRC

9.1	WHOIS	148
9.2	WHOWAS	148
9.3	WHO	149
9.4	NOTIFY and ISON	151
9.5	NAMES	151
9.6	Finding the Operators of a Channel	152
9.7	Network Services	152
9.8	Finger	153
9.9	Finding Someone's Location	154
9.10	How *Not* to Be Found	154

10

CREATING AND MANAGING A CHANNEL

10.1	Creating a New Channel	158
10.2	Channel Operator Status	158
10.3	Channel Modes	159
10.3.1	*Mode b (Ban)*	*160*
10.3.2	*Modes i (Invite-Only) and I (Invitation)*	*160*
10.3.3	*Mode k (Key)*	*161*
10.3.4	*Mode l (Limit)*	*161*
10.3.5	*Mode m (Moderated)*	*161*
10.3.6	*Mode n (Noexternal)*	*161*
10.3.7	*Mode o (Operator)*	*162*
10.3.8	*Mode p (Private)*	*162*
10.3.9	*Mode s (Secret)*	*162*
10.3.10	*Mode t (Topicsetbyops)*	*162*

10.3.11	Mode v (Voice)	163
10.3.12	Viewing a Channel's Mode	163
10.3.13	Mode e (Exception)	163
10.3.14	Multiple Mode Changes	163
10.4	Creating a Private Channel	164
10.4.1	Inviting	165
10.5	Kicks and Bans	165
10.5.1	Correct Use of Host Masks in Bans	166
10.5.2	Ban Problems	168
10.6	Server-Generated Mode Changes	169
10.7	Channel Security	170
10.7.1	Nethacks	170
10.7.2	Flooders and Cloners	172
10.7.3	Colliders	174
10.7.4	Secure Auto-Ops	174
10.7.5	If a Takeover Does Happen	176
10.7.6	Be Careful Who You Op	177
10.7.7	Suspect until Proven Guilty	178
10.8	Channels with No Operators	179
10.9	Desync	180
10.10	Channel Services and Registration	182
10.10.1	Undernet's X and W and Similar Services	183
10.10.2	DALnet ChanServ	183

11

ENHANCING A CLIENT WITH SCRIPTS

11.1	What Scripts Are	187
11.2	Why Use a Script?	188
11.3	Selecting a Script	188
11.4	Obtaining a Script	189
11.5	ircII Scripts	189
11.5.1	Phoenix, TextBox, and Atlantis	189
11.5.2	PurePak	190
11.5.3	LiCe	190
11.5.4	JoloPak	190
11.5.5	Generic Scripts	190
11.6	mIRC Scripts	191
11.6.1	LiOn, QPro, vyxx, and a Few Others	192
11.7	Write Your Own!	192
11.7.1	Aliases	192
11.7.2	Events	193
11.7.3	Conditions	194
11.7.4	User-Defined Variables	194

| 11.7.5 | Server Numerics | 194 |
| 11.7.6 | Practical Scripting Tips | 196 |

12

IRC OPERATORS

12.1	Who They Are	201
12.2	What They Do	202
12.3	How Did They Become IRC Operators?	203
12.4	Finding IRC Operators	205

13

CTCP

13.1	CTCP Explained	207
13.1.1	Sending CTCP Requests	208
13.1.2	Replying to CTCP Requests	209
13.2	CTCP Commands	209
13.2.1	PING	210
13.2.2	VERSION	210
13.2.3	FINGER	211
13.2.4	TIME	211
13.2.5	ACTION	211
13.2.6	ECHO	212
13.2.7	CLIENTINFO	212
13.2.8	USERINFO	212
13.3	PRIVMSG and NOTICE	213
13.4	Customizing CTCP Replies	214

14

DCC

14.1	DCC Chat	218
14.1.1	Initiating a DCC Chat	218
14.1.2	Accepting or Denying a DCC CHAT Request	218
14.1.3	Communicating over a DCC CHAT Connection	219
14.2	File Transfers via DCC	219
14.2.1	Offering a File via DCC	220
14.2.2	Receiving an Offered File	220
14.2.3	Resuming Interrupted Transfers	220
14.2.4	File Servers and XDCC	221

14.3.2	What's This DCC Server Thing?	223
14.3.3	Sound-Related DCC	223
14.3.4	More DCC Options and the Big Secret	224
14.4	DCC from Behind a Firewall or Proxy	224

15

SERVER AND NETWORK COMMANDS

15.1	LUSERS	227
15.2	LINKS	229
15.3	ADMIN	230
15.4	STATS	230
15.4.1	STATS C	230
15.4.2	STATS H	231
15.4.3	STATS I	231
15.4.4	STATS K	231
15.4.5	STATS L	231
15.4.6	STATS M	232
15.4.7	STATS O	232
15.4.8	STATS T, Z, and D	232
15.4.9	STATS U	232
15.4.10	STATS Y	232
15.5	INFO	234
15.6	TIME	234
15.7	TRACE	234
15.8	VERSION	235
15.9	Other Server Commands	236

16

ODDS AND ENDS

16.1	IRC over the Web—Java Clients	239
16.2	Writing a Client	240
16.3	IRC via Telnet	241
16.4	IRC for the Sight-Impaired	242
16.5	Jupitered Servers	242
16.6	Online Help Services	243
16.6.1	Getting Help with Windows Clients	245
16.6.2	Getting Help with Unix Clients	245
16.6.3	Getting Help with Mac Clients	247
16.6.4	Getting Help for Other Clients	247

16.7	The Protocol	247
16.8	Other Types of Real-Time Online Communication	248
16.8.1	Web Chat	248
16.8.2	Talk	248
16.8.3	WWCN	249
16.8.4	ICQ	249
16.9	IRC for Other Platforms	249
16.9.1	Amiga	249
16.9.2	Atari	250
16.9.3	MS-DOS	250
16.9.4	VMS	251
16.9.5	OS/2	251
16.9.6	WebTV	252
16.9.7	BeOS	252

17

ABUSE AND SECURITY ISSUES

17.1	Flooding	253
17.1.1	MSG, NOTICE, and CTCP Floods	254
17.1.2	Nick Floods	254
17.1.3	Topic Floods	255
17.1.4	Public Floods	255
17.1.5	DCC Floods	256
17.1.6	Mode Loops	256
17.1.7	Leavejoin Floods	256
17.2	Hacking	256
17.3	Channel Takeovers	257
17.4	Harassment	257
17.5	Spoofing	258
17.6	Password and Credit Card Number Thieves	258
17.7	Denial of Service Attacks	259
17.7.1	Nukes	259
17.7.2	ICMP Flooding and Smurf	261
17.8	Spam and Mass Messaging	262
17.9	Account Security	263

18

INSTALLING, RUNNING, AND OPERATING
AN IRC SERVER

18.1	System Requirements	266
18.2	IRC Server Software	266
18.3	IRC Daemons	267
18.3.1	Ircd/hybrid (EFnet)	267
18.3.2	Ircu (Undernet)	268
18.3.3	Ircd 2.9 and 2.10 (IRCnet)	268
18.3.4	dal4.6 (DALnet)	269
18.3.5	Conference Room	270
18.3.6	Others ircds and Platforms	270
18.3.7	Adding Services	271
18.4	The ircd.conf File	271
18.4.1	A: lines (All ircds)	271
18.4.2	M: lines (All ircds)	271
18.4.3	I: lines (All ircds)	272
18.4.4	Y: lines (All ircds)	273
18.4.5	O: lines (All ircds)	273
18.4.6	C: and N: lines (All ircds)	273
18.4.7	H: and L: lines (All ircds)	274
18.4.8	K: lines (All ircds)	274
18.4.9	P: lines (All ircds)	274
18.4.10	R: lines (All ircds)	274
18.4.11	D: lines (EFnet) and Z: lines (DALnet)	275
18.4.12	V: lines (IRCnet)	275
18.4.13	Q: lines (EFnet, Undernet, IRCnet)	275
18.4.14	Q: lines (DALnet) and U: lines (Undernet)	275
18.4.15	E: lines and F: lines (EFnet)	276
18.4.16	T: lines (Undernet)	276
18.4.17	D: lines (IRCnet and Undernet)	276
18.5	The MOTD	276
18.6	IRC Operator Commands	277
18.6.1	OPER	277
18.6.2	KILL	278
18.6.3	CONNECT	279
18.6.4	SQUIT	280
18.6.5	DIE	281
18.6.6	RESTART	281
18.6.7	STATS	282
18.6.8	TRACE	282
18.6.9	REHASH	282
18.6.10	DEOP	283

18.7	Monitoring a Server	283
18.8	The Price of Power	284
18.8.1	*Channels*	*285*
18.8.2	*IRC Cops*	*285*
18.8.3	*. . . And Justice for All*	*286*
18.8.4	*Bots*	*286*
18.9	Networking	287

19

IRC ROBOTS

19.1	Description of a Bot	290
19.2	Uses for Bots	290
19.3	Types of Bots	291
19.4	Eggdrop	292
19.4.1	*Obtaining and Installing the Eggdrop*	*292*
19.4.2	*Running the Eggdrop*	*293*
19.5	Combot	293

20

THE SOAPBOX AND MORE

20.1	The Users of IRC	296
20.2	Privacy and Anonymity	296
20.3	Censorship	297
20.4	IRC Addiction	299
20.5	Pornography on IRC	301
20.6	IRC and Software Piracy	302
20.7	Kids on IRC	303
20.8	In Conclusion	304

A

NETWORK AND SERVER LISTS

A.1	Table of Networks	307
A.2	Servers and More Networks	309

B

TERMINOLOGY 313

C

COUNTRIES ON IRC AND DOMAIN DECODER 321

D

USEFUL ADDRESSES 327

E

SERVER NUMERICS 338

F

SAMPLE SERVER CONFIGURATIONS

F.1 Basic Configuration (hybrid 5.3 Server)   339
F.2 Advanced Configuration (Bahamut Server)   342

Index

PREFACE

Hello, and welcome to *The Book of IRC*. In this episode . . . sorry, I got carried away. What I really want to say is welcome to the unique world of communication we call IRC, and that I've done my best to create a book about Internet Relay Chat that is not just informative and also technical, but easy to understand and use.

In this effort, I've received help from many people, and special thanks are due to some of them: Dr. Joseph Lo who, when not neck-deep in research, took the time to contribute great material for Macintosh users; Alice Loftin, for editing out some of my worse grammatical blunders, adding substance and content to some of the chapters and being supportive throughout; M.D. Yesowitch for reviewing text that was sometimes, well, not exactly top of the line and coming up with some great improvements; Gail Nelson for making sure I stayed between the lines (and appropriately admonishing me when I didn't); the team at No Starch Press, who have been very understanding (and inordinately tolerant) of my frequent transgressions of deadlines; Josh Rollyson and the mysterious Swede known as Queux; and several more individuals, who have in their small ways helped this book with their input and contributions.

Whether I've succeeded in creating a book you will find truly useful and helpful is for you to say and your comments are welcome at **comments@bookofirc.com.** Please note that the volume of comments may not permit me to reply to each one individually, but all will be read and considered for the next edition.

Changes in the IRC world will be rapid, and there is a Web site for updates that occur after the release of this book. It's not reasonable to believe that this book will be up to date forever — that's a practical impossibility since IRC (and the Internet as a whole) is an ever changing world. Take the time to visit the book's Web site at http://www.bookofirc.com/, where the latest updates to the book's contents will be posted, and some things that simply did not fit into this book are covered — and possibly much more, as time allows . . .

I hope this book will answer most (if not all) of your questions about IRC and everything around it. And remember, if there's something you think is missing, just let me know . . . and don't be afraid to ask questions. There are many good people on IRC who are willing to help. Who knows? It might even be me that you run into.

Alex Charalabidis
November 1999

0

INSTRUCTIONS FOR INTERNET DUMMIES

This is not meant to be a book about using the Internet. There are many fine books out there that will serve a "Internet dummy" much better than this one, if only for the simple reason that they were meant to be books about using the Internet. Still, I'm taking into account the fact that many readers of this book, even some who have an Internet connection, may have only a superficial acquaintance with the Internet and could use some help with getting connected or understanding more about it. If you're already hooked up and know your way around, skip ahead to Chapter 1 if you prefer. But I still suggest you skim through this one and see if there's anything you can use.

I don't even take for granted that the reader owns a computer. Many people use one at work but have seen no reason to purchase one for themselves. In fact, this was the case with me; I bought my old, used Atari 1040 STF (a fine machine indeed) with hooking up to the Internet in mind, although I did get to play some really hot games on it (while I no longer have it). In retrospect, my employer probably wouldn't have minded if I had hijacked the machine at work for Internet purposes— but your employer may not be so agreeable.

0.1 Help! Where's the On Button?

If you belong to the category of people who are neither computer savvy nor Internet wise, most of the information you have (good and bad) about the Internet comes from the media, and more likely than not companies providing Internet access have bombarded you with advertisements. If we count the advertising campaigns of companies like CompuServe and America Online (AOL) and the legendary quantities of free trial disks sent out (zillions would be a fair estimate), we might say the Internet has reached everyone—if not on their computer, at least in their mailbox. Indeed, in countries like the United States, AOL deprived the computing community of a never-ending supply of free floppy disks when it switched to sending out CDs instead.

Neither of these sources (media and advertisement) is sufficient for gaining adequate knowledge about connecting to or using the Internet. The media don't seem to notice the Internet unless there's a controversy about it that they can exaggerate enough to present to the public as news. Advertisers oversimplify things and hype them up as much as they can—often more, largely because they can get away with it. If you sometimes get the impression they think you're stupid, you're right. Fear not! You have *The Book of IRC*. It may not turn you into a computer guru overnight, but you'll get straight answers for a change. This is where some of the misconceptions and rumors end.

For the rest of this chapter and in some of those that follow, we'll deal with getting an Internet connection and setting it up for use with Internet Relay Chat. We'll take a close look at the most common methods of connecting to the Internet and Internet Relay Chat services, as well as the necessary equipment.

0.2 Equipment

First of all, you'll need access to a computer (tell me if I'm stating the obvious). You can use IRC and the Internet from practically any computer. The difference is that newer, more powerful machines are capable of handling a number of different tasks while connected, whereas older ones (pre-1990, mainly) can only act as a terminal connected to a more powerful computer in a different location; they depend largely on the resources that computer offers. If you don't have a computer, consider whether you intend to use it for more than just the Internet and what you expect from it.

If you want the full package, including pretty pictures, high-speed connections, the ability to play the latest games, and everything else modern computers can do, you should opt for a recent model capable of handling just about anything. If you'd rather start with the most basic package to see if you like using it (or to find out whether IRC is the thing for you), a text-based environment will do just fine. You can find an older, used machine dirt cheap or even dig one up for free from your company's surplus equipment storage room. If you find you don't like IRC, a no-frills machine makes a fine typewriter, offers you plentiful games, and gives you access to the whole wide world of the Internet. These days you can get even fairly powerful used or reconditioned machines for a decent price.

If you plan on buying a new computer and don't think you have the expertise to select the right one, ask a knowledgeable friend to help you out. You should thoroughly scrutinize your prospective buy and not take the salesperson's word for it, or you might end up buying the kitchen sink whether you like (or even use) it or not. The computer market is full of white elephants—machines packed with gadgets you may never want or need, but could end up paying for anyway. Salespeople are doing a good job when they sell you one of these, but it doesn't look good on your bank statement.

Regarding the bells and whistles they will inevitably offer you, try to make a good guess of what your needs will be over the next couple of years. Contrary to the popular myth that computers are obsolete by the time you leave the store, a well-equipped modern machine provides you with all the power you need for a long time. Think . . . do you need that ultra-snazzy-jazzy sound system? Can you live without the latest in gaming gadgets? Personally, I'd opt for a bare-bones system and make my own selection of choice gadgets, but then I'm a professed geek who enjoys building computers out of spare parts. It's a fact that you can get a decent deal on packages that include these options and avoid the hassle of installing them yourself (and trying to make the more obstinate ones work with your computer)—plus you'll have a warranty that says the box will work *with* them in it. And you thought buying a car was bad! Make sure the deal includes an *operating system* (OS — the layer of programs that actually lets you communicate with the machine) such as Windows or the Mac OS.

The computer, regardless of its other capabilities, must have a telecommunications device (its equivalent to a phone), which will usually be a *modem* (modulator-demodulator, for the acromaniacs out there). Either a card or a box (depending on whether it's inside the computer case or attached to it by a cable), this little device converts data from your computer into signals capable of traversing a telecommunications line. It also converts incoming signals back into something the computer can understand.

Regardless of what type of modem you choose, don't pinch pennies on this piece of equipment. Major brands such as Zoom or US Robotics will be more expensive, but also tend to be far more reliable than the nameless bargain modem. External modems are more expensive and require a separate power supply, but they're easier to move or take apart and generally have a helpful, independent function display of their own. New computers tend to come with one installed, though you won't often get a brand-name modem in a "package deal" machine.

Modem speed is another factor to consider. You usually have a choice between speeds of 33.6 and 56 Kbps (that's kilobits per second). If your salesperson calls it "kilobytes (rhymes with "bites"), either you're getting an incredibly good deal, or he doesn't have a clue what he's talking about and you should make an excuse and get out of the store. This figure is the maximum speed at which your modem can shovel data down a line. Higher is better, but ordinary connections cannot handle speeds higher than 53 Kbps under ideal conditions, so 33.6 isn't such a bad choice.

One more absolutely necessary item is a working telecommunications line—a regular phone line will do just fine. Low line quality can seriously impede the functioning of your network connection, though. If you plan to spend long hours on the Internet or transfer a lot of data on a regular basis, you may need a dedicated phone line. In this case, getting a more expensive ISDN link is worth the investment, since it can accommodate much more traffic—provided you also have the *hardware* to take advantage of its capabilities.

Cable lines and *DSLs* (Digital Subscriber Lines) are becoming increasingly available and offer much faster speeds than your average modem connection. However, other cable modem users and TV usage from other people on the same line can strongly affect the performance of a cable link. DSL is probably the connection type for the future (it's basically just a regular phone line with a twist), but it isn't widespread yet and it costs a fair bit more than a regular modem connection. Even in major cities, it may be available only in limited areas. Either of these two options generally requires special hardware and considerable setup fees. If you choose one of these options, however, you can do without a modem.

More recently it's become possible to connect to the Internet and IRC via a TV set with some additional hardware or even a games console. I will not go into details about this means of connecting, since they don't use a full computing environment, and the companies selling the equipment should provide setup instructions. The IRC software that accompanies these devices is extremely poor in features and functionality and won't satisfy even the most undemanding user for long. Depending on future developments in this area, a future edition of this book may cover it.

0.3 Computing and the Internet for Beginners

First and foremost, always remember that the computer is only a machine! Computer phobia is all too common and quite unjustified. A computer is as dumb as any other machine, and if a human doesn't tell it exactly what to do, it sits there like the pretty (or ugly, depending on your personal aesthetics) piece of inanimate silicon, plastic, and metal it really is. When a computer appears to have a mind of its own, as it often will, and refuses to listen to human reason, it's not trying to intimidate you, even though this is precisely what it achieves. The cause of this behavior, though undiscovered, is widely believed to be the work of gremlins. Now there's an explanation I can live with.

Second, the Internet—and especially IRC—is definitely *not* an environment for total beginners. Anyone wishing to use the Internet, and IRC in particular (which involves more technicalities than most of the Internet), should have at least a basic degree of familiarity with computers.

In short, if you don't comprehend the meaning of terms like *directory, file,* or *reboot,* you should learn more about computers before attempting to use the Internet. A good, basic book will do just fine. This will save you and other users a lot of frustration. In the IRC environment, you do most of your communicating with humans, not machines, and newcomers are more welcome when they're visibly trying to educate themselves instead of blundering about trying to "do the Net thing" without blowing up their machine. A friendly attitude gets you a lot of help from more-experienced users, but their patience is not limitless.

If you know nothing about computers, please, please learn to operate yours before getting onto the Internet. You will often find it necessary or desirable to install new software or hardware on your machine or perform other important maintenance tasks, so it's essential that you be familiar with enough of the basics to handle such relatively simple things.

And remember (once more)—a computer is a machine, a bit more than a glorified calculator, but essentially a number-crunching device. It's about as complex and intricate as machinery comes, but if you can drive a car, you can probably handle a computer with the same ease (well, almost) after a bit of practice. Fortunately or unfortunately, taking part in everyday road traffic requires a license, while using the Internet doesn't. It may well be said that a networked computer is just about the most complex device you're allowed to operate without training or a license.

In the same way you need a driver's license before rolling out of the garage, don't venture out into the Internet traffic without knowing how to operate your "vehicle." This might sound like elitism coming from someone who's been around a while, but in my experience ignorance, rather than redundancy, causes the most damage and annoyance on the Internet.

0.4 Internet Service Providers

Owning the equipment and software for connecting to the Internet is one half of the deal. The other half is getting a link through which you can connect. Unless you're fortunate enough to have free Internet access from a university or your workplace, you'll have to buy an account with an *Internet service provider* (ISP), often referred to simply as a *provider*. Nowadays, with ISPs springing up faster than mushrooms in the dark, you're likely to have a wide selection of providers—especially in larger cities, where the number of options available may reach well into three digits.

If you have an Internet connection you can use or borrow for a while, an extensive list of ISPs is available via the *World Wide Web* (http://www.thelist.com). Otherwise, the Yellow Pages and computer or Internet magazines should be a good source of information—the Yellow Pages may be more helpful, as they're more localized.

Your best option is to ask around. If you have friends in the area who are already connected, they can probably give you a more objective view of the quality of a provider's services. If you don't have someone to guide you, you will have to rely on other channels of information.

Magazines generally have ads for large providers with *POPs* (points of presence) in many places; advertising hype, which you can disregard, fills these ads. Unless you're very unlucky or in a really remote place, you'll easily locate the voice phone numbers of one or more ISPs in your area. Larger providers may have a toll-free number staffed by salespeople, while smaller ones more often have someone who also deals with customer or tech support making the sales contacts.

Naturally, each provider will try to talk you into buying from itself. Allow the rep to rattle off the virtues of the establishment, then ignore what he or she just told you and try to establish the individual's attitude and level of knowledge. You probably hate random salespeople patronizing you over the phone as much as I do. Some of them use tech talk to impress and confuse the less knowledgeable—a time-honored sales tactic.

Pay more attention to helpfulness and don't let the salesperson impress you with jargon and promises of the glorious benefits coming to customers of that particular provider. Also don't let numbers and statistics dazzle you—after all, you care about good Internet service, not surveys or promises. In fact, you're very likely to discover that small providers take better care of their customers and are more flexible, fast, and efficient in dealing with problems.

0.4.1 Connecting to the Internet via a PPP Dial-Up

PPP is by far the most common way of connecting today. Using special software, your machine connects to the Internet by dialing your ISP's telephone number. The machine responding to incoming calls identifies you after you send it a unique user ID and password. It then assigns you an *Internet Protocol* (IP) address, thus making your machine a part of the Internet. The majority of providers draw from a pool of IP addresses (which a competent authority assigns to the provider) to give you a random address that no one else is using at the time you call in. If your provider uses this method, you have a different IP address each time you connect. This is known as a *dynamic* IP system.

Other providers give you the same IP address each time you connect and maybe even assign a unique Internet name to your machine. This is a *static* IP system and often costs a bit more. Your ISP should supply you with the software and instructions necessary for connecting in this fashion; make sure it does so before you buy an account, and don't forget to ask for its customer support phone number in case you get stuck.

PPP is a good, fairly simple way of connecting for the Windows, Macintosh, and Amiga platforms (if you're using Unix, DOS, or an Atari machine, it's much more technical and not suitable for the beginner). It has the advantage of putting all your Internet programs on your own machine so you can modify the setup at will. Its main drawback is the relatively slow speed of modem connections.

0.4.2 Connecting to the Internet via Dial-In

This was the most widely used method of connecting before PPP took over. Most ISPs no longer offer plain dial-in connections, though BBSs and providers wishing to offer an extra service for lower-tech users still use it. Be sure to check whether your intended ISP offers a dial-in service if this is how you plan to hook up.

With a dial-in account, you use a simple terminal program to connect to your ISP's number. After you log on, this program makes your system a terminal of a machine the ISP owns and maintains (these machines almost universally use Unix-type multiuser operating systems).

An account that entails using a Unix machine from a command line is called a *shell account*.

A dial-in account is an excellent way of connecting for users with low-end machines (not everyone owns a Pentium). Even old machines like Atari STs and PC-XTs can easily connect to the Internet if they act as a networked machine's terminal. The advantage is that such an account requires minimal local resources and little configuration, and you are not responsible for maintaining the networked machine.

Dial-in is also ideal for people with old, slow modems, for whom using PPP would often be agonizingly slow because the modem communicates with the provider's machine less efficiently than when it acts as a terminal. The drawback is that you usually depend on the ISP's staff for updating and configuring the machine and software available on it, and you may not have access to useful utilities. If you prefer to work in a graphical environment or have trouble understanding text-based systems, it's likewise probably not for you.

0.5 Starting Out on the Internet and Using Basic Services

Before starting out with IRC, I recommend that you familiarize yourself with a few of the basic, easier-to-use parts of the Internet. You'll soon encounter one or both the World Wide Web and FTP when searching for information or obtaining essential files. First, though, we'll have a look at the most common services offered on the Internet—sooner or later you'll make use of these, whether in conjunction with IRC or not.

0.5.1 Using the World Wide Web

The World Wide Web is what less knowledgeable people think of as the Internet. Actually, it's no more than a system of linked documents (called *hypertext* documents), which has grown to immense proportions and now contains millions upon millions of pages, covering just about every topic our literate species has written about. If you're in need of information, this is the place you should look first. (Hypertext is the same system you encounter in DOS or Windows help files when you select a word in a document and press ENTER or click to call up another document.)

The basis of this system is twofold: *HTTP*, HyperText Transfer Protocol, requests documents and transfers them between machines. *HTML*, HyperText Markup Language, consists of special instructions embedded in documents that control the characteristics of the page, its attributes (color, font size, pictures, and so forth), and also make it possible to call up another page or perform a function by selecting part of the text.

All of this requires special software known as a *browser*. Netscape, Microsoft Internet Explorer, Mosaic, and Lynx are some well-known browser programs; you probably have one of them on your machine.

0.5.2   Using FTP

FTP (File Transfer Protocol) transfers files over the Internet. Designed especially for file transfers, it's much simpler than the Web and often faster. FTP is especially useful for obtaining software, including updates of programs you use for IRC.

FTP client programs are very simple to use and need little explaining. You simply connect to an FTP server machine somewhere on the Internet, downloading or uploading files and disconnecting when they're finished.

A special case of FTP is *anonymous FTP*. Public FTP servers, which allow the general public to access files stored on their system, use this system. Smaller FTP sites are often specialized and offer certain kinds of software, while larger ones offer an incredible variety of files for any conceivable machine and purpose.

When you connect to an FTP server, it asks you to give a user name and a password. If you have a personal account on the FTP server machine, such as one your provider has assigned, enter the appropriate user name and password when asked or even before connecting, if your FTP program has such a feature. If you plan to use anonymous FTP, simply enter **anonymous** or **ftp** when prompted for a user name; use your email address as the password. Note that anonymous FTP servers are likely to have restrictions on the number of users who may use it simultaneously, and may permit anonymous FTP only outside business hours.

0.5.3   Using Telnet

Telnet, one of the cornerstones of using remote machines, is simply a means of connecting to another networked machine. What you can do on the remote machine depends on your access level. Telnet programs are extremely simple to use, as they're little more than a terminal, and some can also double as a regular terminal program and dialer. You use them by entering the address of the remote machine (either on the command line or in the appropriate field, depending on the program) and specifying a *port* to which to connect.

A port is essentially an address on a machine—compare it to a telephone extension, in which a number indicating the extension follows the number of the regular telephone network. The competent authority assigns port 23 to telnet. This means if you wish to connect to the remote machine and log in as a user of that machine, you should specify 23 as the port to connect to.

Connecting to a port other than 23 results in refusal of your connection, since that port might not be open to connections or, if the port belongs to a service other than telnet, it may behave differently than a standard telnet port. Some machines run services meant to be "telnet-table," listen on predefined ports, and interact with users coming in via telnet—however, you would have to know the number of those ports in advance.

Why do you need to know this? This is as much as I can offer on a subject that really falls outside the scope of this book. Let's get on to the subject you really want to hear about.

1

IRC? WHAT'S THAT?

IRC, or Internet Relay Chat, is a multi-user, real-time communication system hundreds of thousands of people all over the world use. That's a lot of long words to describe something as simple as text-based chat, but then it's complex and interesting enough to have whole books written about it. This is the latest and, I modestly hope, the most comprehensive and helpful one to date.

If you're already a regular IRC user, you know how much entertainment and knowledge you can gain from it. I and the people who helped me to write this book hope it will help you understand IRC even better.

If you've never used IRC before, this book contains all the instructions, hints, and rules you'll need. It is the first book to cover IRC in this much detail and is designed for even a total beginner to understand, as well as providing a valuable source of information for the more experienced user. Even for those who really know their way around, here it is: everything you always wanted to know about IRC but never thought of asking.

1.1 So . . . What's It All About?

It's about communication. IRC is yet another facet of the ongoing revolution in telecommunications called the Internet, and one of the most fascinating ones. Sure, it's easy to hook up to an online service, open Netscape or Internet Explorer and do your shopping, gather information on anything from quantum physics to horticulture, or just hop from one "home page" to the next, but that's not all there is to the Internet. IRC makes the most of it by offering something beyond the Web and email: the ability to communicate directly, interactively, and in real time with any single person or group you wish to.

IRC is more than entertainment. It's active communication. You can buy all the latest, greatest, state-of-the-art (and pricey) "interactive" software but you'll still only have a bunch of electrons staring back at you. Instead, you can tune into IRC and its diverse multitude of channels and join an online society made up of real people, not computer-generated aliens to be shot down ad lib, not gremlins inside your computer, not programs made to entertain you at your command. It's important to always remember that IRC consists of real people, with all the faults and advantages that implies.

When it comes to real-time communication over the Internet, you have several options: proprietary systems like the chat rooms on America Online or Prodigy that are available only to members, the likes of Instant Messenger or ICQ, IRC, or local bulletin boards, to name the most widely used means. Each has its advantages and disadvantages, and the choice is not always easy.

I won't try to explain the pros and cons of all forms of online chat; most are designed to be very simple. IRC is special in the way the simplicity of text chat expands to include the parallel transfer of files, which can be used for visual and auditory enhancement of an IRC session.

Nowhere else in the world will you find so many opportunities to mingle with the other occupants of the global village. Be they in South Dakota or South Africa, India or Indiana, the people are there. IRC is where you can see the borders of nationality, race, and creed that confine us in everyday life crumble more readily than anywhere else. You could say it is global warming in its safest form.

1.2 Origin and History of IRC

A system based on a similar concept appeared on the U.S. military network much earlier, although it did not make its way to the broader community. But IRC as it is now known evolved from a program Jarkko Oikarinen at Oulu University wrote in the summer of 1988 (Oulu is a small town on the northwestern coast of Finland). Oikarinen added some extensions to a multiuser form of the classic *talk*, a means of one-to-one live communication between Internet users, which had the drawback of not supporting three-way or group communication. Of course, the original IRC was far simpler than modern versions, which have made IRC one of the most complex systems on the Internet. Although there is no longer an IRC server on Oikarinen's original machine, called the *oulubox*, there is still an IRC server at the original site serving local users.

Very early on, IRC was an entirely Finnish affair and largely geared towards Finnish users. Soon after its creation, IRC was exported, and servers in Oulu and Gothemburg, Sweden, made the first international connection, followed soon by Boston, Massachusetts, although the connections were not stable. In those days, the Internet was still a thing of the future, and many of today's main connections didn't exist at that time. Nor was all communication carried over dedicated lines, especially transcontinental and overseas.

"Internetworking" was more often than not subject to the limitations of the regular telephone network and its tariffs, making it a costly affair that even the fairly affluent educational institutes of northern Europe and the United States couldn't support easily.

Since then, IRC has spread all over the world, together with the Internet's development and as part of it. The number of regular and circumstantial IRC users (people who use IRC regularly as well as those who use it sporadically) is impossible to determine, but probably reaches well into seven digits. So far, people in over 120 countries and territories on all continents have used IRC, and it's arguably third only to email and the World Wide Web (WWW) in popularity. By the way, opinions on the pronunciation of IRC still vary. Some prefer to pronounce it "irk," while others prefer calling it "eye-are-see." Personally, I use the latter, even though historical documents dating back to the early days support the former, and it matches the Finnish pronunciation.

IRC's first claims to fame and recognition came in early 1991, during the military operation to expel Iraq from Kuwait ("Desert Storm") as well as in September 1993, following the coup against President Yeltsin in Moscow, when local IRC users relayed reports of the situation around the world. As far as the general public was concerned, however, it was just "the Internet," and few commentators had the knowledge to describe the means used—that is, IRC. Such reports of local happenings have always been a part of IRC life, but rarely did they lead to publicity and even less often to reaching the public with serious information about IRC. Even nowadays, a number of experienced Internet users and an unbelievably large number of professional technical or support personnel working with the Internet have absolutely no knowledge of the workings or even the existence of IRC.

With time, the complexity of all aspects of IRC has increased greatly, making both maintaining and using it much more complicated and involving its users with a lot more technical details than most other Internet applications.

IRC started out in 1988 with only a handful of users, all of them also involved in developing the software and establishing the rules that now form the foundation of IRC. With the number of educational institutions all over the world connecting to the Internet rising sharply in the early 1990s and, consequently, large numbers of students at those institutes gaining access, the number of regular users grew to reach a maximum of 5,000 simultaneous connections in 1992.

Politics made their appearance in the IRC community pretty soon, however, and it became apparent that not everyone shared the same vision of the future. Some decided to follow their own way, breaking up the first network of IRC servers into smaller ones, although few of these splintered networks survived for long. But the changes have made modern IRC even more complicated, since the existing networks follow a number of different standards instead of adhering to a common set of technical and administrative methods.

Of course, you don't have to worry about that yet—they all still follow a basic protocol, which is the technical foundation of IRC, so you can expect to encounter few problems related to those differences in the beginning. Any problems you encounter at first are more likely to be entirely human in character and origin.

Following the fragmentation of the IRC world into a number of separate entities, the combined user count of these continued to grow at an extremely high rate, even compared to the overall number of Internet users, reaching 20,000 for the largest network in early 1996. With *dial-up* services becoming increasingly available to the public in more and more parts of the world, subscribers to commercial *Internet service providers* (ISPs) have been the major contributors to the increase in users and, particularly in the more technologically developed countries in Europe, North America, and around the Pacific, now outnumber academic users by far. Current trends show that the rate of growth could be as much as 30 percent annually, maybe even more.

On February 22, 1999, EFnet, the largest IRC network, reached the landmark number of 50,000 simultaneous connections. It was the opinion of many in 1992 that IRC had reached its limits with the 5,000 concurrent users seen then. This number is still being revised upwards—it's now acknowledged that there's no telling how high it will go.

1.3 Technical Concept

The keyword in IRC is "Relay." While "Internet" and "Chat" have obvious meanings, "Relay" sounds a bit more mysterious. Let's have a look at the basic concept of IRC in order to discover the meaning behind the term.

IRC, in its simplest form, is made up of two programs—a *server* program that accepts connections and a *client* program that connects to the server.

Of course, it isn't absolutely necessary to use a special program— the server would view a simple network connection between you and the server as a client. However, a client program handles some necessary procedures automatically and provides a better and simpler user interface than the more technical messages the client and server exchange.

IRC servers connect to each other via an IRC *network* of servers. Let's use a very simple model of an IRC network for our example: two servers and two clients. The servers are connected to each other, and each has a client (a user) connected to it. The structure would look like this:

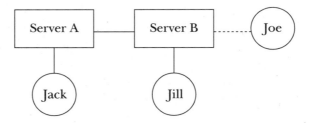

Ignore Joe for now. We'll get to him. Let's say Jack wishes to send a message to Jill. However, their machines don't connect directly. But each connects to a server, which is in turn connected to the server to which the other user is connected. Therefore, Jack can make use of the indirect route that exists between him and Jill. What Jack does is send server A a message. In this message, he will tell server A the message's final destination (Jill) and its contents.

Server A is aware of the existence of Jill, although she's not connected to it directly, and it knows that she's connected to server B. It therefore forwards—*relays*—the message to server B, which in turn sees that the recipient is one of its own clients and sends the message to Jill, who can then read it. Server A also adds the identity of the client sending it (Jack) before relaying it, so the recipient knows who it's from. This transfer of information between the servers and its users typically happens within milliseconds, thus making the exchange of messages swift enough to match that of real conversation.

This is why Jack doesn't need to connect directly to Jill to send his message—the IRC environment permits an almost unlimited number of recipients for the same message and can relay this message to all those users at the same time. IRC permits one-on-one communication, but its real advantage is the ability to communicate with large numbers of people by sharing a common *channel* of conversation.

Let's say we add a third user. Joe is connected to server B, just like Jill is. All three of them join a channel which they decide to call **#the-hill** (naturally). They arrange the channel name by sending messages to each other. Establishing this channel gives them a means of three-way communication. So if Jill wants to tell Jack, "Come, let's fetch a pail of water," and sends the message to the channel instead of sending it only to Jack, all users on the channel receive the message. Joe sees the same message and might decide to go with them—then the world of nursery rhymes would never be the same.

1.4 What IRC Has to Offer

So far, so good, but what makes IRC so exciting and useful? What makes IRC special enough for entire books on the subject? What makes hundreds of thousands of people sit in front of a computer talking to people at the other end of the world whom they don't know and will probably never meet, instead of going out?

In order to understand IRC and realize why it's a good thing, you must try it. Once you connect, it won't take long to discover whether you love it, hate it, or find it nice for an occasional visit. Not everyone is thrilled by it—I've observed that it often does not appeal to people who find it necessary to be in visual contact with the people they're conversing with.

For those who stay after their initial trip to IRC, the rewards can be significant. It's more than just a pastime or something you do during your lunch break. You may soon find yourself arranging virtual meetings (which develop into real ones more often than you'd expect), making new friends, including some you wish you had in RL (that is, "Real Life"), taking part in group projects, such as managing a channel, and having lots of fun. In fact, practically everything in life has an IRC counter-part. It's more than a virtual society—it's a real society with a minimum of re-strictions on your freedom of movement, as long as you follow the very few basic and reasonable rules, which the relevant sections of this book will explain.

IRC, for its longtime denizens and addicts, is more than just a chat system or a meeting place—it can become a way of life. Many people find themselves becoming more active, social, and outspoken in this world where prejudice due to race, sex, or physical appearance is as minimal as can be, given that its users do come from societies where these factors tend to be a major influence on everyday interpersonal communication. IRC can be a very educational experience—you can interact with people you probably would never meet on a real-life social level, people from an amazing variety of backgrounds and culture.

Its high social flexibility is another advantage. Large networks form a single large community—a country, if you like—and smaller network communities resemble towns. The difference is that there are practically no space limitations. The communities can expand indefinitely in theory, so there's no conflict about one community expanding at the expense of another's breathing space. Anyone is free to form his or her own community with like-minded people, or even to build a "city." IRC itself started out as a group of people with an interest or activity in common, and it has been growing outward ever since.

As is the case with all Internet communication methods, IRC has the very important advantage of offering dirt-cheap, real-time communication. It's not the only live chat environment on the Internet, but it is the one with the most versatility and potential uses. Whether for purposes of idle chat or serious discussion, you can communicate directly with numerous people at the same time for no more than your regular Internet connection costs you.

1.5   IRC for Company Use

While it is mainly a recreational environment and often maligned as such, IRC is not without its business uses. Employers may have reason to object to their workforce chatting the workday away on IRC, but this monster can be tamed and put to work for company purposes.

There are already several large Internet service providers that use IRC servers for customer support, either within the framework of a public network or as a stand-alone service. IRC is becoming an acceptable means of offering customer support since it uses minimal resources, does not tie up a company's phone lines, and allows the support personnel to help online while answering telephone calls.

For the same reason, it's also gaining recognition as a potent communications tool within a company, as it will perform well on any TCP/IP-based network and not just the Internet. It provides an ideal environment for intra-company communication and online conferencing and requires very little maintenance once it's set up and running.

At the same time, the low cost of IRC software (in fact, the total cost may be nil) makes it a very cost-effective solution compared to more expensive systems with fewer features and higher maintenance requirements.

In the end, the question is not how much you *can* gain from IRC, because it's there for the taking. The question is what you *wish* to gain, and the options are practically limitless.

Welcome to the world of Internet Relay Chat.

2

YOUR IRC SURVIVAL KIT

There are a few things you really should know before getting on IRC. Save yourself a lot of trouble and potential damage by reading this chapter, which I've packed with advice and helpful hints. You'll need a compass, maps, and emergency rations for the long trip ahead, and here is where you'll find them—so don't skip this essential information.

2.1 Saints and Sinners

You're likely to meet a huge number of people even your first time on IRC—not only those with whom you talk, in public or in private, but also those with whom you share a channel for a while, and still others whose presence you won't immediately notice.

It would be nice to think of IRC as a place filled with good people, but alas, as in real life, this is hardly the case. If you're unlucky, you'll run into some despicable person within minutes of connecting—and you're bound to run into more than one sooner or later. Don't let this discourage you from exploring IRC.

Trust is a good thing—there's no doubt about that. It's the basis of society. In the IRC world, there are a lot of people you can't trust. In a nutshell, trust no one—not because everyone's untrustworthy but because you'll find the results of misplaced trust very unpleasant and damaging, even more so if you use your work machine for IRC.

You'll establish a circle of friends eventually—there's no hurry, so don't try to speed up this natural process up by doing what you're told, whether you understand it or not, in the effort to please everyone. In the meantime, until you're capable of telling the saints from the sinners, you would do well to be cautious. Let's go over some basic rules that will serve you well.

2.2 Safety First

Chapter 17 will cover most of the subjects in this chapter in greater detail. However, you need to be aware of certain dangers long before you reach that part of the book—in fact, before you even connect to IRC. Don't hesitate to flip ahead—the information in Chapter 17 is more technical, but equally useful.

2.2.1 Trojan Horses

Trojan horses have been around on IRC for quite a while now. If you've examined any of the common antivirus packages, you've probably seen an option to include Trojans in the scan.

If you don't remember the story of the Trojan horse, the crafty Odysseus devised this wooden gizmo to take over the ancient city of Troy. He left it at the Trojans' portals, disguised as an item of worship the besieging Greeks had left behind. Actually, it sheltered a troop of Greek soldiers just waiting to get past the city walls and jump out as the Trojans gloated over their prize. This is where computer programs with similar purposes and characteristics get their name.

A Trojan is technically *not* a virus, though it does fall in the general category of nasty items that can attach themselves to your computer if you're not careful. Trojans pose as desirable programs, while viruses generally try to hide. Trojans mainly target Windows machines, but some are designed to compromise the security of Unix hosts.

Trojans are nowadays the number one hazard for uneducated IRC users. The number of people who have "contracted" some kind of Trojan since January 1998, when they became widespread among Windows and mIRC users, is unknown but substantial—enough to show this is by no means an "it can't happen to me" thing. It can happen to anyone.

Almost all somewhat advanced programs for IRC offer the ability to swap files with other users. However, you will also encounter unsolicited offers of files from users you don't know. Look out for these, and *refuse to accept them.* Most will be INI and EXE files, programs your computer or IRC program can run, and in so doing firmly install a nasty program on your computer. Some are cleverly disguised as pictures or contained in Zip (compressed) files.

What do Trojans do? When you accept and run one (double-clicking on the file name usually does the trick), it installs itself somewhere on your computer—wherever its creator has told it to go—and very often poses as a useful program, creates backup copies of itself, and activates each time you run your IRC program or start up your machine. One of the earlier and tamer Trojans installed a file named Winhelper. I bet you would think twice about deleting a file with such a useful-sounding name if you didn't *know* it was actually letting outsiders access your computer or damage your files without your knowing it. Once installed, Trojans often offer unlimited access to your machine to practically anyone. Many also make you unknowingly offer a copy of the same Trojan to other users.

The following is not just an old wives' tale or a horror story—well, maybe it's a horror story, but it *is* true. A friend asked me to take a look at a computer that had been behaving oddly. We turned it on, connected it to the Internet, and sure enough, some programs started to run spontaneously, and others we called up would run with mysteriously slowness or even crash. I got a tipoff from its owner when he told me the CD-ROM drive tray would pop in and out for no apparent reason. That clinched it—I did a basic check on the machine's connections. Lo and behold, I found an unexplainable connection to some machine in Dallas, which judging by its address was clearly a plain old dial-up and not any kind of server.

Apparently my friend had a Trojan that actually *told* certain people his machine's address so they could come and "play" as soon as he connected to the Internet. When we powered up again and reconnected, our next uninvited guest was from somewhere in France.

In other words, it's perfectly possible for someone on the other side of the Atlantic (or the Pacific) to invade your machine, make your CD-ROM drive do funny things, delete your thesis or business accounts (or just steal them), use your computer as a base for illegal operations such as trading child pornography, and wipe out your system to top it off—all within ten minutes. Scary, huh?

Your protection is *knowledge.* Do not accept unsolicited offers of files. Mistrust even those friends send you—there's no guarantee your friend knows enough to prevent such a problem. Reject executable files and scripts altogether unless you're capable of reading and analyzing them. If you don't actually accept and run a Trojan, you are safe. They're like vampires—just don't invite them into your house!

Always remember the first rule about getting files from other people on IRC. If you don't know what it is and can't see for yourself what it does, just say no!

2.2.2 Nukes

Some of the sinners I mentioned earlier employ more straightforward means of making your online life miserable. While you could classify Trojan designers and "pushers" as hackers if they choose to engage in some creative or productive activity (but they don't, so they remain wannabe hackers), nukers are just pre-juvenile delinquents who throw stones through people's windows. Anyone can nuke, but only about 1 in 50 of those who prove their "superior" computing skills in this way has the vaguest idea of how the process works. Actually, even the term *nuke* is a bit high-flown. I simply refer to them as *Denial of Service* (DoS) attacks, and so do law enforcement agencies, since they're illegal.

Nukes are just annoying. They hardly threaten your machine's integrity, but they can easily wreak havoc with your network connection or cause the system to hang and force you to restart it. Windows 95, 3.11 (for Workgroups), and NT users are in a very high-risk category here. Nukes that work on Macintosh, Windows 3.1, Windows 98, and Unix systems are comparatively rare. Of course, new vulnerabilities show up all the time, so by the time you read this book there may well be a new category of nukes. You'll find descriptions and solutions for the most common ones in Chapter 17.

TIP *Several very good websites offer up-to-date information on attacks. They also offer help on patching your system's vulnerabilities. It's a good idea to visit these sites before connecting to IRC and avoid nasty surprises.*

A couple of sites you might find helpful are http://www.irchelp.org/ security/ and http://mirc.stealth.net/.

2.2.3 Insert Card to Continue

All the subjects I am warning you about here are considered criminal acts in most of the civilized world. The last one you should be aware of before connecting is no exception. In fact, it's more clearly defined as criminal, and people have gotten into serious trouble for it.

Here it is, in a phrase: *Never, ever* give your credit card number or password to anyone on IRC! As official looking and convincing as they may seem, none of them are up to any good. Nobody legitimate asks you for your password or credit card number. If someone posing as some sort of staff member threatens you with disconnection if you don't comply, ignore that person. If you do get disconnected, it doesn't result from ignoring that individual—he or she used some kind of DoS attack to make the point. Don't fall for this con trick—log such events and report them to the nearest authority on IRC (see 12.4).

2.3 The Virtual Tourist's Guide to IRC Networks

In Chapter 1, I made a brief reference to the fragmentation of IRC. This requires some explaining before you start connecting to any networks.

The story behind this could turn into a really long novel with lots of sex, violence, and intrigue, and I might be able to make a fortune by writing it under an assumed name, so I'll just stick to the basics here.

IRC servers connect to each other in order to form a network of servers, as the figure in Chapter 1 demonstrated. The point of forming a network is basically to allow people from different parts of the Net to connect to the server closest to them and communicate with others who are doing the same thing elsewhere. A network of servers acts a bit like a postal service: The servers carry the "mail" from city to city in big, fast vehicles, and the user just drops off the message at the local server. This gives the user a faster connection; he or she is using a nearby server, and the faster and more powerful connection of the organization running the server carries traffic between users.

Not everything on IRC takes the form of a network. Many IRCs function quite well with a single server, because of the small number of users, the location, or the ease of managing single servers as opposed to neworks. Their disadvantage is that they depend on a single machine, and faraway users may have slower connections. On the other hand, they don't struggle with bickering server administrators or the need to maintain server-to-server connections. For the sake of simplicity, I'll consider larger services of this type networks, too, even though a single server is not a network in the strict sense of the term.

2.3.1 Formation of IRC Networks

What determines how servers connect to each other? There is no rigid set of rules. Servers link to form a network by mutual consent. So if John is running an IRC server in Seattle and Jane has another in New York, they simply have to agree on some ground rules that apply to both the servers and their users. They then connect the servers, and they're in business as a network. Judy in London, with a server of her own, might agree with their policy and connect her server to theirs so that users in

England also have a local server. Instead of attempting transatlantic connections with their puny modem dial-ups, these people can use Judy's server to talk to the users on John's and Jane's servers. Long-distance and transoceanic connections are much more reliable and faster than they used to be, and Internet routes don't strictly follow geographic criteria, but it's a rule of thumb that you're better off connecting to the closest server possible.

John, Jane, and Judy are now the proud administrators of a network with three servers and choose to name it GossipNet. With a name, the network also has a clearly defined public identity. Anyone who hears of GossipNet and wants to go there will seek a list of GossipNet servers and try connecting to the closest one.

You can link an unlimited number of servers in such a network. Networks with more than 100 servers have existed, and one still does. The higher the number of servers belonging to a network, the more versatility you can expect to find on it—but this is where the dark side of human nature creeps in and spoils the dream.

Let's say GossipNet has grown to include 30 servers in various parts of the world. Widely considered an agreeable place, it has several thousand users. But then disaster strikes. John and Jane have a major fight over which kind of server software to use. Because the programs they propose are not compatible, they can't use both on servers belonging to the same network. They fail to agree, and decide it's no longer possible for them to live under the same roof, but the majority of server administrators share John's opinion.

So Jane takes her server and quits the network. Five more GossipNet servers agree with her point of view and follow her into exile. These six breakaway servers decide to stay together and form a network of their own—and thus BlatherNet is born. As for the users of the servers on each side of the fence, they're just confused and eventually pick the side they feel more comfortable on. BlatherNet could expand and grow to be much larger than GossipNet ever was, or it could fade into obscurity and finally disband. Still, a notion of the "good old days" of harmony remains in the minds of everyone involved.

The names in this story are fictitious, but the circumstances could come about, and the reasons for falling out are often much more trivial.

This is how it's been since the early days of IRC, and this is what I call fragmentation. Instead of one big, happy network of servers with lots and lots of users, there are over 200 small networks. Most of them are quite happy, which is probably better than having one huge, miserable network in which the server administrators hate each other and plot the untimely demise of their enemies, but stay together anyway. It sounds (and sometimes is) like a bad soap opera. The problem you'll have is that you'll need a map to find your way through this maze of networks. Don't worry—you'll run into this subject again in Chapter 6, and Appendix A offers a helpful map of IRC networks.

2.3.2 Bright Lights, Big City

The 200-odd different IRC networks fall into various loose groupings. The first category is the major networks. These are the metropolises on the IRC map. Each has hundreds of thousands of regular users and visitors and a multitude of channels. Diversity is the key attraction of these networks, but as with all big cities, they have bad neighborhoods, thugs, busy main roads (in the form of popular channels), taxi drivers (well, maybe not), and crazy people wandering around preaching the end of the world.

The four big "cities" (in order of relative size) are EFnet, IRCnet, Undernet, and DALnet. Each sees over 30,000 simultaneous connections during peak hours, and they rarely drop below the 20,000-user mark. Almost every IRC user visits one of them at some point.

There are also smaller "cities" that have a different population and definitely more law and order. They tend to be less than half the size of the major networks, and single corporations own them. Talk City and the Microsoft Chat Network are the largest of this kind, reaching 8,000 to 15,000 users during peak hours. They tend not to be as cosmopolitan as the major networks, which have many users from all over the world. Most of the smaller networks' users are North American.

2.3.3 Small-Town World

Not everyone feels comfortable in the metropolitan jungle of the major networks. Many people prefer a quieter, more controlled environment. Others just like to get away from the noise and go to a much smaller network to relax every now and then. The atmosphere of these locations is almost bucolic.

There are many small general chat networks, some really tiny and others quite popular. Very few exceed a maximum of 1,000 simultaneous user connections, but many offer good-quality service and have a loyal following. They're more like the small towns and villages of the IRC map—a place where people know each other and less-experienced users feel more secure.

Quite a few of these small networks call themselves "family" networks. They generally offer registration service for their users, have strict policies on which topics they allow and which they ban. Some even go so far as to offer Web space for their regular users and more popular channels. Almost all based in the United States, they adhere to traditional values in an effort to appeal to more conservative people who are looking for a place on IRC suitable for them as well as their kids.

2.3.4 Foreign Exchange

It's a fact that although English is the dominant language on the Internet, many people speak no English at all, have only a limited grasp of it, or simply prefer to converse in their native tongue. In some countries the cost of equipment and connectivity is very high compared to what users and providers can afford to pay, so international links are poor and local services are in high demand. Even English-speaking countries and regions often have local IRC networks serving users in their area but the majority of these networks are based in a single, non-English-speaking country.

Local and regional networks have sprung up to cater to the needs of these people and are booming like no other part of IRC. Some serve a particular country, others have servers in several countries with a common language. They have become extremely popular with both local residents and expatriates.

Networks of this kind exist in many countries. The largest ones are located in Brazil, Spain, Portugal, and Australia and have many thousands of regular users. Smaller but fairly popular ones exist in Mexico, Italy, Turkey, Greece, Bulgaria, some former Soviet republics, and South Africa. A few more countries are home to fledgling IRC networks that wish to fill the gap in their area.

In other countries, local servers connect to a larger, global network but are very popular with local users. This is the case in the Nordic countries, Japan, Poland, Italy, and several others whose most popular servers exist as part of a major network (primarily IRCnet) or other, smaller global networks.

2.3.5 All Things Special

The fourth distinct category of IRC networks includes everything meant to serve users with a particular interest, of a certain age group, religion, social group, or sexual orientation, and anything else that does not fall in the above three groups of general chat networks. None of them are very large, mostly due to the fact that they have little activity outside the official area of interest.

The possibilities for different topics are limitless. Naturally, the most popular involve computers, operating systems, computer games, and the like. Others, designed for kids, offer a more protective environment and adult supervision. Many services in this category are stand-alone servers.

2.4   Someone Asked Me to Meet Him . . . Where?

You'll often find a reference to an IRC channel on some website, or a friend tells you to look him or her up on IRC. This in itself is not a problem, but becomes one when people neglect to mention which of the umpteen IRC networks they or the channel reside on.

There's really no easy solution to this. You have only three options:

- Connect to a random network and pray it's the right one.

- Connect to every network you know of and see if what you're looking for is there. Start with the major networks and work your way down.

- Ask your friend or the person maintaining the Web page that supposedly mentions the item.

You have the right and the moral obligation to smack your friend for being so vague. It's like saying, "Come to number 24 and ask for Jim," without giving the street name, or saying, "Meet me on a street corner, I'll be wearing pants."

2.5   IRC Clients and Servers

As you saw in the example in Chapter 1—in which Jack, Jill, and Joe were clients connected to servers, forming a network—IRC is based on a client-server model. Naturally, it follows that two kinds of programs are involved—client programs and server programs.

One of these is called an IRC *daemon* (ircd) or IRC server. It runs on a machine connected to the Internet and waits for connections from the clients—that is, connections from other machines on the Internet who wish to use its resources.

The other is a client program that you run on your machine in order to connect to a server. The machines don't *have* to be connected to the Internet—they could be on a local network, too—but for the purpose of this book let's assume they're all part of the Internet.

It is actually quite possible to connect to a server without a special client program (simply using telnet), but that requires some degree of expertise and is tiring because you need to keep sending messages or commands to prevent the server from dumping you.

In practice, it's only useful to people who are actually writing client programs and add-ons. It's strictly for the courageous, technically minded, or desperate, and even advanced users rarely use telnet without good reason. The rest of this book assumes you're using a client program, and mentions "raw" IRC—communicating with a server without the special client program—only where it's really necessary.

There are dozens of different client programs, and I can't describe each in detail, though Chapters 3 to 5 will present all the main options. I'll concentrate mostly on the two most popular clients: *mIRC* for Windows and *ircII* for Unix, with the necessary sidesteps into Mac and *ircle* territory. Over 80 percent of all users use the first two; they essentially represent two different schools, the former more in the department of graphical, Windows-type presentation, lavishly endowed with a host of features of varying usefulness; and the latter offering a spartan interface, flexibility, and speed.

Chapters 3 to 5 cover installation and setup instructions for both programs, as well as a number of popular clients for all platforms. The rest of this book is based on those two clients and mentions special cases regarding others only where appropriate. However, since I intend to describe IRC itself and not limit myself to any particular IRC-related software, you should be able to understand and use IRC with any client by knowing how IRC works.

Of course, there are many more operating systems besides the afore-mentioned three. Some are declining in popularity, others are rising, and a few have a long history but not many users. I can't offer users of those platforms very much—it would take an encyclopedia to cover every client for every platform, and I can't satisfy everyone.

Chapter 16 will help users of OS/2, Atari TOS, AmigaOS, and some other more obscure platforms (obscure as far as IRC is concerned).

2.5.1 Differences among Clients

IRC clients look and feel very different, depending on the platform they use and their individual features. The majority of clients have many fea-tures in common, but also have significant differences. One basic distinction is between text-based clients for environments such as Unix, DOS, or VMS, and graphical interface clients for environments such as Windows or the Mac OS. Another distinction is between clients with a *scripting* language and those that lack one. Scripting capabilities allow a much higher level of customization according to the individual user's needs. Both main clients, which I'll take a closer look at, have complex and powerful scripting languages of their own that allow the user to pro-gram the client to do a lot more than it will out of the box.

Clients tend to have a standard set of commands that mostly conform to the standards of ircII, the first widely used client program. A number of modern clients have added commands of their own, many of which perform multiple commands or special actions.

Not all clients are limited to a particular platform. For example, the Zircon client (not one of the most popular) runs on Windows, Unix,

Mac, and OS/2. Others basically created for use with a particular operating system were ported to another system later on.

2.5.2 Differences among Servers

Ever since IRC ceased to be a single entity and splintered into several networks, the server software in use on each network has evolved separately. The differences are sometimes inconspicuous to the casual observer, but quite often they're very obvious. Each server type has introduced features and/or commands of its own, now unique to that kind of server. I will mention these differences where necessary, but it's almost impossible to know, let alone list, every exception to the rule. The server types I cover are those the four major networks (EFnet, Undernet, IRCnet, and DALnet) use, and I will mention the particular attributes of a server program where necessary.

Most smaller networks use server software identical to one of these or with minor modifications. These are too numerous to cover in detail, so you should obtain any special information directly from those networks after connecting to them.

Keep in mind that commands particular to one type of server do nothing (or do something different) on a different type. These special command sets are constantly being extended by the developers of the server programs and you shouldn't be surprised if you get different results with the same command when you use a different server.

2.5.3 Client Commands versus Server Commands

IRC is based on client programs and server programs that follow certain conventions laid out beforehand regarding the way they "talk" to each other. This set of standards is known as the *protocol*. Both the server and the client must comply with the protocol (speak the same language, that is to say) in order to communicate effectively.

Servers have a set of commands to which they respond if the client makes a request. Clients have one set of commands designed for communicating with the server, as well as a *user interface*, a second command set that lets a human user control it. In many cases, these two command sets don't exactly coincide. The user interface, designed for a user to understand (more or less, depending on the skill of its author), continues to expand, unlike the server commands, which rarely advance.

The average client has a multitude of commands that send very similar commands to the server. It also has single commands that expand to several server commands. The client author may leave some server commands out of the client's command set, seeing no need for them.

When you enter a command, your client converts it into something the server understands and reacts upon. For example, the **PART** command is a server command, but most clients also understand it if the user enters it. However, for the user's convenience (or confusion), many client authors have added a **LEAVE** command to the client, which for some reason has fallen into wider use and does precisely the same thing. The server's command list never added that command, though, so while you can enter either **LEAVE** or **PART**, your client must send a **PART** command to the server. Whether you tell your client to **PART** or to **LEAVE**, the client always tells the server you're "PARTing." You'll never notice this distinction, unless you've gone to the trouble of reading technical documents regarding IRC or are customizing your client with raw scripting (covered in later sections—you really don't need it yet).

The bottom line is, the server does not necessarily know the command your client accepts from you. Knowing the server's command set can be a great help when you're using an unfamiliar type of client or server or writing add-ons for your client.

2.6 Software Licensing

This is a good time to mention the *licensing* of software related to IRC—the terms of use, what you may do with it and what not, and the cost.

Much software for Unix systems—including some clients and most of the server software (ircd) used on the large networks—falls under the GNU General Public License (GPL). Under this license, it may be freely used, modified, and redistributed providing certain conditions are met.

Most Windows and Macintosh clients are commercial and are released as *shareware*. Shareware is "try before you buy" software. You are free to use it for a certain amount of time before paying for it and register yourself as a user. The way this concept is implemented varies. Some software, such as mIRC, is fully functional, and there is nothing to stop you from using it forever without paying. It's an entirely honor-based system, though it is not legal to continue using it after the trial period has expired.

The other three common varieties of shareware are *nagware*, which presents you with a "nag" screen at regular intervals telling you to register; *bombware*, which loses part or all of its functionality after the trial period expires; and *crippleware*, which has limited functionality and turns into a full package only after payment.

Freeware clients are less common and generally not quite as good as the commercial ones. Still, they're functional and cost you nothing.

IRC server software comes in a few different varieties as well, most of them Unix based. There is no IRC server software for the Macintosh platform, and Windows servers are commercial and rather pricey, so most people turn to a free Unix solution for their server needs. If you're using an Amiga or OS/2, you are in luck—there are freeware IRC servers for both.

2.7   Basic Commands

Although they may mean little to you right now, I think this is a good time to start with IRC commands. Most existing clients support these commands. The exceptions are too few to merit extra attention. This section is more helpful if you already have an IRC client installed on your machine.

First of all, there is the concept of a *command character*. A client must somehow recognize the fact that it's receiving a command. The commonly accepted command character is the forward slash (/). On a standard U.S. keyboard, this is the key to the right of the period (.). Modern clients have inherited this convention from their older counterparts. The client in turn sends commands to the server *without* the slash.

Because the slash is so widely accepted as the standard command character in IRC, not all clients allow the user to change it. Even if you can, there's really no point unless you have a good reason not to use it. These clients consider everything not preceded by a command character to be a message.

If you're familiar with the BBSs of old and related forms of online chat, you'll remember how to issue commands by simply starting a sentence with a particular word. With the extensive command set characteristic of today's clients, you would have to remember a long list of words that could not start a sentence. However, you just might run into a client of this kind, so consider this possibility if you're trying to IRC from an unfamiliar machine and the regular commands fail to work.

The basic structure of a command is as follows:

```
<command character>COMMAND <parameters to the command>
```

For example, the **WHOIS** command looks like this:

```
/whois SomeNick
```

There is a command character (/), a command (**whois**), and a single parameter to the command (a user's nickname). There must be no space between the command character and the command, or unexpected things may happen. There has to be a space between the command and its parameters, however. Commands are not case sensitive—you may use capital letters, lowercase, or even mixed case, if such is your desire. **WHOIS**, **whois**, and **WhoIs** all have the same meaning. Some commands accept more than one parameter, while others take none. The command may require parameters or they may be optional.

Here's a summary of commands you can't live without, and a few more you could live without but wouldn't want to:

Command	Required	Optional	Function
NICK	Nickname	Server name	Changes your nickname
WHOIS	Nickname	Server name	Requests information on a user
JOIN	Channel name	Password	Joins a channel
SERVER	Server name	Port	Connects you to the server specified as a parameter, disconnecting you from another you may be using
PART or **LEAVE**	Channel name		Leaves a channel
LUSERS	Server name		Shows information about the server and network
QUIT		Message	Disconnects and exits
MSG	Nickname(s) and message		Sends a private message to that nickname
AWAY	Message		Sets you "away." Use it without the message to cancel "away" status.

That about wraps it up for what you need to know before connecting. If you don't have an IRC client or don't like the one you have, the following three chapters will help you choose one. Just a bit of advice: Don't look for perfection—it doesn't exist in the world of programming. If you have a client, never mind Chapters 3 to 5, and jump to Chapter 6.

3

WINDOWS IRC CLIENTS

Microsoft Windows is the most common operating system in use in homes today, and there are a good number of IRC clients available for use in Windows. mIRC is by far the most popular client, although runners-up include Pirch and Visual IRC. In this chapter, we'll discuss all three of these.

3.1 mIRC

Version reviewed: 5.61 released September 23, 1999
Home page: http://www.mirc.co.uk/
Setup guide: http://www.mirc.co.uk/install.html or
    http://www.irchelp.org/irchelp/mirc/
The most popular IRC client program of this day and age is undoubtedly mIRC. It's stable, easy to use, and has the bee's knees in features—what else could a Windows user expect? Originally written by Khaled Mardam-Bey in 1992, near the dawn of the Internet's "windows dial-up

era," it has since undergone constant updates to reflect users' wishes and needs, as well as the unpredictable developments in the world of IRC servers. The latest version is always available for both 16- and 32-bit versions of Windows.

Users of mIRC make up the majority of IRC population, estimated at 65 to 70 percent of the total. Its usability and software support make it the number one choice for Windows IRC clients. Even those who are not terribly computer literate find mIRC fairly easy to understand and learn its basic functions quickly. It boasts a wealth of features, some common to all but the most basic of clients and some more for the entertainment of the user rather than real function. For example, DCC functions are not only supported in this client, but include a "resume" feature that will pick up where it left off if a user gets disconnected during DCC send or receive transmissions. Of course, this works only if the other party/client also supports the resume function. However, since mIRC is the most common client, this is usually not a problem. Additional features not standard to the IRC protocol include fserve (a multiple file server for DCC), a somewhat customizable *graphical user interface* (GUI), sound, and colored text.

mIRC is *nonags* shareware, which means that you do not get a reminder to register every time you open the client, nor will it cease to function after a given period of time. However, to get the full benefit of support and to ensure continued updates, it's best to pay the small registration fee of $20 (U.S.) or £10 (U.K.).

3.1.1 *Setup and Use*

Setting up mIRC is simple, even for a beginner. Download the program appropriate to your operating system (**mirc561s.exe** for Windows 3.1/3.11; **mirc561t.exe** for Windows 95/98/NT), run the file, and open the program. The first thing you'll see is a splash screen with information about the creator of mIRC and registration information. At the bottom left of the registration screen appears a little check box. Ticking the box will ensure this screen doesn't pop up every time you run the program — thus the "nonags" description.

Because of its overwhelming popularity, I'm going to give slightly more detailed attention to mIRC's setup, including some recommendations, which may also serve as general guidelines with the other clients in this chapter.

I wasn't all too happy with the default setup of mIRC on review. Here's a list of settings I suggest, as well as some items you should check after installing:

Add your info under **File • Options • Connect**. The full name and email address don't have to be correct if you want more privacy.

Most people use the full name (the *realname*, in IRC terminology) for some other description or witticism. Enter the nickname you prefer and an alternative in case the one you want is taken. I suggest you also check the "invisible mode" check box for reasons I will explain later on. You don't need the server list until we get to Chapter 6, so you can ignore it for now.

These are the suggested settings under **File • Options • Connect • Options**:

- Connect on startup: yes

- Reconnect on disconnection: yes

- Popup connect dialog on startup: no

- Move (server) to top of list on connect: no

- On connection failure options, default port number

File • Options • Connect • Local Info. The defaults here are the best choice.

File • Options • Connect • Identd. You should enable the Identd server. Enter your user id (which should match the userid part of the email address you entered earlier). Make System say **UNIX** (*not* Win32), and do not change the port to anything other than 113. The two checkboxes should be checked, largely for security reasons.

File • Options • Connect • Firewall. This is of no use to you if you're not connecting through a firewall. If you do have one, enter its details here. The port will normally be 1080, but some firewalls use 23—ask the firewall administrator.

File • Options • Sounds. This represents event beeps. Leave them off unless you want your computer to beep more than you want it to. They're evil.

File • Options • Sounds • Requests. The default is to not accept sounds. This makes sense since the directory in which the sounds are stored is empty to begin with. Change it when you start building up a collection of sound files.

File • Options • DCC. Leave the default of "ask." Auto-get may sound appealing but it lays you wide open to the risk of receiving nasty files like the ones we saw in section 2.2. Leave everything else in the DCC menu as it is — some options should not be changed until you have a very good idea of what you want them to do.

File • Options • General. This is a collection of odd stuff you will soon want to look at to customize your display. If you hate the dashes between the text lines in the status window as much as I do, this is where you change it.

File • Options • General • Servers. You need neither the finger nor the DDE server, so resist the temptation. You may have a use for the DDE server later on, but the finger server is unnecessary.

The mIRC help files have always been and still are very thorough, although at times you may find it difficult to locate the help for a particular function. Consult the built-in help files first, but if you cannot find what you're looking for, several channels on IRC offer help, such as **#mIRChelp** and **#mIRC**.

3.2 Pirch

Version reviewed: 1.01 (Pirch98): Release date unknown
Home page: http://www.pirchat.com
Download: http://www.pirchat.com/download/
FAQ: http://www.pirchat.com/faqs/
Pirch is (arguably) the number two Windows client, though the difference in popularity makes it a pretty distant follower to mIRC. It lacks mIRC's luster and professional appearance, but remains a powerful client, particularly for advanced users, with a scripting language that is in some aspects superior.

Its large features, pop-up windows, and command lines give it a rather cluttered appearance, so it won't appeal to people who don't have an acre of screen space to devote to it. However, it's technically quite adequate and definitely presents a valid alternative to mIRC. More effort has gone into producing the 32-bit version, and development of the 16-bit version ceased at version 0.87, although that is still functional.

Pirch also supports features not standard in other clients, including the DCC resume function, a file server, text-to-speech (with supporting software), and videoconferencing. The help files for the program are outstanding, with information on how to use both the software and the standard IRC text commands. And unlike the majority of IRC clients, Pirch appeared to have no trouble at all with the **LIST** command on the major networks: Rather than disconnecting due to the load, it pulled the entire channel list without a problem.

3.2.1 Setup and Use

Like other Windows clients, Pirch has a standard Windows installation process. Setting up the connection information, which includes multiple profiles, is fairly straightforward. However, the choice of terms on the dialog screen can be confusing. "Name" refers to the real name, and "Username" requires a full email address. General program options are not accessible until you have connected to a server on IRC, which I found irritating. However, these options do get saved from session to session.

I found the current server list in Pirch hopelessly outdated but editable, and the setup more comprehensive than mIRC's—Pirch sorts the list by separate networks first, then by servers. The downside is that you must close and then reopen the setup screen to save the new server information. Also, the Ident server does not work properly. Regardless of the user name you put into the Ident server box, Pirch sends the user name included in your email address. The help files in this case are inaccurate as well, stating that most servers do not require enabling the Ident server, when the opposite is true.

Pirch is nonags shareware, and registration is $20 (U.S.), which entitles the user to technical support. This client might please experienced IRC users in spite of its quirks, but I don't recommend it for newcomers. Many of its descriptive terms do not match proper IRC terminology, and might therefore prevent newbies from comprehending IRC or communicating their needs clearly when seeking information from help channel resources.

3.3 Visual IRC

Version reviewed: 1.10 Destructo Ware 4 released September 30, 1997
Home page: http://www.visualirc.com/
Setup guide: http://www.visualirc.com/help/setup/
Tutorial: http://www.visualirc.com/help/tutorials/
Alternate tutorial: http://home.earthlink.net/~tm_crazy/
(Author recommended)
Visual IRC, or ViRC as it is commonly called, stood up admirably to the test of Windows IRC clients. In addition to sporting such trendy little toys as voice and videoconferencing, it holds up quite well against other clients in standard operation and features. ViRC is comparable to mIRC, with all the standard functions and several nonstandard ones, including the ever-popular **fserve**, or **XDCC** as ViRC calls it. I only experienced one big problem after I installed it—I could see my own text, but no

one else's! I fixed the bug easily, however, after reading ViRC's help files, in particular the section entitled "What to do if you have problems." The help files as a whole are a little outdated and don't cover some of the newer features, but a quick trip to a tutorial source can answer the vast majority of questions about the program, including these new additions.

ViRC is freeware, which means it costs nothing to use, ever. It is no longer updated. However, the ViRC Web site is continuing to distribute the latest version, and excellent support is still available from the URLs mentioned above and from volunteers in the **#virc** IRC channels on EFnet, DALnet, and Undernet.

3.3.1 *Setup and Use*

Download the zipped file from the distribution site and create a directory for extracting its contents. The rest of the process is simple—just click the ViRC icons in the Programs list, and you're on your way.

Starting up ViRC is pretty simple. The first time you open it, you'll receive the setup screen, which requires input before proceeding. The rest of the setup follows the standard for newer Windows software, with expandable directories and lots of check boxes, not unlike mIRC. And as is the case with mIRC, it's best to go through each section and check your defaults before connecting to IRC for the first time.

The server list for ViRC is quite small, but you can add more servers easily by clicking the down arrow on the server box, opening a server list window. The regular IRC commands, such as **SERVER, WHOIS**, and so forth, seem to work fine, and a few shortcuts are available as well; some you'll find in the aliases section of the program, and others you'll locate by experimenting or asking in **#virc**.

Like many clients, ViRC has a tendency to disconnect from the server when pulling a **LIST** from one of the major networks, and when you place someone on **IGNORE**, you may need to remove the ignored address from the ignore list in the setup.

One thing I really enjoyed about the program was the drag-and-drop option for the four most common mode changes, namely **OP, DEOP, KICK,** and **BAN**. At the bottom of the screen is a Drag and Drop Control Center containing icons for these mode changes. Performing these functions was as simple as dragging a nick (or multiple nicks) from the channel nick list to the appropriate icon—the program did the rest.

ViRC also has tremendous scripting capabilities. Although they're a bit more complicated than mIRC's, you can code in VBscript, JavaScript, and probably any other scripting language you care to install and use. Experienced ViRC users have practically rewritten the program for any number of uses, making their own versions of the program much more powerful.

Overall, ViRC is a great little Windows client and an excellent alternative to mIRC. You certainly can't beat it for the price! On the downside, the program won't address new functions and developments in the IRC world, because it's no longer updated.

3.4 Other Windows Clients

It's really surprising how few decent clients there are for a platform as popular as Windows. Apart from the three we've taken a closer look at, there is Xircon, which enjoys a good reputation, as well as the TCL-based Zircon, which I find totally puzzling but which some users really like. IrcII and BitchX are clients originally made for Unix machines, and the attempts to port them to Windows have been unsuccessful and unpopular, respectively.

One client I *will* warn you against is Microsoft's Comic Chat. Other users will kick, insult, and abuse you all over IRC if you forget to turn off the Comic Chat feature. What's more, in everyone's eyes, you will deserve the punishment. Why? It's widely regarded as a gimmicky toy client for kids who got a computer for their birthday. If you ask a boring old fart like me, it's an unholy creation designed to destroy IRC.

As for the rest of the clients, they are remarkably few, considering the number of people who ask for help writing one. By now there should be hundreds, but it's probably better that there aren't.

4

UNIX CLIENTS

Unix was and is the basic operating system for computers on the Internet, and the IRC world is no exception. Despite the growing use of Windows and other systems on the user level, the majority of machines used for heavy-duty tasks such as WWW or IRC servers use Unix. Many people still rely on shell accounts or run Unix-style operating systems like Linux or FreeBSD on their own machines. The term Unix-style systems (or Unices or Unixes) defines a family of operating systems with similar features and functionality that have evolved out of the original UNIX Bell Laboratories developed in 1969. *UNIX* was Bell's original term, but *Unix* is generally accepted and—semantics aside—will suffice. By the way, the different kinds of Unix are called flavors. This chapter includes some basic Unix commands you really can't live without if you rely on such a system to get on IRC.

For a long time, *ircII*—an IRC client for use on Unix systems—was the standard-setting client and the most widely used one on which others were based. It has spawned a number of variants, some of which have become distinctly different from their "parent."

Less widely used but also powerful clients are available for emacs and the X Window System (a graphical user interface for Unix-style systems, not to be confused with Microsoft Windows). People who prefer to work with Perl will feel comfortable with *sirc*, an excellent Perl client.

This book will discuss ircII more since, besides the fact that it's the most widely used Unix client, almost everything that applies to ircII is valid for ircII-based clients, too. Once you're familiar with ircII, the other, more complicated clients, as well as clients for other platforms, become more approachable.

Now take a deep breath and hang on tight—Unix isn't easy and you're about to jump in the deep end. Still, it's straightforward and logical, so applying simple rational thought to a problem will solve it more often than not. Most of the instructions here apply to people who are using an account on someone else's machine. I'm pretty confident that those of you who run Linux, FreeBSD, or some other flavor of Unix on their own machines know how to install a package. Please don't prove me wrong or I'll have to rewrite this chapter in the next edition.

NOTE *You'll encounter lines beginning with a $ (dollar) character for command examples. This merely indicates a command line (prompt). On your machine it could be a $ (dollar), % (percent), or > (greater than) sign and some text or other characters may precede it. If it's a # (hash mark), you don't need me to tell you what it is, since you're the superuser. Don't tell me—I have a talent for stating the obvious.*

4.1 Getting a Client

IrcII is available from practically every large public FTP or website carrying Unix programs and utilities. Other clients aren't that widely available, but you can find them without too much effort. If downloading isn't your cup of tea (yet), skip back to section 0.4 and check out the basics of FTP and the Web. Appendix D contains a list of good FTP sites.

If you have a disk quota (a limitation on the amount of data you may store on the system), check it by typing **quota -v** at the shell prompt and make sure you have enough space available. Smaller-sized clients such as sirc, smallirc, and tinyirc require a minimal amount of space, but larger clients need much more. You should have at least 3MB free to install ircII (more for the 2.9 and 4.4 versions), and as much as 7MB for advanced ircII-based clients. If you lack the space required, use the system's **/tmp** directory (**cd /tmp**) to download, unarchive, and possibly compile the package. Later, copy only the necessary files to your home directory, making sure you have enough space to hold them. You will need no less than 500KB of disk space for the resulting program file, possibly as much as 1.5MB in case you're unable to downsize the file with the "strip" utility.

The following FTP sites carry practically all Unix clients:

```
ftp.asu.net
ftp.undernet.org
ftp.funet.fi
```

4.2   ircII

Versions reviewed: 2.8, 2.9, and 4.4 series
License: BSD type

ircII is the ideal choice for users who want a client that can grow along with them, adding features as they learn how to use them. It is not a user-friendly client, but simple low-level scripting can easily correct this; a beginner can get the hang of it without much effort. It's essentially a straightforward client capable of development into a complex and versatile tool.

ircII is quite adequate as is, but its main asset is a powerful *scripting* language, enabling a user to configure it to do practically anything with speed and a high level of efficiency. Don't worry about the scripting part just yet—you're not being asked to program a client. Scripting will come in handy, though, as your IRC skills develop. Chapter 11 covers scripting.

You have a choice between the classic version, 2.8.2, and later ones, namely the 2.9 series, 4.4, and 4.4H. Updates are infrequent and each version tends to present new bugs while fixing old ones. 2.8.2 is an excellent choice if you want a rock-solid client with few, tame bugs and don't mind missing some of the cutting-edge features in later versions.

EPIC (this stands for Enhanced Programmable IRC-II Client) is a frequently updated variant of ircII with some added features, including extra commands, color support, and more sophisticated scripting functions. It's a valid option for beginners and advanced users alike, but does tend to lack the stability of regular ircII.

4.3   sirc

Version reviewed: 2.2
License: GPL

This client is written entirely in Perl (a modern and advanced programming language), and therefore requires that you have a recent version of Perl on your system. Its advantages lie in the small amount of space it requires and its almost infinite configurability for anyone who cares to play around with Perl.

The program sirc comes with precise installation instructions and a user-friendly installation interface. As long as Perl is present and functional on the system, installing and using sirc should be easy. Just untar and unzip it, read the instructions, and you're practically set.

Its capabilities include almost every feature other modern clients offer, and a competent Perl programmer can easily expand them. For the adventurous souls who prefer Perl to C and like hacking around, this is the ideal choice. This may also appeal to some Web designers who use Perl anyway.

4.4   BitchX

Version reviewed: 75p1
License: BSD type

BitchX (please excuse our language, but that's really the client's name) is arguably the most popular ircII-based client and actually evolved out of an add-on script for ircII. It was eventually incorporated into the ircII code thus developing a new, unofficial "strain" of ircII that has been evolving separately, diverging a bit further with each release. While the course of BitchX's development has taken it far from the original, though most of the principles of using ircII still apply. Recent versions of BitchX are based on EPIC rather than the original ircII.

BitchX codes most features that previously required scripts into the client, allowing for more speed and ease of use. You can configure almost all display options through variables, and the scripting language is largely compatible with ircII and has had more functions added in the course of development. In its current state, it should be able to perform most functions a user would want without any add-ons. But BitchX justifies its name when you try to configure it.

You should give preference to BitchX only if you're already familiar with running ircII or some other type of advanced client and intend to use it for operating a channel (or even a server—it's becoming increasingly popular with IRC operators as well as regular users). Setting it up is tricky, and I recommend trying it out with a precompiled binary (see 4.5.4) before attempting to install your own client in order to discover the way it works and the settings you prefer. Most of the client development is done on Linux systems, and there may not be a binary available for your operating system. If you can't find one and have another means of connecting to IRC, try asking in the **#BitchX** channel on EFnet (follow the instructions in Chapters 6 and 7 if you don't know how)—generally a number of experienced BitchX users hang out there, including its author.

Documentation in the distribution is insufficient and doesn't cover all aspects of the client, nor is help available for all the functions and commands added more recently. However, BitchX uses the ircII help files by default, so that covers commands the two have in common. Several commands use a different syntax, however, so the ircII help files aren't 100 percent accurate for this client.

The default options are unlikely to satisfy your needs completely, so it's advisable that you carefully edit the **config.h** file (see 4.5.2) and make sure you have enabled what you consider necessary while disabling other settings (such as a link looker) liable to consume excessive machine or network resources or violate server rules. You'll probably also want to create and edit a **BitchX.formats** file to customize the display and offset the psychedelic effects of the gaudy default color scheme. No, really, it's terrible!

You should take one more thing about BitchX into consideration, concerning system resources. Under normal operating conditions, BitchX is more economical with CPU time than ircII, but proves to be quite a memory hog. If you have limited memory available, it may not be the ideal option.

4.5   Installation of ircII and Related Clients

Installation is an often complicated process. You don't have to a Unix guru, but it does help. The following part is for those who can't install a package with their eyes closed and need some help with it. IrcII, EPIC, and BitchX install in practically the same way, so they'll be treated as one here.

4.5.1   *tar, gzip, and Feather*

Most software available on the Internet uses some compression format to reduce storage space and the bandwidth needed for transfers. Zip files and self-extracting executables are very common for DOS and Windows software, while Macs widely use Stuffit. They all serve the same purpose, but nobody has agreed on one format for all platforms.

The compression formats you'll encounter for Unix software are mainly Unix compress (with a **.Z** extension) and gzip (with a **.gz** extension). A more modern form is bzip2, which offers substantially higher compression rates resulting in smaller files, but takes up more system resources (and time) to compress and decompress.

It's likely you'll find more than one package for the same client on the download site you choose. In order to download the correct package, you should know which decompression method is available on your system. If you're not sure, try using the **whereis** command at the shell prompt.

```
$ whereis gzip
gzip: /bin/gzip
$ whereis uncompress
uncompress: /usr/bin/uncompress
```

If the command does not return a path at all but only repeats the name of the command, the utility you tried to find is not on the system. You can also try the **which** command in the same way. Note that gunzip and gzip are two faces of the same coin, but the latter is not available on all systems.

If you have both compression utilities, you should use gunzip because it has a significantly higher compression ratio and you'll save time downloading the package. Good sites should have both the **.gz** and **.Z** versions. If the one you need isn't available at the site you chose, try a different one.

Here's how you decompress a file. If one method doesn't work, try the other:

File Type	Command
.gz	gunzip *file name*
.gz	gzip -d *file name*
.Z	uncompress *file name*
.bz2	bunzip2 *file name*
.bz2	bzip2 -d *file name*

You need not specify the characteristic extension (**.Z**, **.gz**, or **.bz2**). (Note: Remember that Unix is case sensitive. Commands and file names lacking the proper capitalization *will* fail.)

None of these compression utilities merges multiple files into a single archive as PKZip or ARJ do, so you'll need a second utility. Unix-style systems use just one widely, which goes by the name of *tar*. This stands for Tape Archive, originally designed for use with system backups on tape (it has nothing to do with road construction). Users colloquially refer to an archive created with the tar utility as a *tarball*. Such an archive doesn't need a particular extension, but using a **.tar** suffix is a widely accepted convention. Files on many systems can also be decompressed by tar, so you can often use one command to decompress and unarchive a file.

Most files you'll download will combine tar and a compression utility; you can tell which utility from the extension. When in doubt, use the "file" utility, which tells you what kind of file it is.

`.tar`	Uncompressed tar file
`.tar.gz`	Gzipped tar file
`.tar.Z`	Compressed tar file
`.tgz`	Gzipped tar file; it expands to a `.tar` file when decompressed
`.tar.bz2`	Tar file compressed using bzip2

How you unarchive and decompress them depends on the system and the utilities available on it. Not all work in the same way on all flavors of Unix. The basic syntax is:

File Type	Command
`.tar`	tar xvf file name (use this if you've decompressed the file)
`.tar.gz`	tar zxvf *file name*
`.tar.Z`	tar zxvf *file name*
`.tgz`	tar zxvf *file name*
`.tar.bz2`	tar Ixvf *file name*

Full file names are required by tar. You may not omit the **.tar** extension if there is one. Different systems may also require the following:

- Using a hyphen before the tar flags (for example, **tar -xvf**)

- Uncompressing the file before untarring it

You would then see a list of file names scrolling on the screen (unless you omit the "v" from the tar flags). This says which files you're extracting to which path. If you have space restrictions, you may need to delete the tar file once you've extracted the files it contains, in order to make more space available for the installation.

Now you can begin the installation process. The install file included in the client package contains a lot of information. Change to the directory to which you extracted the files (**ls -ld** tells you which one it is). From within that directory, run the GNU configuration script (a shell script, not to be confused with an ircII script) by typing:

```
$ ./configure
```

(In case you're wondering about *feather,* there's no such thing. I just thought it looked kind of cute in the title.)

After extracting the files from the archive and reading the **INSTALL** file, you'll have a choice between the simple way of setting it up or customizing it.

4.5.2 Configuring ircII

You do the quick and dirty way within the directory to which you extracted the source files:

```
$ ./easyinst
```

This method attempts to do most of the tasks the next few paragraphs describe, but has little flexibility. It's a decent choice if you're installing ircII into your home directory and not the system. I believe it's better to do it like this:

```
$ ./configure
```

This method examines your system in order to set up Makefile correctly—the compiler consults this for the compile. It results in a message declaring the process is complete (unless the system has a shoddy setup with which the compiler is unable to work). Then it says you're ready to start the compiler unless you wish to change some of the defaults by editing the **config.h** file in the /**include** subdirectory. This isn't absolutely necessary, but I do suggest editing it and changing certain options in order to make the client more suitable for a beginner or just to add some useful options. Open an editor (any editor—*pico* is more suitable for beginners) to edit the file:

```
$ pico -w include/config.h
```

You can change the options by substituting **#undef** for **#define** or vice versa—**#define** sets an option on, while **#undef** turns it off. Some instructions are in the file. If you don't understand them, leave the options they describe unchanged. You switch other options by alternating 0 and 1, respectively, for off and on, while you set still others with text strings. The settings I recommend changing are the following:

```
#define DEFAULT_SERVER "change.this.to.a.server"
```
Enter the name of the server you'll be using most frequently. This can also be a space-separated list of servers. *Keep* the quotes.

```
#define DEFAULT_CHANNEL_NAME_WIDTH 10
```
Change this to 12 or 15—it will help with channel lists.

```
#define DEFAULT_CLOCK_24HOUR 1
```
Change the 1 to 0 if you don't like "military" time. I'm European and I love it, but civilian Americans generally don't.

```
#define DEFAULT_CONTINUED_LINE "+"
```
Personally, I hate the default + (plus). This is the character you'll see at the beginning of the next line to indicate that it continues, or wraps, from the previous one. I use two spaces instead between the quote marks.

```
#define DEFAULT_DCC_BLOCK_SIZE 512
```
A more reasonable number nowadays is 2048. Use 1024 if you're installing it on your own machine and a 28.8-Kbps or slower dial-up.

```
#define DEFAULT_EIGHT_BIT_CHARACTERS 0
```
You'll need to change the value to 1 if you normally use an 8-bit (extended) character set. This applies to people who use a special character set in their own language.

```
#define DEFAULT_HIDE_PRIVATE_CHANNELS 1
```
Change the 1 to 0. If you keep the 1, you will not see the channel's name displayed in your status bar unless the channel is public.

```
#define DEFAULT_INPUT_PROMPT NULL
```
Setting the value (NULL) to $T> makes the nickname or channel to which you direct your messages appear at the beginning of the input line (unless you perform a command to override this option).

```
#define DEFAULT_LASTLOG 44
```
Change 44 to 500, 1000, or any number you like. This is the number of past messages that stay in the buffer for you to recall with the LASTLOG command.

```
#define DEFAULT_MAIL 0
```
If you do not receive mail on the machine, leave this setting as is. Setting it to 1 tells you when you have new mail, setting it to 2 also shows the sender and subject. I prefer 2.

```
#define DEFAULT_NOVICE 1
```
More-advanced users should set this to 0. Total beginners can keep the 1.

```
#define DEFAULT_SHOW_CHANNEL_NAMES 0
```
Enable this (replace 0 with 1) to see the nicknames present when you join a channel.

```
#define DEFAULT_VERBOSE_CTCP 0
```
Substitute a 1 for the 0. This option displays incoming CTCP requests—more about those later.

You can override all these options later—you are by no means bound to them.

4.5.3 Compile

IrcII and clients based on it are written in the C programming language. In order to create an executable file (binary), you have to convert the C code into something the machine understands. That's what the compiler does for you.

What you'll need in order to do this is access to a C compiler (**cc** or **gcc**). Check for availability by typing **cc** or **gcc** at the shell prompt as you did for the decompression programs. If the result is a message saying "Permission denied," the system has been configured not to allow you to use the compiler (compiling can take up too many system resources, so many system administrators prefer to disable it for the users). The configuration script you'll need also looks for a compiler and complains *very* loudly if it can't find one.

If the configure script didn't complain, you're ready to compile. In case you missed it when reading the **INSTALL** file, here are the basic commands:

```
$ make
$ make install
```

If you're not used to compiling, be aware that masses of computerese gibberish will flood your screen. How fast the flood moves depends on your machine's horsepower. On a 486 or low-end Pentium, it may take as much as half an hour. You'll probably see lines saying "Warning," referring to something the compiler didn't like in the program and pointing to the responsible file and line. You can usually ignore these warnings. However, if **make** exits with a fatal error, you have a problem, and the compile has failed. Such a case goes well beyond the scope of this book, and your best option is to follow the instructions in the next section and consult a good help channel on IRC (see 16.6), or consult your *sysadmin* (system administrator).

4.5.4 Binaries

"Binary? Isn't that a kind of star?" Well, yes, but in this context it has more to do with binary numbers (remember them from school—they have 0 and 1 as their only digits?). Here we're talking about executable files you can run right out of the box.

If you have no compiler, you may skip the section on compiling and configuring and see whether you can obtain a ready version of the program (known as a *precompiled binary*). A precompiled binary must be appropriate for your system. If, for example, you are using a SunOS machine, getting a Linux binary does little good, and vice versa—after all, square bolts don't fit in round holes. If you're not sure about the operating system, type the following at the shell prompt:

```
$ uname -rs
```

Output might look a bit like this:

```
Linux 2.0.34
```

This would mean you're using a machine running Linux, version 2.0, revision (or patch level) 34. This is just an example—it could just as well read "FreeBSD 3.0-RELEASE," "SunOS 5.5," or whichever other flavor of Unix the machine uses. You can generally ignore anything beyond the minor version number (the second part of the second field) so, in this example, you could just say interpret this as Linux 2.0. Often the *major* version number is enough to select a binary, so you might be able to use a Linux 2.1 or 2.2 binary in this case.

Precompiled binaries are generally less widely available. You should only use them as a last resort. Since someone else compiled them, they may have default options that don't suit you, and you'll have to do some extra work to change those options; or the binaries might not work on your machine. I admit I still have a binary that points to a Polish server by default, available on an FTP site (a Polish IRC server administrator contributed it), so look out.

One thing you could try is asking the system administrator for temporary access to the compiler in order to perform this task. Not all *sysadmins* appreciate IRC as much as we do, however, and they may consider it a waste of resources because of its largely recreational use. Few sysadmins will allow a work machine's precious memory and CPU cycles to be hijacked for the purpose of idle chat.

4.5.5 *Setting the Environment*

Applications draw some of the information they need from two sources when you run them. The first source is *environment variables*. They define the properties of the system and a user's general options. Some concern the whole system and many programs need them, while others are entirely up to the user and only one program requires them—they may even be optional.

IrcII and clients based on it use three user-defined environment variables; they are called **IRCSERVER**, **IRCNAME**, and **IRCNICK**. They control your default server, *realname* (this is part of your personal information while you're connected to an IRC server—more about it in Chapter 6), and nickname, respectively, overriding any compile-time defaults. Command line options can override them in turn.

You can set these environment variables from the command line and apply them to the IRC session run thereafter; in this case they disappear when you log out. This is the best way to use a temporary set of environment variables.

For a permanent configuration, you will have to add them to your log-in file—the file read when you log in. Which file this is depends on the system's setup and the *shell* you use.

Shells can be loosely grouped into two families, depending on the commands you need to set environment variables. The first is made up of **csh** and **tcsh**. The second comprises **bash**, **ksh**, **zsh**, and **sh**. Both families include additional variants of the above, which are too numerous to fit into in this book. The most widely used are **bash** and **tsch**. While **ksh** and **csh** are not uncommon, their more modern brethren have largely displaced them.

Use the following command to find out which shell you're using:

```
echo $SHELL
```

I purposely left out the **$** at the beginning of that command line because it is characteristic of a certain kind of shell. The response you will get will be the full path to the shell; you're interested only in the last part—that is, if it says **/bin/bash**, your shell is **bash**. If you wanted to set the **IRCNAME** environment variable, this is what you would do for **csh** and **tcsh**:

```
% setenv IRCNAME "blah blah"
```

For **bash**, **ksh**, **sh**, and so forth, it would be:

```
$ IRCNAME="blah blah"
$ export IRCNAME
```

Proper capitalization, spacing, and use of quotes are essential.

The log-in file to which you add the above lines is not absolute, but can vary from system to system. For **sh**, **bash**, and **ksh** it's usually called **.profile** (note the leading dot). If there exists a **.bashrc** or **.bash_profile**, use it since it takes precedence over the **.profile**. For **csh** and **tcsh**, use **.cshrc** and **.tcshrc** respectively. If there is no **.tcshrc**, **tcsh** falls back on **.cshrc**. In all cases, if none of these files exist in your home directory, create the appropriate one by editing it.

Apart from the basic three variables, some ircII-based clients also understand the **IRCHOST** and **IRCUSER** variables, which are used to define the host name (on a machine that has more than one) and the user name, if it can be changed. Plain ircII understands neither.

4.5.6 *The .ircrc File*

Many programs read a start-up file when you run them and draw some extra information from them. These *rc files* (run command files) are equivalent in function to the INI files Windows uses. Here we'll look at personal rc files with user-specific client commands. Personal rc files are hidden files (beginning with a dot) and reside in the user's home directory.

The rc file ircII reads is called **.ircrc**. EPIC uses the same file. BitchX looks for a **.bitchxrc** but falls back to **.ircrc** if it can't find one. The contents of an rc file can be any set of client commands. It's normally read once a successful server connection is first made. It *can* load before the connection is made, but returns errors if commands in it are also sent to the server.

You can use the rc file to override default client settings—for example, you could set **MAIL** to a value of 1 if the client has been compiled with 0 as the default and you don't like it that way. Apart from **SET**, which you use to change client variables, you can also add **LOAD** commands to load scripts automatically. Although **.ircrc** is really a script and you can include scripting commands like **ALIAS** and **ON** in it, it's good to keep those in separate files you can load from the **.ircrc**. A very simple **.ircrc** file might look like this:

```
SET MAIL 1
SET AUTO_WHOWAS OFF
LOAD blah.irc
```

This changes two variables—**MAIL** and **AUTO_WHOWAS**—and then loads a script file called **blah.irc**. Don't concern yourself with scripts yet, as Chapter 11 is dedicated to them. Note that the rc file doesn't use any command character.

5

IRCING ON THE MACINTOSH

I'm not a Macintosh user, never have been and probably never will be. I will not pretend to be one either. Instead I'll turn over the stage to an expert on the subject. I'm very pleased to have his cooperation and insight as part of this book. Ladies and gentlemen, Joseph Y. Lo and his ultimate guide to Macintosh IRC clients.

5.1 Mac Users Do IRC with Style

As a Macintosh user, you have one of the best environments for IRC. You have access to a user-friendly interface and a wide selection of fast, powerful software. Best of all, you get to IRC on the Mac OS, one of the most robust and fun operating systems in the world.

For the most part, everything you've read about general IRC so far applies to Mac clients as well, except for a few important differences. While most Mac clients support the IRC protocol in RFC 1459, including all of the most commonly used commands, they tend to have many additional features. For starters, all of them, like mIRC for Windows, are *graphical user interface* (GUI) clients. This means that in addition to having text conversations and commands, you can also interact with the program using menus, buttons, pictures, and sounds. This seems appropriate to a Mac IRC client, or else you might as well just telnet to a Unix shell account and use the fast, reliable, text-only ircII client. Another feature common to most Mac IRC clients is that DCC file transfers are set to MacBinary format by default. This is handy if you exchange files only with other Mac users, but it is not compatible with other operating systems such as Windows or Unix. Fortunately, all you have to do is go to each program's DCC options and set it to raw binary mode or the equivalent.

How do you get a Mac IRC client? Most large Internet service providers (ISPs) automatically bundle an IRC client into their software package. The bad news is that sometimes they choose a really out-of-date, buggy client out of ignorance or stinginess. The good news is that all of the better Mac IRC clients are *shareware,* so you can easily upgrade yourself. You can download shareware off the Internet and test-drive it for free. If you choose to keep using the program after a month, you are obligated to pay the program's author a shareware fee of typically less than $30—still much less than a typical commercial program would cost. By registering yourself, you sometimes release intentional restrictions designed to encourage you to do the right thing, and in any case you encourage the author (typically just a regular person who does programming as a hobby) to continue doing good work. Unlike many commercial software programs, all of these Mac clients come with free support and free updates.

5.1.1 *General Downloading Instructions*

So how do you download all this wonderful, inexpensive software? Most ISPs should set you up with a Web browser (typically Netscape or Internet Explorer), which is all you need to download the installation package for each program off the Internet. They should also give you a free program called StuffIt Expander to decode and decompress the installation package. You can usually just select a download link on a Web page. The file gets saved to your disk, and StuffIt Expander launches automatically, producing either an installer program you may execute, or a new folder containing the installed IRC client itself. If this is the case, thank your ISP for doing their job and skip the rest of this section. Otherwise you need to read on, or call your ISP for help.

Most Mac software on the Internet is available in two forms: as a compact MacBinary file of zeros and ones with a name ending in the **.bin** suffix, such as **ircle3.0.sit.bin**, or as a larger but more flexible Bin-

Hex text file with a name ending in **.hqx**, such as **ircle3.0.sit.hqx**. In either case, you need StuffIt Expander to handle these files. If you don't know where that program is, use **Find File** under your Apple menu to search for it on your Mac's disk drive. In the unlikely event that you don't have it, you can get it from Aladdin Systems (http://www.aladdinsys.com/expander).

Once you have StuffIt Expander set up, you need to save the file you wish to download, which normally happens when you select a download link on a Web page. If doing so brings up a long page of alphanumeric gibberish, use your browser's **Save As** feature under the File menu to save that gibberish to your disk manually as a text file. Within the Finder, you may then drag and drop the saved file over StuffIt Expander's icon, and StuffIt should take care of the rest. The result may be an installation program, which you simply double-click to execute, or else you may see a new folder containing the desired programs with their help and support files.

5.1.2 Choosing the Right Client

The following sections describe several major Mac IRC clients. It is a testament to the creativity and talent of Mac shareware programmers that there are so many choices available. While many discerning users consider Ircle the best client, no single client enjoys an overwhelming dominance, as is the case with mIRC for Windows or ircII variants for Unix.

So how do you know which client to choose? I will briefly describe each client below in terms of its design philosophy, unique features, and some pros and cons. It's really a matter of personal taste which client you prefer. You should always look for certain basics when shopping around, which I will refer to as the four S's: speed, stability, standards, and support.

- Speed: The client should be responsive to commands and should not lag your other applications.

- Stability: Under typical use, it should never crash or misbehave.

- Standards: It should support all IRC commands and protocols, thus ensuring that you can interact with other people using similarly standardized clients.

- Support: Finally, whether it came free or you paid for it, somebody must support it, which means they are responsible for releasing updates, fixing inevitable bugs, and answering your questions.

Beyond these basics, remember—this is IRC, not rocket science. Accordingly, the client should be easy to set up and use, have an appealing look and feel so you actually enjoy using it, and support any special features you might fancy. Just don't become too distracted by the rampaging featuritis that has beset most clients, and don't forget your four S's.

What do you need to run these Mac IRC clients? All of them have a reasonable memory size, typically from 1MB to 2MB, allowing them to run on most Macintosh or Power Macintosh computers. Unless otherwise noted, all will run on System 7.0 or higher, though as time goes by more are beginning to require features found in Mac OS 8. If you can browse the Web, you probably have the appropriate networking software for IRC, namely either MacTCP 2.0.6 or Open Transport 1.1 or higher. You of course need an Internet connection, such as a permanent, direct Ethernet connection at your school, workplace, or home, or alternatively a dial-up connection to an ISP.

5.2 Ircle

Home page: http://www.ircle.com
Setup guide: http://www.ircle.com/reference
Another setup guide: http://www.irchelp.org/irchelp/mac
**Scripts, mailing lists, and links to help pages: http://www.ircle.com/
   related.html**

Ircle is the godfather of Mac IRC clients. It has been around the longest and has the most features, making it the de facto gold standard against which all other clients compare themselves. Since the mid-1990s a new author, Onno Tijdgat, has completely rewritten and redesigned it. IRC experts and novices alike consider Ircle a good choice because it delivers well-balanced performance in terms of our four S's. Though it's no speed demon and appears somewhat sluggish compared to ShadowIRC, Snak, or MacIRC, it is among the most stable Mac programs. It adheres closely to standards for maximum compatibility with people using other clients on Macs or even other platforms such as Windows. It accomplishes all these basics and is still reasonably easy to set up and use. As for support, this is where Ircle really shines. It is one of the most frequently updated clients on any platform, and thanks to its longevity and popularity, it offers a wealth of Web sites, free scripts, help channels, and so forth far exceeding the support for all other Mac clients. Figure 5.1 shows a screen capture of a typical Ircle session. (A larger, color version of all figures in this chapter may be found at the http://www.irchelp.org/mac Web site.) The two large windows on the left show simultaneous connections to EFnet **#irchelp** and Undernet **#macintosh**. The top right window serves several different functions: it lists the users in your current channel, includes easy to use mode toggle switches, and has user-configurable buttons for common actions such as op, deop, kick, and ban. The lower right Connections window gives you a very clear interface to each connection. By selecting one row in the list of connections and clicking the **Connect** button, Ircle can connect you to a specific server with the nickname and username of your choice, with optional commands such as joining your favorite channels. Finally, the bottom Inputline window is where you type commands and conversation, with very easy-to-use palettes for color, boldface, or other text formats.

Figure 5.1: A typical Ircle session

Ircle boasts many useful, innovative features. It was the first Mac client to allow simultaneous connections to different networks in different windows, so you could chat on Undernet and EFnet at the same time, for example. It was the first to come up with colored text; graphical "face" representations of the people to whom you are talking, file servers to exchange files, synthesized speech, and video streaming. Ircle also includes many channel protection features normally reserved for advanced scripts, including lists of friends and enemies, with options ranging from giving ops to kicking the person, clone detection, prevention of server ops, flood protection, mass features (op, deop, unban), and automatic logging to a single file or separate daily folders. Most people will be perfectly content with Ircle's many built-in features, though further customization is possible through a scripting environment that uses AppleScript—nice compared to most clients' propensity for inventing their own peculiar scripting language.

Ircle is shareware. You get the usual 30 days of unrestricted use, after which you become limited to ten-minute sessions. This "quitware" approach is intentionally annoying, but the registration fee ties ShadowIRC as the lowest-cost Mac client, and in return you get a professional-quality, well-supported, frequently updated product.

5.2.1 Setup and Use

Download Ircle either in MacBinary format or in BinHex (see section 5.1.1 on general downloading directions) from its home page. Once it is properly processed you should have a folder entitled **ircle <version number>**. Open the folder. The Ircle application itself is called **ircle<version number> US** (note that there is no space before the version number).

For people who want to dive into IRC right away, a folder called Chat Channels contains a dozen or so bookmarklike files, each allowing you to chat immediately in a specific channel on a specific network. Just double-click any of the files and Ircle automatically launches, connects to the network, and joins the channel. This clever and convenient feature is unique to Ircle.

Setting up Ircle to use your choice of servers is a little more work than with most other clients. Launch the Ircle application to see a console window for server messages, a narrow input line area where you issue commands and chat, a user list window, and a connection window, which is where you connect to an IRC server. Experienced IRC users may immediately use the input line to enter commands such as **/server irc.some.server.com** to get connected. Otherwise, use the connection window to create a permanent connection configuration. Within the connection window, each row represents a possible connection. Select the first row and edit it by double-clicking or using the **Edit** button. You may now select a different server and enter your personal information (at least change the nickname from the default). When you close the edit window and return to the connection window, simply select the **Connect** button to make the connection to the desired server. Once connected, you may issue commands such as **JOIN** or use the menus instead.

You can accomplish most of Ircle's functions with simple buttons or menus, or you can use standard commands such as **WHOIS** for more precise control. There are a few deviations from standards. Instead of **PING**, you must use **CPING** to measure the lag between you and a nickname or channel. To ignore somebody who is harassing you, use **/ignore mask**, where the mask is in the **nick!user@host** format. If you just specify a nickname such as **/ignore John**, the command ignores only the nick John. Currently, once you have set an ignore, everything from that mask gets ignored, as there is no facility for ignoring only certain types of messages, such as private versus public. To unignore, you must use **/ignore -mask** (where mask is whatever you specified previously).

There is also a user interface in the Preferences menu where you can set or remove ignores.

The only serious problem with Ircle is its inability to **LIST** channels properly. On large networks such as the Big Four—EFnet, IRCnet, Undernet, and DALnet—trying to list the thousands of channels with Ircle always causes you to disconnect due to the flood of information, while other clients can usually manage the feat if you are on a direct Ethernet connection. On Undernet, you may use server-side filtering to list only those channels with more than five people, which shortens the list sufficiently so that it works (still with inordinate slowness compared to other clients). Fortunately, most large networks have actively updated lists of channels on their official home pages. When in doubt, see Chapter 7 for information on getting channel lists from the Web.

Ircle has some built-in help you may access under OS 8's Help menu, or in Mac OS 7 look for the question mark icon near the upper right of your screen. You can pull down a reference list for commands, or read a list of answers to frequently asked questions (*FAQs*). For more help, be sure to check out the Ircle home page which includes a detailed setup guide, descriptions of the purpose of all the files and folders in the Ircle folder, and links to mailing lists and other help sites.

5.3 ShadowIRC

Home page: http://www.shadowirc.com
Setup guide: http://www.shadowirc.com/support.html
ShadowIRC has quickly become one of the best alternatives to Ircle. It's come a long way since version 0.7, which I characterized as a "geek's client" because its main claim to fame was the use of precompiled C scripts for supposedly faster performance than Ircle's AppleScript scripts. The previous version was also missing many key features, but that has changed. ShadowIRC bills itself as "a small Mac OS IRC client," referring not just to its mere 650Kb of memory use, but also its simpler look and snappier performance compared to Ircle. ShadowIRC is not just Ircle Lite, however, as it is reasonably complete in itself and very expandable. It scores very well on the four S's: it is very speedy, quite stable, compliant with standard commands, and has good support. There is no online help, nor does it have a bundled help manual, but its home page offers extensive help, including setup information and a FAQ.

Let me distinguish between the three kinds of help. By online help, I mean help information built into the client itself, accessible typically via the **/help** command without exiting the client. By bundled help manual, I mean a separate file or application that comes with the default installation of the client, which may be accessed by switching out of the client and into this other file. The home page stuff is one further step removed because it requires going to the Web.

There is no dedicated connection window, with those options inconveniently hidden under two separate items in the File menu instead. There is one Inputline (shown at the bottom) shared for all windows, but without any of Ircle's useful text format palettes.

ShadowIRC's user interface resembles a simplified form of Ircle. The sample session shown in Figure 5.2, which was set up to resemble Ircle, shows two large windows which are connections to EFnet and Undernet. Everything pertaining to each channel appears in one window. For example, the user list is integrated into the right portion of each channel window, so that you can see who is in both channels at the same time (though you have the option of making that a separate window that can be hidden, as in Ircle). You can make the user list narrow to show just the nicknames (as shown in the top window), or wide to show the **user@host** information (as shown in the bottom window). The topic and mode toggle switches are in the bottom of each channel window.

Figure 5.2: A ShadowIRC session

The mode switches are in the corner of the channel window, a subtle shadowing of the letter symbol (such as **T** for ±t) indicates active modes (this is very hard to see). There is no ban list or way to see one. Like Ircle, ShadowIRC allows multiple connections to different servers simultaneously. It tries to support mIRC as well as Mac colors, although unlike Ircle's, ShadowIRC's color scheme actually works. Another cute feature mIRC inspires is the use of pop-ups. Also, by command- or option-clicking a word, you can perform tasks such as copying the word to the input line, sending a CTCP version or Ping, or starting to log.

Speaking of logging, ShadowIRC is the only Mac client with full logging features. In addition to logging everything automatically, like Ircle, it also lets you turn logging on or off manually to record something prospectively. You can even capture everything retrospectively in a certain window to save an event that happened already.

Ircle takes more than three times as much memory as ShadowIRC, so it should be no surprise that you are giving up many features when you choose this smaller, simpler client. Some features you won't find include the file server, sounds for IRC events, CTCP sounds, speech, channel protection (friend's list, enemy list, server op prevention, clone detection, and so forth), and flood protection.

So what about ShadowIRC's famous precompiled plug-ins? On the plus side, they allow you to expand or customize the client to a degree you can't with scripts. For example, plug-ins bundled with the default package implement the server list, user list, and pop-ups. The home page includes links to a dozen or so third-party plug-ins that cover two of the aforementioned missing features (file server and sounds for events), as well other features ranging from mass features to nick completion. On the negative side, the author's push for plug-ins as a faster alternative to conventional scripting is probably misguided, since the speed differential would be noticeable in only a few actions, and these speed claims haven't been verified. Moreover, typical users don't have the requisite C-language knowledge or developer's tools to write or modify these plug-ins. It is unclear how well third-party plug-ins will behave with each other, and there is a real risk of running into back doors and unanticipated bugs when you're using somebody else's prefabricated plug-ins.

The bottom line is, do you want a simpler, faster, less confusing client that has most of the important features? If so, ShadowIRC is worth a closer look. In fact, considering how much it has improved since its last major release, the future of this new client is very encouraging. ShadowIRC is shareware, and after the 30-day free trial it limits each session to 15 minutes before quitting.

5.3.1 Setup and Use

Getting connected requires you to use a typical connection window to select the server you want. Go to the File menu and select **Preferences**, then in the Preferences window select the **Connections** pop-up in the upper left corner. Choose one of the ten connections from the list on the left, then enter at least your nickname and server name. If you know the server name already, enter it in the blank, otherwise use the **Select** button to choose from many networks and servers, which cover all of the Big Four except IRCnet, as well as several smaller nets. You may now use the Open Connection menu under File to open that connection.

You should be aware of some quirks when using ShadowIRC. There is no separate channel list window, so using the **LIST** command just sends the output to your current window. Be prepared for the flood, particularly since there is no **FLUSH** command yet, nor any support for **LIST** parameters such as keyword searching or a minimum number of people. You may **IGNORE** using the full **nick!user@host** mask, such as **/ignore *!*foo@*.aol.com.** You can then remove this with **/ignore -*!*foo@*.aol.com,** but there is no graphical interface, nor is there any way to ignore specific types of messages selectively, such as public ones versus CTCPs.

5.4 Snak

Home page: http://www.snak.com/Snak.html
Snak is another very new Mac client that has rapidly become one of the leading choices, especially for people who find Ircle's four or more windows cluttered and confusing. Instead, Snak puts everything for each channel into one window, including the channel conversation, the user list, and the input area where you type. It's a different look, but the objective is the same: to be the most popular, full-featured Mac IRC client.

To this end—not surprisingly—Snak scores reasonably well in the four S's. It is among the fastest and most responsive clients. It has unfortunately many stability problems, such as occasional crashes and strange bugs, but at least the author has been fixing things quickly. When it comes to standards, Snak goes above and beyond the call of duty, not only using standard commands in everything, but supporting the ircII scripting language, which is very popular and well established among experienced IRC users. To show off this ability, the author encloses the 3,000-line ircII script PurePak, which works with only minor modifications. Support is more of an issue. The client is very new, so there is some risk that Snak may disappear in the future or just fade away, like so many other good programs. On the other hand, when Snak fully implements the ircII scripting compatibility, Snak users can tap into a wealth of existing scripts, and as noted before, the author has been very responsive to support issues.

In addition to the ircII scripting compatibility, Snak has a few other unique features, such as its practical ircII-style ability to try multiple servers per connection. It has the best **IGNORE** capabilities of all these clients. You can create double-clickable setup files that open a custom combination of your favorite connections and channels. An address book organizes information about your IRC buddies. There is also a Guardian adult control feature, which is fairly rough around the edges. (I will defer offering my opinions on such features until discussing the ChatNet client later.)

This Snak session (as shown in Figure 5.3) closely resembles that of ShadowIRC. The two large windows are simultaneous connections to EFnet and Undernet. The user list and input line may be optionally integrated into each window. In this example, the user list is shown on the EFnet window but hidden on the Undernet window, and the detached single Inputline window is shown at the bottom. The number of people in the channel and the topic are shown on top of every channel window, which is very useful. On the other hand, the mode switches are small, barely legible letters in the dark stripe near the upper right corner of each channel window. The Connections window, shown on top of the lower chat window, is similar to that of Ircle but with the unique added feature of supporting ircII-style multiple servers per connection.

Figure 5.3: A sample Snak session

Snak has numerous relatively small bugs, but chances are the author will fix them by the time you read this anyway. It should be noted that the equally young and actively developed ShadowIRC seems much more stable and bug-free than Snak, but then ShadowIRC is a much less ambitious project. As far as missing features go, Snak has no channel maintenance features such as friend's lists and flood protection, and to date lacks a file server.

Snak is shareware, with a gentle reminder at each launch, but no crippled features. It requires Mac OS version 7.5 or newer, Drag and Drop, and the other networking software basics.

5.4.1 Setup and Use

Snak is very easy to set up and configure. When you first launch it, a Connections window appears, offering you the choice of four networks: Chatnet, DALnet, EFnet, and Undernet. To customize any of the connections, select the line (and click the **Edit** button or double-click on the line itself), then enter at least a new nickname, as well as any other network or server information. When you are done, push the **Connect** button. That's it!

For each connection, Snak uniquely allows you to specify ircII-style server lists, so that if it fails to connect with the first server for any reason, it automatically tries the next server in your list, and keeps going until it does make a connection. Likewise, if your current server lags after you connect, you can use **/server +** or **/server -** to go to the next or previous one in the list. The **IGNORE** command works just as in ircII too, which means Snak is the only Mac IRC client that lets you ignore either a nickname or a **user@host mask** and specify the types of messages to ignore. In addition, you can add, edit, or remove ignore masks using a nice graphical interface, with an option to expire the mask automatically after a preset delay.

For more help, Snak is one of the few clients that comes with a dedicated manual, called "Snak Manual." This separate application walks you through the process of connecting, some interesting features, scripting, and a good quick reference list of all commands. Ironically, however, Snak does not have any built-in help, so don't even bother to use **/help** or **search** to find a help menu, and keep the manual handy.

5.5 MacIRC

Home page: http://www.macirc.com
MacIRC is similar to ShadowIRC in trying to provide a simpler, more elegant alternative to full-featured clients such as Ircle and Snak (although its simplified interface can also make it difficult to control). Mac users have always liked MacIRC because of its uniquely Mac-oriented user interface (shown in Figure 5.4), which encourages you to play around with the buttons and menus and discover neat features. While only one channel window is shown in Figure 5.4, MacIRC supports multiple connections. Channel modes and topics are shown at the bottom of the channel window and the input window may be anchored to the upper left of the screen. The window at the right in Figure 5.4 serves different functions depending on which of the four small buttons on top are selected. As shown, it serves as the user list window, displaying a very useful count of the number of users as well as how many are channel operators.

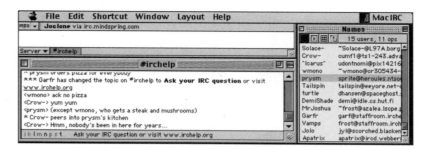

Figure 5.4: A MacIRC session

MacIRC is one of the speediest Mac IRC clients and is very stable. Unfortunately, it is not well supported, lacking help manuals or online help, and offering only a few help sites on the Web. It is also lacking in certain basic features, though these may appear in future versions.

MacIRC is shareware, and is the only Mac client with no disabling or nagging at all. MacIRC does require many elements from more recent system software versions, including OpenTransport and Appearance Manager, both of which come with Mac OS 8. If you are still running version 7, you might not even be able to launch MacIRC.

5.5.1 *Setup and Use*

Getting started with MacIRC requires some minimal IRC experience, since there are no shortcuts and no built-in server list. If you are an IRC newbie, the read-me file does suggest a few servers and describe how to get connected step by step. Otherwise the connect window is self-explanatory: You enter your nickname, your user name, and the server's host name, and you'll find yourself connected blindingly fast.

MacIRC has many stylistic quirks. The **MSG** and **NOTICE** commands and the TAB key all engage the equivalent of **QUERY**, whereby everything you type subsequently is sent to that person only, until you disengage this feature by clicking on the highlighted **Msg** button. This is annoying if you just want to send somebody a quick message or notice. A single window serves multiple duty in displaying the lists for channel users, connections (both to servers and DCC connections), and channel bans. You toggle these three types of lists with unlabeled buttons, while MacIRC ignores the corresponding text commands such as **/who #channelname** and **/mode #channel b**. Likewise, you display and set channel modes with very small, closely spaced switches that look good but aren't very practical. None of these flaws is unbearable, and you may even prefer this setup, but it does take some time before you stop asking, "Where is such-and-such feature again?"

5.6 ChatNet

Home page: http://www.elsinc.com/chatnet.html
ChatNet is unique among Mac clients in that it's commercial software, though that may be mere semantics, as the setup section below explains. ChatNet stands out for three main reasons: its unabashedly nonstandard user interface, AppleTalk chat, and kid-friendly monitoring features.

First of all, ChatNet's user interface will look familiar to anybody who has used chat programs from major online services like AOL (see Figure 5.5). This means an all-in-one window for each channel containing the channel text, user list, and input area. (For the record, ChatNet predates Snak in this approach.) Several common commands are available as large buttons on the left, such as Private and Whois. On top of each channel window are the topic and channel modes. The modes are uniquely translated into English text, which doesn't necessarily help, since "no outsiders" isn't really much more informative than "+n" to newbies. The user list and input line are both integrated into the same window too, with no option to detach them like you can in Snak. When you use ChatNet, almost everything you do tends to pop open a new window, which can be extremely confusing, as illustrated here by the five separate windows for (clockwise from top right) whois, console, channel list, and two private conversations. To make things either more convenient or confusing, depending on your taste, the type and location of buttons on the left also change depending on what type of window it is.

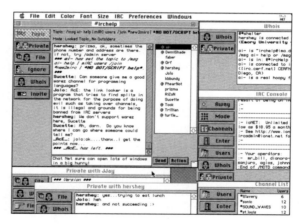

Figure 5.5: A sample ChatNet session

The irony is, your screen tends to get even more cluttered with ChatNet than with any other Mac client, because practically everything you do, such as **MSG** or **WHOIS**, pops open a new window, with no options for redirecting such output to your frontmost window or console. In fact, an incoming DCC file transfer request triggers three new overlapping windows, which you can't even see at the same time: a totally unnecessary private (**QUERY**) window, a DCC transfer status window, and a file save dialog box (you don't get to decide first if you want the file or not). Inexplicably, many people actually seem to like this setup.

The interface itself has a non-Mac aesthetic, like a program ported over from DOS (even though that is not the case). The buttons and menus often look strange or appear in unexpected places. Enlarging a window causes several screenfuls of the existing text to scroll off the top. Perhaps most important, ChatNet tends to rename almost every standard command in an attempt to make IRC more newbie-friendly. For example, **JOIN** becomes an **Enter** button, and channel modes like **+tn** translate into **Locked Topic**, **No Outsiders** (the latter **+n** mode actually means that nobody may **MSG** the channel from outside it, so in this case the translation is misleading). In my opinion, this makes it harder for newbies to learn, since they can no longer rely upon the wealth of existing help resources (including this book), which support those standards.

The second standout feature of ChatNet is its completely unique AppleTalk chat. You can chat with people from your school or company over local AppleTalk networks. There is no need to setup a local IRC server, nor does each Mac need connections to the Internet. Teachers and parents don't have to worry about outsiders barging in to make trouble, and the local network is faster and more robust than IRC. By encouraging kids to write, ChatNet can be a useful learning tool.

Finally, ChatNet was the first to provide kid-friendly censoring features, which may appeal to parents and teachers. The ChatGuardian feature restricts the kind of channels a kid can join and censors inappropriate language from those he or she does join. The ChatWatch feature is like a wiretap, recording all the kid's conversations for review later. These tools may provide some protection, but in my opinion they are more trouble than they are worth. First of all, I have yet to find a kid-controlling tool that kids can't figure out how to evade faster than adults can learn how to set it up. There are already kid-friendly chat servers out there that require screened registrations, on which adult supervisors monitor all conversations. Furthermore, as an educator myself, I believe censorship is no substitute for proper teaching and guidance. Finally and most important, censoring certain words doesn't make IRC safe or even appropriate for unsupervised children.

There are a few other features worth noting. ChatNet does support speech and sound, whereas most other clients (besides Ircle) do not. It is the only client other than ShadowIRC to permit manual logging—that is, it captures channel or private text on demand. As far as disadvantages go, ChatNet is the only major client with no support for multiple network connections, nor does it offer any easy way to add that capability in the future. It doesn't use color to distinguish different types of messages, nor does it support Ircle- or mIRC-style colored text. The rudimentary ignore feature ignores only nicknames. The latest version added the bare minimum of channel maintenance functions, with four buttons to kick, ban, and op or deop (the last two buttons are confusingly labeled as on/off, with the word **op** added to one side). You can ban with **nick!user@host**, but there is no ban list or unban button. ChatNet certainly doesn't have any advanced features such as scripting, friends lists, flood protection, and so forth.

And less we forget our four S's, ChatNet seems sluggish compared to other clients, but it is reasonably stable in spite of an extra system extension. It regrettably flaunts standards and is proud of that fact. The support level remains to be seen for this relatively new commercial company and totally unique client, which mainstream users have not embraced en masse.

5.6.1   Setup and Use

Although ChatNet is technically commercial software, you can still download it free like shareware. Right from the first time you use it, however, it limits you to 20-minute sessions until you pay the registration fee. I found this a major annoyance, as it took me four reconnects just to evaluate it for this review (not counting two reconnects that occurred within a few seconds rather than after 20 minutes). Even worse, each time I had to reestablish my test channels, since ChatNet cannot save such configurations. Updates and support have been free to date, but this company is still relatively new on the scene, so again you run a risk regarding its long-term viability.

ChatNet's installation is by far the most complicated among the clients described here. The AppleTalk chat feature unfortunately requires you to put an additional extension called **MS Listener** in the Extensions folder within your System Folder (even if you have no intention of ever using it). This in turn requires a formal installation and reboot, not necessary for any other IRC client. After downloading and processing, you should see the **ChatNet2.1.1.sea** self-extracting archive. When launched, it in turn creates a **ChatNet v2.1.1** Files folder containing the installer and manual. From that folder, launch the **ChatNet Installer** and follow the directions for the easy install.

There are no shortcuts for getting started, so you will have to do it the traditional way. If you are a typical home modem user not on an AppleTalk network, don't be worried by the clumsy "AppleTalk network not available" error you'll see when you first start, or by the slight delay on every subsequent start. You should eventually get a welcome window that lets you type a nickname and user name, and select a server-port combination from the pop-up menu (this is really inefficient to scroll through, especially with the large server list that comes by default). When you have those settings selected, click the **Login** button to make the connection.

From here you may use the Create Channel menu, which in turn opens the contradictorily named Enter Channel window, where you can type a channel name, or just use the **JOIN** command and avoid the confusion. Each type of window has its own set of buttons on the left representing typically used commands. The console window has these buttons: **Away**, **Mode**, **Channels** (for **LIST**), **Enter** (**JOIN**), **Users** (**NAMES**), **Whois**, and **Private** (**QUERY**). Each channel window has these buttons: **Topic**, **Private** (**QUERY**), **File** (**DCC**), **Ignore**, **Whois**, **Invite**, and **Mode**.

ChatNet doesn't offer any online help, but it does have a separate manual in the form of a stand-alone DOCMaker application. This is by far the most detailed of all the clients' help documents, as you might expect from commercial software. Whether you are new or have IRC experience, I highly suggest you read the manual from beginning to end and not skip around, since ChatNet has many unorthodox approaches when it comes to configuring and using the client.

5.7 Summary

We have reviewed five major Mac IRC clients, selected for their performance and popularity. Each has its unique features and advantages as well as its disadvantages. Ircle is the classic choice with the most features and support, but it can also seem complicated and overwhelming, at least at first. ShadowIRC and Snak are the new kids on the block, with the most active development and an ever-growing list of features, but they are also rough around the edges. Both have a simpler interface and run fast; ShadowIRC is the leaner client and Snak goes for more features. MacIRC looks good, runs fast, and has a certain flair, but it is missing many features and isn't as actively developed. ChatNet intentionally defies standards for the sake of user friendliness. It has some unique features that make it a valid choice for newbies in spite of its many weaknesses.

For up-to-date reviews of these and many other clients, check out the IRChelp.org Mac IRC client page at http://www.irchelp.org/ irchelp/mac, the Tucows Mac IRC clients page at http://tucows.epix.net/ mac/circmac.html, or the Mac Orchard site at http://www.macorchard. com/chat.html.

6

CONNECTING TO A SERVER

Having installed a client program (or bugged someone else into doing it for you) and familiarized yourself with the theory and basics of IRC (What, you didn't? Go back and start reading!), you are now ready to connect to an IRC server. What do you need first? Why, the name of a server, of course! How do you get one? If you don't have a friend who'll take you by the hand, read on.

Depending on your client, there are different ways of setting the server or list of servers to which you intend to connect. Most clients let you set a default server to which your client automatically connects at start-up. Some also let you specify one or more alternative servers in case you fail to connect to the first. Let's not rush things, though. First of all, you'll need to choose a network, and from its available servers select the one most likely to suit you.

6.1 Selecting a Network and Server, and Connecting

Earlier, in 2.3, we saw how the IRC world became divided into many different entities, each with its own special character. This structure may be confusing, but it certainly adds variety. In order to pick the most suitable network, ask yourself what you're expecting to find on IRC. If you want to hang around, explore a few channels, and meet many different people, one of the major networks is probably the best choice. If you'd rather not jump in the deep end and prefer to practice your IRC skills before venturing into the metropolitan jungle of the large nets, there are numerous smaller nets, with few but friendly users and operators who are willing to help newcomers. If your personal ethics require a controlled environment free of potentially offensive material, one of the smaller U.S.-based networks with strict policies is the ideal choice, often a suitable place for your kids as well.

Browse through the list in Appendix A and pick a network that seems likely to suit your needs. If your first choice doesn't work out, there are always many more. Remember, quantity doesn't necessarily mean quality—even if you're on a network with 30,000 or 40,000 users, you'll rarely contact more than a few dozen people at a time.

Once you find a network, check its server list for the nearest server. This step is not absolutely necessary, but it is probably a good idea. Many networks have a generic server address that takes you to a random server— for example, DALnet has the irc.dal.net address for that purpose, and mIRC users know it as Random US DALnet server on their server list. Don't sweat over it—a generic address will do for now.

On an off-topic note, IRC is mainly a casual chat and recreational environment. You won't generally find serious professional topics such as medicine or law, for the very good reason that although IRC includes many professionals from many different fields, they prefer to frequent channels that focus on general chat or a hobby. After all, would you be want to end a day at work with a visit to IRC, only to devote it to an unpaid rerun of the day's work? I might give out some free advice if a topic related to my line of work comes up in a channel I'm on, but I don't sit and wait for "customers." If you need a professional opinion and can't find someone nearby, Usenet (a collection of email-based newsgroups) is a much better place to look. Besides, nothing prevents an unqualified person from posing as a professional. Following medical advice from someone on IRC who claims to be a doctor is risky at best.

As we saw in 2.5, while the technical part of client-server communication must be consistent (with slight variations, depending on the type of server), the user interface for selecting a server and connecting to it varies from client to client. In this book we'll take a closer look at the means ircII and mIRC use. Most other clients follow one of these two methods.

Whether you pick a description from a menu or enter a server name manually, you should be familiar with the way Internet addresses are built. This way you don't need a menu in order to make your way to a server.

6.1.1 *Internet Addressing*

Two or three parts compose the name of any machine on the Internet, using the following structure:

```
[arbitrary.hostname.]domain.tld
```

TLD is the top level domain. It can be a generic one like COM, NET, or EDU, which implies the nature of the organization using it (that is, company, military, educational). Some of these can be registered and used by anyone, anywhere in the world. In other cases it denotes a country— for example, FR for France or MX for Mexico. The country codes follow the ISO 3166 standard (which I won't address here).

Some countries use their TLD and an extra identifier for the type of organization. For example, COM.TR is a company in Turkey (country code TR), and AC.IL is an educational (academic) facility in Israel (country code IL). Major TLDs using this system include Australia (AU), Brazil (BR), the United Kingdom (UK), Japan (JP), and South Africa (ZA).

To make things even more confusing, some countries use both systems. In Canada and the United States it is also possible to have a state or province code precede the country code—for example, FL.US (Florida) or MB.CA (Manitoba). I've used capital letters for emphasis here, but lowercase is more appropriate, so I'm making subsequent addresses lowercase—there is no practical difference in this case.

The other essential part is the second level domain, which comes before the TLD or identifier.TLD combination. This is a name the site chooses which is registered with the competent authority. Examples are netscape.com (home of Netscape Communications) and demon.co.uk (Demon Internet, a major ISP in the United Kingdom).

Everything before the second level domain is a machine name—an arbitrary choice of the domain's maintainers. Some indicate the function of the machine to which they point: for example, "www" indicates a Web server and "ftp" indicates an FTP server. It's also quite common for a machine name to have a structure of its own, as in irc.cs.cmu.edu, where the person maintaining the domain adds "cs" to indicate that it is part of an internal subdivision. This particular example is the address of the IRC machine at the computer science (cs) department of Carnegie-Mellon (cmu.edu).

Many sites maintaining an IRC server follow the convention of using "irc" as the machine's name. Some typical examples are irc.mindspring.com (an IRC server operated by Mindspring Enterprises), irc.demon.co.uk (the IRC server of Demon Internet, a company in the United Kingdom), or irc.funet.fi (the IRC server of the Finnish University Network).

Many IRC networks have a distinct domain name all their servers share regardless of location, and the machine names might reflect a server's location or the name of the organization running it, as in Las Vegas.NV.US.undernet.org (an Undernet server in Las Vegas, Nevada), webbernet.mi.us.dal.net (a DALnet server at webbernet.net in Michigan), and irc.eu.dal.net (any European DALnet server).

6.1.2   ircII

In ircII, there are three ways of selecting the server(s) the client will attempt to connect to when started. The first is by utilizing a list of servers usually named ircII.servers in the **/usr/local/lib/irc** directory (or wherever you installed the client). The list is read from the top with each server occupying a separate line and is the system's default list. The second method is a list set from your log-in file (usually **.profile** or .cshrc) and uses the Unix environment variable **IRCSERVER**. The section on setting up ircII mentioned both of these methods. The third way, which overrides the previous two when used, is to specify the server on the command line:

```
$ irc SomeNick irc.server.com
```

In this case, you must put the nickname you intend to use as the first parameter, otherwise you can't specify the server. You can also optionally add a port number by appending it following a colon. The command line also supports multiple servers in a space-separated list:

```
$ irc SomeNick irc.server.com:6665 irc.other.net
irc.whatever.com:6660
```

If the client fails to connect to the first server, it automatically tries the second.

TIP *The ircII help files have more to say on this topic:* **/help ircii command_line_options.**

6.1.3   **Graphical Clients and mIRC**

Most graphical interface clients, including mIRC, supply a server list of their own. You can expect this list to be fairly up to date, although you will discover that some of the servers listed no longer exist or have changed networks—this is unavoidable because of the speed with which the IRC map changes. The majority will still be valid. In mIRC, you can find the server list under the File menu by clicking **Setup • IRC Servers**.

The problem with some of these clients is that the visible part of a server's information is usually only a description of it or its location, and not its host name, which is the information you need for an Internet application. For example, "IRCnet: US, MI, Detroit" helps people in and around Michigan select their closest server, but it does not say which server you're actually connecting to.

Here's an example: A subscriber of Mindspring (a large nationwide ISP) who lives in Texas and wants to use EFnet might have several servers nearby. However, that user would be better off connecting to Mindspring's own server despite its being further away, because he will be using Mindspring's internal network all the way and will normally get a faster and more stable connection. So it doesn't really help that the Mindspring server is listed merely as "EFnet: US, GA, Atlanta." Don't worry—you'll soon be expert enough at customizing your server list and finding out which servers are best for you. This is just to show that the rule of thumb about connecting to your nearest server is no more than that—a rule of thumb, and far from rigid doctrine.

With these clients, you simply pull up the server list and select the one you wish to connect to. In mIRC, the program presents the server list by default when you first start the program, and you can set it to connect automatically to a particular server. Otherwise, you can pick one from the IRC Servers menu. Under the same menu, you can view the address of a particular server by selecting **Edit**. This is also where you'll add and remove servers to optimize or update the list.

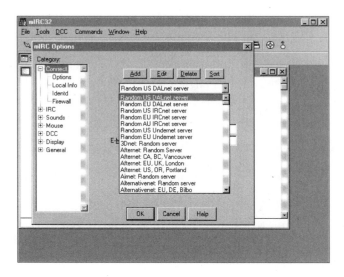

Figure 6.1: List of available servers

If all goes well, you should see a series of notices from the server or the client and have a working server connection within a few seconds. It's not always that simple, though. You may have to work on establishing a set of servers that works for you before being able to connect consistently in the shortest possible time.

When connecting to a server, you are likely to encounter a number of problems. In most cases you'll get a message from either the client or the server. In other cases the connection could simply refuse to work or return an error message that doesn't help at all (mIRC is a bit notorious for saying "connection failed" without telling you why). A lot can go wrong. Next you'll learn of the potential stumbling blocks in your path.

6.2 Things That Can Go Wrong

The process of connecting to an IRC server can yield a surprising number of different errors and corresponding error messages, which can be confusing if you're not familiar with the syntax.

6.2.1 K-Lined, or You Are Not Welcome . . .

The notice "K-lined" means that your address matches an entry on the server's internal list of addresses not permitted to use it; the server disconnects you after detecting this fact. In effect, you are banned from using that server. Messages to that effect can take a variety of forms, but in all cases you will not be able to use the server.

The reason you get for being K-lined is actually an arbitrary message set by a server operator or administrator sets; there may even be no reason at all. K-lines are known as such because the part of the configuration file where the server stores these "kill lines" and checkes upon them with each user connection consists of lines beginning with **K:** (so the correct term is really *K: line*). Not all server operators are kind enough to provide a reason, so it might return no more than a generic "Banned" or "You are not welcome" notice. Don't take it personally—yet. Read on.

The most common reason for being K: lined is that the server's operators have observed misbehavior from users within a group of addresses (of which yours is one), and therefore have decided not to permit any user from that group to use the server. Naturally, if you have never used the server before, it is not your fault, nor is anyone holding you personally responsible for some misconduct. In many cases it affects a specific part of your ISP's addresses or even the entire ISP, and one obnoxious user sharing the same ISP may be causing the problem. This is a disadvantage of using a dynamic address (see 0.3).

Another reason for a K: line could be that you are expected to use a server closer to you in terms of either network topology or geographical location. It doesn't make much sense for, say, a Swedish user to use a server in the United States if there are local servers available in Sweden, and vice versa. K: lines aren't the preferred way of keeping nonlocal users out, but some server administrators use them for that purpose.

In more severe cases, you may get G-lined. Some IRC networks that have a global abuse policy implement *G: lines*, networkwide K: lines (also called global K: lines). On these networks, repeated or extensive abuse from a site may result in simultaneous K: lining from all servers on that network. On DALnet and other networks that use their server software, the equivalent of a G: line is the *akill*. The effect is the same.

Removing K: lines is entirely at the discretion of the server's administrator. Many servers don't take too much care to remove old K: lines, so they may remain in place indefinitely, even for years. G: lines tend to have a set expiration date, which can be anywhere from 20 minutes to a month after it was set, depending on the severity of complaints against the G: lined site or user. Some modern server versions use temporary K: lines, automatically removed after a short while. Unless you're having a really serious problem finding a server, simply remove the server from your list and connect to a different one. Alternately, you may ask one of the server's operators or email the server's admin address (see 15.3) to have it lifted—that is, if they are inclined to do so.

6.2.2 Ping Timeout

Ping timeouts are a common problem on slow connections. Perhaps you connect to the server successfully, but after the initial connection, nothing happens, and the connection closes after a minute or two with the message "Ping timeout." This means the server got no reply from your client from the first **PING**. The server must receive a **PONG** reply to confirm that your client is connected and responding. The cause for Ping timeout may be a slow network connection or a heavy load on the server machine or your own, either delaying the **PING** on its way to you or preventing the reply from reaching the server in the time it should. Network problems are by far the more common cause.

Less common is a problem between certain servers and clients. This used to be a major nuisance, but now—although it hasn't entirely been fixed—newer versions of those particular servers send a message telling you to send a response manually if you are having trouble with Ping timeouts. If the problem is on the server side, try connecting to a different server. You really shouldn't encounter such problems when using modern clients.

If you're having problems connecting to all servers, there's probably something wrong with your machine's or your site's network connectivity. If you're positive the connection to your provider is fine and nothing needs fixing, then your provider's network connectivity is the most likely cause.

TIP *You can use a network diagnostic utility named traceroute to check the network path between yourself and the address you're trying to connect to. It's very simple— here's how:*

IN UNIX `$ traceroute <address>`

IN WINDOWS 95 AND 98 *Click **Start** and open an MS-DOS window. Enter the following: **tracert** <address>*

6.2.3 *No More Connections/Server Full*

This message is not unusual, especially during peak hours. It means the number of connections the server has allotted to your connection class is full. Few servers have a setup that groups all users under a single class. Instead, they define address groups with a maximum limit of users from each group who may be connected simultaneously—for example, by assigning all foreign addresses class 20 and setting a limit of 50 connections for class 20 in the configuration file. In this case, once the quota of 50 users is exhausted, the server rejects all foreign users attempting to connect, with a "Server full" or "No more connections" message, until at least one client of that class disconnects and frees the spot for another.

Another common reason for this message is that you were previously connected to the same server and lost your connection to it, but the server hasn't yet noticed it yet. If the server permits a maximum of one client from any particular address, as many servers do, it detects your attempt to reconnect as a duplicate connection from an address that's already connected. You can either use another server or wait for the previous connection to timeout on the server's side.

6.2.4 *Connection Refused*

The only cause for the "Connection refused" message is that no IRC server was listening for connections on the machine and/or port you tried to connect to. Make sure the server name and the port number are correct and try again. If it continues to return the same message and you're positive about the server's host name and port, its IRC server or machine is having a problem. Connect to a different server—there's no telling how long the server will be down.

6.2.5 *Unable to Resolve Server Name*

This indicates the failure of a name server to convert the canonical name, the "real" name of the server like irc.server.com, into an IP address such as 256.10.2.78. This conversion is necessary for making any network connection.

Canonical names are more for human convenience—networked computers (and computers in general) only understand numbers and need them in order to make a connection. Those numbers eventually change into a string of 0s and 1s, but that's something way beyond the scope of this book. Suffice it to say that your computer is turning everything you tell it into numbers and converting other numbers back into visual signals you can understand.

Failure to resolve server names may stem from a number of different causes. The most common is that either your local name server or the one on which the server's address resides are out of order. Your client sends your query to your local name server, which in turn looks up the name server that holds the records of the server's site (server.com) and then queries it for the IP address matching the canonical name you have given it (irc.server.com). Naturally, your client handles the request and response internally, so you don't notice it—unless it fails.

If this happens with all servers, it's definitely your local server that has a problem. Your ISP's technical staff will fix it, but may not have noticed it. If your ISP is unreachable or can't fix it for a while, your options are either to use an off-site name server, which requires you to know a name server's IP address, or to find an IP address from an existing list of them. PPP users would also have the added problem of having to change the settings of their TCP/IP stack or use a separate lookup program. Therefore, the easier solution is to find the IP addresses of the IRC servers you use most and add them to your list separately.

Note that IP addresses are liable to change without notice (for example, the administrator running the server may decide to use a different machine, or the route through which it connects to the rest of the Internet may change), so it's better to use the canonical names. In the case of IRC networks that use a generic domain name for all their servers (undernet.org, for example is a generic domain name for all Undernet servers), if the name servers serving undernet.org are down, it will be impossible to resolve any of the network's servers. The solution is to use an IP address or regular host name that you know corresponds to such a server. If you don't know any, try asking on one of the other networks' help channel, or try the network's website if there is one.

6.2.6 Illegal Nickname

The server sends this message if you select a nickname that's already in use or if the nickname you chose contains an unacceptable character. Valid characters for nicknames include a to z, A to Z, 0 to 9, and the following special characters: back slash (\), backstroke (`), caret (^), dash (-), pipe (|), underscore (_), left square bracket ([), right square bracket (]), left curly bracket ({), and right curly bracket (}).

Because IRC originated in Scandinavia, many servers consider the following pairs of special characters to be the same due to the layout of Scandinavian keyboards: left square bracket (]) and left curly bracket (}); right square bracket ([) and right curly bracket ({); and pipe (|) and backslash (\). These characters correspond to lowercase and uppercase letters on a Scandinavian keyboard. Because IRC is not case-sensitive, each pair is regarded as being the same character.

The leading character cannot be a number or dash. If the nickname is valid and someone else is using your first choice, you can set most clients to fall back automatically to an alternative nickname. If this also fails or your client has no such feature, the server prompts you to enter a new nickname manually before it will accept you. If you don't enter a new nickname soon enough, the server disconnects you with a Ping timeout (see 6.2.2).

This problem can present itself to users trying to connect to servers or networks running Quarterdeck's IRC server software. Part of this software's nonstandard behavior includes rejecting nicknames that would be quite legitimate on other servers, such as those with an underscore in them. If you can find nothing else wrong with your nickname, try using one made up entirely of letters.

6.2.7 Nickname or Channel Temporarily Unavailable

This message will only show up on servers running IRCnet's server software. In this case, the nickname was recently in use by someone who didn't sign off "normally" as seen from your server. A protective mechanism unique to this type of server prevents use of the nickname for approximately 15 minutes after the user's signoff. You will need to select a new nickname with the **NICK** command (see 2.7) before the server accepts you. You may change back to the original one after the nick delay expires and the nickname becomes available again.

6.2.8 Ending Up on a Different Server

This is not a common problem—in fact, it often isn't a problem at all and may well go unnoticed. If a server is taken down permanently or temporarily, in order to spare the server's regular users the trouble of looking for another server, its administration may choose to redirect people trying to connect to it to a different server. It can be a problem if the server you end up connecting to refuses you with one of the errors mentioned here because of a difference in configuration, or if the server you get redirected to is not on the same network as the one you originally connected to. An example of the latter is what happened to users of America Online's IRC servers. AOL used to maintain servers on all four major networks. In November 1998, it was forced to remove its EFnet server from that network. It then proceeded to take down the servers on IRCnet and DALnet of its own accord, leaving only its Undernet server up. As if this weren't enough of an inconvenience to users, AOL also redirected the addresses of its former EFnet, DALnet and IRCnet servers to point to the remaining Undernet server, so everyone trying to connect to any AOL server would end up on Undernet whether they liked it or not. Needless to say, the company made no friends in doing this.

6.2.9 No Authorization

You can expect this message to appear when you're trying to connect to a foreign server. Also, many servers accept few or no users from outside their domain, and attempts to connect return the error.

If this happens to you while you're trying to connect to a server you normally can access, the most likely explanation is name server failure. The server attempts to convert the IP address from which it detects your connection into a canonical host name, using the same procedure described earlier (see 6.2.5) for lookup of the server's IP address. The difference is that it's requesting the reverse of what you asked for—IP to name instead of name to IP.

Apart from regular DNS problems, some ISPs have simply omitted or neglected adding reverse records for their addresses, not considering it essential to smooth operation. But unlike the case on most Internet connections, on IRC this practice can and will cause problems. Many servers, on the large networks in particular, refuse to accept users whose IP address will not resolve to a canonical host name. If you can confirm this as the problem, ask your ISP to see to it that reverse DNS is enabled. As long as you have this problem, you'll have fewer servers available.

6.2.10 Ident Required/Install Identd/Bad Username

Depending on your local machine, you'll either encounter these messages frequently or very rarely. A number of servers, especially on the major networks, require the presence of an *ident server* on the machine from which the client connection originates—in short, yours. "Install identd" often appears as a K: line reason, too.

If your client is running on your own machine, as is the case with PPP dial-ups, the server looks for this server on your machine. Naturally, few users go to the trouble of installing a separate identd on their machine. The IRC clients usually cover this by emulating it and listening for ident requests in order to send the appropriate response. This is the case with Windows and Macintosh clients.

Ident queries go to port 113 of a machine. Your IRC client, if it's capable of emulating an ident server, listens for incoming queries on this port and, if you have it set up correctly, also send a valid reply, after which the server considers you "idented." Not all servers have rigid rules regarding ident, but it's a good thing to have in place. Developments on EFnet in particular have reduced the number of servers providing access for unidented hosts.

The response sent must match your declared user name, and the ident type should be set to UNIX. This may not be true—for example, in the case of a Windows machine—but tell the server what it wants to hear anyway. If the user name does not match the one you have told your identd to send, the server considers your ident response invalid, unidents you, and naturally refuses you if the server won't accept unidented users. mIRC has port 113 and UNIX set by default under **File • Setup • Identd**. All you have to add is the user ID. If you don't add it, it will be taken from the email address.

Your user name and matching ident response can be practically any arbitrary string of up to 10 characters. An important issue comes into play here, to which you should give thought. Of course, on a machine you yourself run and maintain, you can set your user name to be anything you like and hide your real log-in name, but even if you do, bear in mind that total anonymity is an illusion. Either directly or with the cooperation of your ISP, your identity can be found. By the way, user names such as "me," "ask," or "guess" are considered stupid since they're obviously both fake and unimaginative. Your credibility also suffers from silly fake user names or mixed upper- and lowercase user names. Some servers reject user names like that altogether.

If you aren't the supervisor of the machine running your client, the system administrator must install the identd. If there is no identd and the sysadmin is not willing to install one, that will definitely reduce the number of servers you may use, especially on the larger networks. On a commercial ISP, it indicates a lack of interest in customers' needs. Installing an identd isn't such a big deal and doesn't consume untold of hours of working time. In fact, it's a rather trivial task, and you shouldn't accept any excuses for the ISP's failure to do it. If the machine belongs to an educational or government site and the people responsible for the machine don't want to install it, fine. You can't force them to.

A special case of identd problem involves machines behind a firewall or using a proxy. Because you appear to be connecting from another machine, any identd you run on yours goes unnoticed. Unless the firewall or proxy administrator pulls a few nifty tricks with the configuration, clients from these machines will not be able to ident. This is tricky business—it makes the firewall less effective, and you can't really expect any firewall administrator to bother with it.

6.3 Welcome to the Internet Relay

If all goes well, you make a successful connection to an IRC server. The first four lines you see look something like this:

```
*** Welcome to the Internet Relay Network
SomeNick!george@my.provider.com
*** Your host is irc.webbernet.net, running version 2.9.5/Sc8-
a2/Mr2
*** This server was created Wed Jan 20 1999 at 21:03:58 EST
*** umodes available oirw, channel modes abiklmnopqstv
```

A report on the server's and network's current status follows:

```
*** There are 7444 users plus 28298 invisible and 8 services on 66
servers
*** 159 operators online
*** 19 unknown connections
*** 14582 channels formed
*** I have 2234 clients, 1 services and 1 servers
*** Current local users: 2234 Max: 3068
*** Current global users: 35742 Max: 39293
```

Most of this makes sense, but the rest looks like some computerese conspiracy aimed at undermining your mental health and self esteem. Perhaps we should look at each line individually:

```
*** Welcome to the Internet Relay Network
SomeNick!george@my.provider.com
```

This line means that the server has accepted your connection, and you're now known by the nickname of "SomeNick." It also recognizes you as coming from the host named "my.provider.com," and this host confirms that your user name is "george." Depending on the type of server, it may give your full user mask (see 6.3.2) or just the nickname. Servers running customized software may replace "Internet Relay Network" with the network's name.

```
*** Your host is irc.webbernet.net, running version 2.9.5/Sc8-
a2/Mr2
```

The first part is obviously the server's name, but the second part is rather cryptic. This is the server's "version" and identifies the type of server. In this example it stands for the 2.9.5 basic server version. This server is also running a patch (an add-on or bug fix—in this particular case, an add-on) to add some features to the server that aren't part of the basic 2.9.5 code and that the administrator wishes to have. This is indicated by a plus sign (+) or slash mark (/), followed by the patch's identifier, and is present on a lot of networks' servers. It is often a server requirement.

```
*** This server was created Wed Jan 20 1999 at 21:03:58 EST
```

This doesn't mean the server has existed only since that date and time, but says when the current version of the server software was installed on the machine.

```
*** umodes available oirw, channel modes abiklmnopqstv
```

Oh gosh, more cryptic messages. These two strings indicate the settings (modes) available for users, also known as *umodes* (see 6.4) and *channel modes* (see 10.3) and characterized by certain letters. These strings differ depending on the type of server—for example, umode **r** and channel modes **a** and **q** are particular to an IRCnet server such as irc.webbernet.net, and the rest are present on all but the most divergent types of servers.

The server sends the next four to seven lines to the connecting client, but you can also request them at any time with the **LUSERS** command. They inform you of the network's and server's current status. The total number of users on the network is the sum of visible and invisible users. Unknown connections are nothing more than incoming connections the server hasn't yet accepted and classified. The final two lines are not standard, but many server administrators like to make that information visible.

6.3.1 *The Message of the Day*

At the end of all this information you'll find the all-important **MOTD**— the server's Message of the Day. This text file, stored on the server machine and sent to all successfully connecting clients, describes the server's rules and policies, and sometimes contains useful information and announcements. Despite its name, it's rarely a message "of the day" and will sometimes be months old, depending on how satisfied with its contents the server's administrator is. The amount and nature of the information it contains varies according to how conscientious that administrator is about informing the users of what they should know and of developments in the IRC world.

Although you'll soon become expert enough to get into the habit of ignoring it (I won't throw any stones here—when I started out, it didn't take me long to find out how to make it disappear), you should read it at least the first time you connect to a particular server. Both ircII and mIRC provide a setting that suppresses display of the **MOTD**—this is convenient if you want less noise when connecting, but even a server you regularly connect to offers new and important information once in a while, so you're better off reading it regularly.

TIP *The **MOTD** is often much longer than your screen or window. If your client has a scrollbar in the window, back up to read the part you missed. With ircII and similar clients, do the following:*

```
/set hold_mode on
/motd
/set hold_mode off
```

6.3.2   *Your Identity on IRC*

While you're connected, other users know you in two different ways. The first is simply your nickname, which people need in order to reach you and see you on IRC. It's used as a destination address for messages and an identifier for server queries regarding you.

The second way is more complex and consists of three parts. The first part is your nickname. This is followed by an exclamation mark (!), which serves as a separator between it and the next field, which is your user name. Another separator, an at (@) character, follows. The last part is your host name or the IP address you're connecting from. (As I said previously, host names and IP addresses are equivalent for connecting, but the server treats them as text strings, and therefore they're considered different). The final result looks like this:

```
SomeNick!george@my.provider.com
Nickname!username@host.name
```

This is your identity for sending to the server. Every item the server receives from your connection automatically gets this added to it as the sender's identity. If you send a message destined for a user or another server, this full version will be forwarded to the recipient along with the message. This is your *user mask* on IRC.

6.3.3 Nickname Registration and Ownership

If the network you connected to has a nickname service, you'll be able to reserve a nickname for your own use. Depending on the service's features, you may also be allowed to forbid others to use it in your absence or add personal information to your registration for others to see. Refer to Appendix A for information on the availability of nickname registration services. The usual nickname for this type of service is NickServ, and you can request help on how to use it by sending it a message:

```
/msg nickserv help
```

Just as you may have exclusive use of a nickname by registering it with a nickname service, you may try to use a nickname already registered to someone else. If the nickname's owner has instructed the server to forbid its use by others, the server sends you a notice immediately after you connect or change to that nickname. This notice says that the nickname is reserved and you must either change it or the service will disconnect (kill) you for unauthorized use of a registered nickname or change your nickname to something else. It usually allows no more than a minute for you to change nicknames. If you receive a notice saying something like that on a network you know has no nickname service, ignore it—someone is trying to make you release the nickname so they can use it.

NOTE   *As of April 1999, DALnet no longer allows use of NickServ in this manner. Messages must be directed to nickserv@services.dal.net.*

6.3.4 The Realname Field

Part of your identity will be your *realname*. This did originally contain a user's real name, but nowadays is used more often for displaying a witty comment or the location of a user's Web page. The text in the realname field is quite arbitrary. If you're using a client on your own machine, such as mIRC, you can easily set the text you want to display by adding it to your client's setup. Of course, there's nothing wrong with using your actual name, it's simply common to put something different in the space reserved for it.

If you're using a Unix system, setting the realname isn't that simple, and you'll have to go through the procedure of setting the **IRCNAME** environment variable, which you should already have mastered while setting up your client. If not, please return to 4.5.5 and follow the steps for changing your realname.

6.4 User Modes (Umodes)

All servers permit a user to use certain settings that influence the status of the session. The number and function of these settings varies greatly among different server types, so we'll limit ourselves to looking only at those that are present on most servers or are most important. Setting or removing a user mode for yourself is simple:

```
/mode <your_nickname> +/-<mode>
```

Using the plus (+) before the letter corresponding to the user mode activates it, while the dash (-) unsets it. Omitting a prefix is the same as using a plus sign. User mode letters are case sensitive—**W** is not the same as **w** and may have a quite different effect or may not have a meaning at all.

6.4.1 Umode i

This is the most widely used user mode. User mode **i** (invisible), when set, makes a client invisible to certain types of user listings and scans. It's used for more privacy and to avoid harassment. This is also the solution to the problem of being targeted by spam bots. Many servers automatically set it for a user upon connecting, in which case you'll see a notice that looks somewhat like this:

```
*** Mode change "+i" for user SomeNick by SomeNick
```

You can also set it manually:

```
/mode SomeNick +i
```

Use **-i** if you do not agree with it and the server has set it automatically, or if you no longer wish to be invisible. Some modern clients, including mIRC, allow you to set umode **+i** automatically upon connecting, even if the server doesn't do so.

TIP *To set yourself as invisible automatically after connecting, whether the server does so or not, follow these steps:*

IN MIRC *Go to **File • Options • IRC Servers** and check the **Invisible Mode** box.*

IN IRCII *Add a **MODE $N +i** command to your .ircrc file.*

6.4.2 Umode w

This lets you receive wallops, which are a special type of message servers
or IRC operators send out, usually announcing some network event.
Only IRC operators need to see them, so you might as well leave it off.
On some networks, only IRC operators can receive them, and user mode
+w does nothing for the regular user.

6.4.3 Umode s

Umode s is the perfect way of getting your screen flooded with countless
useless server notices. Umode s sends you all sorts of server notices, and
there are often additional umodes that allow someone to monitor only a
certain type of notice. Trust me—you don't need it.

6.4.4 Umode o

This user mode indicates that IRC operator status is active—therefore
it's available only to IRC operators. Trying to set umode +o is useless,
since it's not obtained with a mode change, but with the **OPER** command (see 18.6.1), which only authorized users can use.

6.4.5 Umode d

Service robots often use umode **d** (*dumb*), which is not available on all
server types. On those networks that do allow users to use it, it prevents
channel text from reaching the client and so is not very useful.

6.4.6 Umode r

Umode **r** is unique to IRCnet servers and others with the same server
software, but unlike other umodes specific to one type of server, this one
can be annoying. The server automatically sets it when a user connects;
it indicates that the server will allow you to use it as a server, but doesn't
give you access to the full, regular command set. The **r** stands for
restricted. This restriction lies in the fact that you may not change your
nickname without disconnecting from the server, and may not use channel operator commands, even if you are given channel operator status.
Perhaps neither of these interests you yet, but it's good to know this,
since you could run into this problem later on. The solution is usually to
use a server that is closer to you geographically. If you already are, use
the **WHOIS** command to check whether your host name is resolving—
some servers impose the restriction on unresolved hosts instead of
forbidding them to use the server (see 6.2.9).

6.4.7 *Other Umodes*

A variety of other modes exist that IRC operators use for monitoring the server. None of these are of any interest to the average user, so you'll do fine without them. Some umodes might be in use on different types of servers, but function differently—**i**, **o**, **s**, and **w** are the only ones you can expect will do the same thing on almost all servers.

The most interesting mode available on several small networks is known as **x**, **a**, or **z** depending on the network. The server can automatically set it, just like user mode **i**, and it hides the first part of your host name by replacing it with some other text. In effect, it fakes a user's host name and thus provides effective protection against DoS attacks, for which the attacker needs to know the target's address. If your small network server automatically sets a mode other than **+i** for you, this is probably it.

6.5 Changing Servers: The SERVER Command

Once you're connected to a server, you don't have to keep using the same one for your entire IRC session. If for any reason you want to use a different server, all good clients support the **SERVER** command, which lets you change servers without having to quit and restart your client. Its use is simple:

```
/server irc.otherserver.net
```

You can also specify a port on the new server other than the default by appending the port number:

```
/server irc.otherserver.net 6665
```

Though typing the command is really simpler, mIRC users can also disconnect first with the connect-disconnect button (leftmost on the toolbar) and then select a new server from the list.

Depending on the client you're using, one of two things may happen: Either your client closes the connection to the current server and initiates the new one, or it holds the old connection until the new one is established. This concerns only the TCP (network) connection—once this has been established, the old connection closes, even if the new server denies you access. If you're using ircII, you can select a server from the internal server list.

This is how it works: Each server you try to connect to gets added to this list with a number; you can view the list by typing /**server**. Then you can use the corresponding number instead of the server's name. You can also add the system's default servers to the internal list by using the **-a** switch from the command line when starting the client.

During your attempt to connect to the new server, you are liable to encounter any of the problems described in section 6.2. Using older versions of ircII, there is one more you may have to deal with. When you connect to a new server, the connection may just hang, leaving the cursor stuck in the top part of the window. After a while you get a message that the connection has failed and you return to the previous one, but your first connection has timed out while the cursor was stuck.

More recent versions of ircII have corrected this problem, but the older versions are still widely used. It affects all versions up to 2.8.2. These versions allow the connections to block the client until the return of a conclusive response (failure or success).

Blocking also means that the client, apart from not responding to your key presses, won't send PONGs in response to the current server's PINGs and the server is very likely to drop it with a ping timeout and lose the connection whether client establishes a new one or not.

6.6   Disconnecting from a Server

At any time, you may close your connection to the IRC server. This is done via the **QUIT** command. Depending on the client you're using, there may be one or more synonyms for that command—for example, **BYE**, **EXIT**, or **SIGNOFF**. In fact, some clients use one of these options rather than **QUIT**.

```
/quit
```

Closing the status window in a graphical client usually does the same, but doesn't confirm that the server has also closed the connection from its side. **QUIT** sends a **QUIT** command to the server and thus makes a clean disconnect by letting the server know you're leaving—otherwise it might take a while to notice that your connection is dead. Using **QUIT** or one of its synonyms, you simultaneously close your client application.

A message with arbitrary content may follow **QUIT** (and other commands with the same effect). If you add no message, it either sends none or defaults to a simple message like "Leaving." Your **QUIT**, plus the message (signoff reason) is sent to all channels you are on at that time. You do not need to leave a channel before leaving IRC. The server's operators may monitor QUITs (and the messages) on most networks. The messages are limited to a certain length, normally about 70 characters, more on DALnet and similar networks.

```
/quit Didn't wanna be here.
```

Technically, the **QUIT** command initiates the closure of your TCP connection to the server and exits the client program. Under some circumstances, though, the connection may be faulty and **QUIT** may not reach the server, or the server's acknowledgment of reception may never reach the client. In these cases, **QUIT** simply shuts down the client program with no visible response from the server's side.

Under ircII, **DISCONNECT** closes a server connection without also exiting the client. Similarly, mIRC, like most other graphical interface clients, allows a simple disconnect when you select **File • Disconnect** or click the leftmost icon on the toolbar.

Disconnections are frequently involuntary, with a variety of possible causes. Your client usually gives you an indication of the cause. Let's have a look at these annoying events, which can happen out of the blue.

6.6.1 *Nickname Collisions*

Nickname collisions are less common than they used to be, since modern servers don't allow collisions, malicious ones in particular, to happen too often. Collisions are still possible, though, especially under bad network conditions, but users can avoid most incidentswith a little care.

A collision occurs if a server detects more than one instance of a nickname on the network. This should not be possible and is a violation of the protocol, so the first server to detect such a thing issues a **KILL** command for one or both offending clients, forcing at least one of them off the network by having the server they are using disconnect them.

Collisions are identified by their characteristic messages, which your client may format to make more understandable. A typical message you might see is:

```
*** You have been rejected by server irc.someserver.net
```

Some very nasty-looking garbage sometimes follows this message. Other users on a channel you were on at the time would see something like this:

```
*** Signoff: SomeNick (Killed (irc.someserver.net <-
irc.server.com(?)))
```

In this case, irc.someserver.net detected the nickname you were using, SomeNick, as in use by two different sources. Depending on the servers' and colliding clients' position on the network, the signoff message may appear in a number of different formats. The example above is a very simple one.

6.6.2 Operator Kill

Unless you're guilty of misbehavior, you should never get disconnected with one of these messages. These disconnections result when an *IRC operator,* a client with special privileges as opposed to a server, issues a **KILL** command for your nickname. The sections on IRC operators, scripts, bots and abuse cover how and why this happens. As a rule, IRC operators do not use **KILL** lightly—your client has violated the servers' or network's rules. Operator **KILL** may appear in two different formats, depending on whether the operator is on the same server as you (local) or a different server (remote).

Some clients exit upon receiving a **KILL** from a local operator. The reason for the kill almost always follows an operator **KILL** command; this can be arbitrary text, but more often states why you got killed. The message you see looks like this:

```
*** You were killed by operator EvilOper (get off my server)
```

Users occupying the same channels see the following, depending on whether the kill was local or remote:

```
*** Signoff: SomeNick (Local kill by EvilOper (get off my server))
```

or

```
*** Signoff: SomeNick (Killed (EvilOper (get off my server)))
```

An operator kill does not prevent you from reconnecting unless a K: line or G: line follows it, in which case you'll see a server notice like those described in 6.2. Automatically reconnecting to the same server after a kill is not a good idea, by the way. Most operators view it as a "bouncy" client that can't take the hint that it's not welcome, and they then set a K: line.

6.6.3 Server Downtime

IRC servers are no more than machines and programs, and therefore are subject to malfunctions, like any computer-related system. If an operator or administrator takes down the server intentionally, you might receive a notice first, advising you to wait before reconnecting or to connect to a different server. If it simply crashes out of the blue, you'll receive no warning.

In either case, the result is the same—you'll appear to lose the connection for no obvious reason. Because it takes a finite time for a server or machine to restart and begin accepting client connections again, if you attempt to reconnect immediately, you won't be able to, and your client will return the message "Connection refused," just hang, or return a network error if the machine has crashed, not just the IRC server on it.

6.6.4   Ping Timeout

Probably the most common signoff for a new user is the Ping timeout. As described in 6.2.2, Ping timeouts result when a server doesn't receive a **PONG** within a certain time after sending you a **PING**. The server sends PINGs are sent at regular intervals if the client hasn't been active—usually between 90 to 240 seconds—and should evoke a **PONG** from the client. If a client fails to respond to a **PING** within a certain time, the server considers it no longer present and closes the connection. mIRC users will see **PING? PONG!** messages in their status window to indicate this is happening; other clients do not. Either way, responses are handled automatically and manual intervention is not necessary.

6.6.5   Connection Reset by Peer

What the heck is a peer, anyway? This apparently cryptic and confusing message is actually quite straightforward. If yours is the client being disconnected, it means the server closed the connection. If you see someone else disconnected with this message, the client closed the connection (in networking, the two connected parties are known as peers), but did not disconnect normally. It isn't really very helpful, since only the end that closed the connection knows the actual reason for the closure. Compare it to losing a phone line. If the other party hung up before the conversation was through without saying goodbye, or mumbled it while hanging up, you won't really know why the call ended. You'll just know the caller is gone and you'll hang up, too.

This type of quit is also associated with some of the DoS attacks (nukes) we went over in 2.2.2 and will encounter again in Chapter 17.

6.6.6   Excess Flood

In order to prevent the server from taking too much of a load from a single client, there is a limit to how much data a server accepts from one client within a certain amount of time. A typical value for this limit would be 1 KBps, meaning the server automatically disconnects any client detected sending more than 1KB of data within a second. There are two possible reasons for getting disconnected like this, and you can avoid them with a little care. A well-configured client is unlikely to get disconnected for excess flooding.

The first reason is that you may really be sending too much data. Sending text files and ASCII art to someone or to a channel may look pretty or help you make a point, but if you attempt to send it all at once, you're likely to be disconnected or, as it's better known on IRC, you *flood off*. The size of the file may be less than the critical limit, but file size increases with the addition of the instructions the server needs (invisible to the user) to forward the message to its recipient(s); your client adds these instructions to each message.

Unless your client has a timing mechanism that leaves an interval between messages in order to slow down the rate at which it sends messages, sending even small files may disconnect you.

The second reason for flooding off is an attack on your client or channel with the intent of forcing your client (and possibly all the others on the channel, too) to send data to the server at a fast enough rate to be disconnected. Flood protection, covered in Chapter 17, can prevent this.

Section 17.1 gives a full explanation of flood attacks. If you do get flooded off, follow those instructions. A properly configured client never yields to this kind of attack, and most modern clients are fairly flood resistant by default.

6.6.7 Kill Line Active

This is the operator kill we looked at earlier, taken a step further. An operator may deem that **KILL** wasn't sufficient or notice that the offending client keeps reconnecting, and set a K: line just like the one mentioned in 6.2.1. The message will be totally unambiguous, saying "Kill line active" or "K-lined," sometimes followed by a reason or the time the K: line is in effect, if it's a temporary one. If you're positive you are not at fault, then you've had a bit of unusually bad luck—the operator set a K: line for some- one else who happens to be sharing a host mask with you while you're connected to the server. Operator-set K: lines are effective immediately and result in instant disconnection of all clients matching the K: line, without allowing them to reconnect. Not all K-lined signoffs are real—some people find it funny to quit with such a message. On DALnet servers the message is "User has been banned."

6.6.8 Other Types of Disconnection

Bad network connections between you and the server cause other less common disconnections. Many of these result in the message "Ping timeout" or "Connection reset by peer," but there are any number of network-related disconnections, such as "No route to host" or "Network is unreachable" or "Host is unreachable." In these cases you should check the connectivity of your local service (for example, if you're unable to retrieve documents from off-site Web servers, your local service has lost its connection to the rest of the world). Ping and traceroute are the tools for doing this, and are widely available from most sites carrying networking software (if you're using a Windows 95 or NT or a Unix system, these utilities are almost certainly present on your system).

If your end of the connection looks all right, the failure is probably on the server's side, and connecting to a new server should solve it. Use the utilities described above to make sure the server you've selected is reachable, since in the event that part of the backbone network breaks down, you may find large segments of the Internet unreachable from where you are. The section regarding abuse in Chapter 17 will cover disconnections caused by network attacks on one of the connected machines (nukes). However, nukes look like the disconnects mentioned here and are often indistinguishable.

Finally, on the largest networks, and particularly EFnet, you may see the message "SENDQ limit exceeded" or something to that effect. This commonly means you attempted to retrieve a list of channels, and the amount of the data sent back was too great to maintain the connection between client and server. If you simply must have a list of every channel on the network, you can try changing servers in search of one that will not disconnect you, or visit http://www.irchelp.org on the Web and view the channel list there.

Now that we've been through all the nasty technical details of connecting successfully to a server and staying there, we can do what we came to do—let's get into a channel to chat!

7

CHANGELS

What has made IRC so popular is the idea of users convening in channels. You may know them as *rooms* from other online chat systems, but the correct term on IRC is *channel*. Still, some IRC services call them rooms, so we'll have to live with the fact that both terms are in use. In a way, the terms describe the difference between the old idea of entering rooms where some sort of party is going on, and the concept of tuning into channels on a forum similar to CB radio.

Instead of everyone connected seeing everyone else and all public messages going to all other users on the network, each user can choose to join one or more channels of his or her choice and communicate only with other users who have selected the same channel.

Channels are identified by a name, which usually reflects the topic of discussion in that channel or the kinds of people that frequent it. The subject matter is entirely arbitrary, as is the name. Anyone can create a channel, name it whatever they like, and talk about anything they care to talk about. The only exception to this is channels on a network that enforces a policy about the kind of channels its users may create—for example, one that forbids sex channels.

In theory, a channel can have as many users as are connected to the network on which the channel exists. If a network has 10,000 clients connected, it's theoretically possible to have all 10,000 on the same channel. Not that you'll ever see any channel of this magnitude on IRC—the maximum number I've actually observed is about 1,000, which is huge enough. Just imagine trying to keep up with the combined messages of 999 users. Channels are highly configurable, though, and it's possible to set up even one that size so as to prevent total and ûtter chaos.

Channels often also have a topic—an description of the channel and its purpose or a comment related to some event on the channel itself. This is the second identifier a channel may have, but is usually not as descriptive as the name. Channels are not required to have a topic indicating what's going on, and many don't. Many channels are quite happy with no topic at all.

Channels can be present and available throughout a network, or their presence may be limited to a single server or group of servers. Global channels, accessible from all servers of the given network, are invariably characterized by a leading hash mark (#) in their name. Local channels, which only users of a specific server may join, begin with an ampersand (&).

A less common type of channel exists only on servers matching a certain mask, but is considered global within this group of servers. Their names begin with a hash mark, but include the server mask, appended following a colon (:). For example, **#friends:*.be** would be available only to people using servers matching the ***.be** mask—Belgian servers, since BE is the country code for Belgium. You won't often encounter these, but they can be very useful under some circumstances. In order for this kind of channel to work on all servers matching the ***.be** mask, the servers must be directly connected.

To summarize this, a channel named **#ThisChannel** is global, whereas you can only reach a channel named **&ThatChannel** from one server. Channels beginning with **&** on different servers can have the same name, without interfering with each other. Finally, you can only reach a channel with the name **#Canadians:*.ca** from servers matching the mask ***.ca**—Canadian servers in this example.

A fourth type of channel has a plus (+) prefix, and is not available on all types of servers—only Undernet and IRCnet servers support them. This kind of channel has the added characteristic of disallowing channel management commands and is actually a very old feature that has been reintroduced without too much success. The purpose of modern-day plus channels was to offer an environment without the channel politics and power play that usually results from having a power structure, as is the case with global channels. The newest versions of IRCnet servers have an additional form of channel beginning with an exclamation mark (!), but so far most clients don't support them, and they are obscure in function and purpose.

As a matter of convenience, all channels I mention from here on will be regular global channels unless otherwise stated.

Global channels are the majority, and have many more potential uses and problems. We have already seen the different IRC networks that are not related to each other and have no interconnection. Likewise, a channel on one network may have a counterpart on another that shares only its name. For example, the EFnet **#irchelp** channel is totally different from the Undernet **#irchelp** channel—each has its own settings, rules, users, and operators. In some cases, the same people maintain channels with the same name on various networks, and these channels look similar. Each must be joined and maintained separately, though, and of course they require separate server connections.

Now let's see how to find and join a channel.

7.1 Obtaining a List of Available Channels

All servers keep the current channel list in memory, and most allow a user to retrieve a large part of it. This is done using the **LIST** command.

Depending on your client, you may also be able to sort the list and limit it to a group of channels with common characteristics. The server, although it keeps a complete list of channels—the number of which may well exceed 20,000 channels on the largest network—also keeps track of secret channels that don't appear in a list. The operators of these secret channels have added a setting telling the server not to divulge any information regarding them or their users (see 10.3.9).

Depending on the network, between 30 and 60 percent of all channels are secret and therefore are missing from the list. This accounts for the difference between the number of channels you receive in a listing and the total number you may have noticed in the output of the **LUSERS** command (see 15.1).

The basic syntax of the **LIST** command is simply

```
/list
```

and the response looks a lot like Figure 7.1.

Depending on your client, the information appears either in your main window or in a special channel list window.

Figure 7.1: Using the LIST command

In Figure 7.1 above, you see a small list of channels. The number following the channel name is the number of users currently on the channel, and the text after the number is the channel's current topic. If the name of a channel is longer than ten characters (including the hash mark), many clients will truncate it. You have to change your client's settings to make it display full channel names that are longer or to make it show more of the names.

Of course, the list may already be too large, so you may want to see less of it anyway. Most clients allow you to limit the number of channels displayed: They filter the list for channels with characteristics you define by adding some parameters to the **LIST** command. Not all of them will apply to all clients, but you can expect a good client to support most of them. Some of the flags and parameters **LIST** is likely to support are as follows:

-topic	Shows only channels that have a topic set.
-min X	Skips all channels with fewer than X users.
-max Y	Skips all channels with more than Y users.
-wide	Displays a list with full channel names and the number of users. The topic, if any, is ignored.
#channel	Shows the list entry for #channel only.
string	Shows only list entries containing string in the channel name.

Examples:

/list -min 5 -topic	Shows all public channels with at least 5 users and a set topic.

/list -max 25 #a*	Shows only global channels with less than 26 users and beginning with the letter A.
/list -min 10 -max 20	Shows all channels with over 9 and under 21 users.
/list #joyride	Shows the entry for the channel named #joyride, including its topic if it has one. If this channel is set secret, you would have to be on the channel in order to see it in a list.

LISTing is often easier said than done. You may encounter a variety of problems while trying to get a list of channels.

7.1.1 Disconnecting When Using LIST

Oops—you asked for a list, got 150 or 300 channels, maybe even none, and got booted from the server. This is an extremely common problem, especially on regular dial-up connections to one of the major networks. It results from a combination of the speed of your connection to the server, the server's setup, and the size of the list itself. On the larger networks, there may be as many as 10,000 channels on the list the server returns. This is a hefty amount of data, and a regular dial-up connection often has trouble handling it.

The disconnection occurs when data waiting to go to a destination exceeds the maximum the server's configuration allows, *or* when it takes the client so long to receive the list that a Ping timeout occurs. Each server sets the values for the maximum amount of data to queue for a client and the Ping interval separately, which explains why you can use **LIST** with no problems on one server while you get disconnected on another.

If the maximum amount of data allowed is less than the size of the list, many connections, especially dial-ups, can't absorb the excess data fast enough to bring the contents of the buffer below the maximum allowed. Often the server's administration may not be aware of the problem—server administrators tend to have very fast connections to the server, and most of them rarely use **LIST** since they know their way around well. Sending an email to the server (see 15.3) asking its administrators to raise the limit for your connection class may prompt them to solve this problem.

Trying to reduce the amount of data by requesting a limited list will not help—for any listing concerning more than an individual channel, the server sends the whole list, and your client sorts it and displays the part you want to see.

Since it's generally easier for servers to provide a solution to this problem on their end than to ask all users to increase their connection's bandwidth (which would be unrealistic, considering the extra cost for both bandwidth and hardware on the user's end), server administrators often cooperate if you bring the problem to their attention. As far as the server software is concerned, only the Undernet and DALnet code and versions based on it do a limited amount of filtering the list before sending it to the client, thus making it possible to reduce the amount of data a server returns.

Since you're probably not inclined to wait the hours or days it will take the server to fix the problem, you should try a few more servers on the network and see if any return a list without disconnecting you.

7.1.2 Strange Channel Names

Once you get a large list from a server, you'll probably notice a number of channels with what appear to be nonsensical names made up of sequences of strange characters. The majority of these are actually quite normal channels. What you are seeing is the ASCII rendition of the Japanese Kanji characters that make up the channel name. These are identifiable as such because they contain many square bracket ([), dollar sign ($), and B characters. Korean and Chinese channels look similar.

Sometimes you'll also see apparently normal names with one or two unusual characters. These are channels that use a slightly different, although Latin-based, character set. Many of these are in a Nordic language; others may be German, French, Portuguese, or Spanish. In order to join one of these, you have to switch character sets, unless your upper character set (character codes 128 to 255) includes these particular characters and you can easily access it. Windows users should be able to reproduce them without too much trouble. IrcII-based clients can produce most of those characters using the **DIGRAPH** command.

Hebrew, Cyrillic, Arabic, and Greek generally translate to a series of vowels interspersed with other characters.

7.1.3 Argh! The List Keeps Scrolling Off and I Miss Most of It

Solving this little problem depends on whether your client can pause during the display of the list. Some older clients aren't geared to handle the length lists can reach nowadays. In other clients, it's simply a missing feature.

If you're using ircII, the process of making the list display one screen at a time is fairly simple:

```
/set hold_mode on
/list [flags] [parameters]
```

This makes the display pause after each screenful of entries. Press the ENTER key to bring up the next screen. If you think you've seen enough,

use the **FLUSH** command to clear the remaining part of the list. Use
/set hold_mode off to keep the display from pausing after every screenful, although it isn't a problem if you leave **hold_mode** on for the whole
session—under some circumstances you may want it on anyway.

With other clients, you'll have to rely on the client's scrolling features,
if any. Most, including mIRC, open a new window to display the list, and
you can use the scroll bar to reach information that has scrolled off.

7.1.4   I Give Up—Nothing Is Working

It's unlikely to happen on the smaller networks, but sometimes on the
larger networks things simply refuse to work for you. Two of the major
networks have a Web service you can contact to get a fairly current list of
channels. EFnet's **#irchelp** team provides one. IRCnet has its own, which
the administrator of the network's main Swedish server creates and hosts.

Both these services are easy to use, updated frequently, and search-
able. Normally they work fine, but they depend on a single server for
the listing they take at regular intervals. Any negative conditions (such
as a *netsplit*—see 7.11) affecting their server at the time they take the list
has repercussions on the list.

Here are the channel listing services on the Web:

http://www.irchelp.org/chanlist	EFnet
http://www.ludd.luth.se/irc/list.html	IRCnet
http://www.liszt.com/	Many other networks
http://users.dal.net	DALnet (You must be a registered user. This allows you to search the registered channel database. It does not show you what channels are active at the moment.)

7.2   Selecting a Channel from the List and Finding the Right Channel

Unless you've successfully limited your search to something very specific, the list of channels you'll get with the **LIST** command will be made
up of a variety of channels with names that may or may not indicate
their nature and subject. You'll probably find many of them uninterest-
ing, silly, or even offensive. At this point we should say something about
the legitimacy of IRC channels. The large networks and their servers
exercise no form of censorship over the names of channels or their contents (see 20.4). The network is legally just a carrier and therefore
cannot and will not be held responsible for any immoral or illegal activities among the people using its services.

The large number of "sex channels" may strike you as peculiar. Many of these are nothing more than pornography trading posts. Others of a more serious nature really intend to deal with sex—some as a meeting ground for those who believe "netsex" is a viable alternative or supplement to real sex, others for discussing fetishes or personal interests, and others for meeting those with matching sexual interests (for example, channels to meet homosexuals, extremely hairy people, obese people, and so forth). In the Internet environment, where many social taboos don't apply and where people often cast their inhibitions aside under the impression of anonymity, this isn't really surprising. Quite a few of these sites are also localized and act as a kind of virtual singles bar.

Channels specializing in the pornography trade have names like **#sexpics** and commonly have a word like *pix* or *pics* in their name (see 20.6). Since they wish to attract customers, they are almost all public and will appear on the list. You can safely assume that channels beginning with a row of exclamation marks or "100%" are pornographic sites trying to stay at the top of alphabetically ordered channel lists. These are generally the seedier ones.

Equally common are a group of channels with the mysterious phrase *warez* written all over them—warez this, warez that, get your warez here, and so forth. These channels are essentially dedicated to the discussion or trafficking of pirated software (see 20.7). Software pirates are extremely active on IRC, and the more prominent and skilled among them form very exclusive groups in an almost guild-like fashion.

Many prominent users on the more populated warez channels are expert IRC users, sometimes decent hackers, who do not care for people looking for illicit freebies. Most networks don't mind their presence—if the law wishes to get them, they are pretty obvious and don't need any pointing out.

In the beginning, you'll probably be more comfortable on a medium or small general chat channel with no more than about 20 users. Chat channels of this kind can become really large, with the number of users well into three digits. This makes them chaotic and almost impossible to follow. Start with one of the chat or bar channels you'll see on the list. Choose one with an attractive, friendly topic, and you're ready to join.

7.3 Joining a Channel

Becoming part of a channel is simple. With the **JOIN** or **CHANNEL** command, your client sends a **JOIN** to your server, which in turn checks to see whether you have permission to join the channel you specified.

Let's say you want to join a channel named **#somechannel** (remember that the hash mark is an integral part of the channel name, and you must use it). The command is simple:

```
/join #somechannel
```

The server runs a brief check on the channel's settings and decides whether you may join it—usually you can for a public channel. If the server accepts your **JOIN** command, you'll see code resembling this:

```
*** Apatrix (apatrix@ircd.webbernet.net) has joined channel
#irchelp
*** Users on #irchelp: Apatrix @Vamps elib @Lindy_ @wmono @Garfr
@MHz @turtle @WishBone @DemiShade @Jolo
*** Topic for #irchelp: Ask your IRC question or visit
www.irchelp.org
*** #irchelp Garfr 917596918
*** #irchelp 884520350
```

This shows you the nickname of all the channel's users, which now include you, and the nickname and host mask of the user who just joined the channel—you again. The lower two lines look a bit cryptic, but this is only because I took the example from a client who does not translate server jargon into something readable. mIRC is more helpful and translates them into something more understandable.

The first of these cryptic lines shows who set the current channel topic and when. The second line is the channel's time stamp, which says when it was created. Both of these times are expressed in "epoch" time—essentially, seconds elapsed since midnight, Greenwich mean time, on January 1, 1970. This is the standard way of timekeeping on the Internet. Most clients by default convert these time stamps into more readable standard (and local) time.

As you see, there are 11 nicknames listed. The number of users could of course be a lot higher and even range into the hundreds, with a screenful or more of nicknames appearing. Note that the at (@) sign before nine of the nicknames is *not* part of the nick, but indicates channel operator status, which we'll look at a bit later on. Other clients, such as ircle, use a different color for nicknames with channel op status (ircle displays them in red). Some clients—mIRC, for example—open a new window for the channel, along with a list of nicknames. Messages sent to the channel appear in the new window, and the channel's vital statistics show up in the status window.

Here you've been told to use **/join #channel**—the complete command line. Depending on your client, there may be one or more shortcuts to joining a channel. You may be able to add the channel's name to a list stored and loaded along with the client, and join a channel by calling up the list and clicking the channel or by using a shorter form of the command itself.

A typical example many clients and add-on scripts use is **/j channel**. Note the lack of the otherwise omnipresent hash mark. The client hasn't left it out—the client will add it and the server will receive the complete **JOIN #channel** command. In the beginning, though, it's better to familiarize yourself with the real commands. This way you can use IRC from practically any client and will not depend on a single platform or client.

Most channels are public and let you join with no more than the **JOIN** command, but this isn't always the case. Let's have a look at the possible snags you may run into.

7.3.1 *No Such Channel*

You're positive that channel exists! Sure it does—but consider what we said a paragraph ago about the correct and full syntax of the **JOIN** command. The channel name you specified didn't begin with a valid character. The **/join #somechannel** command works, and **/j somechannel** might also, but **/join somechannel** will not, unless you have a strange piece of add-on scripting (which you shouldn't) or an ultrasmart client that understands your mistakes and corrects them, which naturally doesn't teach you much.

So, depending on your client, remember to use the hash mark where it's needed. In this case, you forgot it. Oops! Let's try again.

7.3.2 *How Did I End Up on the Channel #?*

You typed a space between the hash mark (#) and the channel name. Try it again without the space. # is a valid channel name on its own.

7.3.3 *Banned from Channel*

This is not unusual, especially if you've encountered a few K: lines while connecting to a server. In such a case you can be fairly sure others consider your provider or host a source of trouble and think its users should be kept off servers and out of channels. You'll get this response to your **JOIN** command if the server sees that your user mask matches an entry on the channel's banned list.

This straightforward message says you're banned from the channel. Less explicit clients just tell you you're "unable to join channel (+b)." This may not seem very enlightening—what the devil is **+b** and how on earth did it get there?

A channel's operators set bans by adding a **+b** setting (channel mode; see 10.3.1) for a certain nickname and/or host mask (see 10.5).

So **+b** means that you are banned from the channel. Channel bans operate independently—each channel has a separate list of bans—and they last until the channel closes or one of its operators removes them.

If you have never been to the channel, obviously you didn't cause the ban to be set. Rather, it was the same local obnoxious user you glimpsed while you were looking at the K: lines in section 6.2.1. If you want to be sure, though, you can look at the channel's ban list when you're not on the channel, with the following command:

```
/mode #channel b
```

Check the list returned and see which entry matches your host mask. If there are a lot of bans affecting whole domains or even *!*@* (which of course matches everything), the channel may have been attacked and taken over.

We'll deal with takeovers later on (see 10.7)—for now, don't panic, just pick a new channel. After all, it's always better to be somewhere where you're welcome. Don't insist on joining the channel. You'll most likely fail—you will just feel frustrated, and the ban will be renewed. Users of large Internet providers like AOL, Netcom, and AT&T are more likely to encounter this problem. The explanation is simple: The more users a provider has, the more idiots and abusers use its services and make the site unwelcome. If the provider also uses an addressing system that makes it hard to ban only a specific part of it, channel operators eventually end up banning the entire site in order to rid themselves of a single annoying user. It's not fair to the rest of the users, but channel operators have this right, and some see it as their duty toward the channel's users. They do as they see fit for the purpose of maintaining order on their channel. AOL users in particular get the worst deal because of the way their dynamic IP addressing works: The pool of addresses from which it draws is immense, and an abuser can have a radically different address each time he or she connects. This doesn't leave channel operators with much choice.

7.3.4 Bad Channel Key

One way those managing the channel safeguard its privacy is by setting a password that the user wishing to join must supply. All servers store this password and compare it with all JOINs for that channel. If the user doesn't supply any password or sends one that doesn't match the existing password, the server forbids the user to join and gives the error message "Bad channel key." If you do know the password—known as the *key* (see 10.3.3)—join the channel as follows:

```
/join #channel keyword
```

7.3.5 Channel Is Full

Another feature used for running a channel is the ability to limit the total number of users the channel may have. In this case, the server checks the current number of users on the channel against the maximum limit set and doesn't allow anyone to join if this limit has been reached.

7.3.6 Kick or Ban after Joining

Because of the limited number of bans a single channel may have, larger channels often also have an informal ban list. One or more clients on the channel, often robot clients, keep their own ban list independent of the current channel ban list, and check each user attempting to join against this list. When the client sees an unwanted user, it bans that person and kicks him or her off the channel automatically. Bans set in this way usually don't last long—most of these robots also automatically remove the ban after a while to avoid cluttering the available space on the ban list and to leave a few slots open for nonregular bans that may be necessary. It's essentially a combination of a ban (**+b**), followed by a **KICK** command (see 10.5)—these are separate commands, so you will first see a ban matching your host mask, then you'll get thrown out of the channel. The command generally looks like this:

```
*** Mode change "+b *!*@my.provider.com" by MeanBot
*** You have been kicked from channel #Somewhere by MeanBot (Go
sit in a corner.)
```

This type of ban happens for the same reasons as a regular ban.

7.3.7 I Joined a Channel on the List and It's Empty!

Unless it was a channel with very few users, who may all have left by the time you read the list and joined, the reason for this appears in the list itself. The client often truncates long channel names (see 7.1), so what you saw was not the full name of the channel but only its beginning.

One example of a channel that used to be particularly confusing was a channel named **#marriages**—users kept joining it and finding it empty, despite the fact that a fair number of users appeared on the list. This is a good example of how a truncated channel name that looks like a complete name can be misleading. Further investigation showed that the name of the channel was really **#marriagesex**, which most of those users had absolutely no intention of joining.

Another cause for this could be a *netsplit* (see section 10.6)—during the time it took for you to receive and read the list and attempt to join the channel, your server disconnected from the rest, effectively emptying the channel as far as your server is concerned. They should be back within minutes—check **LUSERS** (see 15.1) to confirm that it's a split and not some other problem. If the total number of users and server is much lower than it should be or your own servers says it has no servers connected to it, this is the case.

7.3.8 *Nickname or Channel Is Currently Unavailable*

This message is particular to servers running IRCnet code and is technically very similar to the nick delay problem mentioned in 6.2.7. This condition, known as channel delay (CD), occurs when the channel loses its operators by irregular means and is empty—either its last operator becomes the victim of a **KILL** command, or a netsplit leaves all operators on the other side and no users on your side. The channel should open again as soon as the split is fixed and the operators return, as viewed from your server. If they don't return within a certain time (a minimum of 15 minutes), the CD expires and the channel opens again anyway. Each server implements CD individually, so another server will allow you to join if the circumstances causing the delay are not present according to that server.

7.3.9 *Invite-Only*

This means the channel has been set to allow only users who have received an invitation from one of the channel's operators to join. The server checks whether there is an invitation for you to join the channel and forbids you to join if there is none. If you are invited, you see a line like this:

```
*** Inviter invites you to channel #friends
```

The invitation stands for as long as you're connected to the server. If you disconnect from the server for any reason, you'll need a new invitation to join the channel.

Obviously, the users of an invite-only channel desire their privacy and often also set it as secret. Trying to obtain an invitation is more trouble than it's worth, especially if you haven't been on that channel before. You would have to find and contact one of the channel's operators, but you won't get much better results than if you were trying to get into a house when the owners have declared they want no visitors.

7.4   Who Is on the Channel?

Having successfully joined a channel and seen the nicknames of the users on it, you'll probably want to know more about the people who are there with you.

If you just want to see the list of asterisked (*) nicknames again, use the **NAMES** command:

```
/names #channel
```

Some clients let you substitute an asterisk for the current channel:

```
/names *
```

This command returns a list of nicknames the same as the one you saw right after joining the channel. If users have left or joined the channel since you joined it, the **NAMES** list reflects these changes.

WARNING   *Do not use **NAMES** without giving a parameter! If you want to argue the point, see section 9.5.*

If you're using mIRC, you generally won't need the **NAMES** command, since you'll be able to see all nicknames on the channel by scrolling through the list on the right-hand side of the channel window. Other graphical clients display it on the left-hand side.

For a more detailed list of everyone on the channel, you need the **WHO** command. This takes the same parameters as **NAMES**, but some clients allow additional filtering of its output. Here's a typical **WHO** list, assuming you're on channel **#irchelp**:

```
#irchelp Kefka H Anarchy@202.188.232.21 (2 Blood is live in its
purest form)
#irchelp Apatrix_ H@ alc@egnatia.ee.auth.gr (6 Agent of Chaos)
#irchelp Nyctea H satan@sb100b-312.cc.tut.fi (8 Nyctea scandiaca)
#irchelp zaoli H ~zaoli@zaoli.umo.cz (9 dA blue power)
#irchelp pht H@ svobodam@irc.vsp.cz (9 Michal *pht* Svoboda)
#irchelp Rince H@ rince@serpens.swb.de (6 Auf dem Datenhighway to
hell...)
#irchelp Engerim H@ engerim@kip.sateh.com (8 Thomas 'Engerim'
Kuiper)
#irchelp EmleyMoor H@ philipr@admin.irc.demon.net (7 Phil
Reynolds)
#irchelp DemiShade H@ demi@idle.cs.hut.fi (5 Jani Joki)
#irchelp MHz H*@ mhz@irc.webbernet.net (1 Hold your flame till
your dream ignites)
```

```
#irchelp Neverm_nd H@ bart@relics.org (1 Bart Crombe)
#irchelp Apatrix G*@ apatrix@ircd.webbernet.net (0 Web Net IRC)
*** #irchelp End of /WHO list.
```

Right, let's try and make some sense out of these cryptic lines. The first bit is obviously the name of the channel and the second is the user's nickname. The fourth bit should be the address, but what on earth is the rest?

In the third column, you'll see one or more characters explaining the user's status as far as the server is concerned. It contains one of two characters—either **G** or **H**—to indicate whether that user has declared himself *gone* (used the **AWAY** command to indicate his or her absence from the keyboard) or is *here*. This doesn't mean much, since many people never bother to set themselves away when leaving. I often forget to set myself here again when I return.

One or more of the following characters may follow the leading H: or G: an at sign, an asterisk, and a plus sign. The at sign indicates that user is an operator of the channel. The asterisk stands for IRC (server) operator. Finally, the plus sign means the user has a voice on a moderated channel (see 7.6). Depending on the type of server, you may also see a couple of different characters, most commonly a **d**, which means the client is in "dumb" mode and is not following the channel's conversation. This mode is used mainly for service robots and is available only on Undernet and similar networks.

The final part in the parentheses is no more than the ircname or real name (see 6.3.4), but the number in front of it is less easy to explain. This is the distance between your server and that user's server, measured in server hops—how many server links connect you and the other user. For the client performing the **WHO** command, the value is always 0, since there is no way in the world it could be on a different server than itself. Whether you see the number depends on the client's setup.

7.5 Channel Operators

I've made many references to channel operators and attributed mysterious powers to them, such as making a channel secret or kicking people out. What are channel operators and what's so special about them? Are they people? Are they machines? Are they something else we dare not imagine?

Channel operators are users with certain privileges on a channel. They control the channel by using a special set of commands that can change the channel's settings or modes (see 10.3) and topic, invite people to the channel, or remove unwanted users. They are usually called *ops* for short—other terms are *chanops* or *chops*. We'll settle for the most widely used expression, ops, from now on.

Ops don't appear on a channel magically. Something has to make a user a channel operator. There are three ways of obtaining channel op status. The first is being the first user to join a channel, in which case the server automatically gives you ops. The second is getting assigned op status by a user who already is an op or by identifying yourself to a channel server that will check whether you are an authorized user and, if so, assign you op status. The third method, possible only on networks with a channel service, involves identifying yourself to the service with a special password. A user with ops is basically just a channel setting that means this user has operator privileges. An at sign prefixes that user's nickname whenever it appears in conjunction with the channel.

Channel ops last as long as the opped client is present on the channel. If the user leaves the channel for any reason, he or she must obtain ops again by one of the means mentioned above.

A channel may have any number of ops—from no op at all, to every user having ops. Only the number of users on the channel limits the potential number of ops. Having a channel with no ops can be a problem, though. Without ops, no one can change the settings of a channel, or remove obnoxious users from it. In Chapter 10, I'll show you how to become a channel operator by creating a channel.

The power of a channel operator over the channel is absolute and subject to control only by other operators. Unless another op questions the op's actions, he or she is free to change the modes, kick people, ban them, and give out ops to others at will.

Some networks with a channel service allow a hierarchy of ops on a channel and permit a *super-op* or *founder* to assume a higher level of control (in which case the rule of absolute power applies to a single person). Apart from that case, the ops of a channel are equal and may also *deop* each other—that is, remove operator status from a user who is an op at the time. This technically also changes the channel's settings (makes a mode change).

You might wonder how a channel keeps its operators with people coming and going all the time. In the case of larger channels with a lot of regular users, there are enough people to keep at least one regular operator on the channel at all times.

Many channels, especially medium and small ones, rely on a different method of keeping the ops on a channel. You'll soon encounter one of the tools for doing this.

7.5.1 Channel Bots

Bots (short for robots) are the prime tool for maintaining a channel op at all times even if none of the regular users is on the channel. Also known as *automatons* (*automata* if you're into linguistic semantics), IRC bots are programs with a variety of uses, not all of them innocent. They are used most widely as channel management tools.

A channel bot doesn't look any different from a real live user on IRC. Technically, it's a client. Its purpose is to sit on a channel day in and day out and perform channel management functions, either by monitoring channel events and reacting to them or by following instructions from users authorized to send it commands.

The bot needs to maintain a constant network connection, so most bots run on Unix machines with such a connection, independent of whether their owner is logged into the machine or not. Dial-ups are generally not suitable for running bots, since they require constant use of a phone line to stay connected. Also, the bandwidth of a plain modem connection is generally a fraction of that of a machine with a permanent link, making a bot (or any other client on it) less stable and more susceptible to attacks. Since one purpose of bots is to ward off possible attacks on a channel, this can be a strong liability. Cable and DSL are better options.

Since all too often people use bots for much more than just channel maintenance, many servers have a policy forbidding users to connect bots and a standing order for the server's operators to "shoot on sight" or even K: line (see 6.2.1) any address found running one. Another reason for this is the large number of badly configured bots: They can mess up channels and cause users to look for the server's operators to kill it off; they use up network resources by triggering loops; and "vanity" bots hold an entire channel and take up a full-time connection that real users might need during peak hours.

I have nothing against bots on principle. As an IRC operator, though, I've had many opportunities to observe how people use them to harass others. In my opinion, the problems bots create are at least equal to the benefits users gain by their presence. It's simply not feasible to sort them into good bots and bad bots, so banning them all is a valid option many server administrators resort to so they can curb abuse.

A well-configured bot can help maintain a secure channel. You can even program them to entertain or inform a channel's regulars and visitors with funny automated responses or timed announcements. Chapter 19 offers more information about bots and setting them up.

You can usually identify a channel bot by the way it remains in the channel saying nothing or limiting itself to obviously automatic responses. Another characteristic is that they may immediately op a user upon joining, announce the user's presence, or send joining people an automated message (which isn't really smart but is quite popular).

Bots are special programs that act as unsupervised clients on IRC. With the high level of sophistication of some modern clients and add-on scripts, these programs are often as effective as a bot. The line between a high-powered script and a bot is growing thinner all the time, and many users already prefer the script method to keep their channels going.

7.6 Moderated Channels and +Voice

Moderated channels don't quite fit the common definition of moderation. On a moderated forum such as a mailing list, a person who acts as the moderator must approve contributions, and may forward or reject a posting. Moderation on an IRC channel merely allows some users to send messages to it and prevents others from doing so. The sender of a message must be an operator or approved by an operator, but the message itself is not submitted for approval before it's sent to the channel.

Moderated channels are used for IRC classes, news channels, guest lectures, IRC weddings, and other events where attendance is expected to be high but the channel owners want to keep the traffic low. Some IRC networks such as GlobalChat have guest lectures where the moderator and the guest lecturer have voices. When you submit a question, the moderator approves the question by typing it to the channel, and the lecturer answers it on the channel.

Moderated channels have an additional setting permitting only certain users to send messages to the channel. Those who may speak on a moderated channel are its operators and those users to whom they have given a *voice*. This voice is a channel mode, like operator status, but permits the user to speak without giving him or her full operator privileges. On the **WHO** list, a voiced user appears with a plus sign in the same place as an operator's at sign. Ops can give or remove the voice just as they can channel ops, and the voice is also valid for as long as the client is on the channel.

A user can have a voice and ops at the same time. This is really redundant, since an op has a voice anyway and is useful only if the user's ops are taken while still on the moderated channel. As long as the user has ops, the voice is not visible, but is known to the server. If the ops are removed and only the voice remains, the server displays the plus sign indicating the user has a voice.

7.7 Channel Events

In addition to the messages sent to the channel by the people on it, many others appear, and some look very cryptic. These notices are known as *events* and indicate a change in the channel's user list or characteristics. Let's have a look at the various notices you may see while on a channel—mIRC users normally see some of them in the status window, but can set the client to display some or all in the channel window as well by selecting **Options**, then **IRC Switches** from the File menu.

7.7.1 Mode Changes

These are notices indicating a change to the channel's settings (modes). One of the channel's operators usually performs mode changes; these may be one of the changes I've already mentioned or others I'll discuss later.

A typical mode change looks like this:

```
*** Mode change "+m" on channel #Somewhere by ChannelOp
```

This says what kind of change was made on which channel and by whom. In this example, the mode change was **+m**, which means moderated mode. The op named **ChannelOp** added moderated mode to the channel named **#Somewhere**. I will explain the mode changes and what each of them means in detail later (see 10.3).

In some cases a server rather than a user may make the mode change. This is a consequence of net joins, which I'll take a closer look at in section 7.11.

On networks with channel services, one of these services may make the mode change, following instructions from the channel's owner or another authorized person. The service robot isn't necessarily visible on the channel.

7.7.2 Joins, Parts, and Quits

Each time a new user joins the channel or an existing user exits by either leaving the channel or quitting IRC altogether, the channel will be sent a notice describing the change.

A typical join notice looks just like the one you saw right after joining the channel and contains the nickname and host mask of the user joining and the name of the channel he or she just joined:

```
*** Brenni (s@ti33a95-0182.dialup.online.no) has joined channel
#irchelp
```

In the same way, the server also announces a user's departure from the channel:

```
*** Brenni has left channel #irchelp
```

As in this example, not all clients display the **user@host** of the user leaving.

As we saw earlier, when a user quits IRC, any channel he or she is on is sent a notice. If the user adds a message to the quit, this also appears here. As with regular parts, some clients show the host mask of the client signing off while others don't.

```
*** Signoff: Hello41m (Quit: Leaving)
```

7.7.3 Nick Changes

If any user on the channel changes his or her nick with the **NICK** command, the channel will show this self-explanatory message:

```
*** Guest53962 is now known as sOuLfLy
```

7.7.4 Kicks

Kicks appear if one of the operators decides a user should not be on the channel and uses the **KICK** command.

```
*** GENTELMAN has been kicked off channel #chatzone by Dafinka
(idle 120 min)
```

This tells the channel who got kicked by whom, on which channel, and why. The explanation in the parenthesis is meant to inform the channel's users and its other operators of the reason for the kick. It can actually be arbitrary text and is just as often used to add smart comments for the entertainment of the channel if the actual reason for the kick is obvious. Many channels object to people idling—sitting on the channel saying nothing for a long time—and will kick them after a while.

7.8 Leaving a Channel

You leave a channel by simply using the **PART** or **LEAVE** commands, whichever your client supports, or closing the channel window if your client opens separate windows for each channel. If your client (and the server) supports it, you can also leave a parting message in the same way you leave a message with **QUIT**. If it doesn't, you might be able to add this feature with an alias or send it with a raw server command. Chapter 11 deals with aliases and other scripting commands.

Whether you use **PART** or **LEAVE** is not important as long as your client understands both. But the server needs **PART** (**PART** is a server command, while **LEAVE** is only a client command and changes to **PART** when it's sent to the server), so if you intend to use a raw server command to leave a channel, you must use **PART**. (Remember the example I used in 2.5.3.)

This is the simplest form of a command to leave a channel:

```
/leave #somewhere
```

If your client lets you substitute an asterisk for the current channel, **/leave** * makes you leave your current channel.

Some types of server also let you add a parting message just as you can with **QUIT**.

7.9   Joining Multiple Channels

Most clients let you join more than one channel at the same time. If your client does, you can be on as many channels simultaneously as the server permits. The number is usually between 10 and 14 but can also be higher—not that you'll often find yourself following conversations on 14 channels.

You can join more than one channel with a single **JOIN** command, or you can join them one at a time. The **JOIN** command takes a comma-separated list of channels:

```
/join #somewhere,#elsewhere,#nowhere
```

If you do this, you'll see a multiple version of the events you saw when joining a single channel—three different **NAMES** lists, three **JOIN** commands for your client, and three new windows will open if you're using a client with a window for each channel.

IrcII users may have to change one of the client's settings in order to join more than one channel. This command is **/set novice off**. If **NOVICE** is on, joining a channel automatically makes you leave the previous one. Add this setting to your **.ircrc** file as described in section 4.5.6 on setting up the client if you're confident you can handle multiple channels.

7.9.1   *Switching between Multiple Channels*

The conventional way of changing channels without leaving any is to **JOIN** the channel again, although you're already on it. This makes that channel the current one. On a client with separate windows for each channel, you simply select the window corresponding to the channel to which you want to switch. With ircII, you need another line of low-level scripting using the **BIND** command.

The **BIND** command lets you bind a key press to a function. In this case, the desired function is called **switch_channels**. Select a control key that you aren't using for anything else (I suggest CTRL-\) and bind it to the function with the following line:

```
/bind ^\ switch_channels
```

Note that a caret (SHIFT-**6**, **^**) represents the CTRL key. If you press CTRL-**back slash** (**^**), the client cycles through all the channels you're on until you reach the one you want. This is another command you should add to your **.ircrc** file.

An mIRC user can also define hot keys to perform functions like this.

7.10   Channel 0

The only channel not characterized by a leading symbol is the single channel many call "the salt of IRC," because this is the channel every user automatically joins when connecting. This channel is known as *channel 0* or the *null* channel. Every client connecting to a server finds itself in channel 0. From there on the client can proceed to join other channels, or remain there and communicate with individual users.

Channel 0 is also different as far as communications go. On this channel other users are visible only if they have usermode **-i** set, and you can't send public messages to it. Many commands you can use on normal channels will also fail to work. If you choose to join channel 0 while you're on any other channels, you'll leave those channels. **JOIN 0** is a nifty way of simultaneously leaving all the channels you're on.

7.10.1   *The Channel #2,000 Trick*

Some less well-meaning people like to entertain themselves by conspicuously sitting on a channel named **#2,000** or something else with a comma in it and inviting others to join that channel. Remember, though, that the comma is a separator and not a legal character in a channel's name. Joining channel **#2,000** makes you join channel **#2** and channel **000**—and you just saw what channel **0** does. How did those people get onto that channel?

The answer is simple: The comma is not a comma. I don't know the purpose of having a comma-like character (identical to a comma but not a comma) in the character set, but this is how things are. You can bring up this special character with the ALT-**0130** key combination under Windows (you can also view it in the Character Map). IrcII users can produce it with the comma-comma (**,,**) digraph. This proves that what looks like a duck and quacks like a duck isn't always a duck.

NOTE   *mIRC versions 5.5 and later prevent you from joining a channel this way. Its author decided people were having too much fun "playing" with newbies.*

7.11 Netsplits and Lag

It's time to meet a legendary figure who will follow you throughout your IRC career and keep turning up like a bad penny: the Lag Monster. No one has ever seen this insidious creature, but it is believed to lurk in the lines and gobble data packets as they pass by. The result of this is the annoying phenomenon known as *lag*. You can usually tell when this beast is nearby because your messages take longer and longer to reach your friends—you're lagged! According to rumor, the lag monster sometimes eats whole servers and spits them out (too much silicon in the diet is not good, even for a horrible monster). Let's investigate the activities of the most hated creature on IRC.

7.11.1 Netsplits

While this phenomenon is not directly related to channels, you're bound to encounter a netsplit sooner or later while you're on a channel and you may wonder what it means and what causes it. Some of the events you may have observed so far could also be related to netsplits. They affect the whole network, including channels, and result from server connectivity problems, servers or their machines going down, or operator intervention in the network's routing.

Users on a channel can detect a netsplit from the characteristic quit messages. If you see one or more users sign off with the names of two servers as the quit message, this indicates they were on the other end of a server link that just broke. The names of the servers tell you which link that was. On IRCnet and similar servers, the quit reason contains the server on your side of the split (which is still visible to you) and the server of the user who's "signing off." All other server types show the broken link.

A netsplit occurs when two servers lose their link for any reason. When this happens, a server or group of servers loses contact with the rest, and both parts function as separate networks. Let's look at a small network diagram to make it clearer:

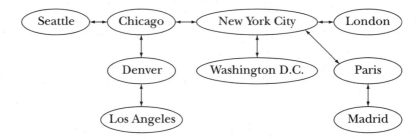

Say the link between New York and Chicago breaks. As a result, Chicago and all the servers behind it (Seattle, Denver, and Los Angeles) lose sight of New York and everything behind it (Washington, London, Paris, and Madrid), and vice versa. In effect, this creates two separate networks. One side sees all servers of the other side disconnect and all clients on those servers signing off as a result. A client on the Paris server can no longer see a client on the Denver server, and vice versa. Here's another example: The link between Denver and Los Angeles drops. Now Los Angeles is alone. Exactly the same result applies in this case—what changes is the proportional size of the split parts.

In a more serious case, the New York server would crash and consequently drop all its links. The network would split into four pieces: Washington and London are both alone; Paris and Madrid form a small network of their own; and Seattle, Chicago, Denver, and Los Angeles form another part. No part can see what's going on with the others. They don't even know that the rest of the Net is fragmented too (unless an observer noticed that the reason was a server crash).

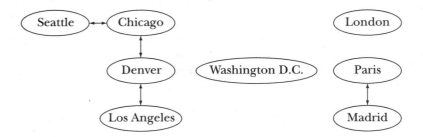

If the New York server doesn't return within a few minutes, the remaining servers refer to the part of the configuration file containing the server connections they can make. In this part (the C: and N: lines, see 15.4.1) the server checks for lines telling it to autoconnect to a particular server under certain conditions, and then attempts to make the connection if these conditions are met (that is, if the server has no connections at all).

This is so netsplits can be fixed automatically on the server's end and require minimal human intervention. Let's say Washington's server is configured to link to Chicago in the absence of New York's server; likewise for Paris, and London automatically links to Paris. These servers each activate their autoconnection in order to bring the network back together despite New York's missing server. The final result would look like this:

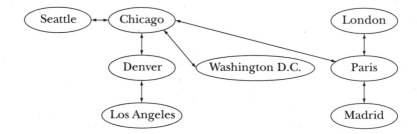

With New York successfully bypassed, the integrity of the network is restored. As this happens, each server transmits its status, users, and channel modes to the others, which then add whatever is missing to their information and inform the channels concerned about users rejoining it.

Changes made to a channel's modes during the time the servers were not connected on one part go into effect for the rest of the network. This important process is called *syncing* and is necessary to avoid confusion and disagreement among servers regarding the channels' and users'status—the net-pathological condition known as *desync* (see 10.9).

This affects channel topics and keys, so you could have different keys and topics on the same channel, depending on what part of the network you're on. If the topic or key is set while the information can't be transmitted (during a netsplit or in the lag preceding a netsplit) the servers will not negotiate it, but each part of the Net keeps its own version of the topic or key until a change is visible to all servers.

7.11.2 Server-Server Lag

Lag is another network problem that, while it's not directly related to channels, can be as much of a nuisance as netsplits. Lag and netsplits often go hand in hand; one may cause the other, leading to a vicious circle that can create tremendous chaos on a big network if it affects a large part of the Internet, including some of its central servers. A high load on the server machine, resulting in slow processing of network traffic, can cause lag, but more often it is due to a network fault that slows down the transmission of data between servers. As a result, the servers on one or both sides of the defective link start queuing data destined for the other end, putting all new messages at the end of the queue. This results in delayed transmission.

If this happens to a centrally located hub server that has a lot of both inbound and outbound traffic, such as server 3 in the example in section 7.11.1, it affects much of the network's communication. If the amount of data queued for a single destination server exceeds the maximum permitted by the server's configuration, the server closes the link to the other server, resulting in a netsplit.

When the link is restored, all client and server connections, which one side or the other considers to have quit, are retransmitted, along with information about the channels' users and modes. This is a large amount of data, and if the destination server does not receive and process it fast enough, it can end up queued, in which case we have a new round of lag and the potential for more netsplits. If the servers' automatic connection features fail to create a new working set of links, the network's IRC operators have to intervene and work around the problem by placing the lagged servers at a less central point of the Internet and using alternate servers as the main hubs.

7.11.3 *Client-Server Lag*

Another cause of delays in message transmission is client-server lag. You can detect this by using **CTCP PING** (see 13.2.1) on yourself. If this command returns a long time, the problem is either the network connection between the client and the server or a heavy load on either of the two machines.

Following a net join, the servers don't resend some information, mainly to reduce the amount of data transferred during the sync. Most types of server will not resend users' away status and channel topics, so you would have to reset these after the rejoin in order to be visible throughout the network. While you may not even notice the fact that the away status doesn't propagate, you'll often observe that you can't see a channel topic other users on the same channel say is there, or vice versa.

8

COMMUNICATION

Now that you've successfully made a connection to an IRC server and joined a channel, you're likely to see all sorts of different messages, strange and plain, scroll down your screen. It's quite all right to remain silent for a while and simply follow the conversation. Once you get the gist of the current topic and think you have something to contribute to the discussion, you'll also want to know how to send messages to a channel or individual users. However, first you must be able to read the messages you're receiving.

With this I don't mean taking English 101 again (or whichever other language you might be trying to follow a conversation in), but identifying incoming messages as what they are and reacting or not reacting according to their nature and content. We'll start by looking at the possible messages you may receive while on IRC.

Of course, you shouldn't ignore a greeting directed at you after you join. If someone says "Hi!" right after you join and it appears to be directed at you, just reply by typing a greeting of your own and pressing ENTER. You may end up in a conversation right away, which isn't really a problem—after all, that's what you came for—but you need to familiarize yourself with everything that goes on within a channel before getting deeper into conversation.

8.1 Types of Messages You May Receive

There are a number of different kinds of messages you'll receive, each with its own significance and use. Different message types are characterized by their appearance—either they show up on a certain part of the screen or they contain certain characters indicating their nature. Your client affects how they look as well. Here's how to identify the various message types.

8.1.1 Public Messages on a Channel

These are the probably the first messages you'll see, and they're what IRC is all about. Any user can send a message to the channel if the channel's settings permit it (most channels do). A public message appears in your main screen or channel window like this:

```
<Greeter> Hello there!
```

The user nicknamed Greeter sent this message to the channel. The angle brackets (< >), which characterize a public message, contain the nickname of the sender. The message itself follows.

If your client also opens separate windows for nonpublic messages, these may also appear in brackets in the corresponding window, rather than appearing in a different display format in the public message window.

8.1.2 Private Messages

It's possible to send a message to a single user or selected group of users without having to join a separate channel. If you have any experience with BBSs and similar chat systems, you'll know this as *whispering*. The recipient of the message will see something like this:

```
*Whisperer* Hi! This is a private message that only you can see.
```

The asterisks (*) around the nickname mean this is a private message, not visible to anyone else on the channel. You don't even have to be on a channel to receive such messages. If you're running a client that opens a new window upon receiving a private message and dedicates it to the sender, there may be brackets around the messages. In this case the window in which private messages appear identifies them as such. In fact, they may appear in a number of different formats depending on the client, but will always be noticeably different from public messages.

8.1.3 Notices

A bot or other kind of service (such as a nickname or channel service) sends notices, usually as a response to something you sent but sometimes with informative content. Some people like to use them to confuse new users by sending them as an unusual kind of private message. On DALnet, this has developed into an epidemic. I don't know why, but people on that particular network tend to use notices instead of regular messages, probably because a lot of mIRC users don't want a new window popping up for every person with whom they exchange private messages. It does have the advantage of not returning the away message when you **NOTICE** a user who has set himself /**away**.

Another reason you see so many notices is that DALnet and, more recently, EFnet both support a special type of notice that gives you the option of sending a message only to the channel's operators and/or those who have a voice in a channel. This type of message displays to the recipients as a plain **NOTICE**. It is indistinguishable from a normal **NOTICE** unless the sender makes it clear it's gone only to ops by adding some text to that effect.

You can send a **NOTICE** to a channel, single user, or selected group, just as with private messages, but they appear different. Generally not used in personal communication, they appear in either your status window (for most Windows clients) or the main window, with the following format:

```
-Noticer- Thank you for joining us.
```

Note the hyphens (-) characteristic of notices. Most clients share this convention. mIRC users see them in their status window by default.

8.1.4 CTCP Requests

CTCP stands for *client to client protocol* and is a form of private message I'll describe in detail in Chapter 13. Their display and handling depends very much on your client. CTCP is a message requesting information in the form of an automatic response from your client.

Incoming CTCP requests in mIRC appear in red in your status window with the nickname of the sender and the keyword of the request in square brackets ([]). For ircII, a CTCP request states that it's CTCP, so as not to be confused with other kinds of messages.

```
*** CTCP TIME from TimeLess
```

```
[Timeless TIME]
```

This means a user with the nickname TimeLess sent a CTCP request to you with the keyword **TIME**. If your client doesn't recognize the **CTCP** command, it may tell you that it's received an unknown CTCP or ignore it altogether. Depending on the client, the target of a CTCP (a channel, your nickname, or a group of users) may display along with the CTCP request.

You should not respond to CTCP messages—after all, their point is to elicit an automatic reply.

8.1.5 DCC Requests

DCC requests are a form of CTCP, which in turn is a form of private message. If you think this is complicated, wait until you get to Chapter 14, which describes DCC in detail. DCC is a means of file transfer and private communication independent of the server or network.

You see a message that you have received a DCC request and describing the type and source of the request. It also contains extra information your client will need if you accept the DCC request, but this does not normally display. The message could also take the form of a small window that opens and asks whether to accept or decline the request.

If you're not sure where the DCC request is coming from, refuse it. Especially if it's a **DCC SEND** request (a file offer), be wary, since the data received could present a security hazard to your client or machine. Sending files meant to render the receiver vulnerable to attack or permit others to access the machine is an increasingly common method abusers use to gain control over someone's client or machine. Don't be afraid of offending someone by refusing a **DCC SEND** (or **CHAT**) offer.

8.1.6 Wallops

Whether these are common or rare depends on your network. There are two forms, one from IRC operators and the other from servers. Regular users can't send wallops. You will not receive any unless you have user mode **w** set, and you don't really need it.

Typical forms of wallops are the following:

```
!Barron*! Behave or I'll jupe the lot of you
```

This means an operator with the nickname Barron sent the message as a wallop. The contents could be anything a normal message would contain. The asterisk indicates an operator rather than a server or regular user sent it (not that regular users are allowed to send wallops nowadays—it's really a redundancy).

```
!Hacker! Possible clones (8) from dialup-34.netabuse.com detected.
```

The above may be from an operator, but in some cases—as in this example—it originates from a service robot with the nickname Hacker, informing the network's operators of certain events or warning them of potential or actual abuse.

```
!ircd.nl.net! Remote CONNECT ircd.webbernet.net 5550 from delta
```

You will occasionally see this type of wallop if you have usermode **w** set. What's happening here is that server ircd.nl.net is informing the network that it received a **CONNECT** command from the operator whose nickname is at the end of the notice (delta) to attempt to connect to server ircd.webbernet.net on port 5550. This is a routing intervention the operator considers necessary in order to correct a network fault.

A similar message appears if an operator orders a server to disconnect from another with the **SQUIT** command, and the operator's reason for breaking the connection follows. A server sends a wallops when the operator issuing the command is not connected to that server.

8.1.7 Operator Notices

Occasionally, if an operator thinks the server's users should be informed of something, he or she sends a private message or notice to all users on the server. This message looks identical to a normal private message or notice. Usually only the contents identify it as server-wide. Some clients, though, recognize it as such and append the mask of the group of recipients to the operator's nick, thus making it clear that the message was directed at all users of a server. Do not reply to operator notices unless they explicitly ask you to.

Operators sometimes use server-wide CTCPs or private messages to detect unauthorized bots, and replying to them could result in your being considered a bot and getting killed or K: lined.

8.1.8 Local Machine Messages and Talk Requests

On a Unix machine, a broadcast message from a user on the same machine or the machine's superuser (root) may interrupt you. There is a Unix command to forbid such messages from reaching you. Only messages from root override this setting and will always reach you. Messages from root usually concern machine downtimes or usage policy, and you should pay attention to them. To prevent messages from reaching you, add the command **mesg n** to your log-in file (**.profile**, **.cshrc**, or whichever you use). You can also use this command or its opposite (**mesg y**) from the command prompt or from within any client supporting a command such as ircII's **EXEC**.

Also, on Unix machines running a talk daemon, you can reach users from any machine on the net by using a talk client. Talk is a simple form of communication for one-on-one direct conversation. Abusers sometimes use talk to create havoc on a user's display with a program named *flash*. You can prevent this with the **mesg n** setting described above, but you will also be unavailable to any normal talk request.

A regular talk request appears in the bottom part of your main window saying there is an incoming talk request, and tells you what to type in order to respond and establish a talk connection. If you want to accept the talk, you have to quit ircII first or open a new screen or **xterm**, if you are able to. Flashes look like a lot of garbage telling you that you have a talk request from your own address, and parts of the screen start to blink. Set **mesg n** immediately without quitting and restore the screen with the **CLEAR** command or by pressing CTRL-L:

```
/exec mesg n
```

```
/clear
```

If you want to talk to the user who sent you a talk, you can send **/DCC TALK user@host** to the user and talk through the IRC window. To send messages to the talker once you've completed the talk handshake, type **/msg @user**. This applies only to ircII. Both EPIC and BitchX have removed this function; you will have to use the conventional way of opening a new terminal in order to reply (or quit IRC first if you cannot open additional terminals). Additionally, it conflicts with op notices used on DALnet and EFnet, where the target of a message can begin with an **@**. You'll probably be more interested in op notices, but in order to use them with ircII, you will have to resort to Chapter 11 and write an alias to override the old function. Don't sweat over it yet.

8.1.9 Actions

You'll often see someone on a channel "doing" something. A leading star characterizes this action, followed by a third-person description of the user's action or an emotional state he or she would like to describe in this manner. You can also use actions in private messages, where they'll appear in a query window or with an asterisk–angle braket (*>) prefix to indicate the action is sent privately and not to the channel.

```
* Joe is a pink bunny.
```

Joe can say it of himself. If anyone else wanted to say that Joe was a pink bunny, it would look like a regular public message. A properly written action looks like a sentence with the sender's nick as the noun. A bad action is the sender's nick followed by something grammatically unsound or incoherent. That can also happen.

8.1.10 Server Notices

You shouldn't normally see a server notice unless you've asked to see some or all types of server notices by joining a channel or setting a user mode that makes the server send you such notices. They are intended to inform interested operators or users of events concerning the server or network.

Technically, they are a distinct class of message, and you can expect your client to treat them differently from regular notices when displaying them. In the beginning, you shouldn't encounter any at all—later, if you're interested in the way servers run, Chapter 18 contains most of the information you'll need to know.

8.1.11 I Joined a Channel and Nothing's Happening!

This is not an unusual occurrence. It could indicate some network, client, or other technical problem, but more often than not there's simply nothing to see. Even if there are 15 or 20 users on the channel, don't panic! Many people leave their client on a channel even while they're away; some of the idle clients may be bots. Joining a channel and meeting silence isn't all that odd, especially if you join a channel in the middle of the night or when everybody is (or should be) at school or at work. Don't expect the absentees to have set themselves away. Most of them will still show as here, largely because not many people pay attention to setting themselves away when they're not around.

Many people also use multiple channels and sometimes don't pay attention to the rest when they're talking to a particular channel. They could have the channel's window hidden when they're not following it and check on it periodically. You're not being scorned—in fact, very soon you'll find yourself doing the same thing.

8.2 Etiquette

There are no formal rules regarding the contents of your messages, but you should keep two rules in mind when talking to others on IRC or sharing a channel with them. I suggest you take these basics of etiquette (or "netiquette," as it is often referred to) to heart:

1. Show others the same courtesy you expect them to show you.

2. Use common sense.

Always remember that your messages are going out to *people*—humans with their own ideas, emotions, levels of tolerance, soft spots, and all those other psychological quirks that make the human animal so intriguing. As in real life, you probably won't be able to avoid the odd faux pas, and you might even be glad others can't see your face turning a deep beet-red color. This doesn't mean you have to be quiet and behave as if treading on eggshells. You can be conversational and active without offending people all the time. Disagreements and the odd fight are a part of life, but insults aren't necessary.

Some other points you should remember in order to avoid be coming unpopular are the following:

- Don't repeat the same message over and over. If you mistype a message, don't correct and resend it. Leave it as is if the message is understandable, or send only the correction. A common way of correcting oneself is resending the mistyped word or phrase followed by the word **even**.

- Don't flood the channel by sending large text files.

- Excessive use of colored text and highlights is generally unwelcome.

- Barging into a channel and doing an "age/sex" check isn't generally appreciated.

- Using actions all the time looks silly.

- Advertising your channel or Web page usually gets you kicked out.

- Stay within the channel's topic of conversation.

- ASCII art may look smart, but few people really appreciate it. Sending too much of it will probably get you kicked out of a channel.

- Experimenting with ASCII art on a channel in the midst of a conversation isn't polite. Create a separate channel (see 10.1) and test it there.

8.3 Ignoring Messages

You're bound to encounter someone who appears to have no sense of netiquette or politeness at one time or another. Some of these people react well if you tell them their conduct is inappropriate, but others don't. If you're an operator of the channel, you can silence the more obnoxious ones by kicking them out. If you're not, or if someone is pestering you with private messages, you can silence them with the **IGNORE** command—BBS veterans know this as "forgetting." The use of **IGNORE** is very different from client to client.

IGNORE is a client function and filters received messages. On the other hand, the **SILENCE** command, available on DALnet, Undernet, and similar servers, has the advantage of reducing the load on your own client by letting the server do the dirty work. It instructs the server to block messages from the user(s) you want to ignore rather than sending them to you and letting your client sort out the mess.

8.3.1 Ignoring with ircII

You can use **IGNORE** with either a nickname or a host mask. In most cases, the nickname is enough. People who are more persistent in their attempt to annoy you can get past this kind of **IGNORE** by changing nicknames. Clients trying to get you disconnected through flooding are best ignored by their **user@host mask** right away. In an emergency, you can also ignore all messages by ignoring the address ***@*** and the message type **ALL**. The basic syntax of the command for ircII is:

```
/ignore <nickname|user@host> <type>
```

The message type can be one or more of the following:

ALL	Everything
MSGS	Only private messages
CTCP	Only CTCP messages
NOTICES	Only notices
PUBLIC	All public channel text

WALLOPS	Only wallops
CRAP	Odd stuff like nick changes, joins and parts, and so forth
NONE	Removes someone from the ignore list

You can specify multiple types with a space-separated list—for example:

```
/ignore Loser msgs notices ctcp
```

You can stop ignoring single types of messages or exclude them from **ALL** by preceding them with a hyphen:

```
/ignore Loser -notices
```

This would stop you from ignoring notices from the user with the nickname Loser, but would still keep msgs and CTCPs from the same user on ignore:

```
/ignore Loser all -public -crap
```

This would make you ignore everything except public messages and what falls in the **CRAP** category (that is, you'll still be able to see the user leave the channel). BitchX users should use **nick!user@host** format for the **IGNORE** rather than ircII's nick or **user@host**.

8.3.2 *Ignoring with mIRC*

The command, again, is **IGNORE**. However, mIRC uses a different format for adding switches to include or exclude certain types of messages. It's also able to ignore a user's host mask by entering only the nickname in the **IGNORE** command.

```
/ignore [-switches] Nickname|nick!user@host [type]
```

If you want to ignore a user's address instead of just the nickname, you must use the full **nick!user@host** format, using asterisk (*) and question mark (?) wildcards where appropriate.

The following switches are recognized:

-c	Public messages
-i	Invites
-k	Color in messages is ignored
-n	Notices
-p	Private messages
-t	CTCP messages
-uN	Will automatically remove the IGNORE after N seconds

Using the **-r** switch removes the **IGNORE** from the nickname or host mask.

The type of **IGNORE** is optional. If you don't specify any, only the nickname is used. If you use one of the following numbers, mIRC ignores more than just the nickname:

0	`*!user@host.domain`
1	`*!*user@host.domain`
2	`*!*@host.domain`
3	`*!*user@*.domain`
4	`*!*@*.domain`
5	`nick!user@host.domain`
6	`nick!*user@host.domain`
7	`nick!*@host.domain`
8	`nick!*user@*.domain`
9	`nick!*@*.domain`

Note that using a type makes mIRC query the server for the **user@host** matching the nickname. Under conditions of lag or during a serious flood, this is probably to your disadvantage—it would be more efficient to manually enter the mask you want to ignore.

8.3.3   *The SILENCE Command*

This command is available on Undernet and DALnet servers. It sets a server-side ignore—that is, messages from the address or user you want to ignore never reach you; the server blocks them.

Not all clients directly support the **SILENCE** command—you might have to use **RAW** or **QUOTE** in order to send it; otherwise **SILENCE** will do just fine.

```
/quote silence +blah@blah.com
```

The plus (**+**) prefix activates a server silence while the hyphen (**-**) reverses it. DALnet and Undernet servers both automatically convert **user@host** into **nick!user@host**. You cannot silence a nickname on DALnet—it must be a **user@host**. Using **SILENCE** with your nick as the only parameter, or using no parameter at all, displays the list of addresses you have silenced.

8.4   **Sending to a Channel**

Sending to a channel is the simplest form of communication. Anything you type that is not a command goes to your current channel or window.

The contents of the message can be absolutely anything, though both the client and the server can restrict the message length.

8.4.1 Sending to a Channel While Not on It

You won't need to do this much, if ever, and it's more often than not ineffective. Almost all channels are permanently set not to accept any messages from users who aren't actually present on them. If you do want to do this, the command is **MSG** (which is actually a private message) with the channel's name as the recipient. This is because public and private messages are identical as far as the server is concerned, and the target can be a channel as well as a user.

```
/msg #Somewhere Hey! Let me in!
```

You can expect channel **#somewhere** not to accept messages from outside the channel, in which case the server returns the error message "Unable to send to channel."

Messages sent to channels from people who aren't on the channel can take a variety of forms. Unix clients generally present it like this:

```
(Joe/#SomeWhere) Let me in!
```

Version 5.61 of mIRC, which was the client's current version at the time of writing, as well as earlier versions, make no visible distinction between a message from a user on the channel and one from outside. This is an omission I hope subsequent versions fix since it's confusing to see a phantom user not on the nickname list sending messages to a channel.

This event can have various causes; either the channel does not have mode **n** set (see 10.3.6) or you or the user sending the messages are desynced from the channel.

8.4.2 Communicating with Multiple Channels

If you've joined more than one channel and are taking part in the conversation on all of them, you'll need a means of directing each message to the right channel. While you can do this easily on clients that have a separate window for each channel—you just switch to the window required—there are also other ways of doing it.

One way is using the **MSG** command seen above in 8.4.1. In this case you will be on the channel even if it isn't your current channel (the current channel concerns only the client—as far as the server goes, you're just present) so the server accepts the message and sends it to the channel. If you're using ircII, you've already seen how to switch between channels (see 7.9.1)—this is more convenient than using **MSG**—just switch to the channel you wish to use and send a public message as you would normally.

Sometimes you want to send a message to all the channels you're on—for instance, to say you'll be away for a few minutes. The **MSG** command can take multiple recipients in a comma-separated list:

```
/msg #somewhere,#otherchannel Away for a few, don't go away!
```

Both channels receive an identical message regardless of which is your current one. The **AMSG** command simplifies this procedure in mIRC:

```
/amsg Away for a few, don't go away!
```

NOTE *On servers running EFnet's 2.8.21/hybrid-6 version, you may no longer use multiple targets for any type of message.*

8.5   Sending Private Messages

Private messaging is the primary use of the **MSG** command.

```
/msg nickname shhhh... they can't hear us!
```

And indeed, they can't. Try sending yourself a **MSG** and seeing what it looks like on both ends. You can also use **MSG** for sending a private message to multiple recipients with a comma-separated list, as for multiple channels.

8.5.1   Using QUERY

QUERY is a client command to facilitate sending private messages without having to use the **MSG** command for each message. Clients have replaced this command by opening a new window for each private communication, but the change has led to confusion regarding the term *query*. Simply sending a user a private message is not a query. Using a dedicated window for sending messages to a user without having to use **MSG** for each message is a query. I think the name of the command was a rather unfortunate choice by the authors of early clients since the word doesn't reflect the function performed. For ircII, **QUERY** works simply like this:

```
/query <target>
```

The target can be a nickname or channel. To close a query, just type /**query** while in the query window.

If you're using mIRC or another graphical client, simply close the query window belonging to the user with whom you've ceased corresponding.

8.6   Strange Characters in Messages

Sometimes you'll notice unusual characters appearing on your screen or people saying things that can't possibly be in a human language. Depending on the kind of characters you're seeing, there are different explanations.

If seemingly random strings of characters are reeling across the screen, you are either being flooded or, if you're connected to your host via a simple terminal, line noise is affecting your modem. Sequences of text with many dollar sign (\$), **B**, and square bracket ([) characters or word-size strings made up largely of vowels are likely to be non-English channels, as discussed in 7.1.2. If a user spouts a stream of gibberish and then signs off, chances are he or she fell victim to line noise and lost the modem connection. You can expect single unusual characters to be part of a foreign Latin-based character set such as Swedish, Finnish, or Portuguese, as occurs in channel names.

8.7   Colored Text and Highlights

Some clients are capable of sending and reading bold, inverse, underlined, or colored text by adding certain control characters to a message. While these can add to the effect of a message, they are client specific, and clients of a different type than the sender's may not support them, resulting in garbage on the receiver's screen. You should avoid them unless you're really certain they're appropriate. The IRC community generally frowns upon excessive use of highlights and color, especially if you're sharing a channel with users whose clients don't support these elements.

Different clients use different control codes for the same highlights; don't ask me why. When mIRC introduced highlights and color in version 4.7, for no apparent reason it diverged from the standard set by ircII (the first client to support highlights), and other clients followed it. The result is a double set of standards—you can expect clients other than ircII and mIRC to follow either one. Regarding color, clients almost universally follow mIRC. This color is *not* real ANSI color—it is exclusive to the IRC clients that support it.

8.7.1   Using Highlights with ircII

Bold, inverse, and underlined text are all supported by ircII. More recent Unix clients based on ircII are also capable of reading ANSI and mIRC color—ircII requires extra scripting to display or filter out color-related codes. Certain control characters surround highlighted text, depending on the type of highlight. These characters are (the ^ character means that you press the **CTRL** key along with the letter or underscore):

^B	Bold
^V	Inverse
^_	Underlined

When adding highlights to a message, the relevant characters appear in inverse on the command line as you type them. While underscore almost never fails, bold and inverse might need some extra attention with some systems and clients. Inverse might require you to press **^V** twice before the character appears, both at the beginning and at the end of the text, to highlight it. Bold sometimes requires a new key binding if **^B** is bound to a different function.

```
/bind ^B self_insert
```

The **SELF_INSERT** function inserts the actual control character in the text with the key press, rather than performing a function assigned to it. Add that line to your **.ircrc** file. You'll rarely need it for the other highlights. Remember to close the highlight by also adding the appropriate control character at the end. You can combine any of these highlights by enclosing the text to highlight between more than one pair of control characters (making sure the pairs close in the reverse order of their opening). Some types of highlights or combinations might fail to appear on some terminals.

NOTE   *As of version 4.4H, ircII supports mIRC-style color. You can turn its display on or off with* **SET COLOR ON/OFF***—the compile default is off. To use color, follow the guide in the next section, replacing the* **^K** *key with* **^C** *(you will need to bind it to* **SELF_INSERT** *as with* **^B** *above).*

8.7.2 *Using Highlights and Color with mIRC*

The mIRC client recognizes color, bold, inverse, and underline, providing you're using version 4.7 or later. On older versions, the corresponding control codes appear as blocks instead. For bold, inverse, and underline, mIRC follows the same conventions as the ircII client, although the actual keys you use to produce highlights are different. To send highlighted text with mIRC, enclose the text within a pair of the following control characters (the caret (^) means you press the CTRL key together with the letter):

^B	Bold
^R	Inverse
^U	Underline

You can insert plain text in fully highlighted sentences with **^O**.

Color is a bit more complicated. You create color codes with the **^K** key press, followed by a number indicating the color, and optionally a comma and another number denoting the background color. You should leave no spaces between the codes and the text or between CTRL-**K** and the codes. After pressing CTRL-**K**, you see a black block, after which you enter the numbers.

Here are the color codes you can use:

Code	Color	Code	Color
0	White	**8**	Yellow
1	Black	**9**	Bright green
2	Dark blue	**10**	Teal
3	Dark green	**11**	Cyan
4	Red	**12**	Blue
5	Brown	**13**	Magenta
6	Purple	**14**	Dark gray
7	Orange	**15**	Light gray

Examples (I've purposely left spaces between the components to make them clearer):

^K 5	Brown text on the default background
^K 15,1	Light grey text on a black background
^K 0,0	White on white

Some people use it to exchange pseudo-invisible messages. Anyone not displaying color can still see the message.

You can use color in almost any text, including channel names, channel topics, your real name, quit messages, and private messages. You *can't* use it in your nickname. You can technically use color in your user name, but this is highly irregular and considered very lame—most servers deny you access if you have control codes in your user name.

8.8 Smile!

Smileys are all those funny character strings such as **:-)** that sometimes follow messages. They are meant to convey a facial expression. Many are widely used and universally understood, while only some users or channels recognize others. Still, you can usually guess their meaning by looking at them. With a bit of imagination you can also create your own. Here are the most common smileys. If you can't immediately see the analogy to a facial expression, hold the page sideways and look again.

:) or **:-)**	The classic "smiley"—a smiling face. The original smiley had the nose, but lazy typists never use it
:(or **:-(**	The frown
;) or **;-)**	A wink and a smile
8) or **8-)**	Smiley wearing glasses or bug-eyed smiley. More common than you'd expect
:-o or **:-0**	Surprise or shock
=:o	One of the funniest. Really surprised, shocked, or unbelieving
(:	Left-handed smiley. Not very common but confusing
>:(	Frown or angry face. No, it's not called a "frowney"
>;)	Sly wink. Up to mischief, probably
;o)	Another smile, believed to have originated in Holland
};)	Truly evil
:-I	Stern or neutral

8.9 Actions

Actions are easy to use and add much in terms of expressing oneself. Excessive use of actions, however, looks amateurish, and you should use them only when appropriate. You perform an action via the **ME** command, which is a client function almost universal to all clients.

```
/me <third-person description of your action>
```

For example:

```
/me hides behind the couch.
```

Technically, the **ME** command is a form of CTCP. This is important to know for scripting (Chapter 11 will clarify this). You can also send an action as a private message with the **DESCRIBE** command or by performing the action with **ME** in a query window. Actions don't work within a DCC chat. An additional mIRC command lets you send the same action to all channels you're on:

```
/ame will be back soon.
```

8.10 Common Abbreviation

You'll often see some messages that look like secret codes people are exchanging to hide things from you. These are actually acronyms or abbreviations for commonly used messages, and each has a definite meaning. Some people also prefer to use these in lieu of bad language. Let's have a look at the most widely used of these messages:

asl or **a/s/l**	This is a request for your age, sex, and location. You don't have to reply.
afaik	As far as I know
bbiaf/bbiam/bbiaw	Be back in a few/flash/minute/while
bbl	Be back later
bbs	Be back soon
iirc	If I remember correctly
im(h)o	In my (humble) opinion
l8r	Later
lol	Laugh(ing) out loud
re	Hello again or re-hi. Indicates recognition after a short absence. Mostly used when rejoining a channel.
ro(t)fl	Rolling on (the) floor laughing
ro(t)flmao	Rolling on (the) floor laughing my a** off
r u m or f	Are you male or female. A silly but common way of asking a question that's rarely appreciated. People who keep asking everyone this question are called "morfers" because they have a fixation with "m or f."

rtfm	Read the f***ing manual. The "m" is sometimes
	replaced with d (docs), s (source code), or p (page).
wb	Welcome back
wtf	What/where/who/why the f***

8.11 Autogreets

After you've received an autogreet, usually in the form of a notice, after joining a channel, you might want to use one yourself. This would require a bit of scripting (with **ON JOIN**) and we'll have a look at it in Chapter 11. Autogreets, while increasingly common, aren't really liked because once the first impression wears off, they look fake and insincere. Using autogreets can also generate a lot of unnecessary traffic following netjoins, apart from the more obvious annoyance of greeting the same people again and again. A genuine, typed greeting is much more welcome.

8.12 Keeping Track of Events by Logging

Many clients allow you to keep a log of events and messages by writing them to a file as they appear, from which you can retrieve and read them later. Logging is a client function.

8.12.1 Logging with ircII

IrcII has two variables for logging that will tell it when to log and which file to log to. Set the **LOGFILE** variable to the file name you're using, and set **LOG** on to start logging and off to stop. If you're using multiple windows, you can log them separately with **WINDOW LOG**, and the client appends the name of the channel or query to the file name for identification.

```
/set logfile irc.log
```

```
/set log on
```

Or change to the appropriate window and type:

```
/window log on
```

If you use /**set log** instead of /**window log** while using multiple windows, everything from all windows ends up in the same file. If a logfile already exists when you start logging, the new messages are appended to it.

8.12.2 Logging with mIRC

To do this, simply click the box in the top left corner of the window containing the contents you want to log, then click **Logging**. A checkmark appears next to Logging. Do exactly the same thing to cease logging.

Alternatively, you can use the **LOG** command

```
/log on
```

```
/log off
```

from within the window you want to log. Under the File menu, select **Options • IRC • Logging** to configure the way it logs items, and specify the directory where the logfiles are kept.

8.13 Communication Problems

You might sometimes encounter strange problems when trying to communicate with a user or channel. While bad network connections or channel settings often cause these, some are also client-side problems.

8.13.1 Can't Send to Channel

Either you're trying to send to a channel that doesn't permit messages from outside while you're not on it, or you're trying to send to a moderated channel without having a voice (see 7.6). If you're getting this message even though your text is appearing normally on the channel, the cause could be desync (see 10.9). Note that your client makes the message appear after you've sent it—the client doesn't receive the message from the server. This means you'll see the message in the channel's window even if the server rejects it. To be sure a message has been received by the other user(s), you'll have to wait for a response from one of the other users on the channel.

8.13.2 Text Is Scrolling on a Single Line

This problem is unique to Unix and ircII clients. Try changing your terminal settings—vt100 is the terminal emulation you should be using. Having it set to ANSI often causes this particular problem. After changing the terminal emulation, log out and log in again.

If that fails to correct the problem, try this:

```
/set scroll off
```

```
/set scroll_lines 1
```

```
/set scroll on
```

If you're really unlucky, you have a "dumb" terminal and will have to make do with having the new text overwrite the old once the screen is full. These terminals are increasingly rare, though.

8.13.3 I Can't See My Nickname before My Messages

This is entirely client dependent, and easy to fix. Some clients do show your nickname by default, while others do not.
For mIRC, follow these steps:

- Go to **File • Options • IRC**.

- Check **Prefix own messages**.
  For ircII, add the following line to your **.ircrc**:

- ON send_msg "*" echo <$N> $1-

This concerns only public messages—you don't need to change anything for other kinds of messages.

9

FINDING PEOPLE ON IRC

People come and go on IRC at a rate that would put Grand Central Station to shame, and more often than not they leave no forwarding address. You'll sometimes want to find another user—someone who disappeared in the middle of a conversation, someone you met with whom you forgot to exchange email addresses, someone to help you out with a problem, or you might simply want to know whether a friend of yours is online. On other occasions, you may want to see the occupants of a channel without having to join it. In this chapter we'll look at the tools available for locating someone on IRC. Several of these commands are also useful for channels.

Be forewarned that IRC servers respect their users' privacy, and if people don't want to be found, they can't be. They can sit on a server outside all channels and not exist as far as nearly everyone else is concerned—with the exception of IRC operators.

9.1 WHOIS

If you already know a user's nickname, you can use the **WHOIS** command to see the information the server has about that nickname. **WHOIS** works whether a user is invisible or not. It also shows you any public channels this user is on, except secret channels. You can also use **WHOIS** to check a user's idle time by requesting the **whois** information from that user's server.

```
/whois server nickname
```

You can substitute the nickname for the server, as with other commands (mainly those covered in Chapter 12):

```
/whois nickname nickname
```

Many people have found it convenient to write an alias for this "double **whois**," and it's also present in most reasonable *scripts* (often with the alias "WII"). This form of **WHOIS** requests the **whois** information from the user's server (or any other server, but servers other than the one that user is on will normally show no more than yours does). You can also use it as a diagnostic tool for detecting **desync** by comparing a user's **whois** information as different servers see it. Don't worry about the reference to scripts and desync right now, though—just remember it when we get to the relevant sections.

If you have a rough guess of the nickname you're looking for, **WHOIS** supports wildcards on most servers. Wildcards (to introduce something you'll encounter a lot further down) are special characters that substitute for others, as follows:

A question mark (?) stands for any single character except no character.

An asterisk (*) stands for any number of any characters, including none.

9.2 WHOWAS

WHOWAS helps you when the user you're looking for is no longer online or has changed his nickname while out of your sight. You can use

WHOWAS to find out the last instance the server saw a nickname, and quite often also the last few times. Unfortunately, **WHOWAS** information doesn't last long. Exactly how long the server stores information about the past use of nicknames depends on its setup and the nickname turnover (meaning the total instances of nicknames used and retired again). A large network during high-traffic hours may store **WHOWAS** information for no more than half a minute. On networks with little traffic, it may last more than a day.

WHOWAS works only with nicknames. There is no way of using this command to detect the last time a user from a particular address was on. Actually, you'd use **WHOWAS** to obtain the last address from which a nickname was seen. It returns any **away** message the user had at the time of quitting or changing nicknames, but none of the channels he was using.

9.3   WHO

In many cases you won't know what nickname the user you wish to locate is using. This is where the **WHO** command is useful. You must have some other information about this user in order to use **WHO**. Let's say you remember that the user hangs out on some channel that has the word *ball* somewhere in its name. Note that **WHO** never returns information about invisible users (those who have user mode **+i** set [6.4.1]). So if your friend is invisible, **WHO** is of no use to you.

NOTE   *More and more users on the large networks are now invisible, either because they set themselves as **+i** or because the server to which they're connected sets all users as **+i** by default. The percentage of invisible users on the major networks ranges from about 50 percent on DALnet to over 85 percent on EFnet. Much of this desire for privacy is due to the immense number of pornography-advertising spam bots messaging all visible users and forcing them to use **+i** to avoid those messages.*

```
/who *ball*
```

This will return a number of irrelevant things, since **WHO** will show you any visible user with the string *ball* in the user name, host name, nickname, server name, or real name. If you aren't careful to use a string that matches a large server as well, you'll get a lot more than you bargained for. Try to be as specific as possible. Wildcards in a channel name will not work—you must use the full name of the channel, including the prefix (pound sign, plus sign, or ampersand).

If a channel is secret, **WHO** will tell you nothing about its users, and the command fails to return any information at all, whether your friend is visible or not. You'll be a lot better off using a part of the user's address, as much as you remember, but allowing for dynamic addressing.

For example, if you recall the user's host mask as **nick@dialup11.nyc.whatever.net** or you get that address using **WHOWAS** (see below), the **dialup11** part is obviously dynamic and therefore should be wild-carded since your user may have dialed in again and been assigned a different address. So you can use the rest, which consists of a geographical identifier and the domain name. Not all providers use such identifiers—you might have to use just the domain name.

```
/who *.nyc.whatever.net
```

If there are any users matching that mask and not invisible, you will receive their **WHO** information. This is the most common way of using **WHO**.

WHO scans the channel name, nickname, real name, user name, host name, and server name for any string you specify. It's important to remember that it treats the user name and host name as separate parts, and your client adds the at (@) character you see between them, so you shouldn't use that character in a **WHO** query.

If you're lucky and have a client that supports flags for **WHO**, you can select which parts of the **WHO** output to search for the string. It's very useful to limit the list, especially if the string you're searching for is likely to return many irrelevant entries. Here are the flags ircII uses (which other clients supporting flags should also use):

Flag	Type of Result
-name	User name
-nick	Nickname
-oper	IRC operators only
-chops	Channel operators only
-host	Host name
-server	Server name only

For example, to find your friend whose host mask is **nick@dialup11.nyc.whatever.net** with the user name flag, you would type:

```
/who -name *nick*
```

and the results will be only those with the string **nick** in their user names.

NOTE *As of this writing, the mIRC client does not support **WHO** flags, so the above is irrelevant for that client. The same applies to many other clients.*

9.4 NOTIFY and ISON

Many clients allow you to maintain a list of nicknames of which you wish to be notified if they join or leave IRC. How you set up such a notify list varies from client to client, but the way it works is identical. If there is a notify list, your client periodically sends **ISON** commands to the server, asking it whether the nicknames on the client's notify list are present. The server replies with the nicknames present. Your client compares the reply to its internal list of nicknames present (as the last **ISON** saw them) and notifies you of changes to the list, telling you which nicknames it has detected that were previously absent and which ones are no longer there.

NOTIFY works on nicknames only. You can't use it for addresses or host masks (this used to be possible with **NOTE**, a practically obsolete command very few servers now support). Since anyone could use the nickname you have on your list, you should check the host mask of the nickname, either with **WHOIS** or by scripting a line that checks it with **USERHOST**.

You can also use **ISON** independently of **NOTIFY**:

```
/ison nick1 nick2 nick3 ...
```

The reply might look somewhat like this:

```
*** Currently online: nick1 nick3
```

The server's reply mentions only the nicknames that are present— it will not tell you whether this or that other nickname is signed on. That's the task of your client's notify system.

Note that **NOTIFY** is a client function, while **ISON** is a server command. Some clients (notably ircII, which added an **ISON** command only in recent versions) don't support **ISON** as a user command, so you'll have to send it as a raw server command, using the **RAW** or **QUOTE** command.

9.5 NAMES

NAMES is actually of little use in finding users, but you can use it for a rough check of a channel's users. Again, as with **WHO**, unless you're on the channel yourself, invisible users and users on secret channels will not appear.

*Do not use the **NAMES** command with no parameter—it will return all visible users on the network and place an unnecessary load on your connection, possibly also resulting in the server's disconnecting you. You may safely use it on networks with a small number of users. However, if you try it on a major network you'll recoil in shock and stare at the scrolling screen in horror. This is not a newbie error. Everyone does it by mistake every once in a while, including yours truly. And, yes, I hate it when that happens!*

*If it happens to you, type **/flush** to clear your buffer. You may, although it's rare, lose a message someone just sent you if you do this. Generally speaking, it's worth it. But if a conversation you were having suddenly ends, it might be because that person is waiting for you to answer a lost message. Usually just saying, "Did you say something to me? I missed it," will put you back in the messager's good graces.*

9.6 Finding the Operators of a Channel

You'll sometimes want to find a channel's operators in order to receive the channel's *key* or ask to be unbanned or invited. For this, you can use both the **WHO** and **NAMES** commands, again with the limitations of secret channels and invisible users. If your client supports a flag allowing you to list only channel operators, use it.

If a channel is closed with a password (key) or requires an invitation (invite-only), chances are its occupants do not wish to be disturbed. Consequentially, the channel will most likely also be secret, and all attempts to see its users from outside will fail. It's really best to take the hint and go to another channel.

9.7 Network Services

If the user you're looking for has a registered nickname on a network that provides a nickname service (usually called *NickServ*), you can try requesting information about that nickname from the service. More often than not, it will say when it last saw the owner of the nickname using it and at what address. A common syntax for querying a service about a nickname would be:

```
/msg <service> info <nickname>
```

but this may vary from service to service. Send the service a help message if you're in doubt. If the same network also has a memo or note server, usually under the predictable name of MemoServ or NoteServ, you could also use this to leave a note for that person.

Here's a sample output of an information query on DALnet:

```
NickServ- *** LART is Web Net IRC
NickServ- (Currently on IRC) For extra info /whois LART
NickServ- Last seen address: apatrix@ircd.webbernet.net
NickServ- Last seen time: Thu 01/07/99 06:58:50 GMT
NickServ- Time registered: Wed 04/08/98 15:49:44 GMT
NickServ- Time now: Thu 01/07/99 06:59:06 GMT
NickServ- This user will not receive memos
NickServ- *** End of Info ***
```

This information says that the nickname LART is currently in use and gives the address of the person using it. The second line would be missing, were he not on DALnet at the time. Depending on the user's preferences, there may be additional lines containing information about those preferences. Note that unlike the vast majority of users, this unsociable individual will not accept memos, so you couldn't use DALnet's MemoServ to send him a note.

9.8 Finger

The finger command is strictly for users on machines with a finger daemon—basically meaning multiuser Unix machines. It is not an IRC command, but a separate protocol. Some clients are capable of sending a real finger query (as opposed to *CTCP finger,* which, being CTCP, queries an IRC client—more about CTCP in Chapter 13) and displaying the reply. This is another confusing ambiguity of command names, but we must remember that commands such as **finger**, **ping**, **who**, and **whois** actually predate IRC and gave their names to those IRC commands with similar functions.

If you know the other person's user name on the system, finger the whole address, as in **george@my.provider.com**. This does not necessarily match the user's email address, since the email address often contains only the domain, while finger must target the user's host.

You must direct finger at a specific machine. If you don't remember the user name, try requesting a list of all users logged into the machine.

Do this by fingering **@host.name**—for example, **finger @my.provider. com**. Many systems demand that you give a user name in a finger query, and refuse to give you this information. Most ISPs refuse to respond to finger queries altogether.

If you do get a reply, the amount of information returned varies depending on the finger daemon's setup, but often says when the user last logged into the machine or whether he is currently on. Even if the user is logged into the machine, it doesn't necessarily mean he is using IRC at the moment. He could be anywhere or nowhere on the Internet. Consider sending a *talk* request or an email.

9.9   Finding Someone's Location

Finding out where a user is located is often as simple as using the Unix command **whois**. **Whois** is the nominal ancestor of the IRC command with the same name, and is a separate protocol requiring a client in order to query a **whois** server about a domain or IP address. The relevant technical document is RFC 954, for those who care about Internet esoterica. In many cases you'll be able to deduce a person's location from the host mask if this includes a geographic identifier or has a characteristic country code.

Often, though, especially with North American sites, this is inconclusive, and you'll want additional information. Use a regular finger client or a special **whois** client (available from good software sites) to ask a **whois** server where the user's domain is registered. More often than not, the user's whereabouts are in the same city or close to the place where the domain is registered. You can also use **whois** to check where an IP address is registered.

The three main **whois** servers contain the data for the three primary zones:

```
whois.ripe.net (Europe, Middle East)
whois.arin.net and whois.internic.net (America)
whois.apnic.net (Asia, Pacific)
```

They also have a Web interface if you lack a client to perform the query. **Whois** doesn't really fall within the scope of this book, though, so that's the last we'll be hearing of it for now.

Naturally, nothing is simpler than asking the other person. Most people will tell you where they are with no fuss whatsoever.

9.10   How *Not* to Be Found

That's all fine and dandy, and someone who doesn't want to be found can't be found, right? All right, pal, now tell *me* how to do it! I don't want to be bugged, get it?

Well, since I've given away all the secrets of digging up people, I guess it's only fair that I tell you how to hide out on IRC.

First of all, you should know that you are visible under all circumstances to anyone with whom you share a channel. There is no way around that. You're also visible to all operators of the server you're using—on some networks, operators of other servers can also see you regardless of your status. There is no avoiding this either. You can hide from everyone else. Note that it's considered highly unethical for server operators to divulge information to a regular user if that user would be unable to obtain it on his own. So don't worry—you can rely on their discretion.

If you're on no channel at all, simply setting yourself as +i does the trick. If you've locked yourself into a secret channel, chances are you're pretty safe from detection there as well. It's a bit more tricky if you're sitting in a large public channel. Anyone may join it and find you there, including people who suspect you might be there. The same goes for any channel you're known to frequent. If you really want to keep nosy parkers from finding you on such a channel, you'll have no choice but to ban them. Naturally, this would require channel operator status. Chapter 10 has more on that. If you're really paranoid about being found, you may end up having to leave the channel.

10

CREATING AND MANAGING
A CHANNEL

So you've been in and out of channels, meeting folks, chatting, and getting the hang of IRC. Now you'd like to start a channel of your own for your friends to join, and you need to know how to create and manage it. Or maybe you're regular enough on your usual channels for the ops to consider you a suitable candidate to become one of the channel's regular ops—now you need to know how to use your newly gained powers to run the channel. Well, this is where the really technical part of IRC begins. Everything up to now will look like child's play.

10.1 Creating a New Channel

Any user can create a channel using the **JOIN** command (see 7.3). Let's say you want to create a test channel called **#MyTestChannel**:

```
/join #MyTestChannel
```

Boy, that was simple. If you join a channel and the channel does not currently exist, the system creates this channel with you as its only user and operator. Although you're alone, you're in charge of everything. Talk about being your own boss!

Once you've created a channel, it's identified by its name and nothing else. If you want your channel to have a different name from the one you initially used to create it, you'll have to repeat the procedure and create a channel with the new name. If there are other people on the channel who want to move over with you, they have to join the new channel.

Trying to create a channel can return a few errors—remember channel delay (see 7.3.7) and getting the channel name wrong (7.3.1).

Say you try to create a channel by joining it, and instead of becoming its operator, you lose your op status immediately after joining and a topic for the channel gets set automatically, despite the fact that you are the only user on the channel. If this happens, you are on a network that has a channel service, with which it's possible to register and own a channel name, and the channel you tried to create is registered to someone else. In this case, you have no choice but to choose a different name for your channel.

You may join an empty channel and simply not get operator status, even if you're the first user to join and there is no channel service on the network. For this there can be two possible explanations, depending on the type of server:

On a network using IRCnet server code, it means the server has restricted your connection (with umode **r** [see 6.4.6]). Change to a server that won't restrict you and try again. On most EFnet servers you cannot obtain channel op status while the server is split from the rest of the network.

10.2 Channel Operator Status

As we saw when we were looking at the definition of channel operator (see 7.5), they have certain powers other users of a channel don't have. Now that you're a channel op, you can use two new commands:

```
INVITE
KICK
```

Two more now give you more options:

```
MODE
TOPIC
```

In the following sections we'll look at the **KICK**, **INVITE**, and **MODE** commands separately and explain their uses. Nothing changes with the **TOPIC** command save that you can restrict its use to channel operators.

10.3 Channel Modes

This is the most complex part of channel management and something a good channel op knows by heart. If you've only just become the op on a channel, you should read this part carefully and create a test channel to practice on. Often it helps to ask a friend to join the channel, too, and be your guinea pig while you experiment with modes and other channel op commands.

Let's take a look at the possible modes a channel may have. Depending on the type of server, there may be a few additional ones particular to that type and of varying usefulness. We'll concentrate on the modes available on all kinds of servers—those mentioned in "RFC 1459," the document describing the IRC protocol.

Newly created channels have no modes set and always need you to add the required modes after creation. You can set some channel services to create the modes automatically if someone joins a registered channel while it's empty, or to reset them periodically. Most clients display the current modes of a channel in the status bar or in the channel window's caption.

You set or unset channel modes by prefixing their characteristic letter with a plus (+) or minus (-) sign, respectively. If you provide no prefix, the server assumes you mean plus. The characteristic letters of the modes are case sensitive—they must be lowercase. This is because the servers are allowing for future extensions to the protocol, which might assign a different meaning to capitals and lowercase. A limited number of servers recently introduced capital mode letters, but until this becomes a standard, you'll almost always be using lowercase.

The general syntax of the **MODE** command is the following:

```
/mode #channel <[+|-]letter> [parameter]
```

If your client supports the asterisk (*) as a substitute for the channel's name, you can also use this with **MODE**.

Nickname changes do not affect modes. You can change your nick as often as you like, and both your user modes and any channel modes applying to you remain in effect.

A channel's modes are lost when the last person in a channel leaves it and it's empty. If you registered the channel on a network that supports registration, you often can have the channel service store a set of modes and automatically set them for you when someone joins the empty channel. Section 10.10 describes the most common forms of channel service, but first you need to know how to set up and run a channel.

10.3.1 Mode b (Ban)

Mode **b** sets a ban forbidding any user to join the channel whose mask matches the string you added as a parameter if added and lifts the ban on that mask if removed. Bans are an important part of channel management and require accurate use to spare your channel unnecessary trouble from unwanted users who won't take the hint that they're not welcome. For this reason we'll take a separate, closer look at bans and their correct use later (see 10.5.1).

Mode **b** with no parameters is the only mode a nonoperator or even a user who isn't on the channel can use (although some less conventional modern kinds of server no longer permit this). This special case of the **MODE** command takes the plus prefix or no prefix and no parameters and allows a user to view the channel's ban list. It's of no importance whether the channel is secret or not.

> **TIP** *DALnet and IRCnet servers also silence a banned user, so that user can send nothing to the channel. You can use the ban to silence a single user without having to resort to moderation (see 7.6).*

10.3.2 Modes i (Invite-Only) and I (Invitation)

Mode **i** is invite-only mode. If a channel is **i**, only users invited by a channel op may join. This is an example of a mode with both a capital and a lowercase significance.

```
/mode #somewhere +i
```

In order to join a channel, a user must now obtain an invitation from one of the channel ops. IRCnet servers also allow you to use **I** to permit some users to join without an invitation. Mode **I** takes a user mask as its parameter, in the same way mode **b** does.

10.3.3 Mode k (Key)

As we've already seen, the "key" of a channel is a password, without which no one is allowed to join. To set a password, you add the **k** mode (**+k**) with the password as its only parameter. If you wish to remove this mode, you must use the exact password in the same way with the **-k** mode change.

```
/mode #somewhere +k onlythebrave
```

EXCEPTION   *On EFnet (newer servers), the key is not a required parameter for mode **-k**.*

10.3.4 Mode l (Limit)

This limits the possible number of users on the channel to the number given as a parameter to the **l** mode change. The number isn't necessary to remove the **l** mode.

```
/mode #somewhere +l 30
```

Anyone trying to join after the limit has been filled will be told the channel is full and stopped from joining.

EXCEPTION   *On IRCnet servers, you can use mode **I** to let someone join regardless of the limit. On Undernet servers, a user invited with the **INVITE** command can join regardless of the presence of a limit.*

10.3.5 Mode m (Moderated)

You can set a channel to allow only its ops and certain other users (those a channel operator gives a voice) to send to it, while the rest can only listen. Mode **+m** adds this setting and **-m** removes it, allowing everyone to send.

```
/mode #somewhere +m
```

10.3.6 Mode n (Noexternal)

Mode **n** is one of the two modes practically no channel lacks. It disallows messages to the channel from any user who hasn't actually "JOINed" it.

10.3.7 Mode o (Operator)

Probably the most widely used mode is **o**. This assigns or removes ops from a user. The parameter to this mode, whether set or unset (op or deop), is always the user's nickname.

```
/mode #somewhere +o MyFriend
```

10.3.8 Mode p (Private)

Mode **p** is rarely used but still possible on all server versions. It does not permit a channel's name to show on the channel list, but returns other information a user may request. The wide use of mode **s**, with which it's mutually exclusive, has made it almost obsolete.

```
/mode #somewhere +p
```

EXCEPTION *On EFnet (newer versions), mode +p makes the channel not receive KNOCK notices.*

10.3.9 Mode s (Secret)

Mode **s** is a common setting that makes a channel return no information about its users and not appear on the channel list. A secret channel does not appear in its users' **WHOIS** info either. As mentioned under mode **p**, modes **p** and **s** are mutually exclusive—you can have either but not both. If you try to add one while the other is present, the server automatically removes the existing one before setting the new one.

```
/mode #somewhere +s
```

But if mode **p** is on, when you set mode **s** you see this change:

```
*** Mode change "+s-p" on channel #somewhere by drYad^
```

EXCEPTION *In accordance with the new function of mode p on EFnet, modes p and s may no longer be mutually exclusive there.*

10.3.10 Mode t (Topicsetbyops)

Set mode **t** to prevent users who aren't channel ops from changing the channel's topic. This, along with mode **n**, is the most common mode. On a channel that is **-t**, any user may use the **TOPIC** command to change its topic.

```
/mode #somechannel +t
```

10.3.11   Mode v (Voice)

Mode **v**, as we saw in 7.6, is unnecessary without mode **+m**. It takes the nickname of the user being given or taken away the voice as a parameter.

/mode #somechannel +v Voiceless

Hmm . . . now Voiceless will have to change his nick.

10.3.12   Viewing a Channel's Mode

Another special form of the **MODE** command is used to see what modes a channel has.

/mode #irchelp

The reply will look like this:

*** Mode for channel #irchelp is "+tnl"

This is the best way to find out if a secret channel exists without having to join it. It will not return any parameters affecting the modes (for example, how high the limit on a **+l** channel is).

EXCEPTION   *On EFnet,* **MODE** *#channel now also shows the limit set with +l.*

10.3.13   Mode e (Exception)

Mode **e**'s function is identical to **b**, but it has the opposite effect. Mode **b** forbids a mask from joining, and mode **e** permits it to join despite a ban. A **nick!user@host mask** is the only parameter it takes. This mode is currently available only on IRCnet and EFnet servers.

10.3.14   Multiple Mode Changes

You can set more than one mode with a single **MODE** command. For this purpose, we'll separate modes into two categories according to their descriptions above: modes that take a parameter (**b**, **k**, **l**, **o**, **v**, **e**, and **I**) and modes that do not require one (**i**, **m**, **n**, **p**, **s**, and **t**).

You can combine any number of nonparameter modes in a single mode change. Depending on the server's version, the maximum number of parameter modes you can set simultaneously is three or four, sometimes even more. Although the protocol specifies three as the number, many servers have raised this to four or even more. If you send more than the maximum, the server ignores every mode change beyond the last permitted number and only accepts the first three or four. You may combine modes that require a parameter and those that don't, as long as the number of parameter-taking modes doesn't exceed the limit.

The modes can be any combination and order, but multiple mode changes need a slightly different syntax and are subject to a few rules:

- You need the plus or minus prefix only once if the changes applied are all one or the other. Example: **+snt**

- Multiple mode changes of the same kind are possible for modes **b**, **o**, and **v**, regardless of prefix. Example: **+ooo** or **+oo-o**

- Mode **v** cannot be combined with mode **o** in most cases.

- You must give parameters in the exactly same order as the modes requiring them. Example: **+oob nick1 nick2 lamer!*@***

- For mixed plus and minus mode changes, a prefix is required before the letter, unless the letter preceding it has the same prefix already applied. Example: **-s+nt**

- Modes **s** and **p** are mutually exclusive. See exception above.

- If the modes in a multiple change conflict, only the last of the conflicting modes applies. Example: **+o-o nick nick**

- Some server versions do not permit redundant mode changes (setting a mode that is already active for the channel).

- Mode characters can also be separated by **<space>**.

10.4 Creating a Private Channel

To create a really private channel, you use channel mode **s** and either **k** or **i** along with it. Whether you use any of the other modes is of no importance and a matter of personal preference. You should set mode **s** first as soon as possible after joining in order to make the channel secret and make it disappear from your **WHOIS** reply and the channel list.

Whether you use **i** or **k** depends on how you want people to join the channel—you can give them the key and let them join whenever they like or require them to get an invitation from you first. If you want people to find you so they can ask for an invitation or key, you should either use a nickname they know you by or set umode **-i** so they can find you with **WHO** (see 9.3).

A channel you make private in this way is as secure as a private message; no one outside it knows even its name. If someone who shouldn't have finds your channel, consider the following possibilities:

- He or she did a **WHOIS** on you between your creating the channel and setting it **+s**.

- Someone who knows of the channel told that person.

- Your name for the channel was predictable (that is, your usual nick).

- He or she wanted to use the channel independent of you and didn't know you were there.

This is why you also set it **+i** or **+k** (or **+ik** if you like to complicate things). You can also use **+l** to strictly limit the number of users your channel may have. Actually, though, more than one of **k**, **i**, and **l** is overkill and essentially redundant.

10.4.1 *Inviting*

If you're an operator of your channel, you can use the **INVITE** command to ask a user to join it. If your channel is set **+i**, you must use it before they can join. **INVITE** has the (often confusing) peculiarity that, unlike all other channel commands, it gives the user's nickname as the first parameter, not the channel's name.

```
/invite Outside #Inside
```

User Outside now sees an invitation and, if the channel is **+i**, also has permission to join. Note that an invitation is only good for as long as the user invited is connected to the server. If he or she disconnects for any reason, the invitation must be repeated.

10.5 Kicks and Bans

If you've tried asking someone nicely to stop annoying or offending the channel and have gotten no results, you'll be forced to use the **KICK** command to remove the user from the channel by force.

```
/kick #somewhere Loser please stop being annoying
```

The user with the nickname Loser is now history. If that person was also a channel op, he or she has lost op status. There is no rule forbidding an op to kick another op out. As a matter of fact, when feeling particularly playful, channel ops have been known to have "kick wars," kicking other ops with a cute message, getting kicked, rejoining, and regaining ops, and doing it all over again. Be careful not to create hard feelings, though. In the above example, the reason given for the kick is "please stop being annoying." If you supply no reason, the server uses your nickname as the kick message.

The user loses ops and voices whether he or she leaves a channel normally or gets kicked. Like all other channel commands, you can substitute an asterisk for the current channel if your client supports it.

Even using the asterisk, you'll often find that you need to remove a user from the channel fast. You should write an alias to make the kick command shorter—more on aliases in section 11 below.

If the user who was kicked won't take the hint that he or she isn't welcome and returns to bother the channel again, you'll need a ban—channel mode **b**.

You have to follow the ban with a kick since **MODE** and **KICK** are separate commands and you can't send them to the server with a single action. Nor will setting a matching ban automatically remove a user from the channel. So you'll set the appropriate ban and then kick the offender.

Remember: Ban first, kick second. If you kick before setting the ban, nothing prevents the user from rejoining the channel until you set the ban, and he or she can easily be back by the time you've placed the ban—then you'll have to repeat the kick.

10.5.1   *Correct Use of Host Masks in Bans*

Bans are tricky in that the ban mask must be precise, or else it will be ineffective. Also, now that dynamic addressing and clients that permit arbitrary user names are so common, more persistent losers can avoid certain bans and need a new ban setting. It does happen that someone is so bent on annoying you that he or she drops the server connection, changes user name, and reconnects or even hangs up and dials in again to get a new IP address. It may sound crazy, but these cases of serious social inadequacy are common.

With more experience, you'll be able to make an educated guess regarding which parts of a user's mask are variable. Some look like Unix hosts, whose users are generally easy to get rid of with a single ban, and others are obviously dial-ups, which are a nuisance to ban effectively without banning too large a group of users. Strings such as "ppp," "dial," "max," and a few numbers in the first one or two parts of the host name are typical of dial-ups and need more care.

What the server checks before matching is the ban against the user's full mask—in the format of **nick!username@host.name** (see 6.3.2). The most limited ban would be one containing the offender's precise nickname, username, and host name. Of course, since users can change nicknames with a single command, and user names, and often parts of the host name as well, are mutable, you'll need wildcards in the right spots. Too few let the culprit in, while too many risk banning a larger number of users than is necessary, maybe even some of the channel's regular users.

Two wildcards are possible in a ban: the asterisk (*) and the question mark (?). If you don't remember their meaning, here's a reminder:

- The asterisk stands for any number of any characters, including none at all.

- The question mark stands for any single character, but not for no character at all.

You can place wildcards anywhere—they don't have to be at the beginning, end, or middle.

- The asterisk wildcard is good for very variable parts of a mask, such as the nickname.

- The question mark is useful for fine-tuning a ban to avoid locking the wrong people out.

Let's say the user appearing as Loser, with the address Ihateyou@dialup-7.chi.loathsome.net, is being a nuisance. The exact ban for Loser would look like this:

```
/mode * +b Loser!Ihateyou@dialup-7.chi.loathsome.net
```

Well, since he could change his nick to something else and rejoin because the mask will no longer match the ban with the changed nick, we should ban him regardless of the nick he's using. What was the wildcard for any number of characters? Right, the asterisk. So let's replace the nickname in the ban mask with an asterisk.

```
/mode * +b *!Ihateyou@dialup-7.chi.loathsome.net
```

Looks much nicer and is definitely more effective. But this one has made up his mind to cause you as much inconvenience as possible. So he disconnects from the server, changes his user name, and returns. Hmm. I guess we can't take the user name for granted either. Fine, Loser, suit yourself.

```
/mode * +b *!*@dialup-7.chi.loathsome.net
```

Try beating this, jerk! Well, sorry to disappoint you, but you can't be smug yet—he's still got another chance. He actually goes to the trouble of disconnecting from his ISP and dialing in again, hoping the system will assign him a different address. And he succeeds: He's now Loser!YouSuck@dialup-11.chi.loathsome.net and marches into your channel as if he were invited. Sigh. Okay, the "dialup-" bit is characteristic. The number changes. The "chi" part is probably a geographical identifier for Chicago—even he won't go as far as dialing long distance to annoy us (at least we hope he won't). So I think we're safe with this one:

```
/mode * +b *!*@dialup-*.chi.loathsome.net
```

Gee, had I known it would take so long, I'd have banned that one from the beginning.

It basically comes down to experience. Identify the variable parts of a user's mask and guess how far this user intends to go. An experienced channel operator would have used the last ban or even something slightly wider (like dropping the "dialup-" part, too). If the channel has no regular users from loathsome.net or has had trouble with them before, you could be lazy (and very effective) by banning the whole site:

```
/mode * +b *!*@*.loathsome.net
```

NOTE *While in this example the user was unable to change the geographical identifier without dialing long distance, this is not set in stone. IBM.net is a notorious example of how some providers assign addresses unrelated to a person's physical location. I can only presume it routes a user to any available node if the local one is full, even one in a different state. While its users may find this convenient, that method can cause a major headache in dealing with abusers on IRC. AOL (aol.com) is even worse because addresses are taken from an immense pool with no form of identifier.*

10.5.2 Ban Problems

Problems with ineffective bans aren't just embarrassing to an op who's frantically trying to get rid of an abuser, but also endanger a channel under attack, since often much depends on being able to get the attackers off the channel fast. You may see two scenarios: The server appears to have accepted your ban, but they keep coming back despite it; or the server doesn't seem to be accepting your ban. For each of these conditions, there are two possible reasons.

If you're seeing the mode change for the ban, but it doesn't seem to be working, first check the ban mask. If it isn't accurate, remove the ban and place the correct one. This can happen if you use an alias to ban or kick and ban, which adds an asterisk before the user name to allow for an ident-related character such as a tilde (~) leading the user name, whether such a character is present or not.

This is a questionable feature in some scripts If the user name is longer than nine characters, the additional asterisk definitely brings it over the limit of ten characters, the maximum for the user name field in a ban. For example, putting an asterisk before the username "mumbo-jumbo" would make the ban you send contain an eleven-character user name, causing the server to drop any characters beyond the tenth. So the user name the server would ban would be "*mumbojumb"—which does not match. If you're positive about the ban's accuracy, the problem is likely to be a channel desync (see 10.9), which is more serious and really tough to deal with.

If you're sending the ban and the server isn't reacting, the problem is with the bans currently in place for the channel. Some servers allow you to have no more than 20 bans for a channel (this can become more under strange network conditions, so don't be surprised if you do see over 20). Check the number of bans on the list and remove as many as needed to bring them under the limit of 20. Make sure you remove the less important ones first. On IRCnet the total is 30 for **e**, **b**, and **I** modes combined. EFnet allows you 25 bans.

The other cause can be that one of the existing bans is too similar to the one you're trying to set. This is a problem with the server code—a bug nobody has worked on eliminating. Annoyingly, this happens if you're trying to extend a ban by placing a broader one than is already in place for the site—necessary if an abuser starts appearing from different machines of the same provider after you've already banned him or her from one, and you have to ban the whole domain. In this case, first remove the previous ban and then set the new one.

Another annoying thing can happen while you're trying to remove a ban. You remove it, and shortly afterward the server resets the ban. This can happen a few times in a row and results from bad network conditions. Lagged servers that eventually split off from the rest fail to see your mode change and continue to see the ban as present. When they rejoin in the syncing process, which we'll have a closer look at in the next section, the ban is restored to the channel on your server, too.

10.6   Server-Generated Mode Changes

You'll often see a server apparently giving people ops. This follows a netjoin and is part of the process called *syncing*. Nethacks are attempts to exploit this and obtain channel ops against the will of the current ops. No, the server hasn't gone crazy and is not giving out ops to whoever asks for them. Those who do get server ops have (normally) already gotten ops from another legit source before the split happened.

Following a netsplit and subsequent rejoin, your server sees all users who were on the other side of the split and hence not visible from your server as signing on again and joining the channel. While they never did sign off (from their point of view you and everyone else who was still visible to you signed off) and their server views them as opped, yours doesn't see that and considers them newly joined nonops. The same applies for you as seen from their server. So the servers try to fix such a discrepancy by negotiating the modes of a channel if they aren't the same on both sides. They "sync" the channel so that its modes are the same on all servers of the net. This is basically done cumulatively—each of the negotiating servers accepts what the other tells it is a mode for the channel if it's missing (remember that ops and voices are channel modes), so that both servers end up with the same set of modes for the channel by adding whatever the other tells them to.

If you recall the channel's modes and ops before a brief netsplit and compare them to those after the rejoin, you'll often find them to be identical. The sync also includes mode changes the operators of either side performed while the netsplit was in progress, and forwards these to the other side. For example, if you set a ban during the split, the sync sends the ban to the rejoining servers.

Nethacks are attempts to obtain ops on a channel by creating the channel on a server that is split off and has no users. Since none of the channel's users are on that server, two things happen: The channel's users will not see the split, since splits make their presence known only when it affects one or more users of the channel, and the fact that, since the server views the channel as empty, it will also give ops to a user who creates it. The intruder then gets ops for all servers when the channel syncs after the netjoin, and hopes to catch the regular ops unaware and deop them—which brings us to . . .

10.7   Channel Security

This is a very important part of running a channel, especially on networks with no channel service. Here are descriptions of how to keep a channel as trouble-free as possible.

10.7.1   Nethacks

Nethacks are only a tiny part of a phenomenon practitioners have developed into a science—and the best of them have advanced it to a fine art. This is the science of harassment, and in this case it involves seizing control of a channel by obtaining op privileges against the will of the current ops.

Channel services that enable users to register and effectively own channels have put an end to this practice on many networks, since the owner or another authorized user can quickly regain ops using the service.

While channel ownership services are in high demand, and most small networks have one, two of the major networks and a few of the minor ones don't run such a service. They stick to the tradition demanding that the current operators be considered the only authority over a channel. Although there have been great improvements recently in the mechanisms preventing nethacks, "hacking" ops is not impossible, and some people still consider it a form of sport. I put "hacking" in quotes, since it has nothing to do with real hacking.

"Hacking" ops on IRC is at best a juvenile and antisocial occupation, and definitely shouldn't be associated with what serious hacking experts are capable of. While not necessarily legal or condoned, the work of hackers has been the major contributor to modern computer security by detecting and pointing out security holes in every conceivable system, and even those who don't approve of it respect it. "Hacking" ops is unimaginative and destructive. The two major nets lacking a channel service (EFnet and IRCnet) use different methods of preventing nethacks, and we'll have a look at these mechanisms now.

Some types of server also unset modes upon a netjoin (deop someone, for example). This feature is part of the system known as TimeStamp (TS), and is not part of the basic server code but of its patches, which servers on EFnet are required to use and which most other networks have implemented as well. Channels and nicknames get assigned time stamps when they're created (hence the name), which the servers compare against each other while syncing. If one part of the channel has a different time stamp from the other (which is bound to happen when a channel is newly created on one side of the split), the one with the older stamp is considered the "real" channel, and its modes are authoritative. New channel modes brought from the "new" channel are reversed. Users on the older side will see no changes, apart from the join of the clients on the rejoined part of the net. Many EFnet servers will *not* grant ops on a newly created channel while the server is split.

The other method is nick delay/channel delay (ND/CD), which we've already encountered in 6.2.7 and 7.3.7—it is used on IRCnet and is partially implemented on EFnet. This system tries to prevent the conditions that would permit nethacks and collisions by making the nick or channel unavailable for a while following irregular signoffs and netsplits, rather than allowing the nethack attempt but reversing it when the servers rejoin, as TS does. Both methods have their advantages and problems, but in practice EFnet's TS system, implemented on every server of the network, is significantly more effective in preventing intentional nick collisions and channel takeovers. It also has the side effect of making it well-nigh impossible to restore ops on an opless channel.

While there are nethack prevention systems even on networks with no channel service, nothing is totally foolproof. Unusual network conditions can permit takeovers or collisions, and it's up to the channel's operators to secure their channel against attack.

Before approaching management of channel security, you should make sure you have a secure and attack-resistant client. With regular nethacks less easy, abusers tend to direct their attacks at the operators' clients more than ever. You may be an expert channel op, but if your client is susceptible to attack, you won't be around to defend your channel.

Another important point is having a secure machine. With more and more flood-proof clients, abusers now resort to attacking the ops' networked machines instead (see 17.7), and you should give much attention to securing your machine against such attacks. It goes without saying that a channel where an op is infected with some sort of Trojan (see 2.2.1) allowing anyone to take over his client is lost if anyone cares to make use of the Trojan to control an op client.

10.7.2 Flooders and Cloners

Probably the most common method of harassment and takeovers since the early days is flooding, particularly clone floods. The number of widely available scripts with such "features" is large and rising as the authors of popular clients (primarily mIRC, the most widely used client) enhance them with advanced scripting features permitting creation of such. With this turn of events, even the humble Windows dial-up turns into a considerable tool for abusers.

Floods are mostly used to try and force the channel ops' clients to disconnect and ideally do the same to all other clients on the channel. This makes it possible for the attacker to gain channel ops by re-creating the channel once everyone has been flooded off and the channel is empty. A flood-proof client is the best protection.

Flood nets are a greater menace since they're coordinated attacks by more than one user. Often the attackers use egg-drop bots with special add-ons. These are generally more powerful since they can be networked, thus achieving better synchronization, and also tend to have more computing power and bandwidth behind them.

To combat floods successfully, you should be able to identify the type of flood and react to it fast. A **+m** mode change for the channel is often very effective since it stops the attacking clients from sending their flood to the channel. An additional mode change to **+i** also prevents more of them from joining. These simple mode changes are much faster than looking up the attacker's mask and banning, especially if more than one host is involved. Then you can kick the attacking clients while the **+i** mode prevents them from rejoining. You may set the ban at leisure once they're gone, and remove the **+im** mode so the channel can resume its normal operation and the friendly clients disconnected by the flood can rejoin. A hot key to set mode **+im** in an emergency isn't a bad idea.

If you have a bot on the channel, you should set it to detect and react to floods and also to multiple joins from the same address, if it supports such functions. Bots are generally designed to be flood-resistant, but could often do with some tweaking in that direction through the configuration. Chapter 17 covers the different types of floods and ways of dealing with them.

A good preventive measure against clone floods is using mode l as a standard setting on the channel. Make the limit high enough to allow for plenty of users, but low enough to prevent massive numbers of clients from joining. If your limit is reasonable, you can easily have as many users on the channel as you like and still reduce the potential damage from clone attacks. This method has served me well, and I strongly recommend it.

Since we mentioned clones, we should also look at the meaning of the term. Recent advances in biotechnology and their media coverage have made this a very trendy word, but people were cloning on IRC long before the guys in the white coats cloned a sheep. Clones on IRC are multiple connections from the same user or machine. Depending on the servers' tolerance for multiple connections, a user may be able to connect 5, 10, or a few dozen clients. It's not impossible, since many clients allow "raw" server connections, used for cloning.

Because of the time and accuracy required, users rely on scripts to connect the clones swiftly to the server. An increasingly common form of clone is the *distributed* clone. This clone tries to mask itself from the servers' operators by spreading all over the network, connecting only one or two clones to each server on its list, and it is indeed harder to detect.

Clone floods, as the term implies, are instances in which the attacker uses clones to flood—which is just about the only thing they're good for. The reason these sad individuals use clones to flood is because 10 clients can send data to a server 10 times faster than a single client. It wouldn't be hard to use a single client to send data at the same rate, but one client would never survive it because of the servers' limits on the rate at which a client may send data to them. So if a single client sent at the rate of nine lines in a given period, the server would boot it for flooding if the server's limit were a rate of 8 lines for a single client. But 10 separate server connections (clones) could each send eight lines, since the server views them as separate clients and permits each individual the maximum limit. So a set of 10 clones could send as many as 80 lines at a time without risking disconnection, whereas a single client would be allowed only 8.

10.7.3 Colliders

Attempts to get rid of the ops by causing nick collisions are more difficult to deal with. These attacks can be so swift that everyone is out within minutes and the channel becomes vulnerable to a takeover. On smaller channels it can take no more than seconds for a skilled collider to get rid of everyone.

Your first reaction upon seeing suspicious collisions (see 6.6.1) on a channel is to set the channel **+s**, yourself **+i**, and change nicknames, thus eliminating the possibility of being hit by an attacker who isn't on the channel. Take a **WHO** list and check it for users who have been a problem in the past or whose presence is suspicious. If invisible users on a **+s** channel still collide, there is definitely a spy on the channel informing the collider of the channel users' nicknames. Kick and ban any suspicious users—you can apologize *later* if you're wrong about them. Kick every user you don't know personally and won't vouch for if you have to.

Collision attacks are speedy and you must act fast. In this case it's better to be safe than sorry (you can be apologetic later). Change your nickname frequently for as long as you're not sure the spy is off the channel. The surest way to find the collider's identity is by identifying the part of the network or server the collisions are coming from and connecting a client to it. If there is a very lagged server in that group, the collider may be using it. Once you're there, use **WHOWAS** and **WHOIS** on a few of the collided nicknames. More often than not, you'll find they've come from the same host apart from the addresses of your channel's regular users, and you'll very likely see a client with that host mask lurking on the channel.

Once you've gotten rid of the collider, send your evidence to the server the collider was using, if you were able to identify the address. Collisions make a server look bad on the network, and admins will generally react to complaints.

10.7.4 Secure Auto-Ops

Neither of the aforementioned are the greatest risk to a channel's security, though. Careless opping causes most takeovers. Sometimes it's someone faking an address belonging to a regular—not impossible, but rare compared to cases of genuinely sloppy opping and criminally misconfigured auto-op lists.

Many channels use auto-op lists so the regulars can get ops without having to ask for them. Most scripts also contain such features. They are anything but foolproof and should be left to the more experienced users to set up. Still, even with a decent level of security and all the precautions, secure auto-ops are a myth. Use a password system instead.

For identifying the regular ops, you can divide users' host masks into two categories—those that are easily copied and those that are harder to fake. The more secure addresses are those with a steady host name and idented user name—meaning, basically, shell accounts. These can be on an auto-op list with the lowest risk of an imposter's assuming the address, unless the account itself is hacked. Ident is important in this case, since it's much harder to fake an idented address (normal "IP spoofs" can't ident themselves). Spoofs are not common nowadays, but I will not swear that you'll never run into one.

Dial-ups are a different kettle of fish as far as auto-ops are concerned, and can be anything from fairly secure to begging for trouble. You should take much care to use the fewest possible wildcards in the host mask on the auto-op list; use the same methods as for bans. Some ISPs may give their users a static host name like myhost.demon.co.uk, which is as secure as a shell account as far as the address is concerned and may be so even with a variable user name. Again, ident is important—unidented address should not be auto-opped. Dial-up users should always have ident enabled before you give them ops, for more security against fake addresses.

In adding users to a bot's auto-op list, follow the above rules and do not rely on the bot's add user functions, since these generate insecure entries on the list by allowing unidented users and wildcarding that's too large a part of the host name. This is especially risky with users from very large ISPs. One typical example of such a high-risk ops list included host names like *.netcom.com, *.aol.com, *.att.net, *.ibm.net, and other comparably large sites. Since those sites have immense numbers of dial-up users matching those masks and each of them can assume any user name, such a list would effectively have half the Internet on auto-op for anyone who cared to use the user name on the list. The above are real examples taken from an actual ops list and not uncommon. Don't be lazy about it—manually enter the address to add.

If you want to be even more security conscious, put only the bare minimum necessary for running the channel on the auto-op list, like the bots and the most secure addresses, and make the rest use a password to get ops. All good bots support passworded ops, and some of the better channel management scripts do, too. Passworded ops offer the highest possible level of security without going to great troubles and being too paranoid.

Another point I can't repeat often enough: *Do not ever* op someone by nick alone. Nicks are the easiest thing in the world to fake. If you're not positive of the user's identity from the conversation on the channel, check the host mask first. Even if you are, it's a good habit to always do a **WHOIS** before opping someone. All too often someone wanting to take over plants a bot on the channel with the nick of a regular who isn't on at the time, then waits for a sucker to give it ops—after which the bot deops everyone while its owner rubs his hands in glee. Giving out ops based on the nick alone amounts to almost criminal negligence.

One more word regarding protection—various scripts include a feature describing itself as "nethack protection." This considers any user joining the channel and getting ops from the server as an attempt to hack ops, and deops that user. Nethack protection is not for the clueless. Turn it off unless you're capable of making it recognize all regulars and not deop them. Few things are as embarrassing as rejoining a channel after a split and deopping everyone. Two or more bad net-hack prots on the channel can cause serious instances of desync (see 10.8).

Now that we've gone to so much pain to make sure our auto-ops are safe, let's throw it all out the window in the light of address spoofing. Not everyone can do it, but someone who can is capable of assuming any host name he or she wishes to *and* be idented. The servers can prevent this, but there is no guarantee that all servers on a network will be secure. If you suspect someone of being an address spoofer, use /**stats L nickname** (note the capital L). This returns an IP address. Use your lookup command (**nslookup** or /**dns**) to resolve that IP address. If it doesn't match the user's address, congratulations—you have gotten yourself a spoofer. The IRCops of the servers the spoofer is on will probably be interested.

So the bottom line remains: Don't auto-op at all if you can avoid it. Write a script that exchanges passwords before opping.

10.7.5 If a Takeover Does Happen

So they finally managed it—you're now locked out of your channel after your attackers got ops, deopped everyone, and kicked the lot of you out. Of course, you're trying to think of ways to get the channel back.

The traditional way of dealing with the problem is simply to let the culprits have it, create a new channel, and invite everyone to it. Of course, this isn't that effective for larger channels whose name is a point of reference. It helps if the regulars have an agreed place to fall back to, but newer users and people who might be interested in the channel would have a hard time finding it. Letting them have it for a while is not the fastest way of getting a channel back, but it's probably the most effective—they'll eventually get bored and leave it.

One thing that will not work is using the same methods they used. Since they managed to take over, you can bet they're familiar with anything you might try and will be prepared for it. What's more, they may have escaped detection by the operators when using questionable means that are against the servers' rules, but you might not be that lucky when you try to strike back. An operator will not accept a channel takeover as an excuse for a counterattack—if the server's policy defines the methods you use as abusive, you're asking for a **K:** line as much as the takeover people did, and may well end up with a lost channel and a few **K:** lines. IRC operators almost universally hate being dragged into channel disputes. If they gained ops by means such as clone floods or collisions and you have a log of their actions, you could try mailing the server's admin address asking for redress. Of course, if the takeover happened because of an op's carelessness or stupidity, the regulars will have to pick the mess up themselves.

Much depends on the reason for the takeover—whether it was a disagreement between the regulars resulting in one party throwing the other out (known as an op war), an attack from someone who holds a grudge against the channel, a takeover from someone who just found your channel attractive (which amounts to no reason at all), or a battle in an everlasting fight over the channel. As motives vary, so does the duration of the takeover and the willingness or reluctance of those holding it to give it back.

Op wars are generally resolved fairly soon—within no more than a day—and everyone returns to the channel, gets ops again, and lives together happily until the next op war.

Someone who takes over the channel just for the sport will generally lose interest soon after having spoiled someone's fun on IRC—they often stay on the channel only as long as they can negotiate with its regulars from a position of power or get a good fight. These are the social dropouts trying to blow their chance of using IRC creatively. Shamelessly playing up to their egos by conceding victory and acknowledging superiority sometimes works miracles. The workings of the human mind are mysterious, and you might be able to use them to your advantage. Some of them will actually listen to reason and just need a break to become part of a group—nobody really enjoys being a loser.

If someone took the channel as an act of revenge against its users for some real or imagined offense, they usually won't be that easy to get rid of. Your best chance of getting it back as soon as possible is to ignore them. The less annoyance you show, the less effective their actions will seem to them.

If the channel is the object of a fight between rival groups, none of which is willing to concede, you'll probably never find a solution. Wars of this kind have been known to go on for years, even with control over the channel changing hands at regular intervals.

Takeovers rarely have an easy solution, but force is not the way to deal with one. Don't panic—stop to consider the best way to get it back.

10.7.6 Be Careful Who You Op

As one old-timer used to say, "A channel that ops together stays together." This romantic notion has its share of truth, but, while the world could be a big happy place full of honest ops, we must also bear in mind that trust does have its limits and the world has more crooks than saints. The truth in this statement lies in the fact that you should cast aside personal disagreements or keep them private in favor of keeping the channel going.

Whether you created the channel and others joined afterward, or you became part of the op team on an established, popular channel, people are relying on you—not only to handle possible emergencies, but also not to put the channel at risk by opping the wrong people. Some people shouldn't be trusted with ops, and letting one of these people have them can jeopardize the normal operation of the channel.

Again, as we said in section 10.7.4, never op someone who looks like a regular if you're not sure it's really that individual. As convincing as they may be, always check their **WHOIS** before giving out ops and make sure it does match their known host mask, especially with unidented clients, since lack of ident is almost universal to spoofed (faked) addresses. If you're still not sure it's the right person, it does no harm to leave them opless unless you urgently need another op on the channel. If you have a bot from which regular users can get ops on request, let them use it.

Mistrust op beggars. Whether they try to convince you by smooth talking, demanding, or pathetic whining, consider it a principle not to give them ops. The channel will decide if it wants them to be ops. On practically all channels, op beggars get a warning and are kicked off the channel if they insist. Less patient ops kick them off right away.

Don't op people just because they're friendly. Even if their intentions are the best, some people don't learn how to run a channel. More than one channel has suffered from regular and very friendly users who are incompetent channel ops.

10.7.7 *Suspect until Proven Guilty*

In your career as a channel op, you'll also encounter suspicious clients on the channel. As a channel op, it's within your rights to remove them from the channel even if you're not 100 percent certain they're misbehaving.

For example, some of your users, especially less experienced ones, may start quitting with "excess floods." Set the channel **+s**—if the flooder is outside the channel he or she will no longer be able to see its clients with **WHO**. If it continues, scan the channel for suspicious clients—nonregulars who aren't talking at all, known troublemakers, and so forth.

Less directly annoying but more insidious are takeover bots that lurk on the channel waiting for a chance to gain ops. Ban these upon detection. Be especially wary of any botlike clients sitting quietly on the channel pretending to be part of the decoration.

You will also have to look out for people infected with Trojans (see 2.2.1). While they generally don't constitute a direct threat to the channel, outsiders may use them to gain information about the channel without ever joining it. Many Trojans also autosend themselves to everyone who joins or parts a channel, thus spreading the disease. Send these people to some good Web page with a "cure" and don't be too scrupulous about kicking them out. They present a health hazard.

Another category of suspect clients whom I consider guilty by default is not as easy to spy. They take advantage of misconfigured proxy servers to hide their real identity. You commonly see them from machines with "proxy," "gateway," "gw," or "gate" in the host name, though many aren't that obvious. These clients are almost always unidented, apart from some that appear with a "root" user name; a very few have a different, idented user name. They're up to no good.

10.8 Channels with No Operators

Whether through accident, carelessness, or malicious activity, it sometimes happens that a channel finds itself with no ops. If you don't have a channel service on the network that you can use to give someone ops, you'll have to resort to one of two methods to regain ops.

The first method—and the more effective one, if applied correctly—is to clear the channel by having everyone leave it so that it can be restarted, with the first user becoming its op. This is best done when there are few users on the channel and all are regulars. The more users there are on the channel, the harder it is to get them out. Often there are highly frustrating scenes with everyone trying to get ops first and trying to rejoin the channel before it's been emptied. You end up a nervous wreck because you're doing exactly the same as everyone else and achieving precisely the same result—zip. Stay outside for a while and let someone else get the ops.

This method fails if there is a bot on the channel and it's not configured to regain ops on a channel if left alone and opless, plus there is no user present with the level of access to make the bot leave the channel. This is one more instance of a misconfigured or inferior bot making a nuisance of itself; an unauthorized bot runs a serious health hazard when the users finally have to ask the server's operators to kill it off so they can regain ops. They usually get a gratuitous **K:** line for the bot thrown in with the deal.

The second way is less conventional and requires a combination of expertise and luck—not necessarily in proportion. Find a split server and re-create the channel on it to get ops. If there were no ops on the channel before the split, the server's protective mechanisms will not be activated (since there are no legit channel ops to be protected), so you can do it. However, on EFnet you can reckon with the majority of servers not allowing you do this at all.

Remember that using link-looker scripts to find a split server can get you into trouble with the server's operators. While some channels survive for a fair amount of time with no ops, the inability of its users to remove abusers means they cannot resist attacks. In the meantime, the attackers may also be trying to get ops using the method described above.

10.9   Desync

Desync is a condition of varying severity in which different servers of a network view the channel as having different users and/or modes. Mild forms of desync may just involve a missing ban or two, while serious cases can make a real mess of the channel. Many different modes on the servers can get involved, and one part of the network might even have no ops, while the rest sees the channel as it should be.

The problem more often than not stems from nethack attempts and op wars, with some mode changes made before a server is ready to accept them. Dumb scripts that clueless channel ops use, containing something called "net-hack protection," can create the same kind of mess and are in fact the most common reason for it. If there is also a lot of lag, it could become bad enough to render the channel useless. In some cases, bad network conditions with much lag and many splits can be the sole cause of a desync, with mode changes sometimes not propagating across the whole network. In that case, channels can be missing a few modes.

You can fix milder conditions where there are still ops on all parts of the network by checking the modes carefully. You ideally make changes from a client that all parts of the net see as an op. If there are only users with ops on different parts of the net, they should op each other first. If a globally recognized op doesn't make the mode changes, the desync will propagate to include modes set by the user, whose op status is also subject to the desync—meaning that half the net will not recognize the user as an op and will ignore the mode changes. The optimal way of getting rid of a desync like this is for the user with ops on all servers to clear all modes and reset those needed.

Now the question arises: How do you know you're desynced?

You should suspect desync if some of the users are receiving error messages they shouldn't. If someone's told "You are not a channel operator" when trying to perform an op function, and that user is certainly an op, you're desynced. The same holds true when someone is told "Unable to send to channel" while you can see him or her and the channel is not moderated. This second message doesn't necessarily indicate a mode desync. It could also mean that the user isn't on the channel at all, according to some server, and should leave and rejoin so that all servers see the **JOIN** and consider the user on the channel.

You won't notice bans that aren't working until you come under attack and someone keeps getting past it. There's no easy answer to this one—try to find one of the attacker's server operators to get him killed before he does too much damage.

The messages indicating there's desync somewhere often have the name of the first server the discrepancy appears on. This server is the "desync point." That and all servers beyond it from your point of view don't see the same modes for the channel as you do. If you can't immediately see the desync point in one of these messages, look for a server on which one of the channel's users has detected desync and where you know there is desync relative to yours. Use the **TRACE** command (see 15.7) to see which servers are between you and the desynced server. If the desync is about a user present on the channel or about an op, use the **WHOIS** command to compare what each server sees (see 9.1):

```
/whois <server> <nickname>
```

If you see yourself as an op, use your own nickname and check whether all servers think you're an op. Do this for each server in the chain. The first server to return something different from your own is the desync point. From the other side of that server, the server you see as preceding it in the server chain is the desync point, since if queried it would return something different from what those servers can see. Even more complicated but rare cases are three-way desyncs—three different sets of modes or users on three different parts of the net. The same methods of correcting desync apply to these as well, but take more time to implement and check. It's just as well this kind of desync is rare.

Now let's have a look at the more serious cases in which a part of the network sees no ops at all. If it follows a takeover attempt, there may even be modes like **+imk** that make the channel useless or unreachable on that part of the net. Desyncs like this can be fixed only if the desynced part gets an op for the channel. Getting ops from your side is impossible, since according to the desynced server no mode change from that side would be valid.

In many cases, a netsplit in the right place, followed by the rejoin and sync, will eventually correct this. This sounds slightly paradoxical— one fault fixing another—but if the split affects a server on which there is an opped client, after rejoining this client will be assigned ops throughout the network during the syncing process, and therefore appears as an op on the desynced servers, too. Then the restoration can begin from that client. Wow, two wrongs can make a right after all.

Say you can see the channel's modes according to the desynced part of the net by doing a **/mode #channel** from one of the desynced servers, and there are modes that aren't present on your server but need removing. A client that is opped on both sides (presuming that whoever got the ops also passed them on to the rest of the regular ops) has to set the offending modes and then unset them. On servers that don't allow redundant mode changes and reopping users, the client with the ops (and no other) must deop and then reop everyone.

Desync can also result from a semisuccessful takeover attempt. In this case the network divides into two parts, each having its own set of modes and users but different ops. Users on either side see the effects of the desyncs. This situation can also result from misconfigured net-hack protection, in which case the resolution is to have each side manually do what the server would have done if the stupid scripts hadn't kicked in, and set the missing modes on each side. If the two sides are not friendly to each other, though, this situation will result in a networkwide guerrilla war, with each side trying to propagate its own modes across the net and gain more ground with each netsplit while preventing the other side from doing the same. If the network is stable, with little lag and few splits, this could result in a stalemate that lasts for days.

As you see, there's often no easy solution for desync, and chance can play a large part in finally getting rid of it. The best solution is prevention. Don't let it happen if you can help it.

10.10 Channel Services and Registration

Channel services have become very fashionable ever since the concept of formal ownership of channels independent of the owner's presence was introduced. Today, channel services have become the norm, and are present on two of the major networks and most of the smaller ones in their bid to attract users by also catering to their proprietary whims. While considered an integral part of IRC life on these networks, they remain controversial on the rest. This indirect form of channel management (indirect because it allows you to make settings without actually being on the channel) is becoming increasingly popular as a way of maintaining a channel without the help of bots. It's also easy to use compared to the hard-core channel management we went into in the rest of this section. But what is considered its main feature—allowing channel ownership—is also its main drawback.

The channel is under the total control of an individual, who can easily overthrow any pretense of democracy and collective management. Networks that will register a channel to a number of users, as Undernet does, are a bit more open, but the oligarchy that method creates is subject to the afflictions particular to that political system.

Each network tends to have its own version of channel service, matching the network's ircd and containing the features that particular network wishes to offer its users in terms of indirect channel management. Appendix A lists the availability of such services on each network.

10.10.1 Undernet's X and W and Similar Services

This is the older kind of channel service—very hyped-up bots that enjoy special privileges with the servers. You don't normally do channel registration directly with the service, but rather with an email or Web application for use of its services. Undernet's channel service bots, nick-named X and W, are available to a channel with a group of users sharing its administration. Find information on how to register and how to use these bots at the Undernet Channel Service website (http://www. cservice.undernet.org). For small networks using a similar form of services, you should check their websites or ask for an administrative or help channel on the network itself. I do not wish to rehash what the fine online documents at the Undernet site explain much better, nor do I have anything to add.

10.10.2 DALnet ChanServ

DALnet is the only one of the major networks that offers easy and unconditional channel registration. ChanServ is the twin of NickServ and depends on it for information, as do other services.

In order to register a channel with ChanServ, you must have (and be using) a nickname registered with NickServ (see 6.3.3); if you do not have one, now is the time to register. Channel registration depends on the nickname—if the nickname expires or is dropped, all channels registered to it are also lost.

Many small networks use the same system. Most of them use their own custom service software, while others use EsperNet services—a rare public release of such a package, originally developed for the small EsperNet network. The basic principle behind all of them is the same, but in terms of features and usage they are as divergent as the server code, and there is no standard command set. You can, however, expect the basic commands to work in more or less the same way.

DALnet servers have an additional command set in which the name of the service is the name of the command. This is helpful in preventing messages meant for a service from getting sent to impostors by mistake. So instead of

```
/msg ChanServ <ChanServ command>
```

it would be

```
/chanserv <ChanServ command>
```

and the server would take care of delivering the message to ChanServ. The same concept applies to other services. You can expect this to work on all networks running the DALnet ircd. Others may have it as well.

For a list of ChanServ commands on the network you're using, send the service a **HELP** command, such as

```
/chanserv help
```

or

```
/msg chanserv help
```

The output will look a bit like this:

```
-> *chanserv* help
-ChanServ- ***** ChanServ Help *****
-ChanServ- ChanServ gives normal users the ability to keep hold of
a
-ChanServ- channel, without the need for a bot. Unlike other IRC
networks,
-ChanServ- channel takeovers are virtually impossible, when they
are registered.
-ChanServ- Registration is a quick and painless process. Once
registered,
-ChanServ- the founder can maintain complete and total control of
the
-ChanServ- channel. ChanServ will stop monitoring a channel if no
Op enters
-ChanServ- the channel for 20 days or the founder's nick expires.
-ChanServ- For more information on a command /msg ChanServ help
<command>
-ChanServ- Core Commands:
-ChanServ- REGISTER–Register a channel
-ChanServ- SET–Change various channel configuration settings
-ChanServ- SOP–Maintain SuperOp channel operator list
-ChanServ- AOP–Maintain AutoOp channel operator list
-ChanServ- AKICK–Maintain the channel AutoKick banned user list
-ChanServ- DROP–Drop a registered channel
-ChanServ-
-ChanServ- Other Commands:
-ChanServ- IDENTIFY ACCESS OP DEOP
-ChanServ- INFO INVITE MKICK MDEOP
-ChanServ- UNBAN COUNT WHY
-ChanServ- ***** End of HELP *****
```

This text is taken from DALnet's ChanServ. Here are the things you should pay attention to: As you see in the notice, there is an expiration date. Unused channels—meaning ChanServ sees no op join them for 20 days—get automatically dropped. It may be more or less on other networks. Channels also expire if the nickname under which they were registered expires or is dropped. Use **HELP REGISTER** to see what you need to tell it in order to register a channel, and make sure you follow the instructions to the letter. You must be on the channel and an operator in order to register. You'll often be asked to identify yourself to NickServ before being able to register a channel.

Write down your password and put it in a safe place. If you give your password to anyone, nobody will be able to help you if the person who has it decides to snatch control of the channel from you. If you forget it, you can bug a special class of IRC operators, the CSops, but they'll expect you to have a fair guess of what the password was and would really prefer it if you didn't require their services at all.

There are three levels of access: founder, SOP, and AOP. The founder is the person who owns the nick under which the channel was registered. SOPs rank beneath the founder, but above AOPs. The founder determines how much access to the channel's settings each class gets. By sending ChanServ the **HELP SET** command, it will show you how to set access levels as well as a menu of channel settings such as a default topic or a URL displayed to people joining the channel. Explore the help menus and find out all you need to know.

Because ChanServ is generally an integral part of the network, operating under the umbrella of a dedicated server, it's also subject to the same outages and failures as any server. Do not take its presence for granted. Learn how to operate a channel manually in an emergency, as this chapter described.

Our next step will be into the realm of pure technicality. The next chapter contains the joys and frustrations of scripting—programming a client. Find out how to become more efficient as a user and operator by enhancing your client with scripts. As I said, this is technical and not for the faint-hearted, but I'll do my best to make it as painless as can be. Basic scripting is really pretty simple and straightforward, but if you really don't care to get that technical yet and don't feel the need for client add-ons, skip ahead to Chapter 12 and keep your sanity.

11

ENHANCING A CLIENT
WITH SCRIPTS

You have no doubt noticed the many references to scripting in earlier sections and are curious about all the things they are supposed to do. Scripting is a form of programming, instructing a client to monitor events and perform some action if they meet certain conditions, or to execute a series of commands. Not all clients support scripting, and those that do each use different scripting languages and different capabilities.

11.1   What Scripts Are

A script is a file loaded into the client, containing settings and commands meant to modify a client's behavior with some degree of automation, or that enable the user to perform commands or sequences of commands with more speed and precision than manual execution would make possible. IRC scripts are used to detect events and react to them automatically, execute conditional commands, shorten processes which would be long and tedious for the user, format the client's output to suit the user's tastes, and do a variety of other things. For those clients that support scripts, there are numerous *script paks*, which are combinations of smaller and larger scripts and settings for the client. Their quality varies from good to garbage — sometimes even a security hazard if loaded. Scripts don't do anything a user couldn't do manually, but they add speed to a procedure, react faster to events than a live user possibly could, and simply make tasks easier.

11.2 Why Use a Script?

This is a good question. People often use scripts of questionable functionality and security just because they've been given the impression that they "need" a script of some sort, without even knowing what they want to be done with one. The truth is that these scripts might look impressive, but do little more than set configuration options a user could easily set without scripting.

Some suggestions to keep in mind: First of all, don't use a script unless you need one and know what you want it for. Check to see whether your client can be configured to do what you want without scripting. Modern clients like mIRC, Pirch, or BitchX are capable of doing many things for which older clients needed a script. In fact, they'll perform better than a client-plus-script combination since the execution of functions that have been coded into the client will be faster.

11.3 Selecting a Script

The standard answer to the question "Which script should I use?" is "Write your own!" But it's a fact that most people, especially those who aren't the most avid IRC fans, have neither the time nor the knowledge to sit down and script. While scripting can be learned (basic scripting is simple), lack of time is a common reason people fall back on ready-made scripts.

Every client with a scripting language will have a number of scripts in circulation. Their quality varies from excellent and highly functional to messy and dangerous. Unfortunately, the latter group is the larger one, so much care should be taken when selecting a script. Naturally, scripts have command sets of their own, which can vary wildly. Apart from a few common commands most script authors seem to find practical, the rest of the bunch can make learning a script as time-consuming as learning to use a client. Widely available scripts often have items in common, mainly because they borrow parts of the code from older scripts.

Most items describing themselves as scripts are really script paks, collections of small scripts molded into a single entity and distributed as such.

11.4 Obtaining a Script

Another good reason for writing your own script or learning enough scripting is that you'll then be able to read a script and understand what it does. There are dozens of potential download sites for any given script, none of them though can guarantee that the script is in its original, undoctored form. Many scripts have Web pages of their own, from which you can download them. I do not recommend running any form of script, however small, that you can't at least look at to spot suspicious code. On the contrary, I strongly advise against running such scripts.

11.5 ircII Scripts

ircII was the first common scripting client. Its powerful scripting language has been one of its main attractions since it first appeared. Over time, users have developed many script paks, more good ones than bad. Most of them date back to 1993 to 1995, and very few are currently maintained. Their longevity, like that of the client itself, is unsurpassed, and some are used even today.

Archives of ircII scripts have become rare with time, and none of the classic old collections work nowadays, due to lack of interest, neglect, or people putting their storage space to better use. You could have a peek at ftp.asu.net for a motley collection of old scripts. I've found most of these to be of little use; a few are useful, but all of these are severely outdated (since I maintain it, I can let you in on the secret that no part of the archive has been added or removed since 1996). However, this may be the only archive with a chance of being updated some time in the future. If you want some good ideas for specific scripts, check out http://www.irchelp.org/ircii/.

11.5.1 Phoenix, TextBox, and Atlantis

Phoenix is one of the best known and widely used ircII scripts. Unfortunately, its availability is much higher than its quality and there are numerous "doctored" versions of it around, which make it risky. Its code is generally cumbersome and slow, loaded with totally unnecessary features.

To quote M.D. Yesowitch in the EBOAI IFAQ, "The author is a nice enough guy, but he can't code."

TextBox is another common script. Easier to use than Phoenix and less messy, TextBox shares its love for useless "smart" features. Again, most of it is a waste of memory; it could easily be reduced to a fraction of its size and retain its functionality.

Atlantis, while having no advantage over the previously mentioned scripts, is also one of the most dangerous scripts in this family, in the sense that there are many copies in circulation to which various malicious additions have been made. Beware.

As you may have guessed, I recommend none of the above. And there are many script paks like those above that offer a fair amount of convenience, little quality, and not enough security.

11.5.2 PurePak

One of the more feature-packed and powerful scripts, PurePak is a better choice than most. It should be used only by more advanced users wanting a script with good configurability and numerous features other scripts miss. Configuring it isn't easy, and beginners should avoid attempts to do so — it could present them with more problems than benefits.

11.5.3 LiCe

One of the very popular scripts, LiCe is set to surpass Phoenix as the most widely used ircII script. LiCe offers few new features but is much more user-friendly than others and has gained in popularity, even among IRC operators. Use it with care (as you should all scripts), since some of its features can create unintentional havoc if used by lazy people who don't bother to configure it correctly. Despite its popularity and many features, I cannot wholeheartedly recommend it.

11.5.4 JoloPak

Now here's a script everyone should start out with. Joseph Lo has created a modern, friendly script pak designed to be changed by its user. No obscure code and traps, just clean, annotated scripting meant to provide an example for you to follow when building your own custom script. Get it at http://www.irchelp.org/ircii/. Five stars.

11.5.5 Generic Scripts

Before you go out looking for scripts, here's a selection of scripts that are packaged with the ircII client and should be located in the **/usr/local/share/irc/scripts** directory (**/usr/local/lib/irc/script** for older versions), to which they are copied during the installation process. Some of them are outdated and useful only with older versions of the client, while others are toylike and do strange or amusing things to your client. A few of these scripts are extremely useful and are often included in the other scripts or paks mentioned above. In fact, with a few aliases and some generic scripts, you can easily build a smart and simple pak for your personal use.

Here are the generic scripts you are most likely to want:

cursor   Allows you to navigate the command line and command history with the arrow keys.

netsplit   Consolidates multiple signoffs and joins due to netsplits and netjoins into single notices and records the nicknames who left in a split.

tabkey   Allows you to use the TAB key to recall the nicknames of previous message or DCC partners.

basical   Contains a basic set of aliases, shortcuts and tweaks, which you can modify to your liking. Not brilliant but very handy and a good starting point.

The first three (and perhaps one or two others), plus a set of uncomplicated aliases and event monitors that are trivial to code, can be combined into a surprisingly good tool of your own. Try it.

11.6 mIRC Scripts

There are many, many archives of mIRC scripts out there. You will find some of them listed on http://www.mirc.co.uk, although I recommend none of them. Unfortunately, there is not much in the way of distinguishing between quality scripts and junk. Do check these archives out, but pay attention to their general attitude towards scripts altogether.

The one archive I can recommend is the one at http://mirc.stealth.net/addons/, which serves useful scripts created mainly by the operators of EFnet's **#mirc** channel and some add-ons and popups that you might find attractive—including smart ASCII art popups that will probably get you kicked out of any channel where you're not a regular, but which you'll nevertheless be tempted to deploy.

11.6.1 LiOn, QPro, vyxx, and a Few Others

These are the minority in the mIRC script world, because they are written by people who take IRC seriously. These scripts and the few like them are the stars of mIRC scripts. They're made with more useability and less warfare in mind, and can actually improve and enhance your mIRC client's functions without turning it into an abuse tool. If you believe you must have a script and aren't inclined to put one together yourself, I'd say this is is the way to go. Their characteristics vary, but what they have in common is solid, functional code and a high level of protection from attacks on your client.

11.7 Write Your Own!

This is always the best option. Scripting for any IRC client is enough to fill any book, and I don't have quite that much space at my disposal here. I also firmly believe that the mIRC and ircII help files are very well written, and people should be encouraged to read them. What I will provide you with here is descriptions of the concepts and tools you'll be using. One more thing you can do is examine an existing script and apply what you found here and in help files to it. In fact, many people start scripting by hacking existing scripts to their liking.

If you use mIRC, the primary section for storing scripts is the *remote*. This is the basic tool for adding functionality to your client. Combined with popups that you can also write yourself (or the lack thereof), you can make it behave like anything from an ircII-like efficiency tool to the ultimate in bee's-knees GUI toys. Startup scripts go in the **script.ini** file which acts more or less like the **.ircrc** file does for ircII.

11.7.1 Aliases

An easy way to group together sequences of commands to be executed with a single command. An alias can act as a reference for another alias and even act as a variable. So, if you wanted to check the server's version and date, you would write an alias containing the **VERSION** and **TIME** commands after each other, separated by a special *command delimiter* (usually a semicolon) to show that one command ends and another begins. Here's what this would look like in ircII:

```
ALIAS VT version;time
```

Case is unimportant. The same alias would look like this in mIRC:

```
ALIAS:VT:/version;/time
```

Notice that mIRC separates the fields with a colon while ircII doesn't really care about spacing. Also note that mIRC requires the forward slash (/) command character even in an alias, whereas ircII does not. These are examples of the difference between different clients' scripting languages. There is no such thing as "IRC scripting" — only scripting in a particular language, that is usually unique to the client. (In both examples above, you'll notice a semicolon is used to separate commands that are to be run in sequence.)

Another common use of aliases is to shorten existing commands. Let's take the **MSG** command as an example. You may think it's already short enough, but lazy people such as yours truly like a command they use so often to be as short as possible. Well, it can't get much shorter than **M** so you could alias **M** to **MSG** so that if you type /**M**, the **MSG** command will be executed. If I had a penny for every keystroke I've saved typing /**M** instead of /**MSG**, my bank account would look a lot healthier than it does now. Any command or command sequence you perform more than once a week could probably benefit from being made into an alias.

11.7.2 Events

You can make your client listen for events with the **ON** command. The type of events is pretty much the same from client to client. Examples of events are: **JOIN** for someone joining a channel; **PUBLIC** for a message sent to a channel; **SERVER_NOTICE** for notices received from a server; and many more. Upon noticing the event the **ON** is meant to intercept, it will perform a command or series of commands in a way similar to an alias. In fact, the command could be an alias instead of a regular command. **ON** events will often have modifiers to control whether the client will react to the event, perform what it would normally do and execute a command, whether it will suppress its normal action and perform only the command hooked to the **ON**, or whether it will perform both and notify the user of its actions. The last form is used for debugging purposes and not used under real operating conditions.

ON is used not only to detect events and react to them, it can also be used to influence the client's display of an event. With an **ON JOIN**, you could format channel joins the way you like to have them displayed. The same goes for any other event. (Hint: Check out the **ECHO** command for displaying your own text.)

ON is the quintessence of automation. Without an event monitor like it, there could be no automated responses, and therefore scripts and bots would be largely nonexistent. The **ON** command set is rather extensive and complex in any modern client so your client's help files (/**help ON**) are definitely the best source of further information.

11.7.3 Conditions

Within both ONs and aliases, you can make your client perform an action only if certain conditions are met. This is illustrated in the way channel control scripts work: Client X joins the channel and is caught by the event monitor **ON** (the **ON JOIN** in this case). This checks whether a particular condition is true or false (predictably, the command is **IF**); for example, is this user's nickname a four-letter word? If yes, then kick him out. If the condition is not met, exit after performing the check. The same **ON JOIN** could be used to perform multiple checks on a joining user before exiting or there could be several different ON JOINs checking the same event.

11.7.4 User-Defined Variables

Conditions and aliases often rely upon variables. If you also had a variable called **KICK_FOUR_LETTER** you could have the **ON** example in the previous section check that. The same variable could be used not only for checking the nicknames of people joining the channel, but also for the messages sent to the channel. If its value is true, every four-letter offender would get kicked. If you felt like engaging in a cussing contest with someone, you could set it to a value meaning false so that the offender would never be kicked. Variables, as the term suggests, are flexible and their value can be changed on the fly. Variable structures can become very complex and combine with aliases and conditions to create something that looks like it makes very little sense to the average user.

While all clients come with their own set of built-in variables, such as **$N** (ircII) or **$me** (mIRC) meaning the client's nickname, users can define variables of their own by assigning them a name and value. These variables can then be used just like regular ones. Of course no client comes with a variable called **KICK_FOUR_LETTER**, so you'd have to add that one to the client.

11.7.5 Server Numerics

Clients can be made to react to numeric replies from the server. As defined in the protocol, there is a fixed set of numerics that are separated into error messages, replies, and other odd stuff. Typically, an error will sent as a numeric in the 400-499 range, a reply in the 300-399 range, etc. Minor variations in the syntax of the same numeric may be encountered from ircd to ircd, but most of them are trivial. Each type of ircd also uses an additional set of numerics for the output of commands or errors particular to that ircd. Therefore, some servers might use the same non-standard numeric for something totally different. A complete list of server numerics can be found in Appendix E.

Here are some examples of what numerics are used for and what they can mean. These numerics are the ones you're most likely to use in a script.

Numeric	Command	Meaning
001	None	Welcome message
002	None	Server name and version

Numeric	Command	Meaning
003	None	Channel and user modes supported
004	None	Time the current version of the server has been running
005	MAP	Server map
221	MODE	Your user modes
302	USERHOST	Client's userhost, oper, and away info
352	WHO	WHO information for a single client
353	NAMES	NAMES list
372	MOTD	MOTD line
375	MOTD	Beginning of MOTD
376	MOTD	End of MOTD
377	MOTD	Identical to 372, different numeric to work around clients that ignore 372
391	TIME	Date/time
421	Any	Command the server doesn't recognize
422	MOTD	Server has no MOTD

No source of information is as good as the client's own help files. IrcII, mIRC, and many others have large sections dedicated to scripting and there are many Web sites that also offer help on the subject.

11.7.6 Practical Scripting Tips

Here are some dos and don'ts, some shoulds and should nots for practical scripting. (Again, my friend Queux was instrumental in helping me put this list together.)

Example 1 (mIRC): Streamlining code

1a. Bad code:

```
if ($nick isop $chan) { set %x = 1 }
if ($nick !isop $chan) { set %x = 0 }
if (%x == 1) { halt }
if (%x == 0) { <do whatever> }
```

1b. Smarter code:

```
if ($nick isop $chan) { halt }
else { <do whatever> }
```

1b is faster because it's based on a true/false outcome instead of first setting a variable, then evaluating it and thereafter executing the action.

1b is not necessarily faster but it is "smarter" and more practical and handy. 1a in this example is rather clumsy.

Example 2 (mIRC): Avoiding unnessecary repetition

2a. Bad code:

```
.unset %tmpshare | .unset %tmpfile | .unset %tmpdir | .unset %tmpwho
```

2b. Smarter code:

```
.unset %tmp*
```

2a unsets a bunch of variables one at a time while 2b unsets **ALL** by running the **unset** command once only and using a wildcard in the variable name. 2b should therefore execute slightly faster and be more practical and functional because it unsets **ALL %tmp*** variables with one sweep — including those beginning with **%tmp** that you might have forgotten to remove earlier.

Example 3 (mIRC): Improving an existing command to reduce the need for repeating it

3a. One of the predefined aliases which comes with mIRC is:

```
/ping /ctcp $$1 ping
```

Using that command you can, in an editbox, type **/ping <nick>** and it will ping that single nick. But what do you do if you want to ping several nicks at once?

3b. A means of overcoming the one nick limitation can be:

```
/ping {
%tmptwh = $1- | %tmptot = $calc($pos(%tmptwh , $chr(32) , 0) + 1)
| :loop
if (%tmptot > 1) {
%tmptwx = $gettok(%tmptwh,1,32) | ctcp %tmptwx ping | %tmptwh =
$deltok(%tmptwh,1,32)
%tmptot = $calc($pos(%tmptwh , $chr(32) , 0) + 1) | goto loop
}
else { ctcp %tmptwh ping } | .unset %tmp*
}
```

With the above lines you can now ping as many as you like simply by typing...

```
/ping <nick1> <nick2> <nick3>...
```

3b simply overcomes the 3a limitation of being able to /**ping** only one nick at the time and should therefore be more functional because it does what is stated above—it lets you /**ping** several nicks at once. Other than saving you the effort of pinging each nick individually, it has no practial function. Note how it applies the rules of example 2 and removes all the temporary variables (**%tmp***) it used before exiting. Remember that this particular one may be uneffective on servers of the hybrid-6 series (mainly some EFnet servers) due to changes in the server code.

Example 4 (mIRC): Don't assume everyone's client or machine work like yours, and presume you don't have their undivided attention

4a. Bad code:

```
splay c:\mirc\sounds\shutdown.wav
```

What if the user doesn't have his/her mIRC installed in **c:\mirc**? What if another wave is being played while executing this line? In either of those cases you will get an error.

4b. Smarter code:

```
if ($inwave == $false) { .splay $mircdir $+ sounds\shutdown.wav }
```

4a tries to play **shutdown.wav** from within a predefined path. 4a code has two basic flaws—it does not check to see if there's another ***.wav** file current being played and it assumes that the wave file **shutdown.wav** resides in **c:\mirc\sounds**. Not everyone installs mIRC in it's predefined path (which is **c:\mirc**) and so for those who haven't done so the command in 4a will fail, either due to the fact that another wave file is being played at the time or due to the fact that it cannot find the wave file.

    4b is much more intelligent and first checks to see if a wave file is currently being played. If not it tries to play **shutdown.wav** from the **sounds** subdirectory of where the running mIRC actually is installed. The real/true path is found using a built-in function—**$mircdir**—which returns the path to the currently running mIRC program. This also covers the possibility of the user having multiple copies of mIRC on the machine.

Example 5 (ircll): Using a script to work around differences between servers

Problem: There are several scripts that send out notices to the operators of a channel, thus excluding mere mortals from the conversation. The mIRC equivalent of this command would be **ONOTICE**. Some servers support this form of messaging directly, while others need a script that will compile a list of the nicknames to be noticed and send the notice. With the advent of hybrid-6 servers on EFnet, this became tricky because they no longer support sending notices to nickname lists, whereas DALnet server supported both so it hadn't been an issue. Therefore:

5a. No longer adequate code:

```
alias wall {
```

Script compiles nicknames into a comma separated list stored in a variable named **tmp.wall.str**

```
^notice $mid(1 500 $tmp.wall.str) [ops:$C] $0-
```

5b. Code that checks the server's version and uses the appropriate form of notice:

```
on ^002 "*" ^assign s_version $7
```

Extracts the server version from the server's greeting (eighth word in server numeric **002**) and stores it in a variable called **s_version**

```
assign nowall 2.8/hybrid-6* dal4.6*
```

Uses fixed list of server types where the regular /**wall** command should not be used

```
alias wall {
if (rmatch($S_VERSION $NOWALL))
```

Matches the **s_version** variable against the **nowall** variable and, if they match, sends a notice to **@#channel**. If not, it reverts to the old method and compiles a list of nicknames.

Thus the command is made to check what type of server it's connected to and act accordingly. If the server's behavior changes again, it may have to be rewritten. These are just the significant lines taken out of context; the remainder of the code is rather long and not important.

12

IRC OPERATORS

Now that you're familiar with channel ops and the way channels are run, let's have a look at a mysterious and even more powerful figure in the IRC world: the (gasp) IRC operator, known also as IRCop, oper, or server op.

You've never seen one, only heard the rumors about their godlike powers. Who are they? Where do they hang out? Do they even exist, or are they just a legend, IRC lore from the times when the Net was young?

12.1 Who They Are

Although often rated as very elusive creatures with magical properties, IRC operators do exist and really aren't that magical although some appear to be under the impression that they are. On the larger networks, the ratio of opers to users is rarely more than 1 in 200. This figure is larger than the actual number of opers present at any given time. Quite a few are idle clients left online 24 hours a day regardless of the operator's actual presence, and some are the servers' own robots, which monitor the server, gathering statistics or sending the human opers notices about server events.

IRC operators are nothing more than regular users who happen to have special privileges on one of the network's servers. They are distinguished by the asterisk (*) mark in **WHO** output if they've set oper status on, and a **WHOIS** on them returns a line saying this user is an IRC operator or something similar. Often the MOTD will identify the opers for that server.

Note that a few vain users like to impersonate an IRCop by placing the phrase "is an IRC operator" in the realname field. IRCop status appears on a separate line in the **WHOIS**—not where the realname field should be. Even smarter ones set themselves as **AWAY** and construct the away message to wrap at the right point to make the message appear at the beginning of the next line. No go—the real IRCop line appears *above* the away notice if there is one. It also looks silly on clients that don't wrap the line at the desired point. If you're trying to look like a vain wannabe, this is a prime way of achieving it.

There are two kinds of IRCops—local and global. Local operators (locops) only have operator privileges on their own server, while global opers may use certain commands for remote servers as well. This is because locops don't appear as operators outside their own server—the server doesn't relay the fact that the user is an oper to the rest of the net, so none of the other servers consider the client an oper and therefore they will not accept privileged commands from that client. You will only see local operators if you are on the same server they are. Before someone asks—no, a female oper is not an operette.

12.2 What They Do

IRCops monitor the servers and network and intervene if necessary to correct a network fault, remove an abuser, or modify some of the server's settings if the situation requires it. Most of the time, though, they lounge around like any other user—after all, no one is more of a user than the person who runs the server. This section is dedicated to the understanding of the way the servers are run and the people who make IRC work from behind the scenes.

IRCop powers vary depending on the policies regarding oper powers and conduct of the network and server for which they are operators, and are far from having unlimited powers. They are often subject to a strict set of rules concerning the use of oper status. Opers enforce the server's policies stated in the MOTD and ensure that those violating them are warned or removed from the server. This does not mean they are or act like IRC "cops," a term often and wrongly applied. Law enforcement is not an oper's task. Taking care of the server is.

An oper may, in addition to the tasks mentioned above, have control over services on those networks that offer them, or deal with user queries regarding just about everything under the sun—often irrelevant to "opering." Frequently, though, they just hang around in more or less idle chat, often with other operators.

Opering is a generic term for everything an IRC operator does that's related to his/her capacity as an IRC operator. It's a useful bit of insider jargon which I'll use as a regular verb (with *opered* as a matching adjective) for lack of a better term. When you set your operator status on, you *oper* yourself and you have entered the state of being *opered*; when you're lurking on a server watching the bots go by, you're *opered*; when you kill off the evil bots, you're also *opering*; when you connect split servers, you're still *opering*. If you ask some opers, to oper is a state of existence, not an activity at all and certainly not a mere verb. They would do well as Zen masters.

On large networks with no channel service, there's a common misconception that operators substitute for the lack thereof by performing channel management tasks as a part of their duties. This is just about the wildest myth on IRC. What an oper is *not* allowed to do is use operator privileges for channel management (that is, **/kill** a channel op he doesn't approve of). If the network wishes to implement advanced channel management or ownership, it installs a channel service.

Consequentially, if an oper says he or she can't help you with a channel-related problem, believe it. Oper status does not imply superior channel op powers. Even if an oper does have powers over channels, it's via legitimate and strictly regulated use of a channel service or a special command set, and not via standard IRC operator commands. Where this option is provided, a hierarchy permits only a certain class of opers to perform such tasks.

Oper status, while giving a user extended powers, has its limits. In fact, as a result of having those powers, opers are subject to more restrictions than a channel op or another user, while they're also charged with the responsibility of keeping the server and network in working condition. It's a highly overrated position and the subject of numerous speculations and myths.

That's how things really are.

12.3 How Did They Become IRC Operators?

"So . . . how did they gain these magical powers?" You're not fooling me! I know you still think opers are something very special and grand. Now wipe that guilty look off your face and admit you want to be an IRCop, too.

Here's how it happens.

The first operator of a server will be its administrator—the person who holds the account under which the IRC daemon is running. This person, within the limits of the network's general policy and any rules the owner of the ircd machine may have set, is the only one who may appoint or remove operators. The server admin is also the source of any authoritative answers regarding the server and is also the official contact person for anything concerning his or her server.

Most active opers tend to be hard-core IRC addicts with years of experience. Others represent the server machine's owners—either employees of the company that owns the machine or members of the faculty for a server that an educational institution owns. Some will be operators or admins of other servers on the same network. Depending on how selective the server's admin is, there may also be a "vanity oper"— someone who doesn't need to be an operator, does no real oper work, but fancies strutting around with a decorative asterisk and somehow got an admin to bestow oper status. You should take some issues into consideration before taking up duty as an oper.

Operating a server is not easy and it's often a rather thankless job. Users who don't like your style will flood, flame, insult, and accuse you of all sorts of crimes (usually meaning you caught them up to some sort of mischief and /**killed** them). You should also keep logs of your actions to compare them against the server's logs in case you do get a mean accusation trying to discredit you. Opering is sometimes exciting but also stressful. Remember, once you accept the job, you may never get rid of it, although you may wish you'd never have taken it . . . but of course you'll become as addicted to opering as you are to the rest of IRC.

First, asking for oper status out of the blue is definitely not the way to get it. Asking what you need to become an oper evokes the response that you don't qualify since you lack the knowledge. Anyone wishing to become an oper is expected to have been around the virtual block and know about the inner workings of IRC.

It's all a matter of chance, actually. In the course of your IRC life, you'll probably meet an admin or two at some point or even be in regular contact with one when you share a common channel. If you happen to bump into an admin who needs an oper and is of the opinion that you'd be suitable, that person might ask you to do it. This means the admin considers you an experienced user with a sound knowledge of the network and its workings, and expects that you'll stick to the rules— use your oper privileges correctly, not embarrass your admin with senseless or abusive kills or busybody routing interventions, and of course keep a discreet eye on the server and its users while you're around.

12.4   Finding IRC Operators

Before looking for an IRC operator, make sure you have a valid reason for contacting one. Most IRC operators also use IRC like everyone else, and don't want interruptions from users wanting things for which they aren't responsible. Many have even stopped responding to users' messages altogether and use elaborate scripting to filter them out. Although this is rather sad, they often have a point: Ignorant users may bother them about areas that aren't their concern. For example, asking an operator to restore a channel on a network like EFnet or IRCnet, which don't permit operator intervention in channel affairs, does little more than annoy the operator (who has probably already heard this request from others 20 times in the last hour).

In many cases, you shouldn't contact just any operator, but only the one who handles the server your question or complaint relates to—this can be a bit tricky with servers in masked domains, since all appear under the mask of a single server. For example, there are three IRCnet servers in Australia, but as far as the rest of the network is concerned, they are all under the mask of ***.au**. From any other server on that network, all you'll see is ***.au**. If you check the server ***.au**, it always shows whichever one of the three is directly connected to the rest of the network, and its operators may well be unable to help you with something regarding one of the other two.

There are several ways of finding an IRC operator:

```
/STATS o <server>
```

This shows possible nicknames and host masks of the server's operators. Then you can use whois to check whether they are on. If you have a complaint about a client on a particular server, substitute the client's nickname for the name of the server, as we showed before. This spares you the trouble of having to do a **whois** on the offending client first, and also queries the client's server, even if it's behind a mask.

Client	Command
ircll:	/WHO -oper <server>
mIRC:	/WHO <server> o

If your client supports the -oper flag with who, you can use this to see a server's present operators. Of course, invisible opers won't appear, since this is the limitation of the **who** command. **WHO -oper 0** (or **WHO 0 o** for mIRC) will search channel 0—everywhere—for operators of all servers.

/who 0 o is a server-side command and not all types of servers support it. Unfortunately, mIRC's who command is poor in features, and one of the other options is often preferable.

Probably the most effective way of finding a server's operators is the **trace** command. Among other data, it shows all opered clients on the server, whether they're invisible or not. Look for the lines beginning with **Oper** in the trace output. If none appears, the server has no active operator online at the moment.

```
/TRACE <server>
```

A less conventional but often effective way of finding an IRC operator is by joining one of the network's operator or administrative channels if you know any, and publicly asking if any operators of the server in question are present.

Briefly stating the nature of your question or problem might get a faster response. If you get no reply immediately, it doesn't mean you've been acknowledged and ignored—one of the other operators present might be looking for the one you need, or perhaps the operator you wanted saw your message and went to look into the problem before responding. The name of some networks' operator channels are included in the network information under Appendix A.

EFnet users have a fast and effective way of looking up a server's operators, a feature added to the servers recently:

```
/STATS p [server]
```

This lists all operator clients and their idle times, saving you the trouble of sifting through trace output and performing a whois on each one of them. If you specify no server, you'll query your current server. This is another command in which you can substitute a nickname of someone using the server for the actual server name. The server's MOTD may contain a list of operators.

13

CTCP

Now we'll be getting a bit more technical. You don't absolutely need to know all the techie stuff in this chapter, but you'll be lost without knowledge of the basic CTCP command set. If there's something you don't understand ("What the heck's a PRIVMSG?"), don't freak out over it. This chapter will find explain everything.

13.1 CTCP Explained

CTCP stands for Client To Client Protocol and describes a set of commands a client responds to automatically. The basic command set is part of the client, and every advanced client permits user-defined CTCP commands and often has additional commands particular to that client. To the server, CTCP is no different from **MSG**, since technically the two are the same type of message, for which the server command is **PRIVMSG**.

Let's expand on **PRIVMSG**. This part is not required learning. If you're intimidated by jargon, feel free to move on to the next section. We saw earlier (see section 2.5) the difference between the commands you send your client and those the client sends the server. The server's limited command set isn't enough to provide for all the users' wishes and needs—indeed, it doesn't have to. Therefore, several commands you use will actually translate into the same server command.

Only the client distinguishes between a normal **MSG** and a CTCP message, so it's the message contents that allow the client to recognize it as a CTCP command. The defining characteristic is a CTRL-A (symbolized by **^A**) character at the beginning and end of the message.

When receiving a message that begins and ends with **^A**, a client sees that message as CTCP and acts accordingly. This is not part of the IRC protocol, but a convention client authors added later. When they introduced automation (because they thought it would be cool, not because there was a dire need for it), they had to use some convention, since the only option for sending messages from one client to another on the server level was the **PRIVMSG** command, and there were no plans to expand the server's command set just to accommodate that. Besides, supporting CTCP on the server level would be a contradiction in terms. Therefore they settled for a signal inside the message itself, which another client would interpret as a command.

13.1.1   *Sending CTCP Requests*

The normal way of sending a CTCP query is with the **CTCP** command:

```
/ctcp <target> <command> [parameters]
```

For example:

```
/ctcp Joe ping
```

Many clients and scripts support simpler forms of these commands, such as /**version** and /**ping** for /**ctcp version** and /**ctcp ping**, respectively. Some, such as mIRC, allow you to use the CTCP command set from within a pop-up menu when you right-click a nickname.

Since the server doesn't see this type of message as different from a normal message, the sender can direct it at the same targets as those, including multiple targets. In order to elicit a response from the target client, the CTCP command must match one the receiver supports and include parameters it may require for a response. If the command fails to do this, the client receiving the faulty CTCP either returns an error response (**CTCP ERRMSG**) or ignores it completely.

13.1.2 Replying to CTCP Requests

To put it simply, you do not reply. You either make your client ignore all or certain kinds of CTCP requests, or you let it reply automatically. There's no reason to respond manually to CTCP—the whole point of it is to provide an automated process of exchanging information.

13.2 CTCP Commands

The set of CTCP commands a client recognizes varies widely from client to client, but almost every client supports the basic ones. For explanatory purposes, the client sending the initial CTCP request is the "sender," and the one to which it's sent, and which reacts to it, is the "receiver." This is the basic scheme as it would appear on an mIRC client in the status window:

You send: `/ctcp Joe version`

Joe sees: `[George VERSION]`

That's all Joe sees. His client replies automatically, unseen to him.

You see: `[VERSION reply from Joe: mIRC32 v5.51 K.Mardam-Bey]`

When a CTCP reply gets sent, the roles actually reverse, but to simplify matters we'll continue to call the client that started the CTCP sequence the sender. Let's have a look at the principal CTCP commands.

In this example, both sides are using mIRC and the messages appear in their status window. The way CTCP messages display varies wildly from client to client. mIRC (and I consider this a disadvantage) by default does not tell you if the CTCP is directed at you personally or at a group of users, as is the case when someone CTCPs a channel or an operator CTCPs an entire server's users. If you want to see the target of the CTCP displayed, you have to script it yourself.

NOTE   *ircII users* must *have a client variable set in order to see the CTCP message they're receiving. If you know you're being sent a CTCP, you're sure you're not ignoring the sender (or all CTCPs), and you still can't see them, you need to issue the following command:*

`/set verbose_ctcp on`

I suggest adding this to your **.ircrc** *file if you didn't set up the client yourself or follow the advice in Chapter 4. Having* **verbose_ctcp** *set off does not affect your ability to return CTCP replies.*

13.2.1 PING

The most widely used CTCP command is **PING**. The sending client generates a time stamp and the receiver bounces it back to the sending client (without adding a time stamp), which compares the reply to the current time. The sender then calculates the difference between the time stamp and the time it received a reply; the result is the round-trip time of the message. **CTCP PING** is the user's main diagnostic tool for detecting lag.

All clients will (or should) return the **PING** unmodified. If the response time is a ridiculous number like 920693456 or -14328, the sender or the receiver has a bug in handling **CTCP PING**, or the receiver is running a buggy script that causes it to return a new time stamp or none at all instead of bouncing back the time stamp it received.

You'll sometimes see people asking you to Ping them. They want you to send them a **CTCP PING** and tell them the result so they can see if they're lagged. Why they would ask someone else to Ping them when it's much easier to send a **PING** themselves is a mystery, but probably stems from the misconception that people don't like to be Pinged. They may want times from more than one person, which they can easily achieve by Pinging a channel instead of a single user. This provides a wider sample of replies and more-accurate individual results.

Your options are to ignore them, humor them, or enlighten them. Obviously, when someone asks you to Ping him or her, it involves the exchange of four messages: one asking you to Ping, your Ping, their receipt of the reply to your Ping, and your message telling them the result.

NOTE *If while using an ircII client you observe that all Ping replies, even the noticeably delayed ones, return a time of 0, add the following line to your .ircrc (the problem in this case is that the client isn't sending out a time stamp):*

```
ALIAS PING //ctcp $0- ping $time()
```

This alias also allows you to use /ping instead of /ctcp nickname ping. $time() is a function which expands to the current time.

13.2.2 VERSION

VERSION is another widely used CTCP command. It sends a **VERSION** request; the response should be the type of client the other user is running. If the other user has some kind of script loaded, **VERSION** may return only the name of the script, from which with a little experience you can deduce the type of client. **CTCP VERSION** takes no parameters.

Nothing on IRC is faked as much as **CTCP VERSION** replies. While many users regard **CTCP VERSION** as suspicious ("What business of yours is my client's version?") and some constantly **IGNORE** it, others simple fake the reply with a bit of scripting. Bots sitting on servers that don't welcome them are especially likely to return a fake reply in their attempt to escape detection by a server's operators. On most clients, you can do this with **ON RAW_IRC**, **ON RAW**, or the equivalent. **ON CTCP**, which many clients support, may not succeed with clients like ircII, which will not allow **ON CTCP** to suppress the default CTCP reply.

Servers generally expect all clients to respond to a CTCP request from an operator, so faking it or ignoring CTCP altogether is not necessarily a good idea.

NOTE *mIRC users should not try to script out the client's version reply. You can ignore it or respond, but do not fake it.*

13.2.3 FINGER

The **FINGER** command isn't used too often these days since many people regard it as snooping, especially if a total stranger uses it. While many choose to configure their client not to respond to it at all, others who haven't done so still may react nastily to receiving an unsolicited **CTCP FINGER**. The response would normally include one or more of the following data: the user's name, email address, and idle time. Why people who don't wish to be fingered allow this command is not clear—probably for the same reason some people leave their curtains open and then complain about lack of privacy.

13.2.4 TIME

The queried client replies to this command with the current date and time of the machine on which it is running. The accuracy of the reply depends, of course, on whether the machine queried has the correct time and time zone set.

13.2.5 ACTION

CTCP ACTION is what the **ME** command really sends (section 8.9). This is why actions don't get treated as public messages even if they're sent to a channel. Clients tend to treat **CTCP ACTION** as a separate type of event rather than an ordinary CTCP or public or private message. Technically, they're just another **PRIVMSG** and just another CTCP. This is something you should bear in mind when scripting, especially if you're handling raw IRC. Most client scripting languages distinguish between an action and other CTCPs, but you can work around this distinction with raw IRC.

13.2.6 ECHO

An almost obsolete CTCP command, this simply bounces back the contents of the message. Some clients, including mIRC, no longer support it since it's of little practical use and CTCP flood attacks often utilized it. You can safely ignore it.

13.2.7 CLIENTINFO

A useful command, **CTCP CLIENTINFO** returns a list of CTCP commands to which the client will respond. You can add the name of such commands as a parameter in order to obtain more instructions on using that command. This command can retrieve information about using a client's automated features; most "live" users (as opposed to bots) don't really appreciate it.

A typical **CLIENTINFO** reply might look like this:

```
*** CTCP CLIENTINFO reply from JackSprat: SED UTC ACTION DCC CDCC
BDCC XDCC VERSION CLIENTINFO USERINFO ERRMSG FINGER TIME PING ECHO
INVITE WHOAMI OP OPS UNBAN XLINK XMIT UPTIME   :Use CLIENTINFO
<COMMAND> to get more specific information
```

This is characteristic of a BitchX client; both ircII and mIRC will return more limited command sets since neither one employs as much built-in automation as BitchX. The number and type of commands may vary greatly from client to client.

13.2.8 USERINFO

This command retrieves some personal information a user wishes known. Exactly what kind and how much information is entirely up to the user. Most clients, including mIRC and ircII, return no information by default, and most users don't care to add any. It is one more CTCP command that has largely fallen into disuse.

If you wish to allow people to see something when they ask for information with this command, ircII-based clients let you set the text you'll return by simply setting the **USER_INFORMATION** client variable. With mIRC it isn't so simple—you'll have to write an **ON CTCP** line in your remote if you want to return anything but a blank message. Also, the default pop-ups don't include it, so you cannot use it by right-clicking a nickname unless you edit the pop-ups file and add it yourself.

13.2.9 Common Client-Specific CTCP Commands

SOUND is used by mIRC and other clients that support sound. The parameter is the file name of the sound the receiver is to play. This requires that the receiver have the sound file on the machine and accessible to mIRC.

Scripts that react to certain events while a user is not present sometimes include **PAGE**, which "pages" the person by beeping, flashing the screen, or playing a sound file.

13.3 PRIVMSG and NOTICE

It's time for a quick rehash of a concept from Chapter 11. An important convention of the IRC protocol is that a client shall not respond to a **PRIVMSG** with another **PRIVMSG**. This is necessary in order to avoid infinite **PRIVMSG** loops, which could occur if two clients were automatically responding to each other's PRIVMSGs. This little example demonstrates how two clients programmed to reply automatically to a **PRIVMSG** (in this case it's a public message, and it could also be a MSG or CTCP) with another **PRIVMSG** can go into an infinite loop:

```
StupidBot (bot@really.dumb.com) has joined channel #DumbBots
<LameBot> Hi there, StupidBot!
<StupidBot> Hello, LameBot!
```

(They automatically greet each other. This is only the beginning. What if they're not programmed to stop responding automatically to each others' greetings?)

```
<LameBot> Hi there, StupidBot!
<StupidBot> Hello, LameBot!
<LameBot> Hi there, StupidBot!
```

. . . Need I continue?

NOTICE, on the other hand, may not get an automatic reply at all, so it is practical and important that a client respond to **PRIVMSG** only with **NOTICE**. Since CTCP is a form of **PRIVMSG**, the same rule applies here: A CTCP request is a **PRIVMSG**, while a response to a CTCP is a **NOTICE**.

As with the **PRIVMSG**, characteristically ^A characters enclose the message contents of the **NOTICE** sent in response to a CTCP query. What we have now is the following:

```
You: PRIVMSG Joe : ACOMMAND parameters A
```

and the reply:

```
Joe: NOTICE George : ▲ COMMAND response ▲
```

These are the raw commands the respective clients send to the server. If you're not feeling very technical right now, skip this message anatomy lesson and pretend you didn't see it. You won't die from lack of knowledge.

Certain inferior clients and/or scripts do not add the trailing **^A** character at the end of the CTCP message. Clients that allow for such "broken" formats may recognize this, but it looks bad on clients that require the correct syntax to recognize a message as a CTCP. These clients display a CTCP lacking the trailing **^A** character as a regular message (public or private, depending on the target) starting with **^A**. Really broken clients not only read such a malformed message as a CTCP, but may also respond to it.

13.4 Customizing CTCP Replies

Some clients allow you to define a custom reply to certain CTCP commands like **FINGER** or **VERSION** from the client's setup. For example, mIRC lets you change the finger reply with no trouble under **File • Options • IRC • Messages** and requires no scripting whatsoever. Others require scripting in order to circumvent the client's default CTCP replies, while more basic ones don't support any of this. If your client lets you set the CTCP replies from a setup menu, disregard the instructions below. When customizing your CTCP replies through a script with raw IRC—if you care to, that is—remember the following rules:

- CTCP replies must begin and end with **^A** characters. You must place the leading **^A** before the CTCP command and the final **^A** following the last parameter. The sender regards any part of the message not enclosed in **^A**, as a regular **NOTICE**.

- A CTCP reply must be a **NOTICE** and not a **MSG** or **PRIVMSG**. If it's a **PRIVMSG**, the receiver reads it as a CTCP request instead of a reply, and you may end up with a loop if the receiver has an equally protocol-breaking setup.

- The first word of the reply message should be the **CTCP** command word.

- If you don't suppress the default CTCP reply, your client will send your custom reply in addition to the standard reply rather than replace it.

- mIRC does not allow circumvention of the **CTCP VERSION** reply. The only way to do this is to use modified versions (hacks) of the client, but these involve unauthorized modifications to the software and I do not recommend using them.

- **CTCP PING** should draw its parameter—the time stamp—from the sender's CTCP request and return it unmodified.

And now, ladies and gentlemen, let us proceed to the next chapter, which concerns DCC, a slightly more technical but equally useful tool for the IRC user. (If I'm sounding like a London tour guide, just tell me and I'll stop.)

14

DCC

DCC stands for Direct Client Connection. This feature is present in most modern clients and allows clients to communicate directly with each other outside the IRC network. What this means is that you can arrange a connection between your machine and someone else's with your IRC client, a connection that will function independently of the IRC servers and network. The answers to "I'm so lagged I want to die, but I just want to talk to my mom" and "Why post my picture on the Web?" are in this chapter— no more scrambling for a new server when yours kicks the virtual bucket, no more messing with email attachments to send a friend on IRC your picture.

Because DCC is initiated through a form of CTCP, DCC requires that both clients be on IRC and visible to each other (on the same network) in order for the initial request, which one of the clients sends, to reach the second client. After the second client has received the DCC request, regardless of whether or not the DCC connection is established, it's of no importance whether the clients can see each other—in fact, if both got disconnected from the IRC network, the DCC request would remain valid. The way DCC is initiated and an established DCC connection is used depends entirely on the clients involved. All clients handle the basic types of DCC in a similar manner, although some newer clients have built-in extensions that others may not handle.

14.1 DCC Chat

Chat is probably the most widely used type of DCC. A DCC chat connection works similarly to a regular "talk" client, the difference being that it does not necessitate opening a separate screen, program, or terminal; you use it from within the IRC client program. DCC chat allows a one-on-one connection with a higher level of security than communications over the IRC server network. Independent chat rooms (as opposed to channels) running on special clients or egg-drop bots also use DCC chat. These rooms are useful for bypassing server lag or communicating with people on different networks through a network of such clients.

14.1.1 Initiating a DCC Chat

All clients capable of handling DCC, graphical or not, should support the following syntax:

```
/dcc chat <nickname>
```

In addition, graphical clients may also have two more means of requesting **DCC CHAT**. The first is a DCC menu from which the user can select the type of DCC and the destination. The second is selecting a nickname from the channel's nickname list (that is, right-clicking on it in mIRC) and choosing **DCC** from a pop-up menu.

14.1.2 Accepting or Denying a DCC CHAT Request

When you're the recipient of a **DCC CHAT** request, either you receive a notice in your main window (text clients) or a small window pops up asking you whether to accept. It's really up to you, but many people consider **DCC CHAT** to be a more intimate form of communication. I think it's a bit like kissing a stranger. When accepting an unsolicited

DCC CHAT request, you're allowing someone you don't know to connect to your machine. That is (as I've said more than once), *not* a good idea.

On ircII and related clients, use the following commands:

```
/dcc chat nickname
```

to accept, and

```
/dcc close chat nickname
```

to reject.

IrcII keeps the pending request forever unless you use **DCC CLOSE**. Fancier clients such as BitchX and mIRC automatically time it out after a while.

14.1.3 *Communicating over a DCC CHAT Connection*

This is another form of communication that depends on the client you're using. Graphical clients open a new window for each DCC session, while text-based clients set them apart by giving DCC messages a different appearance.

Using a graphical client like mIRC, all you do is type your messages in the DCC window, just as you'd do with a regular message (query) session. Under ircII and similar clients, send your messages to the DCC connection by prefixing the nickname with an equal (=) sign, like this:

```
/msg =Joe We are now in DCC.
```

If you also have the tabkey script loaded, you can use it with DCC as well. BitchX automatically adds a **=nickname** entry to your tabkey holder so that pressing TAB after establishing the connection brings up the **=nickname** without your having to receive a message first.

14.2 File Transfers via DCC

The other main use of DCC is for file transfers. With DCC, you can swap files with other users without ever having to go through the pain of installing FTP servers or other file transfer utilities. The only difference you might encounter is transfer speed, since you are often transferring files to or from a machine that offers a slow connection compared to major software download sites. There's no knowing until you try, though. So if you want to send someone a mug shot—sorry, picture of yourself, or trade sound files, this is the most convenient way of doing it.

14.2.1 Offering a File via DCC

Regardless of the kind of client you have, the following syntax should work:

```
/dcc send <nickname> <filename>
```

If the file is in a directory other than your current one, you of course have to specify the path to the file. With mIRC, you can also offer multiple files at the same time by adding more file names to the command line.

14.2.2 Receiving an Offered File

With graphical clients like mIRC, this is generally as simple as clicking on Accept when you see the window offering you a file. Yes, it is possible to accept files automatically, but with all the viruses and Trojans around, you do not want to do this. In fact, I strongly advise you—in your best interest—to resist the temptation of convenience. I know I'm repeating myself, but this is important.

If the same user offers you more than one file, you have to accept each offered file separately.

On ircII and similar clients, use the following command to accept a **DCC SEND**:

```
/dcc get nickname [filename]
```

The file name is not necessary if there is only one offer.

14.2.3 Resuming Interrupted Transfers

What happens when you're transferring a huge file and for some reason you lose the connection? This annoyed IRC users for a long time until someone came up with a solution: **DCC RESUME**. It attempts to pick up where the lost transfer left off, so if you have 509,433 bytes of a file from a previous transfer, it starts transferring from 509,434 instead of making you start anew.

Not many clients support this command, but two of the more popular ones, mIRC and BitchX, include the option. I still think FTP is a more stable means of transferring large files, but not everyone can put files on an FTP server and not everyone wants to run an FTP server on their machine, so DCC is a convenient way of swapping files, especially small ones.

In mIRC, you see a menu when an incoming file matches a file name you already have. This menu asks you whether to overwrite the old file, resume a previous transfer, or rename the incoming file and keep both.

WARNING *DCC RESUME on mIRC and other clients following its lead breaks the protocol and entails the risk of entering an infinite loop like the one we saw in 13.3.*

14.2.4 *File Servers and XDCC*

All major clients can accept and send out files automatically upon request. The first to offer this was ircII, which had a variety of scripts for the purpose. The name of the most popular script was XDCC, a term that stuck. Later on, mIRC came up with its fserve and BitchX invented CDCC, both of which do essentially the same task but are integrated into the client, unlike XDCC, which is just a script.

You must set up file servers very carefully to prevent users from accessing files they shouldn't. By running a file server, you are giving other people access to files on your machine.

There are numerous XDCC scripts around for ircII and EPIC, and it's not possible to evaluate them all. They range from very basic to moderately complex and should provide instructions inside the file. It's a good idea to check the script for back doors, too, if you decide to use one of them.

mIRC has a basic setup that you can combine with scripting to fine-tune its performance and access. Remember that all files you transfer come out of your pocket in terms of bandwidth, so running an fserve on a dial-up isn't always a good idea.

I suggest you create a directory in your mIRC directory and copy the files to which you wish others to have access into that directory. Then, under **File • Options • DCC • Fserve**, enter the full path of that directory in the appropriate field. The defaults of ten simultaneous transfers and five per user in that menu is probably excessive—adjust them to something more conservative, as you don't want every bit of bandwidth sucked up serving files. Of course, if you have bandwidth to spare, there's no problem with leaving the defaults. You also have the option of sending a message to people when they connect to your fserve. To do this, write a text file and enter its name in the second field of the fserve setup menu.

The full help menu for fserve is under **Help • Contents • Other Features • File Server**; all options are listed there. You can set all the parameters of an fserve session from the command line you use to serve a user. Be sure not to serve from directories you do not want others to access—for example, serving C: is not a smart thing to do, since it would let them access any files they liked on your entire C: drive. The same help item contains the commands to use when accessing another user's mIRC file server.

Note that there is no standard way of requesting file server access from other people; it depends entirely on how the other person has configured the client. MIRC clients with that form of automation often respond to !<their nickname>, while XDCC and CDCC on Unix clients are more likely to respond to /ctcp <nickname> XDCC (or CDCC) LIST. Once you're inside the file server, the standard set of commands described in the help file does the trick if it's an mIRC file server. If it's a file server on a Unix client (including egg-drop bots), you can expect it to have a help menu or show you instructions when you connect.

14.3 mIRC and the Science of DCC

Getting DCC to work right is one of the most common problems mIRC users experience. What works on one machine and one connection fails on another. Fear not, there's a solution to (almost) everything. The mIRC team has evolved DCC into a science.

14.3.1 Can DCC GET but Not SEND or CHAT?

This is close to the top of the all-time frequently asked questions list. Say that you can get files perfectly well and accept chat sessions someone else initiates, when you try to send a file or start a chat session yourself, all you get is an eerie silence followed by a timeout. Rest assured, you're not alone in this predicament. Barring the possibility that the problem lies with the receiver, you need to tweak your setup. If you're behind a firewall, take a look at section 14.4 first—that could be your problem.

What to do? Follow these five simple steps:

1. Disconnect from the server.

2. Go to **File • Options • Connect • Local Info**.

3. Clear the "Local host" and "IP address" fields.

4. Check "On connect, always get local host" and "Lookup method: Server." In special cases, you might have to choose to "always get" the IP address and not the local host.

5. Reconnect to the server and try again.

If you're using a proxy or bouncer, this technique will not work, because the server sees the address of the machine you're connecting through and not the machine you're on. If the client is unable to get its local address, you have to enter it manually and keep Normal checked.

14.3.2 What's This DCC Server Thing?

The DCC server can make your mIRC client act like a genuine server for DCC connections. Other clients can connect to your machine if they have your IP address, rather than having to look for you on IRC first or connect to another network in order to initiate a DCC session. You'll find it under **DCC • Options • Server**. It listens on port 59 by default, which is not a problem unless you have a firewall blocking access to that port. In that case, check with your firewall administrator to see what other ports you can use.

You can make the server listen for any or all of the following three types: **CHAT**, **SEND**, and fserve. By default, the DCC server doesn't bother to resolve the address of an incoming connection, but that isn't a big deal. The question remains of how secure this service is, not so much because of the file transfers but because of potential DoS attacks on any open port. Some suspicions surrounded the DCC server's security regarding versions prior to 5.51, so I recommend you take care in earlier versions. I never received official word of a problem, but there was enough smoke so fire seemed a distinct possibility. To view the full list of DCC Server commands, click on the Help button while in the DCC or DCC Server menu—it's a bit hard to find the list from the help menu.

14.3.3 Sound-Related DCC

A lot of people play sounds on IRC. Well, they don't play the sounds, they just tell other people's clients to play them—and that's the snag in the whole sound affair. In order to play a sound, the recipient of the request needs to have the sound file on his machine. Of course, with hundreds and hundreds of different WAV and MID files floating around, the chances that two users have the same set of audio files are remote. Because there are so many, no single person has the disk space to store all the sounds encountered on IRC.

To address this problem, the procedure of asking the person who sent the sound request for the audio file is automatic. In addition to that, mIRC also allows you to send out a sound file automatically if asked, acting as a limited form of file server, as well as automatically request an audio file you don't have. The command for initiating this is **!<nickname>**. I recommend you keep the option of sending the request in the form of a private message instead of sending requests to a channel. Both these options are under **File • Options • Sound • Requests**. Before you throw something at me, I'll stop reminding you of the risks of accepting files from strangers.

14.3.4 More DCC Options and the Big Secret

Under DCC's Options menu, you'll find a set of check boxes defining what happens after a DCC transfer is completed. They don't need much explaining, but it's probably best if you close the windows after completion. Whether you want a beep each time a DCC session ends is entirely up to you.

You will also see a section for timeouts. These regulate how much time your client allows to pass before voiding a **DCC CHAT** or **SEND** request and closing the corresponding port. If the recipient of the request doesn't accept your offer within the specified time, it simply gets cancelled. The DCC get timeout is not as important; it basically just clears the request from the list if you let it time out. To allow for lag that would delay your DCC request on its way to the receiver, don't make the figures too low. A minimum of 120 seconds is reasonable. It also should not be too high, so as to avoid leaving too many pending offers with open ports.

The Big Secret? What secret? Ah, yes, the one I promised in the title. It's not so much a secret as a feature the client's help files don't document. PDCC (pump DCC) actually constitutes a slap in the face of everything sacred in TCP/IP networking. What it does is defy conventions and rules and simply pump data packets down the line as fast as it can, in the hope that they'll all arrive. TCP requires acknowledgement of receipt for the previous data packet before sending the next, but PDCC makes it shovel data down the line almost as fast as your connection can take it. If the packets don't all make it to the destination, you end up with a corrupt file. It's actually surprisingly reliable considering how technically unsound the idea is, so I don't rule it out as an option to speed up your DCC sends. The magic command is:

```
/pdcc <some arbitrary large number>
```

The number is of little importance—most people simply enter a string of five or six nines. Good luck with it.

14.4 DCC from Behind a Firewall or Proxy

A firewall was originally a machine designed to protect other machines from unauthorized access, and this is the strict meaning of the term. Nowadays, they also protect the systems behind them from other kinds of attack. There are also programs that run on the protected machine itself, inspect incoming traffic before letting it pass, and filter it to reject potentially harmful data. These software firewalls are generally over-rated—their inherent weakness is that they allow data to reach the machine in the first place. They're about as good as a bulletproof vest compared to the concrete barrier of a firewall machine.

Most firewalls work on a basis of "forbid all, allow specific"—that is, they reject everything not expressly allowed to pass according to its configuration. Typical firewall setups permit any connection from inside the firewall to an outside host, but allow only certain outside hosts (or all) to connect to a strictly defined set of ports serving a particular purpose.

The problem with DCC is that it is a protocol that uses arbitrary or semirandom ports for its connections. So if your client tells the recipient of your DCC request to connect to port 5532 and expects a connection on that port, this means nothing to the firewall. It sees an attempt to connect to port 5532, thinks "What the heck is that?" and tosses it out.

More than that, if the firewall is on a machine other than the client's, all connections you make appear to originate from that machine and not your own. This makes DCC very tricky. If you have such a setup, there's a good chance you will not be able to initiate DCC connections.

If you're not running the firewall yourself, you don't stand much of a chance of getting DCC to work. For a software firewall such as Conseal on Windows, you may be able to make it work by limiting the number of ports mIRC uses for DCC (use **DCC • Options** and change the range to a number much more limited than the default, such as 5000 to 5005) and letting traffic to those ports pass. With any other setup, read your firewall's documentation carefully and see whether you can make it work. If not, you have to live without the ability to initiate **DCC SEND** and **CHAT** connections. If the firewall is a separate machine and you can run your client on the firewall machine itself, do so.

Well, some of the worst technical stuff is over. Our next step brings us to a command set you'll find useful in seeing what's happening on the server and network around you.

15

SERVER AND NETWORK COMMANDS

These commands are (or should be) common to all servers and supported by all clients. Regular users employ them to obtain information about the network and its servers, and operators use them as diagnostic and maintenance tools as well.

15.1 LUSERS

The command **LUSERS** returns the information sent to each user right after connecting and being accepted by the server, and reports the network status as seen from your current server. This includes the following:

- The number of clients currently connected to all servers of the network (possibly separated into visible and invisible clients) and the number of servers connected. If they are separated into visible and invisible clients, the total number of users is the sum of both.

- The number of IRC operators online (if any).

- The number of unknown connections (section 6.7) on the server, if any.

- The number of clients and servers directly connected to your server.

Additionally, and depending on the server's setup and version, **LUSERS** may also return:

- The current number of local clients and the maximum number of simultaneous connections since the server last started.

- The current total of global clients and the maximum number of clients seen on the network since the server last started.

You can also request **LUSERS** for a remote server or a group of servers. The output depends on what your server sees regarding that server, because your server handles the request locally rather than forwarding it to the remote server for processing. However, some servers, including EFnet servers, require **LUSERS** to request information from the server concerned by duplicating the server's mask in the command line (for example, /**lusers irc.ais.net irc.ais.net**).

Unknown connections, in case you've forgotten, are clients that have connected to the server but have not completed the registration process for acceptance as users.

Here's how to request **LUSERS** information from a remote server:

```
/lusers <server.mask>
```

Example:

```
/lusers *.gr
```

Not all the information it returns concerns that server (some lines contain local stats). The lines you're interested in are the following:

```
*** There are 11 users and 157 invisible on 2 servers
*** 4 IRC operators online
```

You can ignore the rest, since only these two lines are relevant to the server mask for which you requested information; the rest concern the local server. Regarding server masks, if the mask you ask for information from or about is ambiguous, the first server in the list will be queried. The order in which the servers connected to the network, as seen from your part of it, determines the position of the server. For example, if the server irc.ais.net splits off the network and then reconnects, it ends up much higher on the list. This is because the order is from the most recently connected to the oldest, with your server the point of reference at the base of the "tree" structure the servers form. More recently, some smaller networks have reversed this and placed the point of reference at the top of the list. Please, please don't ask me what possessed them to do it.

15.2 LINKS

This command returns information about the way the network's servers link to each other. On some networks, **LINKS** requests are visible to the operators, and repeated **LINKS** may be against the server's policy. This is because abusers used to check for split servers in order to take over channels or collide them.

EFnet servers in particular are particularly paranoid about "link lookers," which, in my opinion doesn't really make sense, since the modern server versions used there are largely secure against abuse that exploits netsplits. The only objection that can be raised against link lookers in this case is that needless repeated **LINKS** commands waste server resources. Just use the command carefully—there's no point in getting banned for behaving like a bot on servers that don't welcome them. Once you join the ranks of IRC addicts, you'll have a hard time convincing yourself, let alone others, that you're not a bot! You may use the command in three ways:

1. To obtain a list of all servers currently linked as seen from your local server. If a remote server is behind a domain mask, you will not see what's behind that mask.

    /links

2. To see a group of servers or a single server with a specific mask as seen from your server.

    /links *.ca

3. To see behind a domain mask by querying a remote server.

    /links *.fi *.hut.fi

This last command asks the server with the mask ***.fi** to return all its links matching the mask ***.hut.fi,** which would otherwise be invisible from outside the ***.fi** domain.

15.3 ADMIN

The **ADMIN** command may include some arbitrary text, anything the administrator wishes, but should return the owner and/or location of the server machine, a contact email address, and the name of the administrator(s).

```
/admin [server.name]
```

If you don't specify any server, **ADMIN** returns the admin information for your current server.

15.4 STATS

This is much more than a single command, since you use it to query a server about a variety of statistics, denoted by a letter. Some of these statistics are privileged to operators and other users may not view them. Which are privileged depends on the server version. It could be one or two, or practically all, depending on how paranoid the server administration and the author of the IRC daemon are. We will not go into obscure types of stats particular to one or two ircds, but will concentrate on those that are (or should be) present in all, and are sometimes (but not always) available to users.

```
/stats <letter> [server]
```

If you leave out the server, the command returns stats for your current server. Possible letters are c, h, i, k, l, m, o, t, u, y, and z. In some cases, capital and lowercase letters return different kinds of stats. Some types of server also return stats on additional letters or even different information for the same letter.

15.4.1 STATS C

STATS C returns the list of lines beginning with C: or N:. These define the servers to which the server connects automatically or following a **CONNECT** command from an oper and information on the port to which it connects. The N: lines you'll see with this command show which servers are permitted to connect and if and how the server will mask if connected to them. Both C: and N: lines are displayed with **STATS C**—there is no special command to view only N: lines—depending on the type of server. IRCnet servers also have lowercase c: lines that indicate the use of data compression for links to the corresponding server.

15.4.2 STATS H

STATS H shows the position other servers connecting may have on the network, as seen from the server. H: lines are for servers permitted to hub (to link other servers behind them) and also show which servers may link behind the one listed. L: lines are for leaf servers, but also indicate the possibility that they may connect a limited part of the network behind them. In practice, only true leaf servers, which have no right to link other servers, generally use L: lines. H: lines define any kind of hubbing permitted.

15.4.3 STATS I

STATS I is the list of all host masks from which the server accepts client connections. They can also include a password (invisible, of course) for privileged users from a site that is otherwise not welcome, direct certain hosts towards particular ports, and determine the connection class of the client (in combination with Y: lines).

15.4.4 STATS K

STATS K is the notorious blacklist listing all unwelcome host masks. In some cases, an admin may just remove the I: line for the host, but in most cases that would affect many more users than setting a K: line for the specific site or domain. It's also popular with lazy admins who can't be bothered with adding more I: lines to replace the rotten one.

Because some servers, particularly on EFnet, have huge K: line lists, to preserve resources the server may not return a K: line list at all. It's not uncommon for a server to have several thousand K: lines, and displaying them to everyone who asks could put a serious strain on the server and network.

15.4.5 STATS L

STATS L displays information about the server's client and server connections. The interesting parts are the first and last figures, which show the sendq and time connected, respectively. L stats are an exception to the **STATS** command's rule of syntax regarding local server stats—to see the stats for both client and server connections, you have to use an asterisk (*).

Also, servers distinguish between the lowercase and uppercase letter. If you use a capital L, the IP addresses of the connections appear instead of the host name. This is useful for tracing spoofers.

Frequent misuse of **STATS L** has caused a number of servers to restrict use of the command to IRC operators.

15.4.6 STATS M

STATS M shows the usage of commands as seen by the server. **PRIVMSG** and **JOIN** usually top the list. This concerns only commands the server recognizes and does not include unknown commands for which it has returned an error message. **STATS M** also returns the number of times each command has been used.

15.4.7 STATS O

STATS O returns the list of the server's operators, including the nickname and the hosts from which they may obtain operator status when connected. A line beginning with an **o:** (lowercase) denotes a local operator, while global operators' lines begin with **O:**.

15.4.8 STATS T, Z, and D

These three **STATS** commands return a variety of network and server-related technical data for diagnostic purposes. These are of no interest to the average user.

15.4.9 STATS U

STATS U returns the server's uptime—that is, the time in days, hours, minutes, and seconds since the server program last started. Some servers also append the maximum connection count.

15.4.10 STATS Y

STATS Y brings up the list of connection classes for both clients and servers. These may be of interest—let's have a closer look:

0	1	2	3	4	5
Y	10	120	0	50	200000

Field 0: The letter Y (really!)

Field 1: The identifier (the number of the class). The Y: line governs the connection rules of any I:, C:, or N: line with this class.

Field 2: The rate at which the server sends PINGs to check the connection (in seconds).

Field 3: For server connections, the frequency with which the server attempts to autoconnect to the server(s) matching this class, if an autoconnect has been set in the C: lines. 0 means it will not autoconnect. For clients, defines the number of clients that may connect from a single address. 0 means no limit. EFnet and IRCnet ircd support this.

Field 4: Maximum number of connections for the entire class.

Field 5: Maximum sendq for connections of this class. If it is exceeded, the connection closes—in this example, if the server has more than 200KB of data waiting to be sent to the client. The number is generally much higher for server connections and is regulated as necessary, depending on the network's total traffic and the hub-leaf relationship to a server, if the Y: line corresponds to a server class.

On IRCnet servers, you see two more fields at the end of the line. They refine the access limits of the Y: line and look something like this:

```
3.1 7.3
```

The 3.1 defines the local limits. The 3 means no more than three clients from the same IP address may use the server, while the 1 places a limit of one client per **user@host**. The 7.3 part defines global limits in a similar way. The server rejects a client if there are already seven users from its host on any servers of the network, and does the same for any **user@host** that already has three instances anywhere on the network.

This is a highly efficient and very flexible method of abuse prevention through the server's configuration. In my opinion, it's one of the highlights of the 2.9 and 2.10 (IRCnet) servers by Christophe Kalt, and I hope other types of server will also implement it in the future.

In all cases except the class number field (1), a field containing a zero means "no limit" if the field represents a limit (such as maximum connections) or "never" if the field is a timer (like the connect frequency).

If your Unix client displays the Y: line with fields separated by colons—for example, Y:0:120:0:200:100000—you may be missing part of the output. To fix this, type **/on 218** *- before sending the STATS Y command.*

15.5 INFO

The **INFO** command is a bit like a credits list in a film, showing the history of and contributors to the ircd the server is running. Some clients have another use for the **INFO** command; in this case you may have to send this as a raw command to receive the **INFO** output. Much of it looks like a pantheon of all the major and minor deities responsible for what IRC has become today. The list gives credit where credit is due—these people, although quite a few of them are no longer around, deserve it.

```
/info [server]
```

If the command doesn't specify a server, **INFO** queries the current server.

15.6 TIME

TIME returns either the current date or the time for the server machine queried—again, if no server name follows the command, **TIME** asks the current server. Note that the output is always in the server's local time. The client command **DATE** also sends a **TIME** request to the server, since **DATE** is not a valid server command. Remember—this is the local time of the *server* and will not match your client's if you're in another time zone. It's very handy for finding out what time it is in another part of the world (providing you know where the server is located).

15.7 TRACE

TRACE shows the route between you and the destination of the trace. Used on a server, it shows the route to the destination, plus the links and operator clients connected to it. With a nickname as the parameter, it traces the entire route to that client, but won't show anything else about the user's server. **TRACE** with no parameters shows the links and opers of the current server.

```
/trace [server|nickname]
```

15.8 VERSION

This command requests the server's version, including information about its configuration. It indicates the compile options, which the server's admin set when compiling it, with a string of uppercase and lowercase letters. Each of these stands for a selected option; the absence of a letter means the corresponding feature has not been activated. The same applies to additional strings a server may return that concern patches the server is running. Used without parameters in ircII-based clients, this command also returns the client's version unless it's sent as a raw server command only.

```
/version [server]
```

VERSION is another command that allows the nickname of a user on that server to substitute for the server's name. It is not related to CTCP version—using it on a client queries its server and not the client itself.

VERSION can find out which type of ircd the network or server you're on is using, in case you're on a network not covered in this book. Some small networks have changed the version string beyond recognition, but others give you a fair idea of what they're running. Most types of servers are based on the old 2.8.21 version used on EFnet, and some have kept that version number. Common types are as follows:

2.8/hybrid*	2.8.21 with modifications by the hybrid team, led by Diane Bruce
2.8.21+CSr*	2.8.21 with modifications by Chris Behrens
2.9.*	IRCnet ircd, older versions
2.10.*	IRCnet ircd, current series
2.9.*+Cr* or **2.10+Cr***	IRCnet ircd with modifications by Magnus Tjernstrom
2.9.*/Sc* or **2.10.*/Sc***	IRCnet ircd with modifications by John Hajek-Doggett
u2.9.*	Undernet ircd, older versions
u2.10.*	Undernet ircd, current series
dal4.4.*	DALnet ircd, older series
2.8.21+dal*	DALnet ircd, even older series
dal4.6.*	DALnet ircd, newer series
2.8.21+th*	2.8.21 (old) with modifications by Taner Halicioglu
2.8.21+digi*	2.8.21 (old) with modifications by Shrihari Pandit
bahamut*	New hybrid-based ircd for for DALnet currently under development

Throughout the book, the versions referred to are the most recent at the time of writing, which are:

EFnet	2.8.21/hybrid-5.3 and 6 beta
IRCnet	2.10.2
Undernet	u2.10.06
DALnet	4.6.7.DreamForge

15.9   Other Server Commands

Some commands are of little practical use, were recently added to the ircd at a later stage, or have been ignored by client authors. There is no client-side support of these commands, so a user has to send them raw to the server, with **QUOTE** or **RAW**.

Many are specific to certain types of ircd or patches run by individual admins. Others are for operator or server-server use. The most common ones are:

KLINE	Used by operators to set K: lines without editing the config file if the server supports it. Related commands are TKLINE (temporary or timed K: line) and UNKLINE (remove K: line), which not all servers support.
HTM	Concerns high-traffic mode, the rate of data transfer at which a server ceases responding to some user commands in order to handle network traffic more efficiently. This is the cause of the "Server load too high" notice you may receive when trying certain server commands such as LIST, LUSERS, or TRACE. Not all server types use HTM.
DLINE	This exists only on EFnet servers and bans an IP address or group of IP addresses regardless of whether they resolve to host names and to what names they resolve. Used mainly for banning contiguous address groups that resolve to host names in several different domains.
GLINE	Sets a global K: line on networks that support it.

HELP   Shows the list of commands the server recognizes. Any other commands sent to it result in transmission of an error message to a client. DALnet-based servers go into much more detail and actually provide a form of help with this command. It is a server command, and you must send it raw, since almost all clients have HELP as a client command.

MAP   Undernet and DALnet-based servers support this command, which returns an ASCII map of the network's current layout, with your server as the starting point. For networks that do not support a MAP command, it's possible to generate such a command using a script such as the imap one included in the ircII package.

16

ODDS AND ENDS

There is so much to say about IRC and everything related to it. Many interesting topics don't warrant a chapter of their own, but don't really fit under any other topic. This chapter is the little box of odds and ends—worthy stuff that didn't fit anywhere else in the book. Enjoy.

16.1 IRC over the Web—Java Clients

To be honest, I don't like Java. I'm talking about the programming language Sun Microsystems developed and trademarked, not about coffee or Indonesian geography. I think Java is too buggy, bulky, and insecure, and it is as excruciatingly slow as software can be, unless you're a power user and use the latest and greatest hardware. However, Java does get the job done when it works and is platform independent.

Where does Java fit in with IRC? Its main use so far has been programs that run by downloading a Web page. These applets, as they are called, can also let someone access IRC through a Web page. You simply go to that page and wait while the Java applet downloads and opens. It then presents you with a screen of options, including your nickname and the channel you want to join. Then it connects you to an IRC server.

Java is not the fastest way of getting on IRC, nor the simplest. It is, however, quite acceptable for people who don't want to run an IRC client while they're already browsing or don't care to figure out how a client works. You need a recent version of Netscape or Microsoft Internet Explorer for Java support, and you must enable Java in the program preferences.

The features Java clients offer range from poor to fair. You generally have very little control over the client's options and cannot join multiple channels or DCC. Because it's hard to get Java right on the programming level, Java clients are also prone to crashes (and they invariably insist on referring to channels as "rooms," but we've already been there). Of all the home-brewed and commercial Java clients I've seen out there, only Qing Gong's IBM IRC Client for Java has impressed me as fully functional, offering a wide range of features as well as integrating well with the browser. It even has a help menu some regular clients would envy.

All in all, IRC over the Web with Java applets is not yet what it could be, nor does it have everything you want in a client. What it is good for is inclusion in a Web page destined for an audience unfamiliar with IRC. By means of this page, people can connect to IRC for specific events, if you're willing to accept some extra load on your Web server. In this case, I highly recommend the IBM client. You'll find some addresses of Web pages through which you can get on IRC in Appendix D.

16.2 Writing a Client

Although there are a multitude of IRC clients for every platform out there, some people are bound to want to create a new one, either because they feel existing clients don't quite satisfy their needs or as a programming exercise in a familiar environment. Apart from the obvious requirements of some expertise in the platform and knowledge of the language they'll be using, everyone intending to write an IRC client must know the following:

- Read the protocol carefully. Always have the RFC 1459 (see 16.7) by your side.

- Start by making your client follow RFC standards before allowing extensions.

- Familiarize yourself with ircd extensions various networks—at least the major ones—implement.

- Be prepared to see ircd breaking the protocol and adapt.

- Pay extra attention to making sure the client does not present a security risk to the machine it's running on.

- Try to adopt the conventions and standards existing clients have set.

And now a message from our sponsors. Okay, I'm kidding, but here's a suggestion: I like free stuff—doesn't everyone?—and I also like free software. Give your client away—we already have enough shareware, payware, and bugware out there. In fact, we have so much that none of the authors make a fraction of the money worth their trouble. Next, if you really want to create a great client, especially on non-Unix platforms, it would be a good idea to consider making it open source. Open source (there's a lot about it at www.opensource.org) means the source code is available to the public and open to peer review. Everyone can see your code, and anyone who cares can make comments or suggestions for improvement. Why non-Unix platforms? That's where the lack is greatest—Unix (and Linux) geeks write open source code all the time. There's a ton of non-Unix software, but very little of it is open source. Consider this option.

End of message. Here's a chance to give something back to your online community. Many years ago, when the Internet was young, people worked on networking and programmed for the thrill and not for profit. That's what made it possible, and that's why it doesn't cost you a fortune. Real end of message. Thanks for your attention.

```
/me gets off the soap box.
```

16.3   IRC via Telnet

A lot has been said about the disadvantages of telnet IRC, but it's still the only means of connecting for some users. People in remote areas with no network connection other than a library or a local BBS with no IRC client on the system are good examples. While sysadmins sometimes question the usefulness of an IRC client or even are unaware of its existence, the presence of a telnet client is generally considered necessary, and it can work for IRC, too. Others forbid the presence of an IRC client on the system, viewing it as a waste of resources. Nobody objects to telnet, so if this is the case, you can telnet to a machine with a client.

The number of telnettable IRC clients has declined over the past few years, but there are still some around. These are usually customized Unix clients, accessible to the public via telnet. There are currently three networks with sites providing a telnet client. You access telnetting to the correct address and port. After this, you're prompted to select a set of options, then you connect to the IRC network the telnet site is serving. The drawback of these clients is that the configuration is preset and the user can't customize the settings. It's more advisable to find a shell account to which you can telnet, and use a regular client from there.

A number of sites offer cheap accounts with no dial-up access. However, if that's not possible either, telnet IRC is an option. It's probably the least desirable way to connect to IRC, but it's useable. Networks with working telnettable IRC clients are the Undernet, DALnet, and Super-Chat. Check Appendix D for the addresses.

16.4 IRC for the Sight-Impaired

So far, the number of sight-impaired IRC users is very low. IRC clients in general are unfriendly toward screen readers, and the contents of IRC itself are often tough to read with the large number of special characters, smileys, and so forth used, and with typing mistakes so common. Still, as long as there is available software, it can be done. Yes, IRC *is* an almost entirely visual environment, but this can be overcome.

Configuring a client for use with screen readers requires a level of expertise the average user or beginner doesn't possess, and it is even harder for someone who doesn't have visual contact with the computer since it involves code—probably the one thing screen readers hate most. Still, it's not impossible. While they're few in number, blind IRC users use special scripts to modify the display and make it more friendly to screen readers. For such scripting, ircII is probably the best client to use since it allows a high level of display customization. MIRC can hook up with a screen reader, but it's definitely not as easy as loading a script into an ircII client.

16.5 Jupitered Servers

This is a peculiar term, since it was really derived from someone's nickname. The matching noun and verb is "jupe" or "jupiter," the former being the most widely used, and the practice is generally referred to as "juping." Jupes are a way of making sure an unwanted server doesn't link to the network and are normally used only when a compromised (hacked) server presents a threat to the network. Less commonly, they are used to practice strong-arm IRC "politics" by effectively forbidding a server to link, even though it is not a security problem.

Although removing the server's C: and N: lines (see 18.4) on all servers is a more effective way of removing a server from the net, you can use a jupe as an emergency measure if the admins who have to change their servers' configuration aren't all reachable.

You implement a jupe by linking a fake server and giving it the server mask of the unwanted server. This is quite possible since the server mask doesn't have to match the host name (the C: lines of the server to which it connects define a network server's mask). As long as this fake server is connected, the network rejects the real (but unwelcome) server's attempts to link, since as far as the network is concerned a link with the server's mask already exists.

You can easily identify such a server on the LINKS list, since its real address in the server logo is localhost, 127.0.0.1, or a host name identical to the server to which it connects, and the logo itself usually indicates it's a jupe.

Jupiter was an old-time IRC operator who holds the rare distinction of having his nickname immortalized in IRC terminology. Back in 1990, when IRC was young and server security wasn't what it is today, one of his pastimes involved taking advantage of the lack of security to impersonate servers and other users. Of course, if he connected pretending to be a server, the real server could not connect—it was Juped! While this didn't always make him popular, he did show why additional security was a good thing to have. He no longer hangs out on IRC, but his nickname lives on.

16.6 Online Help Services

Apart from your client's built-in help, which for many clients is extensive and should cover most of your needs, in the best tradition of the Net, a number of older, experienced users devote some of their time to helping out newcomers. None of them receive a cent for their efforts or the considerable time they dedicate.

You should respect these people and treat them with the courtesy they deserve. Unfortunately, too many new users don't accept this or demand the services they'd get from paid support staff, turning online support into a thankless occupation and reducing the number of those willing to do it.

An old and renowned online help service is the EFnet **#irchelp** channel, run by a group of about 30 dedicated individuals with years of IRC experience (their combined IRC experience is well over a century—wow!). Its sister channel, **#irchelp** on IRCnet, is a bit smaller but follows the same tradition. I'm proud to be a member of those two teams; without them, this book would never have existed. Almost every large network has an **#irchelp** channel, and it's generally a good place to turn to when you're thoroughly stuck.

These helpers are increasingly under pressure as more and more overdemanding new users expect to be spoon-fed the answers to questions that are no more than a click away. But they'll willingly help out with general IRC questions and problems. They do, and rightly so, expect people to have a go at finding the answers themselves, so repetitive questions a user could answer with no more than a little common sense may well evoke a snappy response. They are also the people behind the largest website dedicated to providing information and help regarding IRC. Jim Benson initially hosted and put together this site, now maintained by Joseph Lo (and a cast of thousands) at Duke University. This is the most comprehensive website about IRC and is well worth a visit.

Channels named **#irchelp** are present on all large networks, though they're not necessarily run with the same efficiency or ability to handle all sorts of IRC-related questions. Almost all networks, small or large, have a channel that also provides help to newcomers, often a multipurpose administrative and help channel. In many cases, the server's Message of the Day (MOTD) hints where to look if you need a helping hand on IRC. Many networks also have an **#mIRC** channel, which will help out with the most popular client on IRC, mIRC.

When consulting a help channel, you'll sometimes run into ill-meaning users who try to give you misleading answers that affect your client or machine. Use your common sense in evaluating an answer. For example, a Windows user who believes that pressing ALT-**F4** will do something smart deserves to have his client shut down. It's one of the essential Windows basics that this key press combination closes the active application, and anyone using such a machine should know at least that much before connecting to a network. If in doubt, check whether the person answering is an operator of the channel.

This doesn't mean someone who is not an operator can't give a valid answer—in fact, many help channels rely on experienced users who help out without taking part in running the channel. If someone is deliberately giving out bad answers, the channel's operators usually remove that user from the channel and warn you against following the bad advice before giving you the correct answer.

Channel or nickname services are generally set up to provide help themselves, and you shouldn't need to ask anyone about using them. Usually, simply sending the message "help" to the service brings up a menu of topics. If the service's help menu doesn't cover your problem, check with one of the help channels. Some networks even have a special channel for dealing with problem reports and queries about the services.

Online help services were very popular in the early days, but gradually faded out on all major networks. They mostly referred to the ircII help files and sent them to any user requesting them. There's been a revival of interest in such services, and a number of smaller networks are now running a service, usually known by the nickname HelpServ, that responds to messages asking it for help on various topics. Some networks also run a service called ircIIhelp, providing help for ircII in particular.

Hopefully, readers of this book will rarely feel the need to refer to any of the above services since it covers all topics in greater detail than any online document or service. If you do need help, though, and can't find the answers anywhere in these pages, you know where to go. Who knows—you might find me lurking on one of those help channels.

16.6.1 Getting Help with Windows Clients

First, and before you do anything else in terms of seeking help from others, type **/HELP** to bring up the client's own help facilities. If you're using mIRC, your client includes what is probably the most authoritative and comprehensive documentation any client has. In fact, there are so many resources just a click away that some help channels won't help a person who is unwilling to press **F1** or type **/HELP** and browse a bit.

New mIRC users have an excellent source of information at their fingertips with **/IRCINTRO**, and can call the mIRC FAQ up from within the client. The mIRC FAQ covers 90 percent of the answers to a user's questions; the client package doesn't include the FAQ, but you can download it separately from the mIRC download sites. With the client's built-in help, you should rarely need to ask someone about using mIRC. If the combination of the mIRC help files and this book doesn't offer what you need, even the best help services and channels may not be able to help.

If you still want to ask someone, a number of channels that exist on almost all networks can provide good help with the client. Try any channel named **#mirc**, **#mirchelp**, **#new2mirc**, or a help channel you read about in the MOTD. On smaller networks with only one help channel, you'll usually find experienced mIRC users.

Users of other Windows clients probably won't have such luck. Pirch users should try **#pirch** on EFnet. Where to get ViRC help remains a mystery, and Xircon is more or less unsupported. So with these clients you'll be largely on your own.

16.6.2 Getting Help with Unix Clients

The ircII client's help files deal with just about every aspect of using the client, and you should have downloaded and installed them along with the client itself. Unfortunately, many system administrators neglect to do this, and may not give their users the means to install the help files themselves. If you don't have the help files on your system, you could try to obtain and install them, but this may fail if the client has certain settings that make user-installed help files useless. If you have a disk and/or file quota, the limitations the quota imposes may mean you can't install the help files. Try setting them up in a directory within your home directory, then setting the help path variable (/**set help_path**) to the absolute path of their location. By absolute path, we mean the location of the files in respect to the root directory, as opposed to a relative path, which is based on your current or home directory. The help files are widely available via FTP. Here's an example of the installation process (assuming you have the set of files named **ircii-2.8help.tar.gz**).

First, uncompress and untar the help file, as described in section 4.5. You should see a series of path and file names scroll over the screen as each file is dearchived and put where it belongs. Eventually, you'll have a new directory named "help" within your home directory. Now start up your client and /**set help_path <full path to directory containing help files>**.

If all goes well, typing /**help** should now bring up precisely that—help. On some systems, the client is configured to seek help from one of the now-obsolete help services. In this case the client returns an error message saying there is no such nickname. Try /**set -help_service**, then /**help** again. If it returns the message "No valid HELP_SERVICE or HELP_PATH set," you're out of luck and must rely on remote help services and channels, unless you can recompile the client and change the settings that control the means of getting help. In that case, you can compile a client, which includes the help files anyway. If you use networks that have an ircIIhelp service, use it. On other networks, there is no equivalent. Help channels such as **#irchelp** tend to have a number of expert ircII users who can answer practically any question, and you can also download IRC-related documents from a variety of places—most of these are fairly old and therefore geared to ircII users. And of course, you have this book!

The same procedure works for ircII-based clients such as EPIC and BitchX. BitchX also includes a file explaining many of its unique commands. You can call this filewith /**BHELP** if you've properly installed the client (there should be a ~/**.BitchX/BitchX.help** file). (The tilde (~) in Unix represents a user's home directory.)

IrcII users should install one of the ircII 2.9 clients (I recommend 2.9alpha6 or later, not the 2.9_roof client) or the 4.4 release, since 2.9 and later versions include the help files in the distribution.

16.6.3 Getting Help with Mac Clients

With the decline of the Mac as a highly popular platform and the fact that people more often use it for specific tasks that do not include networking on the Internet, Mac-related help of any kind on IRC has become a rather sad story. While plenty of clients are available for the Mac, their help facilities are often inferior. This may change, though, in the wake of the recent success of the iMac and increased popularity of these clients.

Your best choice for getting help, apart from the files available from www.irchelp.org (which, by the way, a Mac expert maintains), is one of the large help channels—you can only hope that someone in there speaks Mac. Of course, you'll have to put up with the old joke about using Macs as doorstops before you get any help. But even those who have never been near a Mac are aware of the problems Mac users face in getting help, and often try to answer your question unless it's entirely Mac specific. The channel named **#undermac** on the Undernet IRC network has the reputation of being friendly and helpful, and is a good option if you're stuck or can't find any Mac help on the other channels. The same is true of DALnet's **#macintosh** channel.

16.6.4 Getting Help for Other Clients

In most cases, you're alone and must rely on intuition, common sense, and any documentation your client may have. If you do get stuck with client- or platform-specific problems, your best choice is one of the channels where users of your type of machine convene—**#amiga** or **#atari**, for example. You may have to try several networks to find such a channel. People in the mainstream help channels will try to help, but you'll rarely find someone experienced in using your type of machine. It can't hurt to try, but don't have high expectations.

16.7 The Protocol

The IRC protocol is based on a document by Darren Reed and Jarkko Oikarinen, written in 1993. This document, the RFC 1459, is what all client and server authors should refer to. As far as adhering to it goes, that's no more than wishful thinking—I'll explain below. RFC stands for Request for Comments. Many RFCs, like 1459, are authoritative sources of technical specifications and ensure the necessary level of compatibility between different programs. If you ignore the RFC, it's quite likely that server and client programs will not communicate correctly.

While clients must comply with the standards set by server programs, the same doesn't apply to servers. Modern irc daemons often add extensions to the protocol or modify some of the functions described therein.

Apart from forcing clients to adapt to a wider range of different servers, this also makes the different kinds of ircd incompatible. Some of the differences are rather subtle, while others are very noticeable. In the case of some commercial server software, the term "depraved atrocities" might be too mild (I sometimes think a herd of elephants trampling over the server would do less damage).

For example, you can't set up a network so that part of it runs Undernet server code and the other part runs IRCnet code. Even if the servers permit this to happen, which they will not (each will refuse it after detecting the other server's type), it would create problems in server communication and adversely affect the network. Today's ircd authors regard the RFC as outdated, and no type of server is absolutely RFC-compliant anymore. The same applies to client authors, who follow the ircd coders and often exceed them in ignoring standards, protocols, and conventions. The widespread disregard of standards has done the network little good. Of course, replacing the RFC 1459 with a new standard is hardly possible since the variations added on the different irc daemons are numerous and often conflicting, and today's ircd coders are unlikely to get together and agree on common standards.

16.8 Other Types of Real-Time Online Communication

Although IRC is the most popular form of live chat on the Internet, several others enjoy a fairly large popularity. Some are simpler to use and may interest people who have trouble grasping IRC in full.

16.8.1 Web Chat

These are based on Web pages, and you need a Web browser to access them. Point your browser to the URL of such a site, and it calls up a page where users engage in conversations. Chatters submit messages to the page and other users can retrieve them. You follow the conversation by reloading that particular URL, which presents the page with the new messages. Web chat is slow, cumbersome, and a bandwidth fiend, but it's simple to use and allows the chatters to embed links and images in the text.

16.8.2 Talk

Use of the classic one-on-one talk has declined with the increase of online chat environments, where one-on-one conversations are can be held alongside group discussions. The machine receiving the initial talk request must be running a *talk daemon,* which notifies the user of incoming talk requests. You'll rarely find this on the average dial-up machine, but it still shows up on multiuser Unix systems.

16.8.3 WWCN

This new and emerging form of multiuser conferencing looks like a cross between IRC and Usenet. Codewise, it's still at an early stage and doesn't yet offer any special clients (it currently has compatibility with IRC clients), but the concept and protocol are highly promising as a chat medium of the future. Check out http://www.wwcn.org/ for more information.

16.8.4 ICQ

ICQ is not as complex as IRC and, in my opinion, lacks the magic that would make it a full alternative. Nevertheless, it's extremely popular as a background application that enables people to reach others swiftly using unique identification numbers (a bit like phone numbers) without having to go through the pains of searching on IRC. The software itself is not great, and is probably the system's greatest drawback—its bugs and gaping security holes have not inspired confidence. ICQ has fixed these problems, but it still might take a while for the system to shake off its reputation as insecure.

16.9 IRC for Other Platforms

So far I have talked about Unix, Windows, and Mac OS, but these are not the only operating systems under the sun. There are many others, often as good as any of the above, that have outlived their time as a mainstream platform, are just in development, have very specific purposes, or simply never gained wide acceptance. If you use one of these, I hope you'll find the following bits and pieces of information helpful.

16.9.1 Amiga

If I were to cover a fourth platform in detail, it would probably be the Amiga. The continuing popularity of the Amiga and its very loyal base of users and developers keep it alive where others are fading out. Still, it seems to be slowly waning, and software development isn't as vigorous as in its heyday in the late 1980s.

Your choices are basically three: AmIRC, ChatBox, and Grapevine. AmIRC is probably the most popular client for the Amiga. It supports all the basics, emphasizing well-developed standard features rather than modern toys, and provides a stable and secure chat environment. Grapevine, on the other hand, isn't quite as friendly in the installation department and is no longer maintained. Both support scripting and allow their user to create add-ons. However, I have to give AmIRC the thumbs-up, if only because it is still regularly updated. The third client,

ChatBox, is also kept current. It sacrifices appearance for performance and speed, making it a serious option for people with less powerful machines (I know how many old, beloved Amigas are still in service).

Ruling out Grapevine (it doesn't even have a Web page to its name anymore), one of the other two clients should satisfy any Amiga user, as both are complete, up to date, extendible with add-ons, and fairly user-friendly—in short, they're typical, good Amiga software.

16.9.2 Atari

Clients for this dying breed of excellent machines are available but limited. Which one you use depends on the type of network connection you have. Unless you've installed Linux or MiNT, you'll be unable to use a PPP dial-up account because the Atari lacks a PPP driver. STiK, although with each release it promises to add PPP support in the next version, so far offers no such support, and Oasis is an indecipherable puzzle. With Linux or MiNTnet—both of which have high hardware requirements—you will find a very usable IRC client at the same sites where you download the rest of the related software.

If you have hardware limitations, your options are STiK on a SLIP connection with IRC.TOS, which is a basic but fully functional client (provided that you can find an ISP offering SLIP access). For more power, you could in theory go to the trouble of a hardware upgrade and install MiNT or Linux—an expensive option, with much cheaper alternatives in the PC world. The upgrade may cost more than buying an old PC capable of handling all sorts of networking, and doesn't really make sense unless you want to upgrade the machine anyway. The old-fashioned Unix shell dial-in account with an ircII client on your host is still probably your best option if you plan to use a simple ST with less than 2MB of RAM and no HDD. In this case, of course, you'll probably find yourself running ircII instead of a client on your own machine. In practice, on this kind of connection, these low-power Ataris achieve a level of performance superior to most other machines of their generation.

As for the future . . . frankly, I haven't seen an Atari user "in the wild" in ages. It's not very likely that software development will continue, so your options are very limited if you stay with this platform.

16.9.3 MS-DOS

With the various forms of Windows taking over the PC world and the number of clients available for it, few newer PC users even know how to handle MS-DOS. The number of users running MS-DOS clients is negligible, and the few clients written for MS-DOS were abandoned at some point in the past. Most people who still use MS-DOS as their primary operating system prefer a terminal program with a Unix shell account and ircII. With many ISPs offering only true PPP, the lack of freely available PPP software for MS-DOS makes the shell account the only real option.

The only MS-DOS client a number of users still employ is the Worldgroup client for the MajorBBS system. This client is very much nonstandard and offers an interface similar to a BBS chat or teleconference system. As it is commercial and intended for use with MajorBBS, it's not an option for the average user. It's functionally adequate for uncomplicated operations, but too simple to support the needs of a regular IRC user who wishes to enjoy all aspects of IRC. The differences from most clients in the interface and command set are too numerous.

The mere two or three screens of help available with the **HELP** command demonstrate its simplicity. What the help covers is just about all the client can do. To broaden your IRC horizons, you'll need a different client.

16.9.4   VMS

Clients for this platform are few and far between. Even though it has its fair share of geeks and gurus, only one succeeded in bringing an acceptable form of IRC client to VMS. This client is basically a port of the ircII client adapted to VMS reality, and goes by the name of IRCdough—Dough's IRC client for VMS.

The caveat is that you must somehow manage to install it and make it work. Another option is sirc, providing you have Perl on the machine. However, you will probably end up running it in "dumb" mode (limited user interface and display capabilities) because sirc's front end, which is written in C, is unlikely to compile successfully. A few more clients are available, including one called IRCII, but when it comes to VMS, Dough's client is the one to use. To be honest, you should try finding another machine for IRC.

16.9.5   OS/2

Several decent clients are available for OS/2, including a version of Zircon for machines with tcl/tk installed and a BitchX port. The two most popular clients are OPENCHAT/2 and GTIRC. OPENCHAT/2 is a VIO client, while GTIRC makes the best of Presentation Manager and REXX. Both come with all the bells and whistles, including DCC, color, and sound support. If you would like a more common client, you can run mIRC in a WinOS2/32 session. You have an excellent operating system at hand and are blessed with many options. I sound like a fortune cookie, don't I?

16.9.6 WebTV

I know WebTV is a very easy and nontechnical way of using the Internet, but I cannot seriously recommend it for IRC. WebTV is in no way a computing environment, and it shows. The software it offers in lieu of an IRC client is a sorry excuse for one. Its functionality is good for very little other than simple communications. If this is all you want it for, it will do. It joins you to TalkCity by default, which is in itself not bad, but changing to another server is a hassle. It does not support DCC or multiple channels, nor is it capable of identing (this can be very inconvenient when you're trying to use servers that require ident, particularly on EFnet). For any job more complicated than joining a channel, WebTV simply doesn't have what it takes. As far as advanced IRCing is concerned, WebTV is just a little box sitting on top of your TV set.

16.9.7 BeOS

BeOS is a relatively new platform, and not many clients have been written for it. The two that do exist are Felix and Baxter. Neither of them is as fully featured as a Windows or Mac client, but this is sure to change as they develop.

Felix is a bit older and more solid, with a few interface bugs. What I consider its main drawback is the total lack of flood protection—it does not even support ignore functions. Baxter has a cleaner graphical interface and is probably the better option, despite having fewer features. Honestly, anything is better than a client that offers absolutely no protection against idiots and flooders. I hope the author of Felix will endeavor to correct this omission soon, so we can count it among the living clients.

I think you'll agree this chapter is full of happy, helpful stuff. Sorry to disappoint you, but the next one isn't. It's about all the nasty things people do to each other for no good reason. Go figure. Ah well, there's no point in putting it off . . .

17

ABUSE AND SECURITY ISSUES

Every IRC user is bound to encounter at least one form of Internet abuse intended to annoy, disconnect, gain unauthorized access, or simply destroy. Here we'll describe the most common forms of IRC and Net abuse, the methods used, and how to protect yourself. (This chapter is largely a follow-up to section 2.1.)

17.1 Flooding

Flooding is probably the first form of abuse you'll encounter, as it is a favorite of antisocial elements—it requires no imagination and minimal effort. Flooding serves no purpose other than destroying someone's enjoyment, and is usually just annoying; flooders are universally regarded as lamers.

A network desync can complicate flooding and make it a more serious problem. I'll talk about this in more detail below, but the main point is that when a channel is desynced (or when a user is desynced from the channel), the whole channel may not recognize certain properties of the users on it. Your server may think you're an op on the channel, while another server channel doesn't even realize you're there.

Generally, however, channel ops can get rid of flooders if they're attacking a channel. Those who don't have ops will have to rely on their client's **IGNORE** function or leave the channel. Let's have a look at the different types of floods you may encounter on IRC and how to deal with them.

17.1.1 *MSG, NOTICE, and CTCP Floods*

These terms describe floods of any type directed at your client or a channel. Unless the volume of a flood is so great that it fills your sendq and forces you off—which is very unusual, since it requires resources the average flooder doesn't have and increases the risk of detection by IRC operators—the correct use of **IGNORE** can stop it, with no more than a slight loss in connection speed.

Floods using **MSG** and **NOTICE** are little more than an annoyance. Channel moderation and the **IGNORE** command easily stop them. Since **CTCP** is equivalent to **MSG** as far as the server is concerned, setting channel mode **m** effectively prevents the flood from reaching the channel. CTCP floods, however, can disconnect you from the server. Since your client automatically replies to CTCP, a flood may make it send too many messages back to the attacker—enough, in fact, so that the server disconnects you for flooding. You can ignore the CTCPs with **/IGNORE [user] ALL** or with **/IGNORE [user] CTCP**.

17.1.2 *Nick Floods*

This is a very disruptive type of flood; the only solution is to **KICK** and **BAN** the offending clients. You must deal with it immediately since an excess of nick-flooding clones can cause a sendq overflow and client slowdown, resulting in long delays until the kicks and bans take effect. Usually all channel operators must combine their efforts to deal with it effectively. Channel management tools, such as a good bot or script, are a very effective means of handling these problems if configured correctly and programmed to kick and ban nick flooders immediately.

Protective measures include setting a limit on the channel's users with mode **l**, preventing too many clients from joining and creating a hot key or command scripted for the client to stop the display of nick changes. The latter will not solve the problem, but will help by reducing the amount of data displayed and letting you identify flooders more easily. Nick floods also place more stress on the network itself, since the nick changes get relayed to every server on the network, and don't just increase the traffic on the part of the network between the flooder's server and the targets.

Some networks guard against nick floods by preventing more than a certain amount of nick changes in a given length of time, often allowing no more than three changes per minute.

17.1.3 Topic Floods

This is an annoying but easily combated type of flood. You stop it by simply setting mode **t** for the channel—another good reason for having that mode permanently set on a channel. If you're not a channel operator, you may prefer to leave the channel until it stops. If you do not wish to set mode **t**, you can also ban the user from the channel. Be aware, though, that the user can still message the channel if it isn't mode **n**.

17.1.4 Public floods

Public floods are often more effective in annoying people than one might expect. The reason is that the automatic ignore and kick features some protective scripts or bots use often react to other kinds of floods, but not to public ones. If you set a form of protection against public floods, make sure you allow a fair margin for regular channel traffic. People tend to get annoyed when a touchy flood protection script or bot kicks them. If the channel lacks any such protection against public floods and your client won't react to it either, you'll have to **IGNORE** public messages manually from the clients responsible for the flood if you're not an operator. Ops can deal with this effectively by setting the channel **+m**.

One of the pitfalls of a protective script or bot set to guard against public floods is that it tends to check for a certain number of messages within a timespan. Normally, receiving ten messages from one user within a ten-second span might indicate a flood; however, when the network is lagging, ten messages, appropriately spaced from the sender, may hit the receiver like an automated flood.

17.1.5 DCC Floods

These are essentially CTCP/PRIVMSG floods; they pose a potential threat to clients configured to accept DCC requests automatically. Once again, DCC auto-accepts beg for trouble. Ignoring CTCP should work fine for DCC floods as well. Mode **m** also stops this type of flood.

17.1.6 Mode Loops

Flooders sometimes use these after a takeover to render the channel useless, though such incidents are rare. Three clients carry out the most common form of this flood, with two doing **+o/-o** mode changes and the third subject to the changes. This is destructive for the network, as nick floods and operators usually respond to complaints and remove the clients.

Mode loops can also result from misconfigured protection scripts, in which case one of the operators present should deop all looping clients with a single mode change. Mode loops are more destructive under good network conditions, which allow the mode changes to reach the second looping client sooner, letting it reverse the change faster and increasing the rate of mode changes.

17.1.7 Leavejoin Floods

This nasty type of flood disrupts the channel with continuous joins and parts from one or more clients. Setting the channel **+i** and/or banning the offending host(s) is an effective way to deal with it. However, flooders sometimes use it to hit a channel during a desync, since the channel ops trying to ban the flooders may not be seen as ops on the servers the flooding clients are using and therefore the flooders will be permitted to join the channel.

17.2 Hacking

Hacking is possible only if there is a security flaw somewhere. A hacker doesn't create holes, but just uses them—successful hacking means you've proved that you are better informed than the person maintaining the machine you hacked. On IRC, hacking more often targets servers, since clients are rarely exploitable. Using a current but well-tested version of your client is the best way to make sure it's secure—most holes get discovered fairly soon, so a client that has been around a while should be pretty clean. You *should* use pretty modern versions, but there's no need to be on the bleeding edge of technology *all* the time, unless bugs or security problems in older versions make it necessary.

If there is a problem with your client, the access an intruder can gain varies depending on the machine running the client and the nature of the hole itself. In the worst case, that would be full control of the machine and access to other machines.

More common sources of trouble than clients are scripts of questionable quality and commands that give arbitrary access to your client after you type some script someone told you would do such-and-such. Check unfamiliar instructions with a friend, a good help channel, or the client's documentation. If you still have doubts, don't type it. Whenever you're using a script, read it carefully for back doors. If your scripting abilities aren't up to this, you shouldn't be using the script.

17.3 Channel Takeovers

You can mostly avoid these by following the channel security tips in section 7.7. If the channel is taken over and you don't have a channel service for regaining control of the channel, no authority can give it back to you; section 7.5 has already provided the best advice. While takeovers are not approved behavior, operators generally won't act unless they are *certain* there was a malicious takeover and an acceptable log exists to substantiate claims. Even then they will deal only with clients on their own servers.

17.4 Harassment

This means every kind of harassment, including following, stalking, and threats. It isn't very common, but it's not unknown either. Because many different types of individuals may engage in it, one has to deal with it on a case-by-case basis. As with real-life instances of harassment, simply ignoring it is often very effective and thwarts attempts to inspire fear. While it's fairly easy to deal with most cases of harassment, the most persistent and aggressive instances are very tough.

IGNORE almost always does a good job of letting the other party know you're not interested. However, if the perpetrator knows some of your personal details, serious cases can result in regular real-life stalking. The problem is that the identity of the stalker may be unknown (although you can discover it sooner or later).

These more serious cases are usually people who know you personally. Such individuals are also much easier to identify since you can often find information on them locally. Your ISP can cooperate by monitoring incoming requests regarding any personal data (finger requests, for example) to identify their source. In most cases, letting the perpetrator know he or she has been identified stops the behavior, since they tend to do it under the shield of anonymity.

For the most serious cases, ask your friends to help out. You'll find many sources of advice and support; look these up for others' experience in dealing with it. I also recommend http://whoa.femail.com/ as a good source of information for women confronting stalking or harassment problems. You do not have to put up with it. If the stalker is local and is threatening you, go to the police. Stalking—even through the

Internet—is illegal, and you should make your local law enforcement agency aware of the situation.

17.5 Spoofing

Spoofing is not uncommon, despite recent additions to the server code on many networks in an attempt to stop it. It uses essentially simple programs to fake the originating address of a connection. This is often the address of a person the spoofer is trying to impersonate. Usually he or she intends to gain operator privileges on a channel by posing as that person.

The spoof itself is incapable of receiving messages, because the server sends them to a nonexistent address. The server's ident request gets no response, and consequently the message remains unidented. The false address won't reply to CTCP either, and usually times out soon unless the spoof is set up to send PONGs to the server at regular intervals. While the spoofed client can't see messages, its operator can see them and can instruct the spoof to send. In this way, the spoofer can fake an address, gain ops, and instruct the spoof, which now has ops to op him and deop others.

DNS spoofs are less common, but also much less obvious and more effective. A DNS spoof requires access to a domain name server. Having obtained this, a spoofer tries to convince the server that the IP address he's using corresponds to a different host name. It will resemble in all aspects a regular client with an identity, which sees and responds to all messages. The only difference lies in the IP address, which won't be visible in whois information. Spoofers use this type of spoof for channel takeovers and also for impersonating opers and evading bans and K: lines. This is another reason for using ops with passwords on a channel.

You can detect DNS spoofs by looking up the address corresponding to the host name the suspicious client is using, then comparing it to the IP address visible with the **STATS L** command (section 15.4.5). If the two IP addresses don't match, you've just caught a spoofer. The operators of the spoofer's server of residence usually want to know about this.

17.6 Password and Credit Card Number Thieves

A nasty class of individuals tries to steal accounts by tricking people into giving out their password. They identify themselves as some kind of authority—such as a system administrator, an IRC operator, or tech support—and ask users for their password under the pretence of network maintenance or by saying they'll lose their connection if they don't provide the password. Nobody with such authority will ever ask for your account password, especially on IRC.

If you've read this and still give someone your password, it's your own fault. You should report any such messages to the nearest IRC operator and to the user's ISP. Password stealers as a rule get KILLed upon detection. ISPs usually react to complaints about their own users stealing passwords and close the offending accounts.

People trying to get credit card numbers operate in the same manner, sometimes also offering a dubious service such as a pornographic Web site, to which the user is supposed to have access after giving out a credit card number. You should report this practice, known as *phishing*, to an IRC operator and that person's ISP for immediate action. The phisher may already be known and can get into serious legal trouble.

17.7 Denial of Service Attacks

Here's the really nasty stuff. You'd think people would leave you in peace since you're offending no one—but suddenly, out of the blue, your machine starts dying on you as soon as you are in the vicinity of a particular person on IRC. And guess what? He's having more fun than you are. This is a Denial of Service (DoS) attack.

17.7.1 Nukes

Nuke is a generic term for any form of nasty data packet or sequence intended to exploit a known security hole and force the target to crash, reboot, disconnect, or otherwise inconvenience its user. Nukes aren't just not nice, they're illegal.

The existence of exploitable holes has been known for a long time, but Net abusers have used them widely only since late 1997, when the "blue screen of death" epidemic started. At that time someone created and distributed a ready-made program to exploit the problem. Thus it was no longer in the hands of the experts alone, but also available to "script kiddies" who were all too pleased to find out how much annoyance they could cause with a mere mouse-click.

How susceptible you are to nukes depends largely on the type of machine you're using. Macintosh and Windows 3.1 machines are mostly immune to nukes. Windows 95 included some sloppy work on the networking features, which exposed machines to these attacks, and Windows NT machines are vulnerable too. You can patch Windows 95 with the Dial-Up Networking upgrades, downloadable from http://www. microsoft.com. You can protect Windows NT machines with the NT service packs, which include fixes for the problem. Check http://mirc. stealth.net/ for the latest in patches.

Windows 98 corrected the nasty faults that allowed a stroke of the mouse to kill Windows 95. So far, new attacks that work on 98 machines are far and few between, and none have posed a major problem for IRC users. Upgrading from 95 to 98 should put an end to your nuke problems; the fact that there has been no mass slaughter of Windows 98 users a year after its release is encouraging.

Unix is not always immune to nukes. Almost all kinds of Unix machines have seen some form of attack capable of killing them during the last year or two. If you have a home machine running Linux or FreeBSD, stay informed by following a good mailing list or regularly checking a Web site offering news about your operating system. The good news is that it often takes no more than a day for analysis of the problem and release of a patch—a response time very few commercial vendors can match.

Let's have a look at the most common nukes:

Winnuke, aka OOB
> Affects: Windows 95, 3.11, NT
> Symptoms: Blue screen, machine may freeze, cannot restore Internet connection without rebooting

Land
> Affects: Windows 95, 3.11, NT, Mac OS, Sun OS, some BSD
> Symptoms: Freeze, crash

Teardrop
> Affects: Windows 95, 3.11, NT, Linux
> Symptoms: Spontaneous crash or reboot

Click (the original nuke)
> Affects: Any network connection
> Symptom: Sudden disconnection from server

Bonk, aka teardrop2, newtear
> Affects: Windows 95, NT 4
> Symptoms: Blue screen, machine freezes and crashes

Jolt, aka ssping, Ping of Death
> Affects: Windows 95, NT, older Macs, FreeBSD, some others
> Symptoms: System hangs, needs reboot to recover

All these attacks occurred by mid-1998, and operating systems released since then should be immune. Some old versions of an operating system may be immune while newer ones are not, because the vulnerability might lie in features the old versions lack. Variants of the same release of an operating system may react differently.

17.7.2 ICMP Flooding and Smurf

ICMP floods are nothing more than a brute-force attempt to kill your connection by overloading it. Attackers employ the **PING** command to send as many data packets as they can to their target. If in addition the attacker uses a fake source address, he or she has no limit on his capacity to send data because it doesn't bounce back from the target, making it possible to utilize the maximum available bandwidth in such an attack. This also depends on the local network configuration—providers with any sense filter out ICMP packets with fake source addresses and never let such packets venture outside their own network.

Smurfing has nothing to do with little blue creatures living in toadstools in the woods, as in Peyo's famous cartoon series. It is probably the most destructive form of DoS attack. The attacker fools machines on a third-party network into thinking a series of ICMP packets originated from the target of the attack and responding to them. This would be no worse than any old Ping flood if it didn't take advantage of a network's broadcast address—all hosts on a network will reply to anything sent to this address. Unfortunately, many systems administrators have not configured their routers to reject everything sent to the broadcast address from outside their local network. If this is the case, the following (disastrous) sequence establishes itself (the addresses used here are fictitious and used only as examples):

- Attacker is on 222.99.88.77, target at 123.45.67.89.

- Attacker sends a Ping to 214.33.44.255, the broadcast address for the 214.33.44 subnet.

- Attacker fakes the source of the Ping to appear as 123.45.67.89.

- What is sent to the broadcast address, 214.33.44.255, receives replies from all hosts on its network—the more, the merrier.

- All hosts on the 214.33.44 network think they have received a Ping from 123.45.67.89.

- If there are 50 machines on that subnet, all 50 send a Ping response to 123.45.67.89.

Therefore, if there are 50 machines on the third-party network that respond to Pings, what the attacker sends bounces off to the target, multiplied by a factor of 50. If the attacker is capable of sending out a stream of Pings at a rate of 50 Kbps, the "amplifier" sends a stream of 2,500 Kbps to the target. You can do the math for larger figures.

The main problem isn't the attacker. The real problem is the administrator of the 214.33.44 network who allows use of that network as a smurf amplifier. This example would cost him 2.5 Mbps of his bandwidth for the duration of the attack. He might have that much to spare, but you don't. Smurf attacks will hopefully diminish over time as more and more network administrators come to their senses and stop letting attackers use their networks as amplifiers.

Both regular floods and smurf attacks (or fraggle, which uses UDP instead of ICMP but follows the same principle) are illegal. In the United States, they are a federal offense with a penalty of up to four years in jail. Mild cases may result in nothing more than the attacker losing his or her account at the ISP. Smurfers, on the other hand, are likely to be hunted down on a federal and international level since the impact of an attack on the target's ability to serve its customers can be significant.

As for protection, there's not much you can do about incoming traffic except to block it at some point upstream. It's largely up to network administrators to deal with this sort of problem, and you should contact your ISP for ways of counteracting ICMP floods. In the event of a smurf attack, you probably don't need to tell the ISP administrators since it's too obvious to miss.

17.8 Spam and Mass Messaging

While not outright destructive like other forms of abuse, mass messaging is annoying and unwelcome, apart from generating unnecessary traffic for the server it's on and the network as a whole. A number of scripts supporting mass messaging are in circulation, and they usually rely on one of two methods.

The most widely used script connects a bot-like client, which takes a **WHO** listing to see all visible users of the network and then sends a message to all of them at as high a rate as it can manage without being flooded off.

These messages are usually **NOTICEs** and less often **MSGs**. If you have usermode **-i**, which makes you visible on **WHO** searches, you're likely to see one fairly soon on a larger network. Report it to the network's operators—many operators **KILL** such messages upon detection. Others couldn't care less. Smart "spambots" are designed to **MSG** everyone visible except for the IRC operators to escape detection. IRC operators, on the other hand, hate being taken for fools and have devised their own methods of tracking down spammers.

A much more annoying type of mass messaging (using **NOTICE**) comes from file-server clients advertising pornographic services. Both opers and users generally hate these, and reporting them to an oper of the server they're using usually gets them KILLed or K: lined, since most servers classify them as unauthorized bots as well as spammers. Their constant **WHO** scans and repeated messaging generates more traffic than the average once-only spam script.

The other type of spam uses **LIST** instead of **WHO** to obtain the list of public channels. It then joins a channel, sends its message to the channel or to each user individually, leaves, and proceeds to the next one on the list. The type of message spammers are sending—usually an advertisement for a URL, a channel, or an IRC network—often makes them identifiable, along with the fact that they'll be on a number of channels with names in alphabetical sequence. Many of these spam messages meet an untimely death when they blunder into a public channel full of IRC operators. Others lurk on large, popular channels and send their message to every user joining or leaving. It's up to the channel's operators to get rid of them, although an operator of the server they're using might have an interest in doing so as well.

17.9 Account Security

There are some basic rules for keeping your account secure from unauthorized persons. Although your ISP should have informed you of them, many providers don't consider it necessary to give their users instructions on how to keep an account as secure as possible.

Your key to an account is your password. Unless you're sharing an account with someone else by agreement, you should be the only person to know this password. In order to make sure only you use your account, follow this simple set of rules:

- Don't write your password down where others can access it. If you're afraid of forgetting it, write it on a bit of paper and place it in a sealed envelope. Under the monitor is not the best place—it's a little too easy to find there.

- Don't type it in front of others.

- Don't let anyone have it. You can give it to your ISP's support staff if there's a problem with your account, but only over the phone. If you do so, change it as soon as possible. As a general rule, though, tech support won't ask you for it. They should have all the access they need without asking for a password, including the ability to reset a password (setting it back to the original one) if they absolutely have to get in to your account for some reason.

- Change your password at regular intervals. Every two to four weeks is good.

- Never use easy passwords such as first names or dates. Choose a password longer than five characters that combines at least three of these four different types of characters: uppercase letters, lowercase letters, numbers, and special characters. Even if you're sure there is no leak on your side, if your ISP suffers a break-in someone may obtain a file containing your password. While passwords are encrypted in the file, hackers can extract or crack the password with the right tools.

Above all, remember that the terrible things discussed in this chapter may never happen to you. You may never meet an annoying or irritating character on IRC—then again, maybe you will. Don't be paranoid, but always be cautious. Didn't your mother ever tell you not to speak to strangers? There are no stranger people in this world than IRCers.

18

INSTALLING, RUNNING, AND OPERATING AN IRC SERVER

Ascend to the highest echelons of IRC geekdom—run your own server! Whether for business or pleasure, private or company use, now *you* can do it, too. This chapter concentrates on the technical aspects of installing and running an IRC daemon and connecting it to a network. I will assume you're capable of compiling and installing a software package. I consider it absolutely necessary to have that much expertise before you even think of running an IRC server. You don't need to be a Unix guru to set one up, but ircd does require a bit of knowledge, even if you opt for one of the ircds capable of running under Windows.

18.1 System Requirements

An ircd doesn't require huge amounts of memory, bandwidth, or CPU time. In fact, it will run happily even with an 80486/DX33 or equivalent processor and 8MB of RAM.

Naturally, both memory and processor requirements are higher if you intend the ircd as part of a network with a significant number of users. A nonnetworked ircd with only a few users needs even less in terms of resources.

An ircd destined for a major network should reside on a dedicated machine with at least a Pentium-100 or equivalent processor and 64MB of RAM, more if the machine isn't dedicated. These figures will eventually need revising as the network inevitably grows and requires more resources, or if you intend the machine to cater to a large number of users.

Bandwidth is just as important as processor power and memory—that's what can really make or break a networked server. It's not impossible to run a server on a small network with as little as 28.8-Kbps bandwidth. If there is little other traffic sharing the connection, the network can be viable as long as it remains small. For a larger network, you'll need a dedicated link of at least 256 Kbps. Major networks require a minimum of several T1 (1.544 Mbps) links, often more.

18.2 IRC Server Software

Ircd is available for several platforms, but Unix is by far the most preferred operating system. Some ircds run more comfortably on a particular flavor of Unix, but most have a decent level of portability. You can run ircd on Windows 95, 98, or NT, but I have reservations regarding the capabilities of the operating system and its susceptibility to DoS attacks. If you plan to run ircd on Windows, make sure you have patched the machine against all known attacks, and prepare to encounter more. This applies to all platforms, of course, but Windows has the worst record in that department.

It must be said that there is no longer a typical ircd. Most modern servers are based on the old "vanilla" 2.8.21 version with numerous features, hacks, and bug fixes added later, which have made them more and more incompatible. The most popular ircd for new networks is probably the one used on the Undernet (u2.10.06 is the current version) and slightly modified versions of it. This is because it supports Services (NickServ, ChanServ, etc.), which most new networks intend to use, while offering good performance and relative ease of installation.

More-ambitious new networks take the current DALnet or ircu version and customize it to fit their needs. In this way a large variety of ircds have developed, which often present a degree of incompatibility, so a level of uniformity on a network is necessary in order to avoid conflicts between servers. Because of security concerns regarding older ircds, you should get the latest server version. Many older versions have known security flaws, only patched later on.

Still, even with server security at a reasonable level, you'll probably have to make a few more updates for security reasons. It's a good idea to follow related mailing lists, such as an ircd users list specifically dealing with the ircd you're using, or **bugtraq** for information on newly detected security problems and bugs, and to stay generally informed of developments concerning the ircd you use.

18.3 IRC Daemons

Since Unix is the standard platform for running ircds, they are compatible with most flavors of Unix, although some work better than others. Operating systems that are a bit old or nonstandard, such as Ultrix, SunOS 4, or HP-UX, are more likely to present compiling and installation problems, since ircd releases are generally geared toward modern, mainstream systems. Modern operating systems such as SunOS 5.7 or Linux 2.0 and 2.2 usually give you a clean compile and present few problems in running. Solaris and FreeBSD are by far the most popular operating systems on major IRC networks.

In all cases, the **INSTALL** file and the set of files in the **doc/** directory contain more information about the peculiarities of installing each ircd, as well as instructions for specific operating systems, if needed.

18.3.1 Ircd 2.8/hybrid (EFnet)

Versions reviewed: 2.8/hybrid5.3 and hybrid-6 (beta)
Tested on: FreeBSD 3.0, Linux 2.0, SunOS 5.7
Download site: ftp.blackened.com
Hybrid ircd is based on 2.8.21 with an integrated concoction of various patches and hacks. It evolved out of several different series of patches to the 2.8.21 ircd used on EFnet. It performs best on Solaris and FreeBSD, but will run on other systems too.

Compiling it is difficult—you will probably find yourself recompiling a couple of times before getting it right. Hybrid 6 includes a new set of features such as channel mode **e**, the **KNOCK** command, and the controversial rejection of multiple targets for a series of commands.

Its features include numerous monitoring tools for operators, earning it the nickname of "fascist ircd" from opponents of the operator control philosophy. It's designed mainly for powerful machines with high client loads and performs very well under stress. It supports TimeStamp (TS3), restricted connections, and a form of channel delay.

It does not have a Services interface and is recommended for servers that do not intend to offer Services, but that do give operators a high degree of server control. It interfaces well with special server bots (TCMs), giving online operators an additional degree of control.

18.3.2 Ircu (Undernet)

Current version: u2.10.06
Tested on: FreeBSD 3.0, SunOS 5.7
Download site: ftp.undernet.org
Ircu is probably the most popular ircd nowadays. It combines stability with a host of useful features—not necessary, but rather handy—as well as a Services interface. Installation is fairly easy, with a configuration menu that is a bit friendlier than the standard practice of editing Makefile and **config.h**, and the defaults are sensible. You will have to create the **ircd** directory before starting the configuration.

The documentation in the server package is good and kept current. An informative Web site at http://coder-com.undernet.org/ supports it. Ircu has a history of pioneering changes that later made it to other ircds. While not all these changes have caught on, ircu is probably the most progressive ircd in the field of testing new concepts and features. Admittedly, I'm not an avid Undernet user, but I do have to hand it to ircu's creators for making a well documented, stable ircd, with just about every feature you would want or need as a server admin.

18.3.3 Ircd 2.9 and 2.10 (IRCnet)

Current version: 2.10.3
Tested on: BSDI 3.0 and 3.1, Linux 2.0, FreeBSD 2.2.8, 3.0, and 3.2
Download site: ftp.irc.org
2.9 was originally intended to be the successor to 2.8.21 for EFnet, but became a centerpiece in the row that eventually led to the network splitting into two parts, one of which became IRCnet, in July 1996. It emphasizes speed and resource efficiency at the expense of user friendliness and features. Critics regard its code as primitive, but it's perfectly functional and compiles with very little trouble. I've been referring to it as the IRCnet ircd throughout the book, but more precisely, it's the ircd that Christophe Kalt mainly developed, with IRCnet in mind but not expressly *for* IRCnet.

There are several patches to improve its online management and options, but your basic 2.9 or 2.10 version is poor in that department. It supports neither TimeStamp nor channel and nickname services, but includes a unique service interface designed to interact with a special type of locally-run service. This type of service does not appear as a client and can't interfere with remote users or channels in the way the typical channel or nickname service does. Another unique feature is the **iauth** authentication program, which runs as a slave and takes some of the dirty work away from the ircd. One of its advantages is that it can scan connecting clients and reject those using open SOCKS servers.

This ircd is ideal for networks and servers with limited resources, since it's very economical compared to other ircds. If your bandwidth is more precious than your CPU cycles, it's capable of compressing server-to-server traffic, reducing the volume of connect bursts by approximately 60 percent. Its portability is probably the best of any ircd, and it will happily run on almost any platform, including Linux and FreeBSD. At least version 2.9.5 will also compile on Windows NT using Cygwin. I can't tell you what its performance will be under NT, but this ircd is worth a try.

18.3.4 dal4.6 (DALnet)

Version reviewed: dal4.6.7.DreamForge
Tested on: FreeBSD 2.2 and 3.0, Linux 2.0
Download site: ftp.dal.net
I can't say I'm too happy with this ircd or I would recommend it without reservation. The fact is, it could do with a bit of a rewrite. Though it doesn't have many bugs, I find its configurability somewhat below par and its resource consumption horrendous compared to others. Its portability does not match that of hybrid or IRCnet ircd. FreeBSD is the recommended operating system, but it will survive Linux and most mainstream operating systems if you don't make too many demands on it. It's the opposite of IRCnet ircd, placing features above performance.

This doesn't mean it's altogether useless. It's actually a usable ircd, quite capable of satisfying the needs of a small-to-medium network while having an excellent Services interface. It also has a superior O: line setup, through which you can regulate some operator powers without having to recompile. Support for open SOCKS server scanning is optional. Its inadequacies are more obvious on DALnet itself, which has really outgrown the ircd. Otherwise it's a perfectly good option. It should also compile on Windows 32, but I have not tested it myself.

As of the writing of this book, bahamut, the hybrid-based replacement for DreamForge, is still being tested. I do not consider it to be a choice yet; its performance on DALnet is good, but a number of development issues and bugs remain unresolved.

18.3.5 Conference Room

Current version: 1.7.6
Tested on: Linux 2.0 (third-party tests)
Download site: http://www.webmaster.com/
Webmaster's creation has developed into a very respectable piece of software, good enough to stand up and face any more established ircd. Despite my Unix bias when it comes to ircd, I must say this program makes ircd worth running on Windows. Versions of it will run on Windows 32 and various flavors of Unix. You get all the bells and whistles, including integrated channel and nickname services and easy-to-use administration tools, as well as support and a Java client designed to allow people to connect to the server through a Web page.

Its drawback is the price—hefty even if you do not compare it to the zero cost of regular Unix ircds. The $99 for the Windows Personal Edition is acceptable if you want to run a small stand-alone server, but the rest of the price list scares me. The $295 price tag for the Unix Personal Edition, which accommodates no more than 100 clients and isn't networkable, is somewhat steep, and the extra $500 you would have to pay for a networkable version approaches the surreal, even if you do get online and phone support. Running ircd isn't rocket science—support isn't worth such a price difference. Personally, I'd rather put a bit more work into running my server than shell out all that cash when I can get something just as good for free.

18.3.6 Other ircds and Platforms

There are a host of different ircds out there, most of which hack those used on the major networks and run only on Unix. Commercial chat servers from Quarterdeck and Microsoft are adequate. The problem with both of these is that their command sets deviate unacceptably from RFC standards. For Windows, there is also the shareware **wircsrv**, but unfortunately it is no longer maintained and supported. It does have the advantage of having a 16-bit version, but I'm a bit doubtful of the performance you can get from Windows 3.1*x*. A couple more programs describe themselves as ircds, but aren't very convincing. There is no good, free ircd for Windows, but a project tentatively named fircd intends to cover this gap in the future.

The only platforms apart from Unix and Windows for which a working ircd exists are AmigaOS, VMS, and OS/2. I have been unable to locate a copy of the VMS ircd, so I can't really voice an opinion. Both the AmigaOS and OS/2 IRC servers are functional 2.8.21-based ircds, though they aren't developed as intensively as the rest.

18.3.7 Adding Services

Both ircu and DALnet ircd are designed to interface with user services such as ChanServ and NickServ. These services are very popular with users, and most new networks want to have some form of them available. The Espernet services package (Andrew Church on the EsperNet IRC network developed this—hence the name) is one of the very few public releases of such a package—most networks that have developed such a package independently keep it to themselves.

Espernet services interface well with both ircu 2.9 and dal4.4, with a few reservations regarding dal4.6 and ircu 2.10. They're available only for Unix (the author makes it clear that porting services to Windows ranks very low on his priority list), and run on the same machine as a server. They are available from ftp.esper.net.

18.4 The ircd.conf File

Apart from the compile options that control its settings, the server also requires a configuration file named **ircd.conf**. This includes important options and settings, some of which the server absolutely must have to run.

This file comprises single lines, each beginning with a letter characteristic of the option it represents and followed by a colon-separated list of parameters. I recommend reading the **example.conf** file contained in the ircd package (normally in the **doc/** directory) for more detailed information on setting up the **ircd.conf** with the peculiarities of the particular ircd it belongs to. The different conf lines must stick to a particular order to some extent. The **example.conf** file will show you which order to use. You can use an edited **example.conf** and keep the comments if you feel more comfortable having the instructions within the **ircd.conf**. If you do this, do not forget to comment out all example lines.

18.4.1 A: lines (All ircds)

There is a single A: line in the **ircd.conf**, which contains the server's administrative info. It's separated into three parts by colons, corresponding to the three lines (numerics 257 to 259) that, along with the header (numeric 256) make up the reply to an **ADMIN** query. An incorrect A: line prevents the server from functioning. Depending on the ircd, you may need a fourth, blank field—check the **example.conf** for the ircd you have.

18.4.2 M: lines (All ircds)

Your M: line defines the name of your server, a description (the info line you see in **LINKS** and **WHOIS** output), a virtual host if you use one for the server, and a port number your server listens on. Ircu 2.10.06 makes the M: line port the only one to which other servers can connect. Older versions and all other ircds let servers connect to ports with just a P: line. Your M: line must be correct for server connections to work. Ircu also uses a fifth field with a unique server id, probably paving the way into the future since server ids are likely to take over from server names as a means of identification.

18.4.3   I: lines (All ircds)

I: lines are necessary for a server to accept client connections. They allow you to specify who may use the server and, in conjunction with the Y: lines, under what conditions and with what limitations they may do so.

They can also direct clients to certain ports or limit them to using the server only at certain times of the day. Ircu 2.10.06 I: lines can also limit the maximum number of clients (globally) from a single address, a function that is part of the Y: line setup in other ircds.

I: lines work on a drop-through, right-to-left, and bottom-to-top basis. This means when a client connects, the server matches its address against all I: lines one at a time, starting with the right-hand field of the bottom I: line in the conf, and stops when it finds a matching one. If the server finds no I: line match, it rejects the client. It's important to remember to use the correct order in your I: lines. You'll usually want to place the most limited ones at the bottom, where they get read first, and the broader ones at the top. For example, if you had an I: line for ***@*.netcom.com** and a more generic one for ***@*.com**, placing the latter in a position where it would get read before the *@*.netcom.com one (below it) would defeat its purpose, since a connecting netcom.com client would find a match in the *@*.com I: line and never get checked against the other line. The correct sequence, in which I: lines become progressively broader, would look like this:

```
I:x::*@*.com::1
I:x::*@*.netcom.com::3
I:x::paul@wor-ma*.ix.netcom.com::5
```

On IRCnet ircd, lowercase i: lines can be used to restrict the clients matching that i: line. The restrictions are that the client can't use channel operator commands or change its nickname. This is how to impose user mode **r** upon a client.

You can place IP addresses in the second field, which I have marked with an **X**. This is not a significant character—it simply matches no address. You could use any other item that will not match an address, or just leave it blank. The address can either stand alone or have a matching host name in the right-hand field. You can also password an I: line by placing a password in the third field. The fifth field, usually blank, can assign this I: line a particular port.

18.4.4   Y: lines (All ircds)

These are necessary and there must be at least one, but having more can prove very useful for separating the clients and servers, which may connect to you (as defined in I:, C:, and N: lines) into groups. Hardly any server lacks a set of Y: lines regulating client and server connections.

Any server that allows more than local client access or is networked should sort the connections with Y: lines. Use separate Y: lines for client and server connections. Take care when setting up your Y: lines—they must fit in harmoniously with I:, C:, and N: lines.

18.4.5   O: lines (All ircds)

O: lines are not absolutely necessary, but are convenient for running the server from a client connection and for performing global operations on a network. First we must distinguish between the two different types of O: lines—the capital O: and the lowercase o:. Capital O: lines are used for operators with networkwide powers, offering the ability to use **CONNECT**, **SQUIT**, or **KILL** for any of the network's servers and to send global messages and/or wallops. A lowercase o: line limits the operator's powers to the local server (the client's oper status isn't broadcast to other servers). Naturally, the difference between the two is semantic on nonnetworked servers, although some compile options can define or restrict an o: line's powers on the local server, too.

You can encrypt O: line passwords with the **mkpasswd** utility you'll find in the ircd package. In order to use password encryption, you must compile the ircd with **#define CRYPT_OPER_PASS**. If you have enabled this option, you will not be able to use cleartext oper passwords at all.

18.4.6   C: and N: lines (All ircds)

Required in order for a server to link to others, these are therefore essential to a networked server. C: lines specify to which servers your server will connect, either automatically or when ordered by an operator. N: lines specify from which servers yours will accept connections. Both also determine certain other features of the server link, such as masking. C: and N: lines go together—one without the other results in nothing, apart from a few error messages. You must use C/N lines in conjunction with special Y: lines in order to prevent errors generated by attempts at incorrect routing or suboptimal routing.

IRCnet ircd allows compression of server-server traffic. You need to have **zlib** installed on the machine for this to work. In this case, the C:

line has to become a lowercase c: line. You can encrypt C/N passwords just like O: line passwords.

18.4.7 H: and L: lines (All ircds)

Technically not necessary, in practice these maintain order on a network by defining which servers can act as hubs and which can't, thus making sure servers that don't qualify for hubbing a part of the network don't do so. A server must have an H: or L: line on the servers to which it connects in order for those servers to permit it to introduce more servers to the network. These lines also limit the quantity or kind of server your server may introduce. You may need to compile your server as a hub if you wish to link to more than one server at the same time, and other compile options may also be of importance, depending on the ircd.

18.4.8 K: lines (All ircds)

K: lines are technically not necessary, but most server administrators would find it hard to run a good server without them. Their usefulness also depends on the server's I: and Y: lines—if those are well written, the need for K: lines decreases drastically.

K: lines follow the same rules as channel bans, the only major difference being that K: lines use **user@host** syntax rather than **nick!user@host**. You want them to be neither too broad nor too limited.

Weed out your K: lines regularly and delete redundant or stale ones. Too many K: lines take their toll on the server's performance.

18.4.9 P: lines (All ircds)

The P: lines determine which ports are open for connections. Each open port requires one P: line. You can add more P: lines while the server is running, but removing them will not close the port as long as there is still an active connection using it. P: lines can also associate a port with a host or domain allowed to use it.

18.4.10 R: lines (All ircds)

These are rarely used in practice. They allow the server to use an external program before accepting a connection. The only implementation of R: lines I'm aware of is on the Norwegian IRCnet servers, which use them to verify the user name by querying a special service local ISPs run before letting a client connect. Otherwise they are deprecated and on their way to extinction.

18.4.11 D: lines (EFnet) and Z: lines (DALnet)

These perform more or less the same function but have a different name, depending on the ircd. On hybrid, the D: line blocks connections from an IP address or address block, whether this resolves to a host name or not. These lines are often used when K: lines fail because people evade them by using virtual hosts. Although this form of D: line is only used on hybrid, you can achieve the same result using different means on other ircds: On 2.9/2.10 (IRCnet), K: lines perform this function as well as their normal function if an IP address instead of a host is K-lined. On Undernet there are lowercase k: lines for the same purpose, and on DALnet the Z: line is the equivalent. Confused? Me, too.

18.4.12 V: lines (IRCnet)

Only hubs use V: lines, to control the features their downlinks have activated. For example, a hub requiring that its downlinks not be compiled as hubs would use a V: line to prevent it by checking the version of the connecting server and rejecting it if it doesn't fulfill that condition.

18.4.13 Q: lines (EFnet, Undernet, IRCnet)

These are largely a leftover from the times when the only large IRC network was much less organized. Q: lines could prevent a server from connecting. Q actually stands for "quarantine." Q: lines require coordination among the network's servers; otherwise there's a risk of the network breaking up because a server's Q: line isn't present on other servers.

18.4.14 Q: lines (DALnet) and U: lines (Undernet)

The modern use of Q: lines, implemented in DALnet ircd, is quite different. DALnet ircd's Q: lines prevent the use of certain nicknames by non-operator clients. This is useful for preventing users from assuming nicknames they could employ to impersonate an IRC operator, **admin** or **Service**, and is necessary during service downtimes, when wise guys are likely to try to gain other users' passwords by assuming the nickname of a service.

U: lines, implemented in ircu 2.10.06, perform the same function, though with a different syntax. DALnet Q: lines act on a local server level and do not restrict use of the Q: lines nicknames by IRC operators, while ircu U: lines also bind the presence of the nicknames to a server and do not allow their use.

18.4.15   E: lines and F: lines (EFnet)

These are used to bypass other restrictions in the conf. If a connecting client matches a K: line, an E: line entry causes the ircd to ignore the K: line and let the client connect anyway. F: lines do the same, but also bypass class limits so that an F-lined client can always connect even if it is K-lined and its connection class is full. You can also add this feature to IRCnet servers using the **Sc** patch series.

18.4.16   T: lines (Undernet)

This is a really cute feature—though not indispensable, it's nifty and useful. With a set of T: lines, you can send a different MOTD to different connecting clients, depending on their host mask.

18.4.17   D: lines (IRCnet and Undernet)

Servers that autoconnect where they are least welcome make nobody happy. Because the C/N/H/L/Y line combinations do have their limitations (you would think five different config lines could do the job, but they don't), these ircds support D: lines as a means of telling a server under what conditions *not* to initiate a link it otherwise would initiate. This is very useful for avoiding routing chaos.

18.5   The MOTD

The MOTD is not mandatory, but is generally helpful for the server's users and the rest of the network. The contents of the MOTD are more or less arbitrary and normally state the purpose of the server, its policies, the names of the admins or operators, and anything else the server's administrator wishes the users to know. The MOTD is stored in a plain text file named **ircd.motd** in the **ircd** directory and is sent to each connecting client and any others that ask to see it with the **MOTD** command.

Lack of an MOTD file results in the sending of an error message (numeric 422) to the client. You can live without an MOTD, but servers with no MOTD look tacky and poorly run. You can send different MOTDs to different users only in ircu; see below under T: lines.

The contents of the MOTD are up to you, but here are some guidelines for putting together a good MOTD:

- Clearly state the server's rules.

- Huge ASCII server logos are cute. They're also annoying to the user and a waste of resources.

- The longer the MOTD, the less it gets read.

- Include the name of a channel where users can find help.

- I suggest a security advisory regarding Trojans.

- Include a disclaimer saying you are not responsible for content passed through the server.

18.6 IRC Operator Commands

Now that you've made yourself a server and given yourself that O: line, you need to know how to use it.

There are a number of commands only IRC operators can use. They are more or less the same for every kind of server. In this section, I'll look at the basic operating and maintenance commands. I won't go into the realm of commands available to opers on networks that allow them extended powers over channels—if you ever become an operator on one of those networks, more experienced opers will give you extra training. Some commands are also available to users, but give an operator more information. These are the main operator commands. For more commands, see 15.9.

NOTE *All servers allow an administrator to configure the server to limit global or local operators' use of certain commands. The administrator can also forbid some commands altogether and force operators to do the tasks associated with them directly from the server account itself.*

18.6.1 OPER

OPER is the most basic operator command, used to obtain operator status. The user OPERing himself or herself must use this command in combination with a nickname and password while connected from an authorized host listed in the server's O: lines.

```
/oper <nickname> <password>
```

The server checks your host against those listed with **<nickname>** (this will usually be your regular nick). If they match, it checks the password you give against the one stored in the server's configuration file.

Although you must send the nickname that's in the O: line as a parameter to the **OPER** command, you don't have to be using the same nickname at the time. On ircII-based clients, you can also enter the nickname alone, and the client prompts you for the password. As far as the server is concerned, this is no different from the full command, but it offers additional safety, since it prevents your sending the password to someone else (for example, a channel) by mistake. If your client doesn't do this by default, I suggest you write a small script to do so.

If the server accepts the command and identifies you as an operator, you see a message like this:

```
*** Mode change "+o" for user LeetOper by LeetOper
*** You are now an IRC operator
```

Oper status, as the message evidences, is really just a user mode available only to privileged users. If you have only locop status, some ircds set mode **O** instead of **o**. This is of course a contradiction—setting mode **O** for the "little o:" and **o** for the "big O:"—but this occurs because global operator status occupied mode **o** long before someone added a new mode specifically for locops.

Many server versions and patches change the text to something less bland, starting with the old classic, which read, "You are now an IRC janitor. Here's your broom" (which became fashionable again a while ago). My personal favorite was the one on a NewNet server saying, "You are now mentally twelve years old (IRC operator)."

Some fancier clients have a message of their own by default and ignore the server's message. BitchX is a notable example (the notice it shows isn't exactly a model of political correctness—I'll leave it to you to find out what it says.)

NOTE *For security reasons, you should not keep your password in a script. This is so that even if the security of your account or the machine it's on is compromised, the intruder can't retrieve the oper password because you haven't stored it in any file. The weak point of the whole system is that the password is sent to the server as plain text, so it's not immune to discovery. Hopefully some smart ircd coder will devise a system to use encryption on sensitive client-server transactions like this.*

18.6.2 KILL

KILL is a powerful and controversial command. The ability to use this command is often seen as an IRC operator's real power, although this notion doesn't last long—KILL's ineffectiveness will change anyone's mind sooner rather than later. Using **KILL**, an operator can force the user's server to close the client connection, therefore effectively removing that user from the network.

Much debate has gone into the ethics of **KILL** and its appropriate use, but this discussion has never reached a conclusion. In practice, it depends on the rules of the network and individual servers regarding oper behavior, and in some cases on the personal ethics of an individual IRC operator. With the advent of autoreconnecting clients and abuse tools, it's far from effective as a disciplinary measure for abusers and many operators resort to using K: lines instead.

KILLs for users on a different server from the one on which you're an operator (remote kills) get broadcast over the network and appear to everyone monitoring KILLs. KILLs that take place on your own server appear only to other operators of the server and to any users sharing a channel with the KILLed client.

```
/kill <nickname> <reason>
```

You must provide a reason in order for **KILL** to work. It can be any arbitrary text, but server or network policies generally require a valid reason. Many administrators also require their opers to keep records of the actions in a log file for comparison with the server's logs in case the oper's actions come into question. If possible, an oper should also try to record the event for which he or she used the **KILL**.

KILL, like **KICK**, also KILLs a client even if it changes nicknames. **KILL** added this feature fairly early, when abusers discovered they could escape getting KILLed or KICKed by changing nicknames before the operator had time to type their nick; it's known as "KILL chase."

This practice would also enable elimination of nick-flooding clients. In former times, this had a funny (and *really* frustrating) side effect known as the "KILL chase bug," which all server versions should have ironed out by now. Its result used to be that the operator killing a nick-changing client on a remote server would also get booted off the server. I can just see older IRC operators reliving their pain as they read this. Fortunately, newer server versions have fixed this bug.

18.6.3 CONNECT

CONNECT is an important network maintenance command that orders a server to attempt to connect to another server, provided that the other one isn't currently linked to it and that both servers have a valid entry for each other in the C: and N: lines of their configuration files.

The command can go two ways, depending on whether the operator is instructing his or her own server or a remote server to initiate a connection. In order to make the local server connect to another one, use the following:

```
/connect <other.server> <port>
```

To connect two remote servers, one of them must be visible from the operator's server and one not linked at the time you issue the **CONNECT** command. For example, if server A is visible to you, while server B is missing, issue the following command:

```
/connect <server.B> <port> <server.A>
```

You must always specify a port number. **CONNECT** *fails if you don't use one. Notice that the server to connect always goes first, followed by the port number on which server A is instructed to make the connection. Always put the server you can't see first.*

Use **CONNECT** with caution under bad network conditions, since lag can cause network errors and new splits. It is wiser to let the servers' autoconnect feature restore the link unless you know exactly what you're doing. In many cases, it is also better to let a server that's having problems chill out for a while before reconnecting it.

18.6.4 SQUIT

SQUIT (Server **QUIT**) is another network maintenance command to use with extreme caution, since inappropriate use can throw a network into chaos, particularly if the situation is already fragile due to high server loads or a number of unstable links. It instructs the uplink of the server you're SQUITting (as seen from the side of the server where the **SQUIT** originates) to drop the link, thus disconnecting that server and anything linked behind it.

If you **SQUIT** your own uplink, your server disconnects from the network. If you have other servers behind you, they follow. **SQUIT** is basically a way to create a net split artificially. You should only use it on a link that is *really* not working or is heavily lagged, with no recovery in sight. Even then, use it carefully, preferably consulting operators on other parts of the network on how to restore the imminent split. The golden rules of **SQUIT** are:

1. Never **SQUIT** a working link. Simply SQUITting and reconnecting when the links are fast and stable just because the routing isn't optimal is questionable and often asks for trouble.

2. Never **SQUIT** without an alternative. When you close a link with **SQUIT**, you should also have an idea of what to do to reconnect the part you SQUITted, unless you really want the server off the network.

At this point, I'd like to give Vegard Engen special thanks for tirelessly drilling these rules into the minds of newer operators like myself in his capacity as Norwegian IRCnet coordinator and wise old man of IRC. (Never mind the fact that he's actually younger than I am!)

SQUIT is indicated in the case of a visibly compromised (hacked) server. In this case, if its true operators are not present or can't deal with the problem, the intruder may also be able to reconnect the server and use it for destructive purposes, in which case you or someone with access to a hub server may be forced to jupiter it.

18.6.5   DIE

As the term indicates, **DIE** is a very powerful command. Never use it lightly. What it does, very simply, is shut down the server. Many server administrators have the command disabled and will allow server shutdown only from the machine itself.

Use **DIE** to shut down a server *only* if:

- The server or the machine it's on has been compromised (hacked) and is in danger of disrupting the network. Unless you can pinpoint the problem and eliminate it immediately, this might not prevent the intruder from restarting it.

- Its network connection is currently nonfunctional and your server could become a source of abuse (collisions, takeovers, and so forth). In this case you may wish to prevent it from becoming a liability to the network and restart it once its link is restored. A (preferred) alternative is leaving the server up and commenting out (temporarily suspending) the part of the configuration that makes it autoconnect.

Don't use this command except in a dire emergency or a controlled maintenance situation, when it's preferable to shut down the server from the machine. If you really don't want the server to come to life again for a while, you should also disable its watchdog script, or it will restart in a short while. If you don't have the access to do that, **DIE** might not be a good idea. On DALnet, an operator may have to use a special password along with the command, as specified in the X: line.

18.6.6   RESTART

RESTART forces the server to die and restarts the ircd process immediately. Use it only in a real emergency situation, where all other attempts to correct a failing server's behavior have lead to nothing. It's useful in cases where the stress of serving a large number of users for too long has finally taken its toll on the machine (consuming excessive resources and slowing it down), or the ircd itself has presented a bug for which there is no immediate workaround. In the latter case, restarting the server might fix it temporarily, but a bug is a bug and will probably come back. It's better to let the admin restart the server from the machine itself, but **RESTART** is acceptable if the server seems to be about to kick the bucket anyway. Rather than letting it proceed toward an inevitable crash, a controlled **RESTART** is an option if you expect it to do away with the problem. Like **DIE**, **RESTART** may require a password on some servers.

18.6.7 STATS

Certain server stats called up with the **STATS** command may be available only to operators. Which of these stats are privileged depends on compile time options. On some servers all main stats are visible to users, while on others most are visible to opers only.

The type of stats an oper can access is even more varied than the regular set users can see. Consult the ircd's documentation or play around a bit to find out which **STATS** command shows what.

18.6.8 TRACE

The **TRACE** command shows an operator all the server's connections, including invisible users. Some server versions permit this for remote operators too, thus making all users on all servers visible to a global operator. Other servers disable this to give a user more privacy by removing this possibility from the remote opers' powers. Regular users can employ this command as well, but its use is often restricted.

18.6.9 REHASH

A server maintenance command, **REHASH** forces the server to reread its configuration file. It also prompts the server to establish links with servers to which it's configured to autoconnect if these aren't linked at the time. Watching the server closely when REHASHing may help detect faults in the configuration. If you're running DALnet ircd, a periodic **REHASH** is a good idea. This ircd's performance tends to drop a bit while it's running, and the occasional **REHASH** gives it a new lease on life or at least acts like an electronic cattle prod and subdues it temporarily.

REHASH usually follows a change in the configuration, although it's equally possible to do this from the machine itself after editing the configuration file. To do this, send the ircd a **SIGHUP**, assuming the **ircd** directory is your current working directory:

```
$ kill -HUP `cat ircd.pid`
```

You can also look for the process **id** with the **ps** command and
kill -HUP <pid>.

On some servers **REHASH** can also undo temporary changes to the
configuration, which someone might have added with special
commands particular to that type of server—for example, temporary K:
lines. Some commands are intended to allow such configuration
changes from an online oper without making the oper do them internally from the machine.

A **REHASH** is the first step in the four-step problem-solving
sequence—the four R's: **REHASH**, restart, recompile, and if all else fails,
reboot. Sometimes you'll do all the above, but not always in that order.
The fifth R is only for extreme cases—take the machine apart, poke at
the components, and *reassemble* it (a six-pack is optional—this is thirsty
work). Welcome to the reality of systems administration.

18.6.10 DEOP

This command, quite simply, removes oper status. Since it's a user
mode, you see the corresponding mode change:

```
/deop
*** Mode change "-o" for user hotshot by hotshot
```

Setting user mode **-o** has the same effect.

NOTE *BitchX uses **DEOP** as a channel operator command. With this client, and with
scripts that take over **DEOP**, you have to override the client's nonstandard use of
this command. BitchX has replaced it with **DEOPER**. In other cases you can perform the **-o** umode change, **/quote deop** or **//deop**, depending on the client.*

18.7 Monitoring a Server

This is easier said than done. Not only does the type and amount of
information available vary wildly from ircd to ircd, but the way it is presented and accessed changes too. Let's start with the logs. Most ircds
write to several files in the **ircd** directory. Exactly which files these are
depends on the ircd, but **rejects.log**, **users.log**, and **opers.log** are the
most common ones. Some ircds let you change the file names during
the configuration. The first file contains information about every single
rejected client connection; the second logs the successful connections,
quits, and duration of each connection; and the third contains informa-

tion about oper activity. If you have a really small server, none of these is of much importance, since you can easily keep track of events from an opered client. However, on a larger server you need to consult these if you are tracking a particular event. I don't expect you to see anything like the 200MB weekly rejects files I've run across, but that shows just how big these files can get on a large client server.

With an opered client, the way you can monitor your server depends entirely on the ircd. Hybridand ircu offer more in terms of monitoring capabilities, while DALnet ircd isn't quite as helpful. You can see information on these three ircds by setting certain user modes, mainly umode **s**. Additional umodes can increase the amount and type of messages. You can view some without umode **s** using an extra set of umodes, each of which shows only certain types of server notices.

IRCnet ircd, in this aspect, is a different animal altogether. A set of local channels has abolished and replaced umode **s**; we'll refer to these as **&CHANNELS** (to distinguish them from regular local **&channels**). Depending on the type of server notices you wish to monitor, you'll join one of these **&CHANNELS** rather than setting a umode. For example, you can see servers connecting and disconnecting from the network in **&SERVERS**, while operator and server kills get sent to **&KILLS**. **&CHANNELS** have modes **q** and **a** set. This makes them "quiet" (only the server can send messages to them) and anonymous (nobody can see other users on the channel).

This concerns notices about the server's operation. If you for some reason would like to monitor your users' actions, such as connections, nick changes, **LINKS** requests, and so forth, there's a different way to do it for each ircd. Hybrid has the advantage in this case—it's capable of displaying much more information about user actions than other ircds. DALnet lets you watch user connects and disconnects with umode **c** and clients flooding off with umode **f**, but that's about it. You can monitor a few more events through an oper service such as OperServ. IRCnet ircd supports absolutely no monitoring of user connections or actions—if you want such features, the **Sc** or **Fl** patch series will provide some. Ircu offers regular monitoring functions you would expect it to have, and you can also configure it to allow operators to peek inside secret channels.

18.8 The Price of Power

Being an IRC operator, inevitably places you in a position of power and responsibility. How you conduct yourself in your capacity as an IRC operator reflects not only on yourself, but on your server and the network as a whole. Nothing can give a server or network a bad name as fast as an irresponsible, power-tripping oper. Others will forgive incompetence—they'll laugh at you a few times for your blunders, but eventually forget them (that doesn't include K: lining *@* by mistake—*that* will follow you around forever, as some friends of mine can testify). Misusing your O: line for personal power trips brands you as a lamer for longer than you care to know, even if your admin doesn't fire you. Bear with me—I don't often get the opportunity to preach.

18.8.1 Channels

Depending on the network, you may have more or fewer powers over channels. Use them wisely. You're a server operator. Your job is to run the server and keep the network in one piece. Your job is not to run other people's channels for them, especially when they don't want you to. Your O: line doesn't give you the right to ignore the rules of someone else's channel, nor does it entitle you to special treatment.

So when *do* you have some authority over channels? This depends on the network's policy, but if the network has a channel service, chances are IRC operators run it. Users will often come to you with problems regarding the channel service. These problems can range from very simple—they've lost a password and have a fair guess what it was—to complex ownership disputes that drag on for months.

DALnet is the only major network where a special class of IRC operators, the CSops, can directly exercise their judgment and provide immediate solutions to most problems. It would be best if users never needed a CSop, but sometimes they do. Many small networks have modeled their policy on DALnet's, so it's likely you'll be doing these tasks if you take an oper position on one of those networks.

18.8.2 IRC Cops

IRCops are not IRC cops. I've said this before, haven't I? Nevertheless, you will confront many cases in which others expect you to enforce rules. The policy of some networks would actually make you an IRC cop in everything but title. Even on the major networks, I've sometimes questioned myself when telling a user there's no such thing as an IRC cop. Let's put it this way: Cops are law enforcement officers. IRC operators enforce a set of rules that often do not have an equivalent in legislation. While IRC users may break both rules and laws, the IRC operator's task is to take care of violations of the server's rules and leave crime to law enforcement. IRCops are IRCops, cops are cops. Let it remain this way.

The amount and sort of abuse you'll encounter varies from network to network. On all major networks, you can expect the "crime rate" to be somewhat higher than that of the ten largest cities in the United States put together. You'll find yourself thinking, "Just how dumb does this person think I am?" or "This person needs a life" at least five times a day. Brain damaged users will provide you with endless hours of fun and entertainment...*not*. Your problems can range from a single person flooding someone, to an organized gang trying to take down your server and everything within a 100-mile radius. You simply have to deal with each instance on a case-by-case basis.

Your work gets much easier if the ircd provides preventive measures. Hybrid ranks high in this regard, with IRCnet ircd a close second and DALnet way at the bottom of the list. IRCnet and EFnet ircd, as well as ircu to some extent, have added compile and configuration options that allow an operator to detect abuse more easily and prevent some forms altogether. DALnet ircd, on the other hand, is very poor in such features and too dependent on services. DALnet users, however, have more options for protecting themselves.

18.8.3 . . . And Justice for All

You have been appointed judge, jury, and executioner. Any violation of the server's rules mean that you must decide whether sanctions are appropriate and implement them, usually on the spot. Often you have little or no evidence to rely upon.

You don't get many options. For fairly mild violations, you can let it pass, warn the user, kill the problem client(s), or impose a temporary server ban (K: line) on the offender. In more serious cases or with repeat offenders, you may have to resort to permanent K: lines, global K: lines (G: lines or akills), or even sanctioning an entire provider.

Users will sometimes approach you, asking you to address a problem that does not concern you in your capacity as a server operator but rather as a higher authority. Some people just want advice on what to do about their problem; others want you to mediate a dispute, more often than not asking you to judge in their favor. The never-ending stream of supplicants holds a high risk of instilling delusions of grandeur, but that's a risk you'll have to live with—it comes with the job.

I cannot tell you what to do in each case. You have to evaluate the evidence and dispense judgments on a case-by-case basis. It's your choice whether to run your server like a Nazi prison camp commander, a benevolent dictator, the village cop, a janitor, or a good manager.

18.8.4 Bots

If your server allows bots, you can skip this section. All you have to do is weed out the abusive ones when users complain about them. But if you're on a server where bots are forbidden, prepare yourself for lots and lots of bot-hunting fun.

The first question you have to answer is what constitutes a bot. Is a client a bot because of its level of automation? Is it a bot only if the program itself is a bot program? What about borderline cases where a regular client program like BitchX acts more or less as a bot?

There are no easy answers. The definition of a bot is entirely up to you. If you want to use the broadest definition, you could include mIRC file servers, detached clients, and any very idle client. You run the server, so it's your call.

As for the second great question, how to detect bots, that's another story. Bot scripters and coders always come up with new methods of making the bot look like an innocent client, and it's often very hard to detect whether a client is a bot. Needless to say, the bots that do the best job of hiding themselves usually have something to hide.

I'm not familiar with all the advanced tips and tricks of the bot-hunting trade becauseI don't have time to spend my life chasing bots. I employ my own method, which involves the "hunch technique." If it looks like a bot and quacks like a bot (well, you know what I mean), chances are it's a bot. If it doesn't complain when you kill it, so much the better. This method has served me well, but also requires some experience. Use it carelessly and you'll have unjustly K: lined users baying for your blood. You may be better off with traditional methods, which include collecting evidence. I don't guarantee that my unorthodox method will work for anyone else. Your more experienced colleagues will gladly provide you with the tools you need to keep your bot population in check—or at least in constant fear.

18.9 Networking

Running a server is much more interesting if you can also connect it to a network. If you have the equipment and bandwidth to join an existing network, give it a try—many of the smaller networks readily accept serious link requests without much fuss. They usually have an application form on the network's main Web site, asking for information about the candidate's equipment and the prospective admin's experience. If not, the network's main operator channel can often help out.

It's much harder to get a major network to accept a link request. They consider applications based on a server's hardware, often requiring a dedicated machine, sufficient bandwidth (usually multiple T1 lines are the absolute minimum), the local user base of the server's site (meaning that the site has enough users to justify having its own server), and the admin's and operators' experience.

On networks with a form of central administration, a committee reviews applications and votes on them. On networks with no central governing body, you submit applications to administrators of the hub server you're asking for a link.

Submit linking requests to the appropriate email address and clearly state the reasons you have for linking a server, why you wish to link to that particular network, and a description of the resources you can dedicate. An informal discussion with the right people before submitting your request can help, and you should familiarize yourself with the ircd version current on that network by installing it and giving it a test run.

Once you have permission to link, arrange the appropriate C:, N:, and H: lines with your new uplink. Turn autoconnect off while you test the link, in case you don't get it right the first time—it's not very convenient to have a broken server autoconnect while you're trying to fix it. Rely on your uplink admin's experience with the ircd you're running and you'll be all right. All it takes is a bit of patience.

19

IRC ROBOTS

Automation was introduced to IRC clients fairly early. The addition and development of scripting features made it possible to configure a client to do a large number of things unsupervised, following its owner's instructions. While the powerful scripting language of the ircII client made it capable of complex automation, more speed and less consumption of machine resources were both still desirable. So developers created special programs with a minimal user interface, capable of running in the background with coded rather than scripted automation features. Robot programs — already known to be fast and efficient in other fields of Internet programming — proved to be the same on IRC.

19.1   Description of a Bot

A robot—or bot, in common shorthand—is a special form of client. It runs separately in the background and it has a different user interface than other clients. You control a bot through its configuration and by sending commands to it from a regular IRC client. While normal clients send data to the display for the user to see, a bot either writes its output to a file or forwards it to a client on IRC, if so instructed. The user can't employ a bot program as a regular client, but a client with extensive scripting can emulate a bot. A genuine bot is a stand-alone program specially written to provide a high level of automation for tedious and repetitive tasks or for actions requiring speedy performance.

19.2   Uses for Bots

Bots can do practically anything that requires automation. Their most common uses are as channel management tools (see section 7.5.1). Their fast and precise reactions make them much more efficient than human users sending commands manually. Good channel bots can maintain a secure and stable channel by monitoring channel events and reacting to them after consulting an internal list of host masks and operations to accept from each.

Entertainment bots are also popular—users can configure them to respond to messages with a funny message of their own, to send more or less random responses, to welcome users to a channel, and so forth. A common type of entertainment bot is the "bartender" bot, which responds to requests for drinks and even lets you buy other people drinks (after which it asks you to pay the tab). You'll see these bots more often on networks with channel services, where they don't have to perform channel management functions as well, although many common bots do have such additional features. On networks with no channel service, the bartender is often also the bouncer—the same bot is both the entertainer and the guardian of the channel.

IRC operators use other specialized robots (TCMs) to monitor server events and, when they detect specific events they've been configured to observe, inform the human operators. Less friendly bots of this kind are also configured to use **KILL** if they notice a certain type of abuse—in my opinion a questionable practice, because a **KILL** should result from human judgment, not an automated procedure.

Services are essentially a type of bot with a special role on a network, maintaining a channel or nickname ownership database, and performing management commands for those databases. Some are true high-power bots, while others form a much more complicated system, and the network maintains them as an integral part of it.

Since bots offer higher speed and efficiency than regular clients, it's no wonder they're popular with abusers, too. The use of single bots for channel takeovers and floods is not unknown, and abusers use nastier types to generate nickname collisions intentionally. It's also possible to network some modern bot types and use them for coordinated attacks. The power of these "floodnets" lies in the fact that a large number of clients can attack simultaneously, the attacker can use other peoples' bots on the same network to attack, and these bots are generally on better network connections than regular users' clients.

19.3 Types of Bots

As with any program, there are different kinds of bots for each type of machine or operating system. Most bots, however, run on Unix systems with permanent network connections and more bandwidth than the average user's machine.

Nowadays the most widely used type of bot is Robey Pointer's *eggdrop*, available for almost all types of Unix machines and 32-bit Windows systems. This is also the only decent bot for Windows. Provided that your Windows machine can stay connected to the network and survive a DoS attack, it will suffice, though a regular client enhanced with scripts could probably do the job just as well on a Windows machine. Macintosh users aren't quite as lucky—apart from the ShadowBot, the automated cousin of ShadowIRC, there is nothing they can use. Given that the Mac OS, although a good operating system, is not really designed to achieve the sensational uptimes a bot needs in order to be reliable, it's probably best that you consider a Unix solution anyway.

As Unix is the predominant operating system for bots, it has a wide variety of robot programs at its disposal. They range from simplistic, often insecure ones like the vladbot or the johbot, to complex tools like the eggdrop.

Running a Unix bot such as the eggdrop requires that you have access to a Unix machine on which to install it. Not just any old Unix machine will do. You want a stable machine with an equally stable network connection, and you need permission to run a bot on it. Don't take this for granted. If we're talking about an eggdrop, it's one of the worst resource hogs around, and often makes the machine a target for cracking and DoS attacks. Not many sysadmins appreciate seeing such a program on their machine, and many who do tolerate it won't hesitate to kill it off if it becomes a nuisance or an inconvenience—or even if they just need some extra memory on the system.

19.4　Eggdrop

Although this bot is an efficient channel management tool with many factors in its favor, it's extremely unpopular with the servers. Abusers also favor some of its advanced features and can turn into a powerful means of abuse, and many operators on the major networks have a standing "shoot on sight" order for eggdrop bots.

The eggdrop supports *tcl scripting*—one of its main attractions. This is a powerful platform-independent scripting language, often used in conjunction with programs written in various programming languages and in CGI applications on the Web. In fact, the eggdrop will not install without tcl. If you don't have it on the system, you should get it from http://www.scriptics.com and install it before you read further.

19.4.1　*Obtaining and Installing the Eggdrop*

Eggdrop source code is available at many large FTP sites such as sunsite.unc.edu and its mirrors worldwide. I recommend checking ftp.sodre.net in the /**pub**/**eggdrop** directory for a list of mirrors, as well as for the latest version of the eggdrop—1.3.28 at the time of writing.

Before I say anything about installation, here's my disclaimer: You must be able to find your way under Unix—if not to install an eggdrop, to *run* it efficiently. Eggdrops are *not* for newbies. If you're not comfortable using Unix or IRC, I strongly advise against it. You must have some basic skills and be familiar with simple security precautions, or you and your channel may regret ever having said "eggdrop."

First of all, untar and unzip the source package. If you need instructions on how to do this, read the previous paragraph again and reconsider. But because I'm a nice guy and not just a know-it-all, I'll tell you that the way to do it is the same as with regular Unix clients (or practically any Unix software package), and most of the instructions in Chapter 4 apply here. The eggdrop author, Robey Pointer, makes it pretty clear in the **README** and **INSTALL** files, which are the first things you should address, that this is not for newbies. If you thought my advice about knowing your stuff before running an eggdrop was excessive, wait until you see his! These two files also contain very valuable instructions and can troubleshoot many problems you may encounter while trying to install the bot. *Do not* skip them or something very nasty will happen to you. If you'd like to know what that is, read the files. :-)

Untar and gunzip the bot package, type **./configure** and **make**, maybe edit the **config.h** first ... you know the drill. The eggdrop will compile on almost any form of Unix without problems. Even if there are problems, the **INSTALL** file usually has a solution.

19.4.2 Running the Eggdrop

A bot, though it's the most automated creature on IRC, does not run itself. It will not guess what it's supposed to do, nor will it rise from the ashes when it dies, unless *you* have told it to. The eggdrop is no exception. It may act smart but it's not intelligent. It's not even artificially intelligent. In fact, it's downright dumb, like every other bot.

Configuring the eggdrop isn't the easiest thing in the world. Remember one ground rule: When in doubt, it's best to err on the side of caution. Security is the weakest point of the eggdrop, not because the code itself is insecure, but because it's easy to make that one little mistake that will cost you your channel. I was really planning on going into the subject in detail—but honestly, the great help files in the **doc** and **help** directories of the eggdrop distribution would make anything I have to say redundant. The eggdrop's documentation is an example I wish more software authors would follow, even though it would put me out of business as a writer.

Here's another word of caution that applies to other bots. Many servers do not welcome bots. They're providing a free service, and you have probably used it before, so in a way you owe them one. Please respect their wishes and put your eggdrop only on servers that don't mind bots. That's the nice way of saying it. The other way I could put it is: "No bots. Put your bot on my server and you will die a slow, painful death." Well, I myself am not quite that extreme, but some of my colleagues in the IRC operator business strike terror into the artificial heart of every robot within a five-mile radius and aren't as nice about dealing with unwanted bot runners as I am. I'm not very nice about it, by the way.

One last recommendation: Be very, very careful whose bots you network with, if you do network your eggdrop. Give them the minimal privileges needed and trust no one. The more a botnet grows, the more likely it is that the proverbial bad potato will sneak onto it. Experiment with the bot's networking features by hooking up with a friend before joining any large botnet—don't take it for granted that all bots there will be friendly or that their owners will appreciate your presence. Remember this and you'll thank me.

19.5 ComBot

The ComBot, which Chris Behrens authored, is the second most popular bot after the eggdrop. It lacks some of the eggdrop's advanced multiuser and user list functions and is slightly less secure, but compensates with speed, user friendliness, and efficiency at handling multiple channels. The latter characteristic also makes it more economical with network resources, since it happily handles more than one channel without problems—so it can make better use of the connection slot it occupies on the server. Unlike the eggdrop, it cannot network with other bots. That could make it inconvenient if you want to run a channel's bots as a group, but does mean others consider a ComBot less of a threat, since most serious abuse comes from networked eggdrops.

ComBot is what's known as a *C-bot* (like the eggdrop), in that it's written in the C programming language. Although it is possible to run a ComBot without any knowledge of C, I highly recommend a fairly good mastery of it, since you may have to tweak some code.

After you've unzipped and untarred the ComBot file, you should set it up so that you, the bot owner, have access to it in IRC. Do so prior to compiling, since the bot will use the current user list (**Combot.lists**) upon execution. If you're not in the list to begin with, you won't have access to the bot to make changes. Open the **Combot.lists** file in a text editor such as pico or vi and add your address to the user list.

Follow the suggestions in section 10.7.4, when entering addresses in the bot's list. If you have a dynamic IP, you need to use an asterisk (*) in place of the part of your address that changes, but try to use as much of your host mask as possible without wild cards. I also strongly recommend a password, but since passwords are encrypted in the file and therefore unreadable, set your own after the bot is running on IRC. You will likely find a lot of other users listed in the **Combot.lists** file. You should delete these so unknown users won't have access to the bot.

I also recommend printing out the file **Bot.Help** and reading it carefully. If you're going to run a bot, you should know exactly how, and the help file is the place to start. Take your time—read all the bot's files carefully and thoroughly. No bot can protect a channel if the owner doesn't know how it works. When you're confident that you are ready and have edited the files to suit your needs, you can compile and run the bot. This is an extremely simple process: Enter the bot's main directory and type **make** at the shell prompt.

Once you've successfully compiled it, you have an executable ComBot file. Simply type **./ComBot** at the shell prompt to start the bot process on IRC. With luck, the bot will be on IRC, in the specified channel, when you get there yourself. Good configuration and a careful setup should make reliance on luck unnecessary, though. This more or less concludes the technical part of the book. In the next chapter (and the last of the book), some very useful information combined with some opinionated ramblings will, I hope, leave you with few unanswered questions on the subject of IRC.

20

THE SOAPBOX AND MORE

Partly because IRC is part of the Internet, partly because it's an international real-time communication system of potentially vast proportions, when you are on IRC, a variety of issues confront you regarding morals, the law, security, and many other small or large points. The rest of this book has addressed most of them in detail, but some I've touched on only briefly.

I'll try to shed some light on some of the more interesting or controversial issues I haven't previously covered. I base everything here on personal observations, and I don't claim that the rest of the IRC community shares my opinions, but I do believe many may agree with my views—even the more radical ones.

20.1 The Users of IRC

The social background of the people on IRC is very mixed, and varies depending on their location and the technological level of each area. In relatively affluent societies where modern computing technology has reached people's homes, as is the case in North America, northern and western Europe, Japan, and Australia, people of lower education or income have access to the Internet. In low-tech or poorer regions such as eastern Europe or Latin America, generally only students and people at higher income levels have access. This does have some impact on the IRC population, but there is no typical IRC user. Although some ages, nationalities, or professional groups may be more common, people from every walk of life all over the world use IRC.

Two kinds of people who find IRC particularly appealing and represent a fair proportion in the population are people with a multicultural or multinational background and expatriates. With IRC everywhere, it's an ideal and cheap way to stay in contact with all aspects of your national background, get news from home, talk in a native language, learn more about a neglected part of your heritage, and renew your ties to a place or culture. Often these people, upon returning to a less developed homeland or area, bring the Internet and IRC with them. Racism and bigotry are not common in the open world of IRC, though disputes do sometimes spill over from real-life politics. In general, though, people of the most varied national backgrounds coexist and communicate in a way that should provide a lesson for the powers that be.

I don't pretend to be a sociologist, but I do find the sociology of IRC interesting. IRC, in my opinion, should be regarded as a real society. The stereotyped long-haired hacker who lives on beer and pizza and spends most of his waking hours in front of a computer is not the exclusive inhabitant of this domain. All kinds of people are on IRC. As the diversity of its population increases, the face of this society changes. I could go on in my amateur way, but others more qualified have analyzed the sociological aspects of IRC. One of these efforts is Elizabeth Reid's impressive "Electropolis: Communication and Community on Internet Relay Chat" thesis. Although written in 1991, it remains strikingly accurate—I highly recommend it. You can find it at http://people.we. mediaone.net/elizrs/work.html.

20.2 Privacy and Anonymity

One point that has occupied the thoughts of many users in the past, and will continue to do so, is the question of how private those "private" messages really are, and how real their anonymity is.

Messages on IRC are just about as private and secure as anything else on the Internet—that is, essentially insecure. A message can be intercepted and read at any point of its route. Before we get all paranoid about it, instances of such listening in are rare, and the weak points are the users' own machines and their connection to their ISP rather than the server network.

Rules regarding the privacy of users' messages on IRC are strict, and any responsible person acts upon reports of their violation. The most characteristic case is that of a server admin who got caught listening in on users' messages a few years ago—this person lost his admin status and will probably never be an operator again. While it's technically possible to rig a server to eavesdrop on private messages, the network acts fast and decisively upon any evidence of such events. The end user's machine often proves to be the least secure of all machines involved, since the level of security on IRC server machines is generally very high.

If you want to have a higher degree of security for personal real-time communication, DCC is a fair choice since it bypasses the server network. Still, I may not be wrong in presuming that private conversation on IRC is more secure than the telephone system. Using encryption is the best option, but it is not widely available for IRC clients, and the related software is subject to import, export, and use limitations in many countries.

Anonymity is even more of an illusion when it comes to dealing with abuse. Your ISP's records show the times you were on and possibly where you connected to. Under certain circumstances, the law may require its cooperation in identifying you. If you're accused of illegal or abusive activities, various agencies can consult these records, so you are almost always traceable.

For more information about online privacy issues, I recommend the Electronic Privacy Information Center's Web site at http://www.epic.org/.

20.3   Censorship

It's hard to be objective on a subject where you have a fixed stance that's not open for discussion, so I won't pretend to be objective. I base parts of this section on my personal, subjective views, and I do not expect you to share them, though I would be pleased if you did. Humor me.

The United States is the country with the most influence on the Internet, so attempts to pass controversial Internet legislation in the United States are bound to receive a lot of attention. The downfall of the Communications Decency Act was a relief—but, however brief, its ephemeral success generated much discussion and alarm and some of its provisions actually remain in effect. Its successor, the Child Online Protection Act, will probably share its fate when it reaches the U.S. Supreme Court. Don't let the sugar-coated name mislead you—it's about restricting access to content on the Internet. Still, I'm not taking any bets about its success or failure.

As far as I'm concerned, claims of protecting the public from evil influences are a shaky pretense. Nobody is forced to use the Internet. Nobody on the Internet has "evil" forced upon him or her just because he or she is there (except maybe junk email). If you let your kids get porn off the Internet, blame your parenting and not the Internet. In short, if you don't like it, don't use it. And if you heard all this from someone else, believe nothing. You can form your own opinion by using the Internet yourself.

IRC is slightly different from the Internet at large because it's not commercial and it has varying levels of authorities capable of censorship within strict limits. First there are the channel operators—the first form of authority you'll meet on IRC. Channel ops have absolute control over a channel and may exercise censorship over its contents at their discretion. Anyone who disagrees with the policy a channel op sets and enforces is free to leave the channel; in some cases, the channel operator may require him or her to leave the channel (by means of kicks and bans).

You can always create your own channel restricted to those who agree with you. As in real human society, you could do this quite easily when the world was less crowded—although those who chose to create such a society usually ended up in an inhospitable environment that no one else wanted. On IRC there is no such thing as a desert, and you cannot be sent to Siberia. If you don't like the IRC world as it is, you're free to create your own lush, green paradise, which will be as good as you make it.

IRC networks and servers offer their services free of charge. Therefore, they may allow or forbid whatever they please, permit anyone they like to use it, and close it down whenever they fancy. If they wish to censor the contents of a channel, its name, or its topic as part of their policy, they may do so. After all, those networks that do reserve the right of censorship make it clear in their Message of the Day. You aren't paying for their service: it's their right to tell you what you can use it for. Again, you're free to leave if you don't like it.

On the major networks, no form of censorship exists. Whether users and operators agree or disagree with a point of view, a philosophy, a lifestyle, or whatever else is immaterial. Freedom of speech is paramount. People might disagree with what you say, but they can't keep you from opening your own forum of advocacy, and they will get into trouble for trying to. This policy goes for everyone.

20.4 IRC Addiction

On a more objective and scientific note, online addiction (OLA), also known as Internet addiction disorder (IAD), has already become a subject of psychiatric study, otherwise there wouldn't already be several TLAs (Three-Letter Acronyms) for it. Along with the growing number of people using the Internet, the number of those who are more or less hooked is also rising. People have become so entangled in the Web that they rarely return to the outside world and they spend endless hours browsing. Although "Web-oholism" is the most well-known form of addiction, getting hooked on chat lines (be it an ISP's internal system, such as an AOL chat room, or an open forum like IRC) can have an equally destructive effect on a person's social, personal, family, and financial life. It's no less severe than other known kinds of addiction—drugs, alcohol, gambling, and so forth. People have neglected their jobs, their families, and their friends in order to spend as much time as possible—sometimes every waking hour—on IRC.

Apart from the many humorous quips that start, "You have been on IRC too long if . . . ," when you find yourself spending a lot of time on IRC, you should check for the following symptoms:

- "Another five minutes" become hours.

- You're late to work because of your morning IRC session.

- You log on in the morning under the pretence of checking your email and end up on IRC.

- When returning home, you turn on the computer before anything else and log in.

- You lose track of time on IRC.

- You speak more with people online than you do with people living in the same house.

- You start IRCing well beyond your usual bedtime hours.

- Family and friends complain about feeling neglected because of "the damn computer."

- You reject evenings out and social gatherings in favor of IRC.

- You get nervous and snappy if you're unable to get online.

- You tie up the phone line although you're expecting an important call.

- You pay for your Internet access even if you can't afford it.

- You reschedule your day, giving priority to events on IRC.

- Your grades have dropped as a result of too much time online.

- You keep putting things off if they require leaving the computer.

If you're observing one or more of these symptoms, you're likely suffering from some stage of OLA. While you find IRC increasingly enjoyable, the rest of your life goes downhill, until the consequences of neglecting everyday things outweigh the benefits you're gaining from IRC. You feel awful, but now you start using IRC as a means of escape. If you reach this stage, it's serious and you should let someone drag you, if you can't drag yourself, to a professional who's familiar with addictions.

To a large extent, it's a matter of self-discipline. Addictions often indicate dissatisfaction with other aspects of life; you can deal with them by working on the bad parts before the addiction takes over altogether. So the widely used remark "Get a life!" does hold some truth, however offensive you may find it. If your addiction is at an advanced stage, though, or the situation is beyond your control, you usually have just two choices: Seek professional help or stay off the Internet altogether, canceling your account if necessary. Maybe even take both these steps.

As with any kind of addiction, you should never take it lightly or shrug it off as a nonexistent problem. If it's having a negative or destructive effect on other parts of your life, you have to deal with it. Although you're likely to encounter many other individuals with a similar problem on IRC, it's a subject rarely discussed online. There is, however, a Usenet group named alt.irc.recovery; it has little traffic but might be of help. Your ISP may also be willing to cooperate by restricting your access to certain hours of the day or taking away IRC. If you don't cheat by buying another account or borrowing time from friends, that can certainly help.

Of course, I'm not a doctor, so you might like to seek a more qualified opinion. I recommend the site of Dr. Kimberly S. Young, one of the pioneers in the study of online addiction, at http://netaddiction.com/ as very informative and helpful. I'm not convinced that online therapy is the way to go, but it's there if you want it.

20.5　Pornography on IRC

One of the more controversial issues regarding the Internet and its lack of policing is the distribution of pornographic material. In addition to subscriber services and nonnetworked BBSs that sell porn of all kinds, there is a tremendous amount of it freely available to anyone who cares to look for it. It's not quite as widespread on IRC as on the Web or Usenet, but IRC does have its share of people engaging in the trade of pornographic material.

On IRC, opinions are divided between those who tolerate porn and those in favor of censoring it. Outside those networks that have a standing policy forbidding porn, moves to forbid it on other networks have failed due to the widely shared opinion that freedom of expression must be protected on IRC and absolutely no form of censorship should exist. From a legal point of view, the interesting and complex question of applying local laws to a global network or parts of it hinders the enforcement of relevant laws on IRC. Can a person in Russia or Denmark be held liable for supplying porn to a person (perhaps a minor) in the United States? Questions such as this one await answers. While some countries may outlaw pornography or require it to be "on the top shelf" (out of public sight), the legislation of others may permit its free distribution to anyone of legal age. This age is another variable factor.

One aspect, though, deserves closer attention and can have many legal implications. Child pornography, known as "kiddie porn" on IRC, is illegal in just about every country on Earth and generally available only on specialized channels, since the mainstream pornography channels refuse to be associated with it and forbid it. The system tolerates the presence of such pornography because of the rules defining the network and its servers as an unmoderated medium and forbidding any kind of censorship. But child porn remains illegal and those engaging in this trade are subject to investigation by domestic or international agencies, including the FBI and Interpol.

Many people encountering child pornography on IRC find its tolerance puzzling. Channels with names like **#!!9yroldsex or #!!!preteenpix** are in public view—why is nothing done about them?

Server operators and administrators are not law enforcement officers. The fact that a channel has a suspicious name is not proof, and no operator is willing to risk criminal liability by downloading pictures just to see whether they are what the channel name implies. Of course, they lack the means and the authority to apprehend people who actually are trading in child pornography. The final reason is that blundering crusaders are just what real law enforcement agencies need least. Scaring the suspects off can easily blow an ongoing online police operation. In some cases, the law has used IRC evidence to convict child pornographers not only of distributing child pornography, but also of rape, incest, and a host of related crimes. You may not see the law enforcement officials, but they are aware of the Internet.

Still, if you want to take action, you can inform your local authorities. Many countries now have special computer squads capable of dealing with crime involving computers. Site administrators are generally very cooperative since their reputation may be at stake, even if they cannot be held liable for their users' actions. (The issue is currently under review by German and English courts, at least; in some cases, Internet service providers were held liable for their users' actions.) If you think you should strike a blow, contact the police or whatever agency is responsible for child abuse in your country. In the United States, you can call the National Center for Missing and Exploited Children at 800-843-5678 or check http://www.fbi.gov/ for a list of field offices. You can find more information at the Customs Service's Web site (http://www.customs. ustreas.gov/enforce/childprn.htm). In Canada, the RCMP advise that you contact the local RCMP detachment or the police, as well as the ISP concerned.

20.6   IRC and Software Piracy

Another case of illegal activity on IRC is the trade of pirated software. "Warez" channels, numerous on IRC, are as hard to keep in check as pornography channels.

Warez traders are a rather motley bunch, with a form of caste system depending on the hacking or cracking skills of individual traders and the quantity and quality of the items they trade. They may be anything from experienced software pirates to amateurs who just don't believe in paying for software. The best of the bunch make a point of staying inconspicuous, and conduct their business mostly in private. The less likeable wannabe or "warez pup" waves a banner far and wide and engages in dubious activities, usually involving an attempt to display machismo by harassing someone or attacking servers.

While pirating software obviously violates international copyright law, in most cases local law enforcement lacks the knowledge or means to identify and apprehend the traders. If the computer systems involved are in different countries or an individual uses machines outside his country of residence, the problem is even more complex. However, even the most elaborate cover-up is sometimes not sufficient, and in many places legislation against software piracy has become stricter and enforcement better as a result of more pressure from the software industry. Warez traders are not immune to the legal consequences of their actions, even though they may be smart enough to evade authorities for a long time.

Penalties for possession of pirated software range from fines and confiscation of computing equipment to prison terms. Legally, the buyer is as liable as the seller.

20.7 Kids on IRC

With the Internet in schools and homes, many more children have access to IRC than in the past. Although I've seen plenty of youngsters on IRC behaving more maturely than the adults, a degree of care is in order. IRC is basically an adult environment and not necessarily suitable for kids. Altogether, it's a touchy subject, since every opinion voiced clashes with someone's pedagogical ideas.

To some extent a child's behavior depends on how he or she got onto IRC—if the parents forbid it, they can expect kids to sneak online and get up to mischief. We've all been kids—we know how it happens. Once you forbid it—and I challenge you to find a reason a child will accept for not being allowed on the Internet—its attraction becomes even greater. In any case, the younger generation tends to have a strong interest in networked computers and devices with many buttons. Besides, you can expect children to outsmart you when you try to keep them out—today's kids tend to know 10 times more about computers than their parents. If you really want them off, physically lock the computer.

Treating the matter more openly gives you a better chance of keeping your children out of trouble. You should take the time to check things out yourself and choose the places you think are suitable. Supervised sessions are not a bad idea, either—they can be educational and entertaining for both parties.

However, don't use the Internet like television. If you don't have enough time to spend with your kids or want to "keep them quiet," sending them off to the computer is effective but far from safe. Of course, seeing what gets labeled as "children's programs" on TV, I'm not sure the Internet isn't preferable. If you don't let your child use the Internet or IRC based on the reports that it's full of "unsuitable material," you have other options.

First of all, "unsuitable material" may be widely available, but it doesn't magically appear on your hard disk—you have to look for it and download it. A growing number of programs can screen inbound traffic, with a varying degree of efficiency. The problem is that too rigorous screening often blocks perfectly harmless or useful material (one instance reported in Utah blocked access to the Quakers' website—I'd be curious to see what was deemed "unsuitable"), while too lax rules allow much of the forbidden stuff to get through. The conventions these programs use for filtering incoming material are often so ridiculous that whole normal words and phrases get swallowed by mistake. The bottom line here is: If you can't trust your kids to follow a reasonable set of rules, don't let them online.

One more point to consider is that children should not use a networked computer in unsupervised groups, since peer pressure can strongly affect their behavior. They're much more likely to get up to mischief if they're feeding each other ideas or challenging each other to do the forbidden.

Children are as much at risk as adults regarding online addiction. If your son or daughter starts displaying signs of such addiction, you should act fast and decisively by curbing the amount of time spent on the Internet. Granted, there'll be a fight, but you must stop this trend before it becomes serious. Teenagers with feelings of personal inadequacy, a limited social life, or problems at school are at higher risk. They can gain much in terms of sociability and self-esteem by joining the IRC community—I'd even recommend it for this reason—but caution is necessary.

I would also advise great care regarding the "kid" or "teen" channels on the major networks. Although they're popular and give kids a chance to meet people their age from all over the world, these channels are often worse than real life. They can be highly antagonistic and lead to regular dogfights involving the use of every modern network abuse tool—not a very suitable environment for learning to get along with people.

Another potential hazard is that pedophiles frequent and infiltrate some of these channels. This doesn't mean any such channel is a war zone or a nest of pedophilic excess. There are a number of quite good teen channels, especially on the smaller networks, which have all the advantages of IRC without the drawbacks. Along with those networks that have a standing policy forbidding inappropriate channels or contents, Kidlink IRC, KidsWorld, and the ScoutNet network are good places for your kids to meet people their own age under the discreet supervision of knowledgeable adults.

IRC is basically an adult world, but that doesn't mean you should keep kids off it at all costs. Everyone can benefit from meeting people and cultural exchange, and it's a good way to introduce a young person to the world of online communication. Of course, within a week they'll probably know more than you ever will, but that's the way it goes.

20.8 In Conclusion

Despite all its problems, I love IRC. I have gained much from being on it. Although it has its downsides, overall I've found it a positive and enriching experience.

The friends I've gained all over the world; the endless hours of serious discussion and chat; a better understanding of other people, places, and cultures; not to mention my marriage to a fellow IRC addict—all these have left their mark on me. I must admit I've been hooked on IRC since I first stumbled across it, and I have spent some time as an IRC junkie and antisocial troglodyte (just what I was warning you about earlier in this chapter). That has come and gone now, and I can look back and laugh even at the bad times. Yeah, I did go and get a life in the end, but IRC remains part of mine, and it can be part of yours, too.

My final recommended reading item is Ove Ruben Olsen's "The Tao of Internet Relay Chat," which you'll find at http://apatrix.asu.net/irc/docs/tao. To quote from it, "If the Tao is great, then the IRC is running ceaselessly." Let it be so. IRC is good. I hope this book has helped make it good for you, too.

See you online!

NETWORK AND SERVER LISTS

A.1 Table of Networks

The following table lists all the principal networks and the more interesting smaller ones. The letters in the **Type** column are as follows: **G**=General chat, **R**=Regional, **S**=Special interest, **K**=Kids. **F** stands for Family networks, for lack of a better description; these are general chat networks that pay extra attention to providing an environment suitable for the whole family.

The number of servers that a network has is far from steady, so many of these numbers listed are the approximate number of a network's servers.

Distribution is the geographical distribution of a network's servers and users—basically, which part of the world you're more likely to find people from on that network.

The **Port** column indicates on which port you can expect the servers for this network to listen. The three columns before the last indicate the availability of special services with a + (available) or - (not available).

The **CS** column lists Channel Services for the registration and maintenance of channels, **NS** denotes Nickname Services for registering nicknames, and **MS** signifies Memo or Note Services with which to send other users notes while they are away. These services do not necessarily follow the Chan/Nick/MemoServ naming convention; you should check on a specific network to see whether this is the case.

The final column lists one or more channels on the network where you can find online help. Some are not dedicated help channels but places where you can generally find someone to lend a hand or point you in the right direction. Many more IRC networks and information about them can be found at http://www.irchelp.org/networks/nets/.

Name	Type	Servers	Distribution	Port	CS	NS	MS	Users	Help channels
EFnet	G	50	Worldwide	6667	-	-	-	35000-60000	#irchelp,#mirchelp, #help
IRCnet	G	140	Worldwide	6667	-	-	+	25000-55000	#irchelp,#mirc
DALnet	G	35	Worldwide	7000	+	+	+	25000-50000	#dalnethelp,#irchelp
Undernet	G	45	Worldwide	6667	+	-	-	25000-45000	#help
TalkCity	G	15	N.America	6667	+	+	-	5000-25000	#new2talkcity, #tchelp
MSN	G	5	N.America	6667	-	-	-	5000-20000*	#helpdesk
GalaxyNet	G	35	Worldwide	6667	+	+	+	3000-8000	#ircsolutions, #irchelp
WebNet	G	20	Worldwide	6667	+	+	+	3000-6000	#webnet-help
ChatNet	G	20	Worldwide	6667	+	+	-	1500-2500	#irchelp, #beginner
BRASnet	R	70	Brazil	6667	+	+	+	1000-9000	#ajuda
Oz.Org	R	5	Australia	6667	+	-	-	1000-3500	#help
ChatNet	G	15	N.America	6667	-	+	-	1000-2500	#help
AustNet	G	20	Worldwide	6667	+	+	+	800-3000	#help,#mirc
QuakeNET	S	10	Europe	6667	-	-	-	700-1500	-
PTnet	R	?	Portugal	6667	+	+	+	500-5000	#beginner
RedeBrasil	R	20	Brazil	6667	+	+	+	500-2500	#beginner
IRC-Hispano	R	20	Spain	6667	+	-	-	500-4000	#ayuda_irc
StarChat	F	15	Worldwide	6667	+	+	+	400-1200	#help
TrIrcNet	R	5	Turkey	6667	+	+	+	300-1200	#help,#beginner
GRnet	R	20	Greece	6667	+	+	+	250-1000	#help
ZAnet	R	11	S.Africa	6667	+	+	+	200-1000	#beginner
Open Projects Net	S	30	Worldwide	6667	+	+	+	200-400	-
SuperChat	F	6	N.America	6667	+	+	-	100-500	#superchat
KidsWorld	K	6	U.K., U.S.	6667	+	-	-	50-200	#adminland

* Inconsistent count displayed

A.2   Servers and More Networks

And now for a bit more detail: In order to get onto any network, you need a server name. Programs like mIRC and ircle are very helpful in providing decent server lists for your immediate needs, but what happens if you want to meet someone on an obscure server not to be found on any list? What if your client doesn't come with a list?

Networks are listed below in alphabetical order. Server names in bold type denotes a *round robin* address—that is, it cycles through a pool of server addresses in order to distribute the users evenly among servers. Some of them only point to one server now, but may add more servers to the pool later. A port number is listed only if the network does *not* use 6667 as its default port number.

Servers come and go all the time, some even change networks—there's no guarantee that these addresses will be valid tomorrow, but I've listed the more stable ones. Those listings in bold type are "Recommended"— these are small networks that I recommend if you're confused by all this variety and want something to start out with. (The matching deposits in my Swiss bank account are purely coincidental.)

Fairly up-to-date server lists can be found on the Web at http://www.irchelp.org/networks/servers/ and http://chatcircuit.com/webzine/techarea/servers/saintcc.htm. As time passes, networks may disappear, more will come into existence, and some servers will change. These two Web pages will serve you well if the data on this list no longer work.

Name	Comments	Servers
AfterNet	-	**irc.afternet.org**
AlternativeNet	-	**irc.alternativenet.org**
AmigaNet	Amiga computers	**irc.amiganet.org**
AMnet	-	**irc.amnet.org**
Ancients	-	**irc.ancients.net**
AustNet	-	**us.austnet.org** (US), **au.austnet.org** (Australia) **sg.austnet.org** (Singapore), **nz.austnet.org** (New Zealand)
BDSMnet	BDSM	irc.bondage.com, irc.handcuff.com
BeyondIRC	-	**irc.beyondirc.net**
BrasIRC	Brazilian	irc.brasirc.com.br
BRASnet	Brazilian	**irc.brasnet.org**
Castlenet	-	**irc.castlenet.org**
ChatNet	-	**irc.chatnet.org**
ChatPR	Puerto Rican	**irc.chatpr.org**
DALnet	-	**irc.dal.net**, **irc.eu.dal.net** (Europe)
DifferentNet	-	**irc.different.net**
Dominion	Sci-fi	irc.scifi.net

Name	Comments	Servers
DudiNet	Dutch	**irc.dudi.org**
duh-net	-	**irc.duh-net.org**
EdNet	-	**irc.underworld.net**
EFnet	-	irc.ais.net (Illinois), irc.idle.net (California), irc.c-com.net (Texas), irc.psinet.com (Virginia), efnet.sto.telia.se (Sweden), irc.magic.ca (Manitoba), efnet.demon.co.uk (UK), efnet.telstra.net.au (Australia)
EICN	-	**irc.earthint.net**
EqNet	Equestrian	irc.quintex.com
Espernet	-	**irc.esper.net**
FDFnet	-	**irc.fdf.net**
FEFnet	-	**irc.fef.net**
FireStar	-	**irc.firestar.org**
GalaxyNet	Popular with Asian users	**irc.galaxynet.org**, **sg.galaxynet.org** (Singapore), **au.galaxynet.org** (Australia)
GammaNet	-	**irc.gamma.net**
GRnet	Greek	nana.irc.gr, thales.irc.gr
Gumtree	Australian	**irc.gumtree.org**
HanIRC	Hangul Korean	irc.hanirc.org, gauss.tower.wayne.edu
IceNet	-	**irc.icenet.org**
IIGS	Genealogy	irc.iigs.org
IRCity	Italian	irc.ircity.org
IRC-Hispano	Spanish	irc.arrakis.es
IRCnet	-	irc.webbernet.net (Michigan), irc.stealth.net (New York), **us.ircnet.org** (US), chat.bt.net (UK), irc.funet.fi (Finland), **au.ircnet.org** (Australia)
JellyBelly Net	-	irc.jellybelly.net
KidLink IRC	Registration required	see http://www.kidlink.org/
KidsWorld	-	us.kidsworld.org (US), notts.uk.eu.kidsworld.org (UK)
KnightNet	Port 5555	**irc.knightnet.net**
KreyNet	-	irc.track.nl, ircd.vip.fi
LagNet	South African	**irc.lagnet.org.za**
LinPeople	Linux support	see Open Projects Net
Millenia	-	**irc.millenia.org**
MSN	Microsoft Chat	irc.msn.com
MTV	Yack Live	irc.mtv.com
MysticalNet	Recommended	**irc.mystical.net**
Netlink-IRC	-	irc.netlink-irc.org
NewNet	-	**irc.newnet.net**, **eu.newnet.net** (Europe)
NightStar	-	**irc.nightstar.net**
Open Projects Net	Open source forum	**irc.openprojects.net**
Othernet	-	**irc.othernet.org**
Oz.Org	Australian	mpx.oz.org, wollongong.oz.org
PhishyNet	Recommended	**irc.phishy.net**
PTnet	Portuguese	irc.rccn.net, irc.telepac.pt

Name	Comments	Servers
QuakeNET	Quake (the game)	irc.quakenet.eu.org
RedeBrasil	Brazilian	redebrasil.ebt.elogica.com.br, irc.redebrasil.rec.br
RinduNET	Malaysian	**irc.rindu.net**, **irc.my-linux.org**
RusNet	Russian/Ukrainian	rusnet.portal.ru (Russia), irc.lucky.net (Ukraine), irc.crocodile.org (US)
SandNet.net	-	**irc.sandnet.net**
SandNet.org	-	**irc.sandnet.org**
ScoutLink	Scouting	utah.us.scoutlink.org (US), zeist.nl.scoutlink.org (Netherlands)
Shadowfire	-	**irc.shadowfire.org**
SorceryNet	Port 9000	**irc.sorcery.net**
StarChat	Recommended	**irc.starchat.net**, polaris.starchat.net
StarLink	-	**irc.starlink.org**
StarLink-IRC	-	**irc.starlink-irc.org**
Stomped.com	Games, Quake	irc.stomped.com
Stonernet	"Legalize it"	stonernet.org
SuperChat	-	**irc.superchat.org**
Support-Group	Health/personal	discussionssupport-group.com
SurNet	Argentinian	irc.sur.net
TalkCity	WebTV default	chat.talkcity.com
TrIrcNet	Turkish	irc.raks.net.tr
Undernet	-	**us.undernet.org** (US), **eu.undernet.org** (Europe)
UniBG	Bulgarian	irc.gocis.bg, irc.acad.bg
UnionLatina	Spanish/Latin American	irc.lander.es (Spain), irc.terranet.com.ar (Argentina)
Valhall.net	-	**irc.valhall.net**, irc.c64.org
WarpedNet	-	**irc.warped.net**
WebNet	-	**irc.webchat.org**
Wolfnet-IRC	-	irc.wolfnet-irc.org
WorldIRC	-	**irc.worldirc.org**
XNet	-	**us.xnet.org** (US), **ca.xnet.org** (Canada), **eu.xnet.org** (Europe), **au.xnet.org** (Australia)
XWorld	-	**irc.xworld.org**
ZAnet	South African	gaspode.zanet.org.za, irc.ru.ac.za
ZUH.net	Recommended	**irc.zuh.net**
ZW-IRC	Zimbabwean	irc.samara.co.zw

B

TERMINOLOGY

Special thanks to Josh Rollyson for helping compile this short jargonbuster.

/help The first thing you should try. :)

31337 *See* elite.

42 The Answer to the Ultimate Question about Life, the Universe, and Everything (*see* HHGTTG).

action A line of text formatted in a specific manner through the use of the **ME** command (for example, **Nickname is a pink bunny** as opposed to **<Nickname> is a pink bunny**).

ADSL Asynchronous digital subscriber line. A high-speed Internet connection currently available in limited areas only. Performance ranges from ISDN to better than T1 speeds.

ANSI American National Standards Institute. Among other things, it sets a standard for terminal color codes and keyboard remapping codes. Some clients, notably BitchX and Epic, support ANSI color codes.

ASCII American Standard Code for Information Interchange. This is the standard character set almost all computer systems rely on.

Back Orifice Remote administration tool for Windows machines, released by the Cult of the Dead Cow hacker group. Originally used as a Trojan horse, it has now been released as Back Orifice 2000 (BO2K) and is actually a sophisticated administration tool comparable to similar programs released by Microsoft and other vendors. Use of it as a Trojan horse, however, continues to be widespread.

ban To set the **+b** channel mode, preventing a user from joining a channel.

BO *See* Back Orifice.

BOFH Bastard Operator from Hell. Main character in Simon Travaglia's online cult series of the same name. Often describes system administrators and IRC operators with a not-so-amiable attitude toward users. (You must prove yourself worthy, so I'm not telling you where to find it. Search the Net, Luke!)

bot Short for robot. An automated client designed for unattended operation. Not permitted on many IRC servers, particularly larger networks.

channel A group chat on IRC.

channel operator A user in control of a channel. Indicated in most clients by **@** beside their nicks.

CHAP Challenge Handshake Authentication Protocol. A protocol similar in purpose to PAP.

chat room Unit of an online chat service; equivalent to a channel on IRC.

click A denial of service that can cause "Connection Reset by Peer" messages.

client An end-user application in a client-server network computing model. The client implements some processing functions and acts as the interface between the user and the server. mIRC is an example of an IRC client.

cracker A hacker without ethical standards. A cracker's goal is usually to damage or steal data.

CTCP Client-to-Client Protocol. A protocol for simple automatic interactions between clients on IRC. One example of a CTCP command is **PING**, which measures the delay it takes for a message to get from one client to another and back.

DCC Direct Client Connection. A protocol for direct communications between two clients, used for reduced-lag semisecure chats and for file transfer. A CTCP handshake initiates DCC, after which the connection continues independent of the server.

Deep Thought A massive supercomputer built to find the answer to the Ultimate Question (*see* 42, HHGTTG).

Denial of Service (DoS) An attack on an Internet host with the intention of disabling it or reducing its availability. Highly illegal.

dmsetup.exe Widespread Trojan horse that targets Windows and mIRC users.

DNS Domain Name Service. Essential for the translation of IP addresses into host names and vice versa.

eggdrop Most common type of IRC robot.

elite Superior in capability or knowledge. The more substitutions of numbers and symbols for letters an individual uses (for example, *31337)*, the less aptly this describes him or her. Other permutations are "leet, ereet," and their derivatives.

emoticon Sequence of ASCII characters depicting a facial expression—for example, a smiley: 8-)

endless loop Infinite repetition of a sequence that restarts itself once finished. *See* infinite loop.

exploit Means of taking advantage of a known security hole; hack.

flood 1) To send large amounts of data to a user or channel. 2) To send large amounts of data directly to a host on the Internet.

FTP File Transfer Protocol. Designed solely for transferring files over the Internet.

GUI Graphical user interface, in which the user interacts with the computer using visual representations of files, programs, and components.

hacker Often incorrectly used interchangeably with cracker, this term actually means someone with a thorough knowledge of computers and a strong desire for exploration, particularly in the area of security.

hax0r Wannabe cracker. Also known as *script kiddies,* these are users who think they know how to hack but rely entirely on prewritten "t00lz" from security and hacker sites, because they lack the computing skills required to create them.

HHGTTG *The Hitchhiker's Guide to the Galaxy* by Douglas Adams. A cult book among the first generations of Internet users. Required reading.

HNG Horny Net-Geek. This species has infested IRC for many years. Also called rumorfs or morfers because they start conversations with "r u m or f (m/f)," meaning "Are you male or female?"

HTML Hypertext Markup Language, used mainly in Web pages to define characteristics such as display and layout.

HTTP Hypertext Transfer Protocol. The protocol behind WWW sites.

ICMP Internet Control Message Protocol. Protocol for diagnostics and error reporting. Used by utilities such as Ping and traceroute.

infinite loop Infinite repetition of a sequence that restarts itself once finished. *See* endless loop.

IRC Internet Relay Chat. A protocol for two-way, real-time, text-based communications, defined by RFC 1459. *See* RFC.

ircname *See* realname.

IRC operator Person who helps run a server. Please don't bug these people about every little problem; they are overworked as it is.

ISDN Integrated Services Digital Network. Supports higher bandwidth connections than normal phone lines, widespread availability.

kick To remove a user forcibly from a channel.

luser Word play on user and loser; originated at MIT. Slang term that system administrators and IRC operators use, especially those who fall in the BOFH category.

MOTD Message of the Day. Message sent to users after they log in to a machine. Also common on IRC servers.

MP3 A format for highly compressed digital audio files of near-CD quality, short for Motion Picture Experts Group (MPEG) Audio Layer 3. Many MP3 files in circulation are illegal copies of copyrighted material.

Netbus Remote administration tool for Windows machines, mostly distributed as a Trojan horse.

newbie New user who hasn't yet learned the ropes. Hopefully if you've read this far you no longer fall into this category.

nick Nickname. A handle you use on IRC.

nuke Slang term for a type of DoS attack that targets a host's vulnerability to cause a lockup or reboot.

PAP Password Authentication Protocol. A protocol often used on top of PPP to encrypt your ISP passwords before sending them.

POP Post Office Protocol. Irrelevant to IRC; this concerns email.

PPP Point-to-Point Protocol. Primary protocol used for connecting a dial-up user to the Internet. PPP allows a serial link to behave like a network interface.

realname Part of an IRC user's visible personal information. Most client applications display it after the address.

RFC Request for Comments, the standards of the Internet. The RFC for IRC is 1459.

robot *See* bot.

room Incorrect term for channel. *See* chat room.

root Superuser account on a Unix machine.

RTFM Short for Read the Fine (or any other F word) Manual.

sendq Amount of data stored, awaiting transmission.

server The workhorse in a client-server environment. In IRC the server has to process enormous amounts of information and route it to the correct client.

shell 1) A text-based interface for an operating system. 2) An account on a Unix machine.

SLIP Another protocol used for dial-up links, but seldom seen now.

smurf A DoS characterized by massive amounts of ICMP data. This attack involves manipulating another site into acting as an amplifier for the attack. Probably the most disruptive form of DoS, on occasion it brings down entire IRC servers. Because of its disruptive nature, it is the easiest to trace back successfully to its origin.

SSH Secure shell. Similar to telnet, except that SSH offers strong encryption for the connection.

T1 and T3 Also called DS1 and DS3. High-speed Internet lines used mainly by businesses. Bandwidth is approximately 1.5 Mbps for T1 and 45 Mbps for T3.

take over To gain control over a channel through unethical or illegal means.

TCM Texas.net Connection Monitor. A type of robot used mainly on EFnet servers, designed to help IRC operators monitor them.

TCP/IP Transmission Control Protocol/Internet Protocol. Two protocols at the heart of the Internet and IRC. TCP provides reliable connections (that is, it recovers lost data and puts packets in the right order), and IP gets packets to their destinations as efficiently as possible.

telnet A protocol (and applications) for connecting to a remote system over a terminal-type interface.

TLA Three-Letter Acronym. You've seen many in this book.

Trojan Short for Trojan horse. A malicious program disguised as a desirable one.

troll One who trolls. *See* trolling.

trolling 1) Asking questions to which you already know the answers. 2) Looking for trouble. The term finds its roots in the mischievous behavior of the trolls in Scandinavian folklore, who are said to taunt people for their own amusement.

virus A Trojan horse program that spreads by attaching its code to other files.

warez Pirated software.

WinNuke One of the early widespread DoS attacks. Specifically targets Windows 95 systems.

COUNTRIES ON IRC AND DOMAIN DECODER

This is a list of the countries and territories from which users appear on IRC. A small number of countries with very few users may be missing due to lack of reliable reports. The list refers to most by their common English names.

Before the name, I've added the ISO 3166 domain code, which is also the code for a top-level domain. You can find a full list of codes at ftp://ftp.ripe.net/iso3166-countrycodes. Countries are sorted by domain code rather than name since you're more likely to be searching for what country a code corresponds to. Some sites in these countries may appear on IRC under a different code—usually .net or .com.

Europe

AD	Andorra
AL	Albania
AM	Armenia
AT	Austria
BA	Bosnia and Herzegovina
BE	Belgium
BG	Bulgaria
BY	Belarus

CH	Switzerland
CY	Cyprus
CZ	Czech Republic
DE	Germany
DK	Denmark
EE	Estonia
ES	SpainFI Finland
FO	Faroe Islands
FR	France
GE	Georgia
GR	Greece
HR	Croatia
HU	Hungary
IE	Ireland
IS	Iceland
IT	Italy
LT	Lithuania
LU	Luxembourg
LV	Latvia
MC	Monaco
MD	Moldova
MK	Macedonia, Former Yugoslav Republic of
MT	Malta
NL	Netherlands
NO	Norway
PL	Poland
PT	Portugal
RO	Romania
RU	Russian Federation
SE	Sweden
SI	Slovenia
SK	Slovakia
SM	San Marino
TR	Turkey
UA	Ukraine
UK	United Kingdom
YU	Yugoslavia (Serbia and Montenegro)

Some organizations in Russia still use the SU (Soviet Union) domain.

Asia

AE	United Arab Emirates
BH	Bahrain

BN	Brunei Darussalam
CN	China, People's Republic of
HK	Hong Kong
ID	Indonesia
IL	Israel
IN	India
IR	Islamic Republic of Iran
JO	Jordan
JP	Japan
KR	South Korea
KW	Kuwait
KZ	Kazakhstan
LB	Lebanon
LK	Sri Lanka
MN	Mongolia
MO	Macao
MY	Malaysia
NP	Nepal
OM	Oman
PH	Philippines
PK	Pakistan
QA	Qatar
SG	Singapore
TH	Thailand
TW	Taiwan, Republic of China
UZ	Uzbekistan

North and South America (including the Caribbean)

AG	Antigua
AR	Argentina
BB	Barbados
BM	Bermuda
BO	Bolivia
BR	Brazil
BS	Bahamas
CA	Canada
CL	Chile
CO	Colombia
CR	Costa Rica
DM	Dominica
DO	Dominican Republic
EC	Ecuador
GT	Guatemala

HN	Honduras
JM	Jamaica
MQ	Martinique
MX	Mexico
NI	Nicaragua
PA	Panama
PE	Peru
PY	Paraguay
SR	Suriname
TC	Turks and Caicos Islands
TT	Trinidad and Tobago
US	United States of America
UY	Uruguay
VE	Venezuela

Most sites in the United States and many in Canada use .com, .net, .edu, and .org instead of their national domain code. The KY domain (Cayman Islands, unlisted) is remotely administered and users who appear with that domain code probably are not located there.

Oceania and the Pacific

AU	Australia
GM	Guam
NC	New Caledonia
NZ	New Zealand
PG	Papua New GuineaAfrica (including outlying islands)
CD	Congo, Democratic Republic of (ex-Zaire)
CI	Ivory Coast
CV	Cape Verde
EG	Egypt
KE	Kenya
MA	Morocco
MU	Mauritius
NA	Namibia
RE	Reunion
SN	Senegal
TN	Tunisia
UG	Uganda
ZA	South Africa
ZW	Zimbabwe

Pseudo GTLDs

The following countries and territories sell space in their top-level domain to users all over the world, thus acting as generic top-level domains (GTLDs), like .com and .net. This is a source of revenue for small island nations and other less affluent countries. I cannot truthfully say I have seen a user actually located in one of these places. The low registration fees in some of them have attracted many individuals who register a domain for the sake of having one, then appear on IRC with a domain such as outca.st or ji.ms (we call that a vanity domain). Some, because of their particular code, also appeal to companies (for example, TM).

It's possible to have a second-level domain registered in another 50 or so countries that also have a population on the Net and are listed above, even if you do not live there. More uninhabited or sparsely populated islands will probably acquire a virtual population over the next few years. Here's the list of the more common ones (you may never have heard of them).

AC	Ascension Island	Mid Atlantic
AS	American Samoa	South Pacific
CC	Cocos Islands	Indian Ocean
CX	Christmas Island	Indian Ocean
GS	Georgia and South Sandwich Islands	South Atlantic
MS	Montserrat	Caribbean
NU	Niue	South Pacific
SH	Saint Helena	Mid Atlantic
ST	São Tomé and Príncipe Islands	Equatorial Africa
TC	Turks and Caicos Islands	Caribbean
TF	French Southern Territories	Southern oceans
TJ	Tajikistan	Central Asia
TM	Turkmenistan	Central Asia
TO	Tonga	South Pacific
VG	British Virgin Islands	Caribbean

D

USEFUL ADDRESSES

NOTE *If you're using a browser to access sites other than Web sites, remember to add the correct URL scheme, such as ftp:// or news:. Web sites should, of course, begin with http://.*

D.1 Web Sites

dir.yahoo.com/Computers_and_Internet/Internet/Chats_and_Forums/ IRC/Channels/ Another good place for channel listings, even if the URL is uncomfortably long.

ftpsearch.lycos.com The best place to search for specific files by name.

mirc.stealth.net Useful mIRC stuff, good tips on dealing with DoS attacks.

www.bitchx.org Home of the BitchX client.

www.chatcircuit.com Nice site. Newsletters, server listings, lots of help. Maintained by the Chatcircuit IRC server team.

www.dal.net   Official DALnet home page. Everything you need to know about using DALnet.

www.eff.org   Electronic Frontier Foundation. Important information about online privacy, freedom of expression, Internet-related legislation, and many more matters of concern to Internet users.

www.irchelp.org   Probably the best there is. Wide range of documentation and resources, centered mainly on EFnet and IRCnet. Top source of information about Unix and Mac clients.

www.ircle.com   Ircle (Mac client) home page.

www.joecartoon.com   Totally unrelated to IRC, I just think it's cool. :)

www.liszt.com/chat/   Great repository of current channel listings for many networks.

www.mirc.co.uk   The official mIRC home page. Contains links to just about everything you could ever want to know about mIRC. The "links" sections also offers the most complete list of resources in languages other than English.

www.mirchelp.org   Clean, simple mIRC site by the operators of Efnet's #mirchelp channel.

www.mircx.com   Many, many mIRC scripts. Personally, I don't like the way they serve practically any abusive trash you ask them to, but I must give it points for completeness.

www.netway.com/~marci/songs/   Songs about IRC. Just when you thought *you* were a geek.

www.newircusers.com   A very comprehensive and helpful site. Some off-topic stuff.

www.pirchat.com   Home of the Pirch client for Windows.

www.snafu.de/~kl/epic/index.html   Epic's home page.

www.snafu.de/~kl/IRCES/   Announces chat events on various networks.

www.stevegrossman.com/jargpge.htm   Chatters' jargon dictionary. This includes jargon from many other forms of online chat; sometimes it stretches the definition a bit.

www.thelist.com Listing of Internet service providers by region.

www.tucows.com Huge software archive for Windows, Mac, and Linux systems. Mirrors all over the world.

www.undernet.org Very complete and well organized. Good for more than just the Undernet.

www.userfriendly.org Geek humor taken one step further.

www.webmaster.com Home of the number one commercial IRC server software, Conference Room.

D.2 FTP Sites

cs-ftp.bu.edu	Lots of old stuff—this is where to get IRC clients for antique machines.
ftp.asu.net	Maybe the most complete IRC client and server archive; good variety of new Unix client binaries.
ftp.funet.fi	Finnish University Network public FTP, one of the best-established archives on the Internet.
ftp.ripe.net/rfc	RFC repository for the technically minded. RFCs 1459, 1413, 954, and 931 may be of interest. RFC 2324 covering HTCPCP specifications is required reading.
ftp.undernet.org	Comprehensive but largely outdated; wide selection of older ircII binaries for odd platforms.
ircii.warped.com	Warped Communications FTP archive; main ircII download site.
metalab.unc.edu	Huge software archive, has just about everything under the sun.

D.3 Telnet Services

These services are not as popular as they used to be and may be discontinued in the future.

Host	Port	Log-in	Password	Description
telnet.dal.net	23	dalnet	no password	DALnet telnet IRC client
telnet.superchat.org	23	no log-in	no password	SuperChat telnet IRC client
telnet.wildstar.net	6677	no log-in	no password	Wildstar's telnet IRC client for the Undernet

D.4 Newsgroups

alt.irc   Lots of general IRC discussions, announcements, and flame wars.

alt.irc.mirc   Questions and scripts for mIRC.

alt.irc.questions   Good place to get solutions for unusual problems.

alt.irc.recovery   IRC addicts of the world, unite!

alt.irc.scripts   General scripting issues.

E

SERVER NUMERICS

This section is meant to help client coders and scripters find their way through the maze of numeric insanity. It covers the numerics currently used in all four principal ircds and a couple used in common patches. I do not know why there are several different meanings to a numeric, why the same reply has more than one numeric in some cases, or why the same reply sometimes has a different name but an identical numeric. I'll attribute it to communications breakdown among ircd coders—but perhaps it's a conspiracy. The truth is out there. . . .

I have not marked RFC numerics as such, whether they are redundant, deprecated, or used. The fact that a numeric is listed here does not mean it's actually in use. Some are only present in the numerics headers and have no practical application in the current ircd. The list would be twice as long if I included all the strange numerics employed in patches and hacks to these ircds—consult the numerics header of the ircd in question to get the full list.

E=EFnet hybrid-6
I=IRCnet 2.10.2p1
U=Undernet u2.10.05
D=DALnet 4.6.7.DreamForge

Numeric	E	I	U	D	Description
001	✓	✓	✓	✓	RPL_WELCOME
002	✓	✓	✓	✓	RPL_YOURHOST
003	✓	✓	✓	✓	RPL_CREATED
004	✓	✓	✓	✓	RPL_MYINFO
005		✓			RPL_BOUNCE
005			✓		RPL_MAP
005				✓	RPL_PROTOCTL
006			✓		RPL_MAPMORE
007			✓		RPL_MAPEND
008			✓		RPL_SNOMASK
009			✓		RPL_STATMEMTOT
010			✓		RPL_STATMEM
200	✓	✓	✓	✓	RPL_TRACELINK
201	✓	✓	✓	✓	RPL_TRACECONNECTING
202	✓	✓	✓	✓	RPL_TRACEHANDSHAKE
203	✓	✓	✓	✓	RPL_TRACEUNKNOWN
204	✓	✓	✓	✓	RPL_TRACEOPERATOR
205	✓	✓	✓	✓	RPL_TRACEUSER
206	✓	✓	✓	✓	RPL_TRACESERVER
207	✓	✓	✓	✓	RPL_TRACESERVICE
208	✓	✓	✓	✓	RPL_TRACENEWTYPE
209	✓	✓	✓	✓	RPL_TRACECLASS
210		✓			RPL_TRACERECONNECT
211	✓	✓	✓	✓	RPL_STATSLINKINFO
212	✓	✓	✓	✓	RPL_STATSCOMMANDS
213	✓	✓	✓	✓	RPL_STATSCLINE
214	✓	✓	✓	✓	RPL_STATSNLINE
215	✓	✓	✓	✓	RPL_STATSILINE
216	✓	✓	✓	✓	RPL_STATSKLINE
217	✓	✓		✓	RPL_STATSQLINE
217			✓		RPL_STATSPLINE
218	✓	✓	✓	✓	RPL_STATSYLINE
219	✓	✓	✓	✓	RPL_ENDOFSTATS
221	✓	✓	✓	✓	RPL_UMODEIS
222	✓				RPL_STATSBLINE
222				✓	RPL_SQLINE_NICK
223	✓				RPL_STATSELINE
224	✓				RPL_STATSFLINE
225	✓				RPL_STATSDLINE
231		✓	✓	✓	RPL_SERVICEINFO
232		✓	✓	✓	RPL_ENDOFSERVICES
233		✓	✓	✓	RPL_SERVICE
234	✓	✓	✓	✓	RPL_SERVLIST
235	✓	✓	✓	✓	RPL_SERVLISTEND

Numeric	E	I	U	D	Description
239		✓			RPL_STATSIAUTH
240		✓			RPL_STATSVLINE
241	✓	✓	✓	✓	RPL_STATSLLINE
242	✓	✓	✓	✓	RPL_STATSUPTIME
243	✓	✓	✓	✓	RPL_STATSOLINE
244	✓	✓	✓	✓	RPL_STATSHLINE
245	✓	✓		✓	RPL_STATSSLINE
246		✓			RPL_STATSPING
246			✓		RPL_STATSTLINE
247		✓			RPL_STATSBLINE
247			✓		RPL_STATSGLINE
247				✓	RPL_STATSXLINE
248		✓			RPL_STATSDEFINE
248			✓	✓	RPL_STATSULINE
249	✓	✓	✓	✓	RPL_STATSDEBUG
250		✓			RPL_STATSDLINE
250	✓		✓	✓	RPL_STATSCONN
251	✓	✓	✓	✓	RPL_LUSERCLIENT
252	✓	✓	✓	✓	RPL_LUSEROP
253	✓	✓	✓	✓	RPL_LUSERUNKNOWN
254	✓	✓	✓	✓	RPL_LUSERCHANNELS
255	✓	✓	✓	✓	RPL_LUSERME
256	✓	✓	✓	✓	RPL_ADMINME
257	✓	✓	✓	✓	RPL_ADMINLOC1
258	✓	✓	✓	✓	RPL_ADMINLOC2
259	✓	✓	✓	✓	RPL_ADMINEMAIL
261	✓	✓	✓	✓	RPL_TRACELOG
262	✓	✓			RPL_TRACEEND
262			✓		RPL_TRACEPING
263		✓			RPL_TRYAGAIN
263	✓				RPL_LOAD2HI
265	✓			✓	RPL_LOCALUSERS
266	✓			✓	RPL_GLOBALUSERS
271			✓	✓	RPL_SILELIST
272			✓	✓	RPL_ENDOFSILELIST
275			✓	✓	RPL_STATSDLINE
280		✓			RPL_GLIST
281		✓			RPL_ENDOFGLIST
290				✓	RPL_HELPHDR
291				✓	RPL_HELPOP
292				✓	RPL_HELPTLR
293				✓	RPL_HELPHLP
294				✓	RPL_HELPFWD
295				✓	RPL_HELPIGN

Numeric	E	I	U	D	Description
300	✓	✓	✓	✓	RPL_NONE
301	✓	✓	✓	✓	RPL_AWAY
302	✓	✓	✓	✓	RPL_USERHOST
303	✓	✓	✓	✓	RPL_ISON
304	✓	✓	✓	✓	RPL_TEXT
305	✓	✓	✓	✓	RPL_UNAWAY
306	✓	✓	✓	✓	RPL_NOWAWAY
307		✓			RPL_USERIP
307				✓	RPL_WHOISREGNICK
310				✓	RPL_WHOISHELPOP
311	✓	✓	✓	✓	RPL_WHOISUSER
312	✓	✓	✓	✓	RPL_WHOISSERVER
313	✓	✓	✓	✓	RPL_WHOISOPERATOR
314	✓	✓	✓	✓	RPL_WHOWASUSER
315	✓	✓	✓	✓	RPL_ENDOFWHO
316	✓	✓		✓	RPL_WHOISCHANOP
317	✓	✓	✓	✓	RPL_WHOISIDLE
318	✓	✓	✓	✓	RPL_ENDOFWHOIS
319	✓	✓	✓	✓	RPL_WHOISCHANNELS
321	✓	✓	✓	✓	RPL_LISTSTART
322	✓	✓	✓	✓	RPL_LIST
323	✓	✓	✓	✓	RPL_LISTEND
324	✓	✓	✓	✓	RPL_CHANNELMODEIS
325		✓			RPL_UNIQOPIS
329	✓		✓	✓	RPL_CREATIONTIME
331	✓	✓	✓	✓	RPL_NOTOPIC
332	✓	✓	✓	✓	RPL_TOPIC
333	✓		✓	✓	RPL_TOPICWHOTIME
334		✓			RPL_LISTUSAGE
334				✓	RPL_LISTSYNTAX
341	✓	✓	✓	✓	RPL_INVITING
342	✓	✓		✓	RPL_SUMMONING
346		✓			RPL_INVITELIST
347		✓			RPL_ENDOFINVITELIST
348		✓			RPL_EXCEPTLIST
349		✓			RPL_ENDOFEXCEPTLIST
351	✓	✓	✓	✓	RPL_VERSION
352	✓	✓	✓	✓	RPL_WHOREPLY
353	✓	✓	✓	✓	RPL_NAMREPLY
354		✓			RPL_WHOSPCRPL
361	✓	✓	✓	✓	RPL_KILLDONE
362	✓	✓	✓	✓	RPL_CLOSING
363	✓	✓	✓	✓	RPL_CLOSEEND
364	✓	✓	✓	✓	RPL_LINKS

Numeric	E	I	U	D	Description
365	✓	✓	✓	✓	RPL_ENDOFLINKS
366	✓	✓	✓	✓	RPL_ENDOFNAMES
367	✓	✓	✓	✓	RPL_BANLIST
368	✓	✓	✓	✓	RPL_ENDOFBANLIST
369	✓	✓	✓	✓	RPL_ENDOFWHOWAS
371	✓	✓	✓	✓	RPL_INFO
372	✓	✓	✓	✓	RPL_MOTD
373	✓	✓	✓	✓	RPL_INFOSTART
374	✓	✓	✓	✓	RPL_ENDOFINFO
375	✓	✓	✓	✓	RPL_MOTDSTART
376	✓	✓	✓	✓	RPL_ENDOFMOTD
381	✓	✓	✓	✓	RPL_YOUREOPER
382	✓	✓	✓	✓	RPL_REHASHING
383		✓		✓	RPL_YOURESERVICE
384	✓	✓	✓	✓	RPL_MYPORTIS
385	✓	✓	✓	✓	RPL_NOTOPERANYMORE
391	✓	✓	✓	✓	RPL_TIME
392	✓	✓		✓	RPL_USERSSTART
393	✓	✓		✓	RPL_USERS
394	✓	✓		✓	RPL_ENDOFUSERS
395	✓	✓		✓	RPL_NOUSERS
401	✓	✓	✓	✓	ERR_NOSUCHNICK
402	✓	✓	✓	✓	ERR_NOSUCHSERVER
403	✓	✓	✓	✓	ERR_NOSUCHCHANNEL
404	✓	✓	✓	✓	ERR_CANNOTSENDTOCHAN
405	✓	✓	✓	✓	ERR_TOOMANYCHANNELS
406	✓	✓	✓	✓	ERR_WASNOSUCHNICK
407	✓	✓	✓	✓	ERR_TOOMANYTARGETS
408		✓		✓	ERR_NOSUCHSERVICE
409	✓	✓	✓	✓	ERR_NOORIGIN
411	✓	✓	✓	✓	ERR_NORECIPIENT
412	✓	✓	✓	✓	ERR_NOTEXTTOSEND
413	✓	✓	✓	✓	ERR_NOTOPLEVEL
414	✓	✓	✓	✓	ERR_WILDTOPLEVEL
415		✓			ERR_BADMASK
416		✓			ERR_TOOMANYMATCHES
416			✓		ERR_QUERYTOOLONG
421	✓	✓	✓	✓	ERR_UNKNOWNCOMMAND
422	✓	✓	✓	✓	ERR_NOMOTD
423	✓	✓	✓	✓	ERR_NOADMININFO
424	✓	✓		✓	ERR_FILEERROR
431	✓	✓	✓	✓	ERR_NONICKNAMEGIVEN
432	✓	✓	✓	✓	ERR_ERRONEUSNICKNAME
433	✓	✓	✓	✓	ERR_NICKNAMEINUSE

Numeric	E	I	U	D	Description
434		✓		✓	ERR_SERVICENAMEINUSE
435		✓		✓	ERR_SERVICECONFUSED
436	✓	✓	✓	✓	ERR_NICKCOLLISION
437		✓			ERR_UNAVAILRESOURCE
437			✓	✓	ERR_BANNICKCHANGE
438		✓			ERR_NICKTOOFAST
438				✓	ERR_NCHANGETOOFAST
439			✓	✓	ERR_TARGETTOOFAST
440				✓	ERR_SERVICESDOWN
441	✓	✓	✓	✓	ERR_USERNOTINCHANNEL
442	✓	✓	✓	✓	ERR_NOTONCHANNEL
443	✓	✓	✓	✓	ERR_USERONCHANNEL
444	✓	✓		✓	ERR_NOLOGIN
445	✓	✓		✓	ERR_SUMMONDISABLED
446	✓	✓		✓	ERR_USERSDISABLED
451	✓	✓	✓	✓	ERR_NOTREGISTERED
455				✓	ERR_HOSTILENAME
461	✓	✓	✓	✓	ERR_NEEDMOREPARAMS
462	✓	✓	✓	✓	ERR_ALREADYREGISTRED
463	✓	✓	✓	✓	ERR_NOPERMFORHOST
464	✓	✓	✓	✓	ERR_PASSWDMISMATCH
465	✓	✓	✓	✓	ERR_YOUREBANNEDCREEP
466	✓	✓	✓	✓	ERR_YOUWILLBEBANNED
467	✓	✓	✓	✓	ERR_KEYSET
468		✓			ERR_INVALIDUSERNAME
468				✓	ERR_ONLYSERVERSCANCHANGE
471	✓	✓	✓	✓	ERR_CHANNELISFULL
472	✓	✓	✓	✓	ERR_UNKNOWNMODE
473	✓	✓	✓	✓	ERR_INVITEONLYCHAN
474	✓	✓	✓	✓	ERR_BANNEDFROMCHAN
475	✓	✓	✓	✓	ERR_BADCHANNELKEY
476	✓	✓	✓	✓	ERR_BADCHANMASK
477		✓			ERR_NOCHANMODES
477				✓	ERR_NEEDREGGEDNICK
478		✓	✓	✓	ERR_BANLISTFULL
481	✓	✓	✓	✓	ERR_NOPRIVILEGES
482	✓	✓	✓	✓	ERR_CHANOPRIVSNEEDED
483	✓		✓	✓	ERR_CANTKILLSERVER
484	✓				ERR_DESYNC
484		✓			ERR_ISCHANSERVICE
484		✓			ERR_RESTRICTED
485		✓			ERR_UNIQOPPRIVSNEEDED
489			✓		ERR_VOICENEEDED
491	✓	✓	✓	✓	ERR_NOOPERHOST

Numeric	E	I	U	D	Description
492		✓		✓	ERR_NOSERVICEHOST
501	✓	✓	✓	✓	ERR_UMODEUNKNOWNFLAG
502	✓	✓	✓	✓	ERR_USERSDONTMATCH
503	✓				ERR_GHOSTEDCLIENT
504	✓				ERR_LAST_ERR_MSG
511			✓	✓	ERR_SILELISTFULL
512			✓		ERR_NOSUCHGLINE
512				✓	ERR_TOOMANYWATCH
513			✓		ERR_BADPING
513				✓	ERR_NEEDPONG
521				✓	ERR_LISTSYNTAX
600				✓	RPL_LOGON
601				✓	RPL_LOGOFF
602				✓	RPL_WATCHOFF
603				✓	RPL_WATCHSTAT
604				✓	RPL_NOWON
605				✓	RPL_NOWOFF
606				✓	RPL_WATCHLIST
607				✓	RPL_ENDOFWATCHLIST

SAMPLE SERVER CONFIGURATIONS

Lines beginning with the pound sign (#) are comments and not config lines, just as in a real configuration file. Some of the data is of course fictitious, but it is all adapted from real, working configs. I suggest you start by reading the first example, for hybrid servers, regardless of which configuration you'll be using, as it contains information that applies to any setting. If there is a difference, the relevant section will mention it. To get the best idea of how server configurations work, I recommend reading all of them.

F.1   Basic Configuration (hybrid 5.3 Server)

This is a fictitious server, but the config layout follows a real networked server I used to run.

The server needs a name. This should match a valid host name. Leave the second field blank. The third field is arbitrary and can contain anything you like. The fourth field is the default port.

```
M:irc.cia.gov::The secret server:6667
```

Administrative info is required. There are three fields, the last one being the admin's email. This information is sent out in response to the **ADMIN** command.

```
A:Company server:Langley, Virginia:Bill Clinton
<bill@whitehouse.gov>
```

Y: lines are good for you. In this example, the first one is a general Y: line for a maximum of **20** class **1** users, with no (**0**) limit on connections per host or **user@host**. In theory, a single user could fill all the connections. You set a user's class from the I: line. Users have a maximum sendq of about **100KB**, and the server will ping them every **90** seconds. 90 seconds is the lowest value I'd ever use — 120 to 240 is more common, and as much as 300 on a large server.

The second value is for server connections. The maximum of **10** connections is definitely exaggerated unless you have a major hub. The server will attempt to autoconnect to servers in class **2** every five minutes, provided that the C: line has enabled autoconnect. If more than roughly **4MB** of data queues for a class 2 server, your server will drop the link.

```
Y:1:90:0:20:100000
Y:2:90:300:10:4000000
```

This is just about as lazy as you can be. Permit connections from anyone, anywhere, and assign them to class **1**, as laid out in the Y: lines. It's generally a good idea to give your IRC operators separate I: and Y: lines so that they can connect regardless. Actually, hybrid allows for this with F: lines. The only thing that keeps masses of clones from connecting is the fact that the Y: line limits the total connections to 20.

```
I:*::*::1
```

The server's operators — it's not required, but it's convenient for monitoring the server while you're online. Each line is composed of three parts: First, the mask a user is allowed to oper from; second, the password that must be sent along with the **OPER** command; third, the operator's usual nickname, which you must send regardless of whether you're using that nickname at the moment.

You may encrypt the password, providing you have enabled crypted password support while compiling.

Encrypt your passwords with the **mkpasswd** utility in **ircd/tools**. In this example, this is not the case, and the passwords are in plain text — one very good reason to make sure no one but the ircd user can read **ircd.conf**. Notice that Jason's small **o:** makes him a local operator, so he does not enjoy global privileges.

```
O:bill@*.whitehouse.gov:secret:Bill:
O:joe@*.cia.gov:spieslikeus:Joe:
o:jason@*.cia.gov:bbbxxx:Jason:
```

C: and N: lines are necessary for networking. They're a bit similar to I:
lines in design. Here we have a single server connection with the same
server name as the machine's host name. That is, the server at **irc.sen-
ate.gov** (first field) will be announced to the network as **irc.senate.gov**
(third field). The first field *must* be a valid host name or IP address. The
second field is the password — like the O: lines, you can encrypt it or
not, depending on the compile-time options. This is not a very good
example — it's considered best to use different passwords for the C: and
N: lines in the interest of security. The fourth field of the C: line says
whether it will autoconnect. Here, your **irc.cia.gov** server will autoconnect to port **6667** on **irc.senate.gov** at the interval specified in the class **2**
(see the last field) Y: line, if it sees it's not linked.

Finally, the fourth field of the N: line says whether your server will
mask to something on the remote server. For example, if you wanted it
to appear as ***.cia.gov** on **irc.senate.gov** (and any servers that may be
behind that one), you would put a "1" in this field, masking one field of
the host name. For this to work, irc.senate.gov must have ***.cia.gov**
instead of **irc.cia.gov** in both the C: and N: lines.

```
C:irc.senate.gov:link2me:irc.senate.gov:6667:2
N:irc.senate.gov:link2me:irc.senate.gov:0:2
```

K: lines keep unwanted users from connecting. Since this server has an
"open" I: line, a K: line will probably prove to be necessary.

Example 1: Ban user **slobodan** from connecting to the machine
named **president.gov.yu**. The reason displayed to the user will be **Go
away**.

```
K:president.gov.yu:Go away:slobodan:
```

Example 2: Ban all connections from the ***.kp** top-level domain regardless of user name with the reason **No nukes**. (This couldn't be more
fictitious, because North Korea (*.kp) is not on the Internet.)

```
K:*.kp:No nukes:*:
```

Example 3: Ban user **saddam** connecting from anywhere in the ***.iq** top-
level domain. (This is as fictitious as the previous example for the same
reason.)

```
K:*.iq:Not welcome:saddam:
```

Example 4: Ban anyone from the **.ru** top-level domain whose machine does not verify their user ID through ident. This is what the tilde (~) stands for.

```
K:*.ru:Identification required for everyone from Russia:~*:
```

Allow everyone from **.spb.ru** to join regardless.

```
E:*.spb.ru::*:
```

F.2 Advanced Configuration (Bahamut Server)

Here is the genuine config file from WebNet Worldwide's DALnet server (webbernet.mi.us.dal.net), abridged and edited for obvious security reasons. The server . . .

```
M:webbernet.mi.us.dal.net:*:Web Net Worldwide:7000
```

. . . and the admin.

```
A:Asu Pala <pt@dal.net>:Web Net Worldwide:Taylor, MI +1 888 WEB-
NETT:
```

Here are our user and server classes. Class **0** is a generic class for connections matching no other Y:.

```
Y:0:120:600:1:5000000
```

The main user Y: line can handle up to **4000** users.

```
Y:1:300:0:4000:300000
```

Server links. I think the connection frequency of **90** seconds for class **13** is a bit on the high side because of the large number of users this server generally has.

```
Y:13:90:90:1:6000000
Y:14:450:180:0:3500000
```

Y: lines to match a set of I: lines (shown below) for specific users and operators.

```
Y:100:300:0:100:300000
Y:666:300:0:10:500000
Y:906:300:0:10:500000
Y:907:300:0:10:500000
Y:908:300:0:10:500000
Y:909:300:0:10:500000
Y:910:300:0:10:500000
Y:911:300:0:10:500000
Y:912:300:0:10:500000
Y:913:300:0:10:500000
Y:914:300:0:10:500000
Y:915:300:0:10:500000
```

These are the ports on which the server will listen. This server listens on the common **6660 to 6680** range, plus **7000**, which is the DALnet default port, and **7325**, which DALnet uses for server-to-server connections.

```
P:*:*:*:6660
P:*:*:*:6661
P:*:*:*:6662
P:*:*:*:6663
P:*:*:*:6664
P:*:*:*:6665
P:*:*:*:6666
P:*:*:*:6667
P:*:*:*:6668
P:*:*:*:6669
P:*:*:*:6670
P:*:*:*:6671
P:*:*:*:6672
P:*:*:*:6673
P:*:*:*:6674
P:*:*:*:6675
P:*:*:*:6676
P:*:*:*:6677
P:*:*:*:6678
P:*:*:*:6679
P:*:*:*:6680
P:*:*:*:7325
```

This is the I: line under which all mortal users fall. Because of the way DALnet works, there is little call for separating them into classes, so we dump them all under a single I:. This does not do much in terms of preventing misuse of the server through its configuration, but it saves a lot of cycles.

```
I:*@*::*@*::1
```

All these are I: lines for individual users, mainly the server's operators, and for the server's local users. **NOMATCH** and **x** mean nothing by themselves, they simply invalidate the field they're in because they're impossible to match to a host name or IP address.

```
I:24.0.243.128::NOMATCH::1
I:x::*@*.webbernet.net::100
I:x::primetime@*.webbernet.net::666
I:x::pt@*.webbernet.net::666
I:x::kelaynak@*.webbernet.net:906:906
I:x::mhz@irc.webbernet.net:907:907
I:x::girard@*.princeton.edu:907:907
I:x::dredster@*.noc.ionet.net:908:908
I:x::dredster@dredster.ionet.net:908:908
I:x::dj@newton.pconline.com:909:909
I:x::thetaz@*.pconline.com:909:909
I:x::thetaz@*.webbernet.net:909:909
I:x::thetaz@thetaz.org:909:909
I:x::dakal@*lowdown.com:910:910
I:x::apatrix@*.wnm.net:911:911
I:x::rmullen@*thorn.net:913:913
I:x::marci@shell2.mdc.net:914:914
```

IRC operators. All operators have separate I: and O: lines for every address they oper from. I've snipped a few to save space. The strange strings near the end of the line define the privileges of the individual operator and are unique to DALnet ircd.

```
O:primetime@*.webbernet.net:<pass>:pt:rRDhlCckKbBNnAaufoO:666
O:pt@*.webbernet.net:<pass>:pt:rRDhlCckKbBNnAaufoO:666
O:kelaynak@*.webbernet.net:<pass>:kelaynak:arRDhlkKbBufoO:906
O:marsha@*.popsite.net:<pass>:PrincessDI:Oa:912
O:marsha@youngs.ringgold.ga.us:<pass>:PrincessDI:Oa:912
O:marsha@216.1.116.*:<pass>:PrincessDI:Oa:912
O:mhz@irc.webbernet.net:<pass>:mhz:rRDhlkKbBufoOa:907
O:girard@*.princeton.edu:<pass>:mhz:rRDhlkKbBufoOa:907
O:dredster@mud.shadowwind.org:<pass>:Micheal:Oa:908
```

```
O:dredster@dredster.ionet.net:<pass>:Micheal:Oa:908
O:dredster@*.noc.ionet.net:<pass>:Micheal:Oa:908
O:dakal@*lowdown.com:<pass>:dakal:OaRD:910
O:*adam@209.82.128.*:<pass>:kaleido:OaDR:910
O:*nobody@209.82.128.*:<pass>:kaleido:OaDR:910
O:thetaz@twilight.zone.webbernet.net:<pass>:TheTaz:rRDhlCckKbBNnAa
ufoO:909
O:thetaz@thetaz.org:<pass>:TheTaz:rRDhlCckKbBNnAaufoO:909
O:apatrix@*.webbernet.net:<pass>:Apatrix:*:911
O:apatrix@bofh.wnm.net:<pass>:Apatrix:*:911
O:rmullen@*.thorn.net:<pass>:hershey:*:913
O:*@shell2.mdc.net:<pass>:Doogie:OaRD:914
```

The X: line in DALnet ircd contains two passwords, which must be used with the **RESTART** and **DIE** commands, respectively.

```
X:<pass>:<pass>
```

Special U: lines regulate the presence of services and where the server will accept them from.

```
U:stats.dal.net:*:*
U:services.dal.net:*:*
U:services2.dal.net:*:*
```

The C: and N: lines follow the same principle as in every other ircd. The hubs' IP addresses are not publicized on DALnet as a matter of policy, so I've stripped them here as well. Being a leaf, this server will have no more than a single server link at any time, so they are all in class **13**. A hub server would have more different classes.

```
C:<address>:<pass>:enigma.mi.us.dal.net:7325:13
N:<address>:<pass>:enigma.mi.us.dal.net::13
N:<address>:<pass>:toronto.on.ca.dal.net::13
C:<address>:<pass>:toronto.on.ca.dal.net::13
N:<address>:<pass>:quantum-r.ny.us.dal.net::13
C:<address>:<pass>:quantum-r.ny.us.dal.net::13
N:<address>:<pass>:indy.in.us.dal.net::13
C:<address>:<pass>:indy.in.us.dal.net::13
N:<address>:<pass>:chrome.mo.us.dal.net::13
C:<address>:<pass>:chrome.mo.us.dal.net::13
```

H: lines are also the same as they would be everywhere else. This server is a leaf, so it has no L: lines.

```
H:*:*:quantum-r.ny.us.dal.net
H:*:*:trapdoor.ca.us.dal.net
H:*:*:toronto.on.ca.dal.net
H:*:*:chrome.mo.us.dal.net
H:*:*:indy.in.us.dal.net
H:*:*:enigma.mi.us.dal.net
```

DALnet akills are not written to the config, nor are K: lines placed with the **KLINE** command. Thus the only way to implement "hard" permanent K: lines is by writing them into the conf. Here's a good reason for adding comments to your K: lines: I think I set that second one, but I don't remember what for. I will now go and remove it because I can't recall its purpose.

```
K:*.home.com:Use gate.dal.net:~*:
K:62.157.150.46:Go away:*:
```

Broken thing is the actual comment in the config file. To expand on my previous note about adding comments to your K: lines, make sure they also make sense. :) Oh, yeah . . . and date them. The same goes for Z: lines — this particular comment refers to the below Z: line entry. I have to shamefully admit that this is one I added myself.

```
# broken thing
Z:210.162.87.244:
```

Q: lines are nicknames that no user may employ under any circumstances. Only services use them, and the ones with wild cards are meant to prevent impostors from using nicks similar to a service nickname.

```
Q::Reserved:ChanServ
Q::Reserved:NickServ
Q::Reserved:OperServ
Q::Reserved:HelpServ
Q::Reserved:*c*h*n*s*r*v*
Q::Reserved:*m*e*m*o*s*rv*
Q::Reserved:*n*i*k*s*rv*
Q::For IRCops:IRCop
Q::For IRCops:DALnet
```

The comment above the line is another genuine config comment. It's dated and says who set it, though not why. Still, I feel confident about my colleague's judgment — this line sure looks better than the ones I put in myself. Z: lines do the same as EFnet's D: lines and IRCnet's K: lines: They drop connections from the IP address or block regardless of whether and what it resolves to.

```
#Micheal!dredster@fnord.noc.ionet.net Z'd: 38.193.1.98:No reason
(1999/06/11 00.03)
Z:38.193.1.98:No reason (1999/06/11 00.03):
```

INDEX

Note: Italicized numbers indicate illustrations.

SYMBOLS

&. *See* ampersand (&)
*. *See* asterisk (*)
@. *See* at sign (@)
[ ]. *See* brackets ([])
:. *See* colon (:)
^. *See* CTRL key
$. *See* dollar sign ($)
!. *See* exclamation mark (!)
/. *See* forward slash (/)
#. *See* hash mark (#)
-. *See* hyphen (-)
%. *See* percent sign (%)
+. *See* plus sign (+)

A

abbreviations, IRC–related,
    142–143, 299, 313–319
ACTION (CTCP command),
    211–212
actions, 141–142
    definition, 313
    on IRC channels, 131
    overuse of, 132
Adams, Douglas, 316
address book feature of Snak, 64
addresses. *See also* IP addresses
    email, 35
    faking, 174
    finding IRC users', 149
    Internet, 75, 321–325
    secure, 174
    wildcards in users', 149–150
ADMIN (command), 230
    ircd.conf file A: line and, 271
ADSL, definition of, 313
advertising on IRC, 132, 263
afaik, 142
akill (DALnet command), 79
Aladdin Systems' Web site
    address, 57

ALIAS (command), 53
aliases
    case sensitivity of, 192
    creating, for double WHOIS
        command, 148
    ircII generic script for, 191
    for KICK commands, 166
    for pinging, 210
    in scripts, 192–193
    setting modes with,
        in emergencies, 173
A: lines, 271
    sample, 340, 342
alt.irc.recovery, 300
AME (mIRC command), 142
#amiga, 247
Amiga operating systems
    IRC clients for, 249
    IRC servers for, 270
    IRC server software for, 30
    and PPP, 7
AmIRC, 249
ampersand (&), 100
AMSG (mIRC command), 137
anonymity on IRC, 296–297
anonymous FTP, 9
ANSI
    color, 138, 139
    definition of, 313
    terminal emulation, 144
AOL (America Online)
    host masks, 168
    IRC bans on users of, 109
AOPs, 185
AppleScript, 61
    Ircle use of, 59
AppleTalk chat, 68
"AppleTalk network not available"
    notices, 70
arrow keys, ircII script for navigat-
    ing with, 191
ASCII, definition of, 314
ASCII art, 133
asl, 142
asterisk (*)
    with action descriptions, 131
    as channel name, 112, 160
    with KICK command, 166

nicknames surrounded by, 126
right angle bracket (>)
    prefixes, 131
    in WHO command replies, 113
    as wildcard, 148, 167
#atari, 247
Atari operating systems
    IRC clients for, 250
    and PPP, 7
Atlantis (ircII script), 190
at sign (@)
    as field separator, 87
    before nicknames, 107, 114
    and talk request commands, 130
    and WHO command, 113, 150
AT&T users and IRC bans, 109
autoconnects
    disabling, 281, 288
    rate at which IRC server attempts,
        233, 340
    restricting, 276
    setting config options for, 340, 341
autogreets, 142
automatons. *See* bots (robots)
auto–op lists, 174–176
AUTO_WHOWAS (variable), 53
AWAY (command), 32, 113
away messages
    avoiding return of, 127
    to fake being an IRC operator, 202

B

Back Orifice, 314
"Bad channel key" notices, 109
"Bad Username" notices, 83–85
ban lists, 109, 110
BAN (mode change), 38
    to stem nick floods, 254
"Banned" notices, 78–79, 108–109
bans, 108–109
    bypassing with mode e, 163
    definition of, 314
    during a desync, 181
    on different channels, 109
    followed by KICK command, 110,
        165–166

bans (*continued*)
　host masks and, 166–168
　limit on number of, 169
　troubleshooting problems with, 168–169
.bash_profile (Unix file), 52
.bashrc (Unix file), 52
bash (Unix shell), 52
basical (ircII script), 191
Baxter (BeOS IRC client), 252
bbiaf/bbiam/bbiaw, 142
bbl, 142
bbs, 142
Behrens, Chris, 293
BeOS IRC clients, 252
binaries, 50–51
BIND (command), 119–120
.bin files (Mac), 56
BinHex files (Mac), 56–57
BitchX, 44–45
　built–in automation on, 212
　CDCC, 221
　DCC CHAT on, 219
　DEOP command on, 283
　help on, 45, 246
　IGNORE command on, 134
　installing, 45–53
　replying to talk requests on, 130
　startup file, 53
　transferring files on, 220
　version reviewed, 44
　for Windows, 39
BitchX.formats file, 45
.bitchxrc file, 53
BOFH, definition of, 314
bombware, 30
bookmarks for chats, 60
BotHelp file, 294
bots (robots), 290–291
　abuse by, 115
　add–user functions, 175
　and bans, 110
　channel service, 183
　on channels with no operators, 179
　definition of, 314
　detecting, 287
　eggdrop, 172, 291, 292–293
　fake replies by, 211
　floods caused by, 291
　identifying, 115, 286–287
　Internet connections used for, 115

nickname collisions caused by, 291
notices from, 127
versus scripts, 114–116
spam from, 89, 149, 262
takeovers of channels by, 178, 291
uses for, 173, 255, 290
visibility on channels, 117
brackets ([]), 127
browsers, 9
　Save As feature, 57
bugs in IRC clients
　older versions of ircII, 92
　Snak, 65
　Visual IRC, 38
bugtraq, 267
bulletin board systems, 7
bundled help manuals, 61–62
BYE (command), 92
.bz2 filename extensions, 46, 47
bzip2 files, 45

C

Cable lines, 4
　to run bots, 115
canonical names. *See* host names
"Can't send to channel" notices, 144
caret (^) in scripts, 120
C–bots, 294
C compilers, 50
.cc (Unix command), 50
CDCC, 221
CD (channel delay), 111
censorship, 297–298
channel bans. *See* bans
channel bots. *See* bots (robots)
CHANNEL (command), 106
channel delay (CD), 111
channel desyncs. *See* desyncs
channel events, 116–117
　logging, 143–144
　in scripts, 193
channel identifiers, 100
"Channel is currently unavailable" notices, 111
"Channel is full" notices, 110
channel lists, 101–103
　of bans, 109, 110
　obtaining, 61, 101–103
　that scroll offscreen, 104–105
　using modes p and s to keep off, 162

Web sites with, 105
channel mode changes
　availability of channels, determining, 86
　to defend against floods, 172–173
　to destroy an IRC channel, 256
　during a desync, 181–182
　notices about, 117
　rules for multiple, 163–164
　server–generated, 169–170
　on ViRC, 38
channel modes. *See also* MODE (command)
　mode b (ban), 160, 166
　mode e (exception), 163, 267
　mode I (Invitation), 160
　mode i (invite–only), 160, 172
　mode k (key), 161
　mode l (limit), 161, 173
　mode m (moderated), 161, 172
　mode n (noexternal), 136, 161
　mode o (operator), 162
　mode p (private), 162
　mode s (secret), 162
　mode t (topicsetbyops), 162
　mode v (voice), 163
channel names
　with commas (e.g., #2,000), 120
　errors involving, 110–111
　hash mark (#), 108
　length of, 102
　pornography, 106
　strange, 104
channel operators
　attacks on clients used by, 172
　becoming, 114, 158
　censorship by, 298
　choosing other, 177–178
　definition of, 314
　desync, dealing with, 180–182
　duties of, 113–114
　hierarchies of, 114, 185
　identifying, 113, 152
　messages to, 127
　op wars, 177
　powers of, 158
　regaining status as, after losing, 179–180
　security concerns of, 170–179
channels. *See also* multiple channels; secret channels
　access levels for registered, 185

actions on, 131
advertising, 132
#BitchX, 45
&CHANNELS on IRCnet, 284
client maximums, 100
creating new, 157–158
creating private, 164–165
"currently unavailable," 111
definition of, 314
with DNS spoofs, 258
with duplicate names on different
    networks, 101
effect of mode loops on, 256
empty, 110–111
errors connecting to, 108–111
finding particular, 27, 105–106
using help on, 244
identifying moderated, 117
identifying who is on, 112–113
invite–only, 111
#irchelp, 243–244
Ircle bookmarked, 60
joining, 106–108
lists of, on the Web, 105
management of, by bots, 290
#mIRC, 36, 244
moderated, 116
naming new, 158
with no operators, 114, 179–180
number of operators on, 114
number of users on, 100, 101, 102
pinging, 210
pornography, 106, 302
public messages on, 126
quitting, 92, 118–119
registration of, 183–185
sending to, 135–137
sex, 106
silent, 131–132
syncing, 169–170
takeovers of, 176–177, 181,
    256, 257
    by bots, 291
for teens, 304
"temporarily unavailable," 82
time created, 107
topics discussed on, 74
types of, 100
#virc, 38
channel services, 182–185
    bots that run, 183, 290
    creating a channel on a network
        that offers, 158

finding help from, 244
IRC networks with, 307–308
and nethacks, 171
operators in charge of, 285
when to use, 203
channel topics
    current, 102, 107
    that users can't see, 124
chanops. See channel operators
ChanServ, 183–185
    ircu and DALnet interfaces
        with, 271
CHAP, definition of, 314
ChatBox, 249, 250
Chat Channels, 60
ChatGuardian, 69
ChatNet
    about, 68–70
    versus other IRC clients, 69–70
    logging features of, 69
    session window of, 68
    setup and use of, 70–71
    strengths and weaknesses, 71
    unique commands in, 69, 70, 71
    user interface, 68, 71
    Web page address, 68
CHAT offers, 128
chat program interfaces, 68
chat rooms. See also channels
    and DCC, 218
    definition of, 314
    proprietary, 12
ChatWatch, 69
Child Online Protection Act,
    297–298
child pornography, about, 301–302
children
    IRC clients for, 39, 68, 69
    IRC networks for, 25, 26, 304,
        307–308
    using the IRC, 303–304
chops, 114
CLEAR (command), 130
click, definition of, 314
CLIENTINFO (CTCP command),
    212
clients
    bugs in, 65
    channel protection features
        of, 59
    criteria for choosing among, 57
    DCC Chat with, 218–219
    definition of, 314
    differences between, 28–29

enhancing, with scripts, 187–199
help on, 243–247
how they work, 15
Java applets as, 239–240
lag in message transmission, 124
for less–used operating systems,
    249–252
licensing rules for, 30
for Macintosh, 55–71
making invisible, 89
not supporting multiple simulta-
    neous chats, 70
obtaining, 42–43
pinging, 210
preventing attacks on, 172
and screen readers for the
    blind, 242
specifying server lists, 66, 76–78
supporting multiple simultaneous
    chats, 59, 62
supporting speech, 37, 59, 69
trying multiple servers per
    connection, 64
for Unix, 41–53
version information for, 235
for Windows, 33–39
writing, 240–241
client–to–client protocol. See CTCP
C: lines, 273–274
    obtaining a list of, 230–231
    sample, 341, 345
c: lines, 274
clones and clone floods, 172, 173
collider attacks, 174
colon (:)
    as field delimiter on mIRC, 193
    in global channel names, 100
ComBot, 293–294
Combot.lists file, 294
Comic Chat, 39
comma–like character in channel
    names, 120
command characters, 31
    and rc (run command) files, 53
command delimiters in scripts, 192
command lines
    prompts for IRC commands on, 42
    specifying the server on, 76
commands. See also IRC commands
    DCC server, 223
    tar, 47
    Unix directory of, 47

commands (*continued*)
Unix file compression, 45–48
communication on IRC, 125–145
communications devices,
buying, 3–4
compilers, 50
compressed files, 45
Macintosh, 56–57
computers
buying new, 3
lessons for beginnners, 5–6
machine names of, 75–76
needed for Internet and IRC, 2–3
old or low-end, 8
protecting, from attack, 20–23, 172
conditions in scripts, 194
Conference Room (ircd), 270
config.h file, 45, 48
configure (Unix command), 47, 48
CONNECT (command), 279–280
messages following a, 129
"Connection refused" notices, 80, 95
"Connection reset by peer" notices, 95, 314
country codes, Internet, 75, 321–325
CPING, 60
cracker, definition of, 314
credit cards, protecting, 22–22, 258–259
crippleware, 30
.cshrc (Unix file), 52, 76
csh (Unix shell), 52
CSops, 185, 285
CTCP, definition of, 315
CTCP commands, 207–208, 209–213
CTCP ACTION, 211–212
CTCP CLIENTINFO, 212
CTCP ECHO, 212
CTCP FINGER, 153, 211
CTCP PAGE, 213
CTCP PING, 124, 210
CTCP SOUND, 213
CTCP TIME, 211
CTCP USERINFO, 212
CTCP VERSION, 210–211, 215, 235
CTCP ERRMSG message, 208
CTCP floods, 254
CTCP requests, 127–128, 207–215.
See also DCC

customized replies to, 214–215
the ME command and, 142, 211
the NOTICE command and, 213
replying to, 209
seeing, 209
sending, 208
CTRL key
with backslash (\), (command), 120
codes for highlighted text in ircII, 139
codes for text in mIRC, 140
in scripts, 120
cursor (ircII script), 191
Customs Service's Web site address, 302

D

daemons. *See* ircds
dal4.6 (DALnet ircd), 269, 286
DALnet
akill command, 79
channel list, Web site address with, 105
ChanServ, 183–185
CSops, 185, 285
dal4.6 (ircd), 269, 286
DIE command on, 281, 345
extra command set, 183–185
HELP command on, 237
interface with user services, 271
invisible users on, 149
K: lines, 346
LIST command with, 104
#macintosh, 247
MAP command on, 237
MODE b on, 160
most recent version known, 236
nicknames on, querying, 153
NickServ policy, 88
notices on, 127
Q: lines, 275
quit messages, 92
REHASH command on, 282
RESTART command on, 345
sample server configuration for, 342–347
server monitoring capabilities, 284
server software, 266
SILENCE command, 133, 135
size of, 25

telnet capabilities, 242
"User has been banned" notices, 96
Z: lines, 275
dash (-). *See* hyphen
DATE (command), 234
DCC
definition of, 315
file transfers, 56, 219–222
and firewalls or proxy servers, 224–225
floods, 255
Options menu, 224
server commands, 223
servers, 221–222, 223
sound-related, 223
troubleshooting on mIRC, 222–224
DCC CHAT, 218–219
actions within, 142
problems using, on mIRC, 222–223
timeouts, 224
DCC CLOSE, 219
DCC GET, 222
timeouts, 224
DCC RESUME, 36, 220–221
DCC SEND, 220
problems using, on mIRC, 222–223
requests, 128
timeouts, 224
DDE server, mIRC, 36
Deep Thought, 315
"Denial of Service" (DoS) attacks
avoiding, 91
by bots, 291
definition of, 315
detecting, 95, 97
nukes, 22, 259–261
smurfs, 261–262
WinNuke, 319
DEOP (command), 283
using, on other operators, 114
DEOPER (BitchX command), 283
DEOP (mode change), 38
DESCRIBE (command), 142
desync, 123, 180–182
diagnosing, with WHOIS command, 148
flood attacks during, 253, 256
indications of, 136, 144, 169
preventing, 176
three-way, 181

dial-in Internet accounts, 7–8
dial-ups. *See* PPP dial–ups
DIE (command), 281
  in DALnet ircd config file, 345
DIGRAPH (command), 104
Direct Client Connections. *See* DCC
DISCONNECT (command), 93
disk quotas, working around,
  42, 246
distributed clones, 173
DLINE (command), 236
D: lines
  EFnet, 275
  IRCnet and Undernet, 276
dmsetup.exe (Trojan horse file),
  315
DNS
  definition of, 315
  spoofs, 258
dollar sign ($), 42
domain codes, 321
domain names
  components of, 75
  querying whois servers about, 154
  shared by IRC network servers, 76
DoS attacks. *See* "Denial of Service"
  (DoS) attacks
DOS operating systems
  IRC client for, 250–251
  and PPP, 7
Dough's IRC client for VMS, 251
drag-and-drop options on ViRC, 38
DreamForge (DALnet ircd), 269
DSL lines, 4
  to run bots, 115
dumb scripts, 180
dumb terminals, 145
dynamic IP systems, 7

E

easyinst (Unix command), 47
ECHO (command), 193
  CTCP version, 212
echo (Unix command), 52
EFnet
  2.8.21/hybrid-6 ircd standard, 137
  attitude to link lookers, 229
  banning IP address(es) on,
    236, 275
  bans, limit on, 169
  barring KNOCK notices on, 162
  #BitchX channel, 45

  channel op status during netsplits
    on, 158
  hybrid ircd, 267, 284, 286
  invisible users on, 149
  #irchelp, *59*, 58, 101, 243
  IRC operators on, finding, 206
  K: line lists, 231
  MODE command on, 162, 163
  most recent version known, 236
  preventing nethacks, 171–172
  Q: lines, 275
  regaining ops on, 179
  "SENDQ limit exceeded"
    notices, 97
  size of, 14, 25
eggdrop bots, 172, 291, 292–293
  definition of, 315
Electronic Privacy Information
  Center Web site address, 297
"Electropolis: Communication and
  Community on Internet Relay
  Chat," 296
E: lines, 276
elite, definition of, 315
emacs IRC clients, 42
email addresses, 35
emoticons (smileys), 141
  definition of, 315
empty channels, 110–111
endless loop
  with DCC RESUME on mIRC, 221
  definition of, 315
  PRIVMSG, 213
Engen, Vegard, 281
enhanced programmable IRC-II
  client. *See* EPIC
environment variables, Unix, 51–52
EPIC, 43
  and BitchX, 44
  help on, 246
  installing, 45–53
  replying to talk requests in, 130
  start-up file for, 53
  XDCC scripts, 221
epoch time, 107
errors and error notices. *See also*
  bugs in IRC clients; endless loops;
  "K-lined" notices
  "AppleTalk network not avail-
    able," 70
  "Bad channel key," 109
  "Bad Username," 83–85
  "Banned," 78–79, 108–109
  "Can't send to channel," 144

  with channel ban, 168–169
  "Channel is currently unavail-
    able," 111
  "Channel is full," 110
  channel named #, 108
  "Channel temporarily unavail-
    able," 82
  "Connection refused," 95
  "Connection reset by peer,"
    95, 314
  while creating a new channel, 158
  CTCP ERRMSG, 208
  DCC, 222
  disconnecting when using LIST
    command, 103–104
  empty channels, 110–111
  "Ident required," 83–85
  "Illegal nickname," 82
  "Install Ident," 83–85
  "Invite-only," 111
  ircII "HELP_PATH set," 246
  ircII "No valid HELP_SERVICE,"
    246
  KILL chase bug, 279
  without MOTD, 276
  "Nickname is currently unavail-
    able," 111
  nickname missing before mes-
    sages, 145
  "Nickname temporarily unavail-
    able," 82
  "No authorization," 83
  "No more connections," 80
  no such channel, 108
  "PING? PONG!," 95
  "Ping timeout," 79–80, 92, 95
  "SENDQ limit exceeded," 97
  "Server full," 80
  "Server load too high," 236
  server numerics, 194, 331–337
  as symptoms of nuke attacks, 260
  text scrolls on a single line, 144
  troubleshooting for IRC servers,
    283
  "Unable to join channel (+b)," 108
  "Unable to resolve server name,"
    81
  "Unable to send to channel,"
    136, 180
  "You are not a channel operator,"
    180

EsperNet services, 183, 271
etiquette
    IRC rules, 132–133, 141
    when last message is lost, 152
events. *See* channel events
example.conf file, 271
excess flood disconnections,
    95–96, 178
exclamation mark (!)
    as field separator, 87
    in IRC channel names, 101
EXIT (command), 92
exploit, definition of, 315
external modems, 4

F

family IRC networks, 25, 26
    detail on selected, 307–308
FAQs
    Ircle, 61
    mIRC, 245
    Pirch, 36
    ShadowIRC, 61
feather, 45, 47
Felix (BeOS IRC client), 252
field delimiters, 193
filename extensions, Macintosh,
    56–57
files
    decompressing and saving
        Macintosh, 56–57
    decompressing and unarchiving
        Unix, 46–48
    large text, 132
    Trojan horses in, 21
    Unix startup, 53
file servers, DCC, 221–222
file transfers
    via DCC, 219–222
        on Macintosh systems, 56
    between different operating
        systems, 56
    first IRC client to support, 59
    with FTP, 9
    with IRC, 12
Find File (Macintosh program), 57
FINGER (command)
    CTCP version, 153, 211
finger server, mIRC, 36
finger (Unix command), 153–154
fircd (Windows ircd)
firewalls

using DCC with, 222, 223,
    224–225
ident problems caused by, 84–85
using mIRC with, 35
flashes, 130
F: lines, 276, 340
floodnets, 172, 291
flood offs, 96
floods, 172–173
    caused by bots, 291
    combatting, using IGNORE
        command on ircII, 133
    definition of, 315
    indications of, 138
    types of, 253–256
FLUSH (command)
    ShadowIRC and, 64
    to stop a list, 105
    to stop screen from scrolling, 152
"forgetting," 133
forward slash (/)
    as command character in
        aliases, 193
    before commands, 31
    as server patch indicator, 86
founders, 114, 185
fraggle, 262
FreeBSD
    with IRC daemons, 267
    and nuke attacks, 260
freedom of speech, 298
freeware, 30
fserve, 34, 37, 221
FTP (File Transfer Protocol)
    DCC alternative to, 219
    definition of, 315
    using, 9
ftp in Internet addresses, 75

G

gcc (Unix command), 50
geographic locations of IRC
    networks, 25–26, 307–311
geographic designations in
    Internet addresses, 75, 76
G (gone), 113
GLINE (command), 236
G: lines, 79
    reconnecting after, 94
global channels, 100, 101
global IRC networks, 26
global IRC operators, 202, 275, 277

global K: lines, 79, 236
global limits set by IRCnet
    servers, 233
GNU configuration script, 47
Grapevine, 249, 250
graphic face representations of
    other users, 59
graphic IRC clients, 28
    connecting to servers with, 76–78
    DCC Chat with, 218, 219
    Macintosh, 56
greater-than sign command line
    prompts, 42
greetings versus autogreets, 142
GTIRC, 251
Guardian adult control feature,
    Snak's, 64
GUI
    customizable, 34
    definition of, 315
.gz filename extension, 45, 46, 47
gzip and gunzip files, 45–46

H

hacker, definition of, 316
hacking, 256–257
harassment on IRC, 257–258
hash mark (#)
    in channel names, 100
    command line prompts, 42
    in IRC server config files, 339
hax0r, definition of, 316
HELP (command), 237
"HELP_PATH set" notices, 246
HelpServ, 245
help services, online, 105, 243–247,
    308
    types of, 61–62
H (here), 113
HHGTTG, definition of, 316
hidden files, 53
Hitchhiker's Guide to the Galaxy, The,
    316
H: lines, 231, 274
    sample, 346
HNG, definition of, 316
hold_mode, 87, 104, 105
hops, IRC server, 113
host masks
    acceptance of, by IRC server, 231
    in bans, 166–168
    blacklisting, 231

wildcards in, 150
host names
  checking if resolved, 90
  faking, 91
  versus IP addresses for IRC server
    identification, 81, 83
  as part of IRC identity, 87
.hqx files, 57
HTM (command), 236
HTML, 8–9, 316
HTTP, 8, 316
hub servers, 231, 274, 345
Hybrid ircd, 137, 267, 284, 286
hypertext, 8
hyphen (-)
  prefix for SILENCE command,
    135
  setting channel modes with, 159
  before user mode letter, 89

I

+i, setting, 89
iauth, 269
IBM IRC Client for Java, 240
ICMP
  definition of, 316
  floods, 261
ICQ, 249
"Ident required" notices, 83–85
Ident servers
  and channel operator security,
    175
  enabling, 35
  error notices from, 83
  Pirch, 37
ident type, 84
IF (command), 194
IGNORE (command)
  to block CTCP VERSION, 211
  ChatNet and, 70
  to combat harassment, 257
  in different IRC clients, 133–135
  Ircle and, 60
  ShadowIRC and, 64
  Snak and, 64, 66
  ViRC and, 38
iirc, 142
I: lines, 272–273
  sample, 340, 344
  statistics on, 231
i: lines (IRCnet), 272
"Illegal nickname" notices, 82

im(h)o, 142
infinite loop. See endless loop
INFO (command), 234
.ini files, Unix equivalents of, 53
INSTALL (file), 48
"Install Ident" notices, 83–85
Internet
  addresses, 75–76
  basics, 1–10
  versus IRC, 298
  real–time communication via,
    12, 13
  timekeeping on, 107
Internet addiction disorder (IAD),
  299
Internet connections
  for bots, 115
  equipment needed, 2–5
Internet Relay Chat. See IRC
Internet Service Providers. See ISPs
internetworking, 13
invisible mode in mIRC, 35
invisible users, 154–155
  investigating, 149, 282
INVITE (command), 165
  channel operator use of, 159
invite-only channels, 111, 164–165
IP addresses. See also DNS
  banning on EFnet, 236, 275
  connecting to the Internet with, 7
  ephemeral nature of, 81
  finding where registered, 154
  as part of IRC identity, 87
  resolving, 83, 176
  spoofs, 175, 176, 258
    tracing, 232
IRC, 19–32
  accessing through a Web page,
    240
  advantages of, 16–17
  alternatives to, 248–249
  business uses of, 17
  complexity of, 14
  controversies about, 295–305
  dangers of, 20, 74
  definition of, 316
  harassment on, 257–258
  hiding on, 154–155
  identity on, 87, 91, 179
  kinds of users, 19–20, 296
  legislation affecting, 297–298
  obscurity of, 13–14
  one-time use of, 240
  origin and history of, 13–14

pronunciation of, 13
rate of growth, 14
reaching, via telnet, 241–242
standards, 14
topics discussed on, 74
what it is, 11
why use it, 12
IRC addiction, 299–300
irc in a machine name, 75–76
IRC channels. See channels
IRC chat servers, commercial, 270
IRC clients. See clients
IRC commands. See also names of
  specific IRC commands
  basic, 31–32
  BitchX, 45
  case sensitivity of, 31
  ChanServ, 184
  ChatNet versions of, 69, 70, 71
  client, 28, 29–30
  client versus server, 118, 151
  CTCP, 207–208, 209–213
  executing sequences of, 192
  for finding IRC operators,
    205–206
  for finding people on IRC,
    147–152
  for IRC operator use, 277–282
  recognition of, by IRC server, 237
  in scripts, 197
  sent to an IRC server, 232
  server, 29–30, 227–237
  server numeric, 195–196
  shortening, with aliases, 193
  syntax, 31
ircd.conf file, 271–276
IRCdough, 251
ircds, 27, 266, 267–271
  ircd 2.8/hybrid (EFnet), 137,
    267, 284, 286
  ircd 2.9 and 2.10 (IRCnet),
    268, 286
  security measures by, 286
#irchelp, 243–244
IRChelp Web site addresses
  DoS attack info, 22
  IRC network channels, 105
  Mac IRC client page, 71
  server lists, 309
IRCHOST (variable), 52

ircII, 43
  bugs in older versions of, 92
  changing servers with, 91–92
  compilation of, 50
  configuration of, 48–49
  CTCP requests on, 128, 209
  DCC CHAT on, 219
  DIGRAPH command on, 104
  DISCONNECT command on, 93
  fitting text to screen, 87, 104
  help files, 45, 76
    installing, 245–246
  IGNORE command on, 133
  imap script, 237
  installing, 45–53
  joining more than one channel
    with, 119
  logging with, 144
  mIRC-style color, support on, 139
  ON CTCP command on, 211
  options, 48–49
  pinging on, 210
  popularity, 28
  replying to talk requests on, 130
  QUERY command on, 137–138
  scripting for blind users, 242
  scripts, 189–191, 199
  selecting server(s) with, 76
  standards, 42
  switching among channels with,
    119–120
  text highlights on, 139
  text scrolling on a single line, 144
  transferring files via DCC
    with, 220
  VERSION command on, 235
  versions reviewed, 43
  WHO command flags, 150
  for Windows, 39
  XDCC script, 221
ircIIhelp, 245
IRCII (VMS IRC client), 251
Ircle, 58–60
  deviations from IRC client
    standards, 60–61
  help files, 61
  session window, 59
  setup and use, 60–61
  strengths and weaknesses, 71
  Web page addresses, 58
ircname, definition of, 316
IRCNAME (environment
  variable), 51, 52, 88
ircnames. See realnames

IRCnet
  as alternative to umodes, 284
  channel delay on, 111
  formation of, 268
  i: lines, 272
  ircd 2.9 and 2.10, 268, 286
  #irchelp, 243
  limit on bans, 169
  list of channels, 105
  using MODE commands on,
    160, 161
  mode e support on, 163
  most recent version known, 236
  plus channels, 100–101
  preventing nethacks on, 171–172
  Q: lines, 275
  server monitoring capabilities, 284
  server traffic compression support
    on, 273–274
  size of, 25
  STATS Y extra fields, 233
  V: lines, 275
  Web site address with list of
    channels, 105
IRC networks. See also netsplits
  attacks on broadcast addresses
    of, 261
  bandwidth needed by servers on,
    266
  blocking unwanted servers from,
    242–243
  censorship by, 298
  channel lists of, 61, 105, 308
  with channel services, 158,
    307–308
  commands, 227–237
  common server domain name
    in, 76
  for families, 25
  formation of, 23–25
  fragmentation, 24
  geographic locations of, 25–26,
    307–311
  how they work, 15
  largest, 25
  legal liability for users, 105
  linking a server to, 287–288
  list of, 307–311
  maps of, 237
  non–U.S., 26
  number of clients on, 227
  number of servers on, 23, 24
  number of users on, 85–86
  OSs used by major, 267

  selecting, 74–75
  server installation and manage-
    ment for, 265–288
  server–server lag, 123–124
  for special topics, 26
  structure of, 23
IRCNICK (environment
  variable), 51
IRC nicknames. See nicknames
IRC operators
  becoming, 203–204
  channel management by,
    203, 285
  commands used by, 277–283
  CSops, 185, 285
  definition of, 316
  identifying, 113, 205–206
  impersonators of, 202, 258
  IRC servers for, 240–241, 344–345
  lists of, 232
  notices from, 129
  number online, determining, 228
  power-tripping by, 284
  status, determining, 90
  versus real cops, 285–286
  types of, 202
  using KILL command, 94, 96
  what they do, 202–203
  who they are, 201–202
IRCops. See IRC operators
IRC protocol, 29, 247–248
  channel modes in, 159
  importance of, 14
  Macintosh IRC clients' support
    of, 55
.ircrc file, 53
  adding commands, 89, 119, 120,
    139, 209, 210
IRC scripting. See scripts
IRC server administrators
  (sysadmins)
  contact info, finding, 230
  channel takeovers, reporting
    to, 177
  colliders, reporting to, 174
  role of, 50, 204
IRCSERVER (environment
  variable), 51, 76
IRC server masks in channel
  names, 100
IRC server notices, 90, 131
IRC server numerics, 331–337
  in scripts, 194

IRC servers. *See also* autoconnects; ircds; lag; netsplits; umodes
censorship by, 298
checking hops to, 113
choosing which to connect to, 23, 73, 77, 78–79
commands, 29–30, 227–237
configuration examples, 339–348
connecting to, 74–75, 272
   restrictions on, 90
connection information about, 230–234
"Connection refused" notices, 80
default, 51
desync point, 181
differences among, 29
disconnecting from, 92–97
downtime, 94–95
first, 13
host names versus IP addresses of, 81, 83
how they work, 15
hub and leaf, 231, 274, 345–346
involuntary disconnection from, 79–80, 93–97
ircd.conf (config) file, 271–276
jupitered, 242–243
lists of, 76–78, 77, 91
monitoring, 283–284
networking, 287
"No more connections/server full" notices, 80
number of, on a network, 23, 24
operating systems for, 266–267
patch identifiers, 86
reconnecting to, 94
redirection of users among, 82–83
requesting LUSERS info, 228–229
using script to work around differences among, 199
security issues, 267
setting maximum connections for, 340
single versus networked, 23
software for, 30–31
specifying a list of, 66, 92
statistics about, 230, 232
system requirements for, 266
TRACE command for, 206, 234
troubleshooting steps for fixing, 283

"Unable to resolve server name" notices, 81
version information, 86, 235–236
written rules and policies, 86
IRC software licensing, 30–31
IRC users. *See* users
IRCUSER (variable), 52
ircu (Undernet ircd), 266, 268, 271, 284, 286
ISDN, 4, 316
ISON (command), 151
ISP accounts, protecting, 263–264
ISPs, 6–7
and finger requests, 153
ident server installation by, 84
liability for users' actions, 302

J

Java clients, 239–240
JavaScript, IRC scripting with, 38
JOIN (command), 32
   code in response to, 107
   to create new channels, 158
   errors involving, 108–111
   to join a channel, 106–107
   for multiple channels, 119
   shortcuts with, 107–108
JOIN 0 (command), 120
JOIN (event), 193
join notices, 117
JoloPak, 190
jupe/jupiter/jupitered servers, 242–243

K

Kalt, Christophe, 268
Kbps, 4
key. *See* passwords
kick, definition of, 316
KICK (command)
   channel operator use of, 159, 165–166
   notices, 118
   relationship to channel bans (+b), 110, 166
   to stem nick floods, 254
KICK (command), 38
"kick wars," 166
Kidlink IRC, 304

kids
IRC clients for, 39, 68, 69
IRC networks for, 25, 26, 304, 307–308
pornography involving, 301–302
using the IRC, 303–304
KidsWorld, 304
Kill chase, 279
KILL (command), 278–279
   bots using, 290
   error messages after, 111
   IRC operator using, 93, 94, 96
   using on a channel operator, 203
"Kill line active" notices, 96
kill lines. *See* K: lines
KLINE (command), 236, 346
"K-lined" notices, 78–79, 96
K: lines, 78–79, 274
   adding comments to, 346
   bypassing, on EFnet, 276
   global, 79
   operator-set, 96
   reasons for, 83
   reconnecting after, 94
   sample, 341
   server commands related to, 236
   statistics on, 231
k: lines (Undernet), 275
KNOCK (command), 267
   notices, 162
ksh (Unix shell), 52

L

lag, 121
   checking for, 210
   client–server, 124
   dangers of, 174
   and desync, 180
   server–server, 123–124
leaf servers, 231, 274, 345–346
LEAVE (command), 29–30, 32, 118–119
leavejoin floods, 256
leave notices, 117
legislation affecting IRC, 297–298
LiCe, 190
line noise, 138
link lookers, 180, 229
LINKS (command), 229–230
   ircd.conf file M: lines and, 271

Linux operating systems
  IRC client, 250
  with IRC daemons, 267
  and nuke attacks, 260
LiOn, 192
LIST (command)
  disconnection while using,
    103–104
  with Ircle, 61
  output display, *102*
  parameters, 102–103
  Pirch and, 36–37
  ShadowIRC and, 64
  spam use of, 263
  syntax of, 101
  ViRC and, 38
Liszt Web site address, 105
L: lines, 231, 274
  sample, 346
  statistics on, 231–232
Lo, Joseph, 190
LOAD (command), 53
local IRC operators, 202, 275, 277
local limits set by IRCnet
  servers, 233
local machine messages, 130
LOG (command), 144
LOGFILE (ircII variable), 143
logging
  IRC client features for, 63, 69
  with ircII, 143
  with mIRC, 145
log-in files
  commands to add, 130
  selecting server(s) from, 76
  Unix, 52
LOG (ircII variable), 143
logs, server, 283–384
lol, 142
lookup commands, 176
loops. *See* endless loops
l8r, 142
luser, definition of, 316
LUSERS (command), 32, 227–229
  channels counted by, 101
  checking for netsplits with, 111
  network/server status, viewing
    with, 86

M

MacBinary files, 56
machine names, 75–76
Macintosh operating systems
  bots on, 291
  DoS attacks on, 22, 259
  IRC clients for, 28, 55–71, 247
  IRC server software for, 30
  and PPP, 7
MacIRC, 66–67, 71
  interface, 66
  quirks, 67
  session window, *67*
  setup and use, 67
  strengths and weaknesses, 71
  Web page address, 66
Mac Orchard Web site address, 71
MacTCP software, 58
MAIL (variable), 53
make (C compiler commands), 50
MAP (command), 237
Mardam-Bey, Khaled, 33
mass messaging, 262–263
+m (channel mode change), 117
ME (command), 141–42
  and CTCP ACTION
    command, 211
MemoServ, 153
memo services, IRC networks with,
  307–308
mesg n and mesg y (Unix
  commands), 130
Message of the Day. *See* MOTD
messages. *See also* CTCP requests;
  DCC; notices; private messages
  abbreviations used in, 142–143
  away, 127
  barring outside, with mode n, 161
  blocking, 130
  brackets around, 127
  communication problems with,
    144–145
  correcting, 132
  ignoring, 133–135
  local machine, 130
  mistyped, 132
  spam, 262–263
  to channel operators, 127
  to ignore, 128, 129
  types of, incoming, 126–131
Microsoft Chat Network, 25

Microsoft Comic Chat, 39
minus sign (-). *See* hyphen
mIRC, 33–34
  adding mode i to, 89
  AMSG command on, 137
  automatic sound file transfers, 223
  changing FINGER reply on, 214
  changing servers on, 91
  color codes, 140
  CTCP commands on, 213, 215
  CTCP requests on, 127
  DCC, 222, 225
  disconnecting from server, 93
  display of channel events,
    116–117
  FAQ, 245
  features, 34
  files to download, 34
  fserve, 34, 37, 221
  help using, 36, 244
  highlighted and colored text
    on, 140
  hot keys, 120
  ident server setup on, 84
  IGNORE command on, 134–135
  IRCINTRO, 245
  logging features, 145
  menu options, 35–36
  nickname, prefixing messages
    with, 145
  program currently running on,
    path of, 198
  QUERY command on, 137–138
  replying to CTCP USERINFO
    on, 212
  scripts, 191–192, 196–198
  server list, 77
  setup and use, 34–36
  text scrolling features, 105
  transferring files on, 220
  user nicknames, seeing on a
    channel, 112
  screen readers with, 242
  version reply scripts, 211
  version reviewed, 33
  Web page addresses, 33
  WHO command on, 150, 206
  in a WinOS2/32 session, 251
#mirc, 244, 245
mirc561s.exe and mirc561t.exe
  files, 34
mIRC color, 138, 139
#mirchelp, 245
mirc.stealth.net (Web site), 22

mkpasswd utility, 273
M: lines, 271–272
  sample, 339, 342
  statistics on, 231–232
MODE (command)
  channel operator options with, 159
  during a desync, 181–182
  syntax of, 159
  viewing channel modes with, 163
modems, 4, 8
moderated channels, 116
  identifying, 117
  symbol for users with voice
    on, 113
modes, 86. *See also* channel modes;
  umodes
MOTD, 86–87
  definition of, 317
  creating, 276–277
  finding IRC operators with, 206
  help in, 244
  Undernet's T: lines feature
    for, 276
MP3, definition of, 317
MS-DOS IRC client, 250–251
MSG (command), 32, 136
  communicating with multiple
    channels using, 136, 137
  creating an alias for, 193
  versus CTCP command, 207
  floods using, 254
  MacIRC and, 67
  using QUERY instead of, 137
msg @user (ircII command), 130
multiple channels
  joining, 119
  quitting all at once, 120
  sending an action to, 142
  switching among, 119–120,
    136–137
  taking part in conversations on,
    136–137
multiple windows, logging with, 143

N

nagware, 30
NAMES (command), 151–152
  finding channel operators
    with, 152
  nicknames, list of, 112
National Center for Missing and
  Exploited Children, 302

Netbus, definition of, 317
Netcom users and IRC bans, 109
nethack protection feature,
  176, 180, 182
nethacks, 169–170, 170–172
netiquette
  IRC rules, 132–133, 141
  when last message is lost, 152
netsplit (ircII script), 191
netsplits, 121–123
  changes to channel modes
    during, 123
  creating, 280
  empty channels resulting from,
    110–111
  error notices after, 111
  and rejoin, 170
  regaining operator status
    with, 179
network services, 152–153
#new2mirc, 245
newbie, definition of, 317
nick, definition of, 317
NICK (command), 32, 82
nick delay/channel delay
  (ND/CD), 171–172
nickname collisions, 93, 174
  caused by bots, 291
"Nickname is currently unavailable" notices, 111
nicknames
  address for, obtaining, 149, 176
  case sensitivity of, 82
  "currently unavailable," 111
  entering, on mIRC, 35
  faked, 175
  floods using, 254–255
  host masks of, 150, 151
  "illegal," 82
  IRC client variables for, 194
  ircII scripts for, 191
  list of, maintaining, 151
  listing, on a channel, 112
  listing, with JOIN command, 107
  and mode settings, 160
  notices of changes in, 118
  as parameters to the OPER
    command, 277–278
  as part of IRC identity, 87
  preventing use of, 275, 346
  registering a channel with, 183
  registration and ownership, 88
  requesting info about, 152–153
  pinging several, script for, 197–198

  showing, before messages, 145
  "temporarily unavailable," 82
  Unix environmental variable
    for, 51
  color in, 141
nickname services
  bots that run, 290
  help on, 244
  IRC networks with, 307–308
NickServ, 88, 152
  and channel registration, 183
  ircu and DALnet interfaces
    with, 271
N: lines, 273–274
  list of, 230–231
  sample, 341, 345
"No authorization" notices, 83
"No more connections" notices, 80
NOTE (command), 151
NoteServ, 153
note services, IRC networks with,
  307–308
NOTICE (command)
  in different IRC networks, 127
  floods using, 254
  MacIRC and, 67
  mass messaging with, 263
  responding to a CTCP query
    with, 213–213
notices, 127. *See also* errors and
  error notices; messages; MOTD
  autogreet, 142
  of channel mode changes, 117
  with CTRL-A in beginning and
    end, 208, 213
  IRC connection, 85–87
  join, 117
  K-lined, 78–79, 96
  KNOCK, 162
  of nickname changes, 118
  quit, 92, 117–118
  sending, to nickname lists, 199
  server, 90, 131
  server numeric, 331–337
  wallops, 90
NOTIFY (command), 151
"No valid HELP_SERVICE"
  notices on ircII, 246
NOVICE (ircII variable), 119
nukes, 22, 259–261
  definition of, 317
  WinNuke, 319
null channel, 120

O

Oasis, 250
Oikarinen, Jarkko, 13
O: lines, 232, 273
  sample, 341
o: lines, 232, 273
  sample, 341
Olsen, Ove Ruben, 305
ON (command)
  help files for, 193
  making client listen for events
    with, 193
ON CTCP (command), 211
  replying to CTCP USERINFO
    with, 212
ON JOIN (command), 193, 194
  in scripts for autogreets, 143
online addiction (OLA), 299
online help services, 105, 243–247,
  308
ONOTICE (mIRC command), 199
ON RAW (command), 211
ON RAW_IRC (command), 211
ON (scripting command), 53
OPENCHAT/2, 251
open SOCKS server scanning, 269
open source code, 240
Open Transport software, 58
operating systems, 3. *See also* names
  of specific systems
  and IRC daemons, 267
  and nukes, 260–261
operators. *See* channel operators;
  IRC operators
OPER (command), 90, 277–278
opering/oper/opered, 203
opers. *See* IRC operators
opers.log file, 283–284
OP status, 38
ops. *See* channel operators
op wars, 177
OS/2 operating systems
  IRC client for, 251
  IRC servers for, 270
  IRC server software for, 30
oulubox, 13

P

PAGE (CTCP command), 213
PAP, definition of, 317
parameters

to commands, 31–32
to modes, 163–164
PART (command), 29–30, 32,
  118–119
part notices, 118, 119
passwords
  channel, 109, 152, 161
  channel registration, 185
  encrypting IRC operator, 273
  for I: lines, 273
  to identify channel operators,
    174, 175
  for IRC operator commands,
    281, 282
  ISP account, 263–264
  protecting, 22–22, 258–259
  in scripts, 278
  in server config files, 340, 341, 345
  for users excepted from blacklisted
    host masks, 231
  value of, for channel operators,
    258
PDCC (pump DCC), 224
pedophiles, 304
people, finding on IRC, 147–155
percent sign (%), 42
Perl (language), 44
  Perl IRC clients, 42, 44
phishing, 259
Phoenix, 189–190
pico (text editor), 48
pictures
  sending, via DCC, 219
  Trojan horses in, 21
PING (command), 96–97
  CTCP version, 124, 210
  definition of, 315
  floods using, 261
  Ircle version, 60
  rate at which server sends, 233
"PING? PONG!" notices, 95
"Ping timeout" notices, 79–80,
  92, 95
Pirch, 36–37, 245
  FAQs, 36
  features, 36–37
  help on, 245
  setup and use, 37
  version reviewed, 36
  Web page addresses, 36
#pirch, 245
P: lines, 274
plug-ins, ShadowIRCs, 63
plus sign (+)

with channel names, 100
server patch indicator, 86
setting channel modes with, 159
with SILENCE command, 135
before user mode letter, 89
in voiced user names, 116
in WHO command replies, 113
Pointer, Robey, 291
point-to-point protocol. *See* PPP
POPs, definition of, 317
popups
  in IRC clients, 62
  writing, 192
pornographic ads, 263
pornography, about, 106, 301–302
ports, 9–10
  port 23 for telnet, 10
  port 59 for DCC servers, 223
  port 113 ident queries, 84
  setting the number that mIRC
    uses for DCC, 225
  specifying, on IRC servers, 91,
    272, 273, 274, 343
  that must be specified, 280
  used by individual IRC networks,
    307–311
pound sign (#). *See* hash mark (#)
PPP, definition of, 317
PPP dial-ups, 7
  banning, 166
  and channel operator security, 175
  ident servers for, 84
  running bots with, 115
  running fserve on, 221
precompiled binaries, 50–51
precompiled C scripts, 61
prefixes, omitting umode, 89
privacy
  issues, 296–297
  maintaining, with mIRC, 35
  making an IRC client invisible, 89
private messages, 126–127
  actions in, 131, 142
  sending, 137–138
PRIVMSG (command),
  207–208, 213
profiles, multiple, 37
.profile (Unix file), 52, 76
providers. *See* ISPs
province codes, Internet, 75
proxy servers

and DCC, 224
and hiding users, 179
and ident problems, 84–85
PUBLIC (event), 193
public floods, 255
public messages, 126
PurePak, 190

Q

Q: lines, 275
  sample DALnet, 346
QPro scripts, 192, 195
QUERY (command), 67, 137–138
query windows, actions with ME
  in, 142
question mark (?) wildcards,
  148, 167
Queux, 195
QUIT (command), 32, 92–93
quit notices, 117–118
  indicating a netsplit, 121
quitware, 59–60
quota -v (Unix command), 42
QUOTE (command), 135, 151, 236

R

RAW (command), 135, 151, 236
raw IRC, when to use, 28, 212
rc files (run command files), 53
re, 142
realnames. See also nicknames
  definition of, 317
  field in IRC clients, 35, 88
  Unix environmental variable
    for, 51
  in WHO command reply, 113
Reed, Darren, 247
registered channels, 183–185
REHASH, 282–283
Reid, Elizabeth, 296
rejects.log file, 283
relay, significance of, 15
remote (mIRC tool), 192
RESTART (command), 281–282
  in DALnet ircd config file, 345
resume features on mIRC, 34
RFC 1459, 247–248
  channel modes in, 159
  Macintosh IRC clients' support
    of, 55

RFC, definition of, 317
R: lines, 274
robots. See bots (robots)
room, definition of, 317
rooms. See channels
root, definition of, 317
ro(t)fl, 142
ro(t)flmao, 142
round robin address, 309
rtfm, 142, 317
r u m or f, 142

S

salespeople, dealing with, 6–7
ScoutNet, 304
screen, unreadable text on, 138, 152
screen readers and IRC, 242
scripting languages for IRC, 193
script.ini file, 192
script paks, 188, 189
scripts
  aliases in, 192–193
  for blind IRC users, 242
  versus bots, 114–116
  conditions in, 194
  creating, with ircII, 43
  creating, with Ircle, 59
  creating, with Pirch, 36
  creating, with ViRC, 38
  definition of, 187
  dumb, 180
  events in, 193
  for file transfers, 221–222
  generic, 190–191
  guidelines for, 195
  ircII, 189–191, 199
  link-looker, 180
  loading automatically, 53
  maps of IRC networks, creating
    with, 237
  mIRC, 191–192, 195
  numerics used in, 195–196
  obtaining, 189
  poor, 196–199
  precompiled C, 61
  security risks with, 188, 190
  selecting, 188–189
  server numerics in, 194
  tcl for, 292
  user-defined variables in, 194
  uses for, 28, 188, 255, 256–257
  watchdog, 281

writing, 192–199
scroll (Unix command), 144–145
second level domain, 75
secret channels, 101
  creating, 162, 164–165
  finding, 163
secure auto-ops, 174–176
security issues, 20–23. See also
  "Denial of Service" (DoS) attacks;
  floods; nethacks; passwords
  and DCC and encryption protec-
    tion features, 297
  with DCC requests, 128, 218–219
  with DCC server software, older
    versions of, 223
  and eggdrop bots, 292, 293
  on IRC channels, 170–179
  and Ircle channel protection
    features, 59
  mass messaging and spam,
    262–263
  with mIRC auto-get option, 36
  with scripts, 188, 190
SELF_INSERT function, 139
semicolons (;) as command
  delimiters, 192
sendq, 231, 233, 340
  definition of, 317
"SENDQ limit exceeded" notices, 97
SERVER (command), 32, 91–92
"Server load too high" notices, 236
SERVER_NOTICE (event), 193
server numerics. See IRC server
  numerics
server operators. See IRC operators
Server QUIT (command), 280
servers. See also DCC servers; Ident
  servers; IRC servers; proxy servers
  definition of, 318
  whois, 154
service, querying an IRC network,
  152–153
service robots. See bots (robots)
SET (command), 53
setenv (Unix command), 52
sex channels, 106
ShadowBot, 291
ShadowIRC, 61–62, 71
  help features, 61
  logging features, 63
  versus other IRC clients, 62–63, 64
  precompiled plug-ins, 63
  session window, 62
  setup and use, 63–64

ShadowIRC (*continued*)
  strengths and weaknesses, 71
  user interface, 62
  Web page addresses for, 61
shareware, 30
  Macintosh IRC, 56
  nonags, 34
shell, definition of, 318
shell accounts, 8, 175
shells, Unix, 52
shortcut keys. *See* aliases
sh (Unix shell), 52
SIGHUP (command), 282
SIGNOFF (command), 92
SILENCE (command), 133, 135
sirc, 42, 44
slash. *See* forward slash (/)
SLIP, definition of, 318
smileys (emoticons), 141
  definition of, 315
smurf
  attacks, 261–262
  definition of, 318
Snak, 64–65
  bugs in, 65
  lack of help, 66
  session window, /i65/I
  setup and use, 66
  strengths and weaknesses, 71
  user interfaces, 64, 65
  Web page address, 64
Snak Manual, 66
software. *See also* clients; ircds;
  operating systems
  downloading from Internet, 9
  licensing, 30–31
  piracy, 106, 302–303
Solaris, using with IRC daemons,
  267
SOPs, 185
sound, support by IRC clients for, 69
SOUND (CTCP command), 213
sound files, sending with DCC,
  219, 223
spam, 262–263
spam bots, 89, 149, 262
special characters
  in channel names, 104
  the imitation comma, 120
  in messages, 138
  in nicknames, 82
speech support by IRC clients,
  37, 59, 69
spoofs

DNS, 258
  IP address, 175, 176, 232, 258
SQUIT (command), 280–281
  messages after, 129
SSH, definition of, 318
stalking, 257–258
startup files, Unix, 53
state codes, Internet, 75
static IP systems, 7
STATS, 230–234, 282
STATS C (command), 230–231
STATS D (command), 232
STATS H (command), 231
STATS I (command), 231
STATS K (command), 231
STATS L (command), 231–232, 258
STATS M (command), 232
STATS O (command), 232
STATS o (command), 205
STATS p (command), 206
STATS T (command), 232
STATS U (command), 232
STATS Y (command), 232–234
STATS Z (command), 232
STiK, 250
strip (Unix utility), 43
StuffItExpander, 56, 57
Sun operating systems, using with
  IRC daemons, 267
Superchat telnet capabilities, 242
super-ops, 114
s_version (ircII variable), 199
switch_channels function, 119–120
syncing, 123, 169–170
sysadmins. *See* IRC server adminis-
  trators (sysadmins)

T

T1 and T3 lines, definition of, 318
T: lines, 276
tabkey script, 191, 219
takeovers of channels, 176–177,
  181, 257
  by bots, 291
  definition of, 318
  with DNS spoofs, 258
  followed by mode loops, 256
Talk, 248
TalkCity, 25, 252
talk daemon, 248
talk (one-to-one Internet), 13
talk requests, 130

"Tao of Internet Relay Chat" (O.R.
  Olsen), 305
Tape Archive, 46
tarball, 46
.tar filename extension, 47
tar files, 46–47
tar (Unix command) and its flags, 47
tcl scripting, 292
TCMs, 290
  definition of, 318
TCP/IP, definition of, 318
.tcshrc (Unix file), 52
telecommunications devices,
  buying, 3–4
telecommunications lines, 4
  international links, 26
telnet, 9–10, 27
  definition of, 318
  IRC via, 241–242
temporary variables, removing,
  197, 198
terminal emulation, 144
text. *See also* messages; notices
  colored, 138
  etiquette for use of colored or
    highlighted, 132, 141
  highlighted, 138–139
  red, in mIRC messages, 127
  that doesn't fit in screen window,
    87
  that scrolls offscreen, 104–105,
    152
text-based computer systems, 8
text-based IRC clients, 28
TextBox, 190
text-to-speech function of Pirch, 36
thelist (Web site), 6
Tijdgat, Onno, 58
TIME (command), 211, 234
timeouts, DDC, 224
time stamps, 107, 210
TimeStamp (TS), 171
TKLINE (command), 236
TLA, definition of, 318
TOPIC (command), 162
  channel operator options with, 159
topic floods, 255
topics
  discussed on IRC, 74
  current channel, finding, 102, 107
  IRC networks for special, 26, 307
  mode t for setting, 162
  that some IRC users can't see, 124
top level domain (TLD), 75

TRACE (command), 234, 282
during a desync, 181
finding IRC server's operators
with, 206
traceroute utility, 80, 96–97
transfers. *See* file transfers
Trojan horses, 20–22
Back Orifice, 314
danger to channel operators'
clients, 172
danger to channels, 178–179
definition of, 318
troll, definition of, 318
trolling, definition of, 319
tsch (Unix shell), 52
Tucows Mac IRC clients Web site
address, 71
tv connections to the Internet,
4–5, 252

U

U: lines (DALnet), 345
U: lines (Undernet), 275
umodes, 89–91
availability, determining, 86
setting manually, 89
umode a, 91
umode d (dumb), 90, 113
umode i (invisible)
and channel 0, 120
on different types of servers, 91
investigating users with, 149
setting yourself as, 89
umode o, 90
and the DEOP command, 283
on different types of servers, 91
umode r (restricted), 90
and creating a new channel,
158
IRCnet method of imposing,
272
umode s, 90, 91, 284
umode w, 90, 91
umode x, 91
umode z, 91
"Unable to join channel (+b)"
notices, 108
"Unable to resolve server name"
notices, 81
"Unable to send to channel"
notices, 136, 180
uname -rs (Unix command), 51

#undermac, 247
Undernet
channels on, 61
INVITE command on, 161
#irchelp, 101
ircu (ircd), 266, 268
k: lines, 275
LIST command on, 104
#macintosh, /i59/I, 58
MAP command on, 237
mode l on, 161
most recent version known, 236
plus channels, 100–101
Q: lines, 275
server software, 266
service robots, 113
SILENCE command, 133, 135
size of, 25
telnet capabilities, 242
U: lines, 275
#undermac, 247
Web site address, 268
Undernet Channel Service
Web site, 183
Unix operating systems
case sensitivity of, 46
blocking messages with, 130
config.h file, 45, 48
DoS attacks on, 22, 260
filename extensions, 45–48
GNU General Public License, 30
identifying specfic, 50–51
IRC clients for, 28, 41–53
IRC daemons for, 267–271
IRC server software for, 30
obtaining help on IRC clients for,
245–246
and PPP, 7
running bots on, 291
setting the realname with, 88
startup files, 53
tmp directory, downloading
with, 43
Trojan horses for, 20
when text scrolls on a single
line, 144
version numbers, 51
UNKLINE (command), 236
unknown connections, 86
unset (mIRC command), 197
Usenet advantages over IRC, 74
user-defined environmental variables, Unix, 51–52
"User has been banned" notices, 96

USERHOST (command), 151
userid
for mIRC, 35
part of email address, 35
USERINFO (CTCP command), 212
USER_INFORMATION
(variable), 212
user interfaces, 29. *See also* GUI
ChatNet, 68, 71
MacIRC, 66, 67
Snak, 64, 65
user masks
in bans, 166–168
parts of, 87
user modes. *See* umodes
user names
bans and, 169
color in, 141
error notices regarding, 84
Pirch, 37
users. *See also* messages
banning and/or silencing,
78–79, 160
with channel operator status, 114
circumstantial, 13
finding, on IRC, 147–155
invisible, 149
gone or here, 113
graphic face representations of, 59
identity on IRC, 87, 91, 179
invisible, 154–155
IRC operators' powers over, 286
on IRC, 19–20, 296
from large ISPs, bans on, 109
limiting, 161
list of, obtaining with finger,
153–154
locating, 154
maximum, on a channel, 101, 102
preventing, from changing
topic, 162
quantity of users on an IRC
network, 86
regular, 13
removing, from a channel,
174, 178–179
removing, with KICK command,
165–166
sight-impaired, IRC usability
for, 242
with special interests, 26
total, 13, 14
voiced, on moderated channels,
116

voiced, on moderated channels
(*continued*)
who hide identity, 179, 324, 325
women, 257
users.log file, 283

V

V: lines (IRCnet), 275
vanity domains, 325
variables. *See also* environment variables
built-in IRC client, 194
nowall, 199
removing temporary, using scripts, 197, 198
s_version, 199
user-defined, 194
USER_INFORMATION, 212
VBscript, IRC scripting with, 38
verbose_ctcp, 209
VERSION (command), 235–236
CTCP version, 210–211, 215
videoconferencing, IRC clients with, 36, 37
video streaming, IRC client support for, 59
ViRC, 37–38
help on, 245
setup and use, 38–39
virus, definition of, 319
Visual IRC, 37–38
bugs in, 38
features, 37, 38
help files, 38
version reviewed, 37
Web page addresses, 37
VMS operating systems
IRC client for, 251
IRC server for, 270
voice connections, IRC clients with, 37, 59, 69
voiced users on moderated channels, 116
creating, 163
vyxx, 192

W

WALL (command), 199
wallops, 90, 128–129
warez, definition of, 319

warez channels, 106
warez traders, 302
watchdog scripts, 281
wb, 142
W (channel service bots), 183
Web, the, 8–9
Web Chat, 248
Webmaster's Web site address, 270
WebNet Worldwide DALnet server Web site address, 342
Web pages
accessing IRC through, 240
advertising on IRC, 132
with channel listing services, 105
with IRC server lists, 309
WebTV, 4–5, 252
"Welcome to the Internet Relay" messages, 85–86
whereis (Unix command), 46
which (Unix command), 46
whispering, 126
WHO (command)
determining who is on a channel with, 112–113
finding channel operators with, 152
finding IRC operators with, 205, 206
finding users with, 149–150
flags for, 150
parameters, 112
spam use for, 263
WHOIS (command), 32
checking host mask of nickname with, 151
checking server name resolution with, 90
during a desync, 181
finding IRC operators with, 205
finding users with, 148
identifying DNS spoofs with, 258
ircd.conf file M: lines and, 271
and secret channels, 162
structure of, 31
using, before giving out ops, 175–176
whois servers, 154
whois (Unix command), 154
WHOWAS (command), 148–149
wildcards, 148
in addresses, 149–150
in bans, 167
in channel names, 149
security concerns about, 175

WINDOW LOG (command), 143
Windows operating systems
DoS attacks on, 22, 259
help on IRC clients for, 245
IRC clients for, 28, 33–39
IRC daemons for, 270
and PPP, 7
running bots on, 291
Winhelper Trojan horse file, 21
WinNuke, 319
wircsrv (ircd for Windows), 270

Worldgroup client for the MajorBBS system, 251
World Wide Web, 8–9
wtf, 142
WWCN, 249
www in Internet addresses, 75

X

X (channel service bots), 183
XDCC scripts, 221–222
Xircon IRC client, 39, 245
X: lines (DALnet), 345
X Windows IRC clients, 42

Y

Y: lines, 273
sample, 340, 342–343
statistics, 232–233
Unix client display of, 234
"You are not a channel operator" notices, 180
"You are not welcome" notices, 78–79
Young, Dr. Kimberly S., 300

Z

.Z filename extension, 45, 46, 47
zip files, Trojan horses in, 21
Zircon IRC client, 28, 39
Z: lines (DALnet), 275, 346, 347
zsh (Unix shell), 52

PLAYING LINUX GAMES

by AL KOSKELIN

The first complete guide to gaming for Linux users, *Playing Linux Games* covers Linux basics as well as game-specific hardware and software issues. Linux can be a great gaming platform and this book has everything you'll need to get games up and running fast, including dozens of games, drivers, and information files on the bundled CD-ROM. You'll learn:

- How to find, install, run, and troubleshoot games on Linux
- How to get the software or drivers you need to play games under Linux
- How to set up a LAN to play games over a network
- How to install and play the games currently available for Linux (including games for other operating systems that can be emulated on Linux)
- Game-specific tips, techniques, and strategy

AL KOSKELIN studies computer science and writing at the University of Wisconsin-Stevens Point. He is the co-founder of the popular Linux Games Web site (http://www.linuxgames.com).

350 pp., paperback, $34.95 w/CD-ROM
ISBN 1-886411-33-6

LINUX MIDI & SOUND

by DAVE PHILLIPS

Linux MIDI & Sound offers in-depth instruction on recording, storing, playing, and editing music and sound under Linux. The author, a programmer and performing musician, discusses the basics of sound and digital audio, and covers specific software and hardware issues specific to Linux, including:

- A clear introduction to the fundamental concepts of digital sound

- Linux-specific issues including available toolkits, GUI libraries, and driver support

- Reviews of available software with recommendations

- Recommended components for building a complete system including a digital audio player/recorder, soundfile editor, MIDI recorder/player/editor, and software mixer

- Coverage of hard disk recording, advanced MIDI support, network audio, and MP3

- A complete bibliography and an extensive list of Internet resources

- A CD-ROM with dozens of software packages

A performing musician for over 30 years, DAVE PHILLIPS became interested in computers as a means for playing, editing, and recording music. He is an expert in MIDI, Csound, and Linux. He currently maintains several educational Web sites on these topics.

300 pp., paperback, $39.95 w/CD-ROM
ISBN 1-886411-34-4

THE NO B.S. GUIDE TO RED HAT LINUX 6

by BOB RANKIN

This book is a thorough yet concise guide to installing Red Hat Linux 6 and exploring its capabilities. Author Bob Rankin (*The No B.S. Guide to Linux*, No Starch Press) provides easy-to-follow instructions for installing and running Red Hat 6. Through examples and helpful illustrations, the author guides readers through these topics and more:

- Installation — in ten easy steps!

- How to use and configure GNOME — the new Linux GUI

- How to write Bash or Perl scripts and use the Bash shell

- How to connect to the Internet with SLIP/PPP and how to run the Apache Web server for Linux

- How to access DOS files and run Windows programs under Linux

The CD-ROM contains Red Hat Linux 6 — one of the most popular Linux distributions available. It's easy to install and requires minimal configuration — you'll be up and running in a snap!

BOB RANKIN is a programmer and nationally recognized expert on the Internet. He is a columnist for *Boardwatch Magazine* and a contributor to several computer publications. His books include *Dr. Bob's Painless Guide to the Internet* (1996) and *The No B.S. Guide to Linux* (1997).

1999, 402 pp., W/CD-ROM $34.95 ($54.00 CDN)
ISBN 1-886411-30-1, Item #301

STEAL THIS COMPUTER BOOK: WHAT THEY WON'T TELL YOU ABOUT THE INTERNET

by WALLACE WANG

"A delightfully irresponsible primer." — *Chicago Tribune*

"If this book had a soundtrack, it'd be Lou Reed's 'Walk on the Wild Side.'" — *InfoWorld*

"An unabashed look at the dark side of the Net — the stuff many other books gloss over." — *Amazon.com*

Steal This Computer Book explores the dark corners of the Internet and reveals little-known techniques that hackers use to subvert authority. Unfortunately, some of these techniques, when used by malicious hackers, can destroy data and compromise the security of corporate and government networks. To keep your computer safe from viruses, and yourself from electronic con games and security crackers, Wallace Wang explains the secrets hackers and scammers use to prey on their victims. Discover:

- How hackers write and spread computer viruses

- How criminals get free service and harass legitimate customers on online services like America Online

- How online con artists trick people out of thousands of dollars

- Where hackers find the tools to crack into computers or steal software

- How to find and use government-quality encryption to protect your data

- How hackers steal passwords from other computers

WALLACE WANG is the author of several computer books, including *Microsoft Office 97 for Windows for Dummies* and *Visual Basic for Dummies*. A regular contributor to *Boardwatch* magazine (the "Internet Underground" columnist), he's also a successful stand-up comedian. He lives in San Diego, California.

340 pp., paperback, $19.95
ISBN 1-886411-21-2

If you can't find No Starch Press titles in your local bookstore, here's how to order directly from us (we accept MasterCard, Visa, and checks or money orders — sorry, no CODs):

Phone:
1 (800) 420-7240 OR
(415) 863-9900
MONDAY THROUGH FRIDAY,
9 A.M. TO 5 P.M. (PST)

Fax:
(415) 863-9950
24 HOURS A DAY,
7 DAYS A WEEK

E-mail:
SALES@NOSTARCH.COM

Web:
HTTP://WWW.NOSTARCH.COM

Mail:
NO STARCH PRESS
555 DE HARO STREET, SUITE 250
SAN FRANCISCO, CA 94107
USA

Distributed to the book trade by Publishers Group West

UPDATES

This book was carefully reviewed for technical accuracy, but it's inevitable that some things will change after the book goes to press. Visit the Web site for this book at **http://www.bookofirc.com** for updates, errata, and other information.